CW01046478

THE PORSCHE BOOK

a definitive
illustrated history

Other PSL Porsche books

Porsche Racing Cars of the Seventies
by Paul Frère

Porsche 911 Story
2nd Edition
by Paul Frère

To our fathers' memory

THE PORSCHE BOOK

a definitive illustrated history

by **Lothar Boschen and Jürgen Barth**

Translated by Paul Frère
Foreword by Dr Ferry Porsche

 Patrick Stephens, Cambridge

© 1977 Motorbuch-Verlag, Stuttgart
English language translation © 1978 and 1983 Patrick Stephens Limited

All rights reserved. No part of this publication may be
reproduced, stored in a retrieval system or transmitted,
in any form or by any means, electronic, mechanical,
photocopying, recording or otherwise, without prior
permission in writing from the publishers.

First published in Germany by Motorbuch-Verlag, Stuttgart,
under the title *Das Grosse Buch der Porsche-Typen,* von
Jürgen Barth/Lothar Boschen

First published in Great Britain August 1978
Reprinted April 1980
Reprinted February 1981
Reprinted April 1982
Reprinted November 1982
Second Edition October 1983

British Library Cataloguing in Publication Data

Boschen, Lothar
  The Porsche book.
  1. Porsche automobile
  I. Title II. Barth, Jurgen   III. Das Grosse
  Buch der Porsche-. *English*
  629.2'222   j1215.P75

  ISBN 0-85059-559-2

Text photoset in 10 on 11pt English 49
by Stevenage Printing Limited, Stevenage.
Printed in Great Britain on 100gsm Fineblade cartridge
and bound by The Garden City Press, Letchworth
for the publishers, Patrick Stephens Limited,
Bar Hill, Cambridge, CB3 8EL, England.

Contents

Preface

Sentimental reasons played a large part in my decision to translate this book. Porsche was the first established manufacturer who ever offered me a works drive in an important race—and what a race: the 1953 Le Mans 24 Hours! The car I shared with the late Richard von Frankenberg was a beautifully streamlined, pushrod-engined coupé, prominently featured in this book, and with its sister car it made history by being the first mid-engined car ever to run in the famous 24 Hours race, in which it performed well.

Also, Jürgen Barth, co-author of this book, is the son of Edgar Barth, who was my co-driver in a Porsche Spyder—again at Le Mans, but in 1958—and Jürgen himself won the French classic in 1977.

Another important factor that influenced my decision is that (although I say it myself!) I have a better than average knowledge of what has been going on at Porsche over the years, having owned five of their cars (two 356A models, a 911S, a Carrera 3-litre, and a 3.2 which I currently run) and having written three Porsche books, two on racing car development and one entirely dedicated to the 911/930 series. The many contacts with the factory that this has required have not only strengthened the friendly relations which already existed between the Porsche company's management and technical staff and myself, but have also enabled me to get an intimate knowledge of their cars and the men responsible for them. I felt sure that this would help me to fulfil the difficult task of translating what is essentially a reference book, the value of which lies mainly in its absolute accuracy, without letting the authors down. In fact, many points were discussed with them before the work was completed.

Vence, France, May 1983   *Paul Frère*

Foreword to the first edition

When they wrote this comprehensive book, which includes every type of production and racing car built by the Porsche company from 1948 to date, the authors Lothar Boschen and Jürgen Barth succeeded in compiling a work which should be of interest to everyone, not just to 'insiders'.

Owners of our production cars all over the world will be just as happy to read this highly informative book as the innumerable private owners of Porsche racing machinery.

On behalf of the Porsche company which has just celebrated its Silver Jubilee, the undersigned wishes to express his warmest thanks to the authors for their very precious work.

Dr Ing hc Ferry Porsche

8

Introduction

It was surely in the nature of Professor Ferdinand Porsche that, as long as he lived, he was never content with anything he achieved. Whenever he made an invention which was then promptly picked up by someone else, his fiancée, who later became his wife, urged him to sue the imitator and to claim his rights. But Professor Porsche himself never had any urge to sue. He preferred to leave things well alone and if he felt his fiancée pushed him too hard, he just told her: 'Ah, come! I have something much better in my mind anyway!' All through his life, this remained his attitude: whenever he had completed something, there was no rest until he had a new idea or could improve on what he had done. When he designed a touring car, he already had his ideas about how to increase its performance. When the development of a touring car approached its final stages, his policy was to tune it specially and enter it in competitions for which it was suitable, so that the car should have been tested under the most exacting conditions before it was put into production. He himself started by setting the right example: when he designed his early car with electromotors in the wheel hubs, he drove the vehicle in record attempts so that both experts and possible customers would be convinced of the product's quality. This is one reason why Professor Porsche never understood why the big companies in the automobile industry all retired from racing in favour of laboratory development.

As soon as the Austrian-born engineer, who was strongly opposed by part of the German motor industry, started working on the Volkswagen project, he was already thinking of producing a special sporting version of it. In 1935 he produced a completely unscheduled VW drophead coupé based on the experimental saloon version No 2. Two years later came the first open model of the VW 60 series, of which only 30 were made.

From the beginning of the project, there was a good understanding about technical matters between the two German-based Austrians, Ferdinand Porsche and Adolf Hitler. Hitler trusted the car designer from Bohemia and used to summon him to his house in Berlin when it came to finding a solution to technical problems. One of the first meetings resulted in Porsche getting the contract for developing the Auto-Union Grand Prix car, and the commission of a potential winner of the international Berlin-Rome speed event, scheduled for the autumn of 1939, also had its origin in one of their talks.

The official order for the VW-based racing coupé came from the Oberste Nationale Sportkommission (Upper National Sporting Commission), headed by Korpsführer Hühnlein who was also chief of Sports and Motors Sports under the

Hitler regime. He was keen to see the two bodies he led, the OSK and the NSKK (the latter responsible for production cars), acquire fame by achieving spectacular successes.

The first three cars completed, which were prevented from achieving their aim by the outbreak of war, must be considered direct ancestors of the Porsche car.

No wonder that several years later, when Porsche sports cars started running off the assembly line in Stuttgart, a slogan was forged which surely applies to all cars designed by Professor Porsche: 'Porsche—driving in its finest form'.

10

The Company

Born in Bohemia and schooled in Vienna, Ferdinand Porsche came to Stuttgart in 1923. It took nearly 30 years from then, however, for cars carrying the Porsche trademark to be produced in the Swabian metropole. When he founded his own design office in 1930 under the name of Dr Ing hc F. Porsche KG, Ferdinand Porsche initiated one of the most exciting chapters in German automobile history. It is on the drawing boards of this design office that, among others, the so successful Auto-Union racing car and the Volkswagen took shape. After the Second World War the new generation took over and a new era began. Professor F. Porsche died in 1951, but long before his death his son, Dr Ferry Porsche, had laid the foundations for new activities. Starting from VW Beetle mechanical units, he developed a light, fast sports car to be made in small series, the first car called a Porsche. The design office had become a car factory.

The small-scale production soon became larger. In 1951, no fewer than 1,103 cars left the Stuttgart-Zuffenhausen-based factory and found their way to sports car enthusiasts all over the world. It was also in 1951 that Porsche officially participated for the first time in a motor sport event: the occasion was the Le Mans 24 Hours race in France, which the Anglo-German team of Dickie Attwood and Hans Herrmann were to win outright 19 years later, driving a Porsche 917. That victory set the seal on 19 years of continuous economic and sporting successes by the company led from very modest beginnings by Dr Ferry Porsche and his colleagues.

People at Porsche are rightly proud of their tradition, but today no less than yesterday, their main interest lies in progress. They don't sell only cars: they sell technique and progress to outsiders too. This has become an ever more important activity of the company, extending into the fields of touring and commercial vehicles, aviation and armament. Up to February 1972, Porsche KG was entirely the property of the Porsche and Piëch families of which members held key positions. Prominent among them were Ferdinand Alexander Porsche, responsible for styling, and Dr Porsche's two nephews, Dipl Ing Ferdinand Piëch and Dr Michael Piëch, respectively responsible for outside commitments and administration. On March 1 1972, the company was reorganised. The Porsche and Piëch families, owners of Dr Ing hc F. Porsche KG, Porsche Konstruktionen KG Salzburg, and their branches, took the decision to incorporate their European companies into one single organisation. This made approximately 6,200 people, mainly concerned with the development, construction and sale of motor cars (1971 turnover approximately DM 900 million) dependent on a central management presided over by Dr Ing hc Ferdinand Porsche and his sister, Kommerzialrat Louise Piëch. Dr Ing (now Professor) Ernst Fuhrmann was made responsible for all technical matters, while Dipl Kaufmann Heinz Branitzki became responsible for all commercial affairs. Dr Ernst Fuhrmann (born in 1919) had already held an important position with Porsche as a designer from 1957 to 1966, but had later become a member of the Goetze Werke management. He had come back to Porsche in 1971. Heinz Branitzki, born in 1930, came to Porsche in 1965 from the Carl Zeiss company to take the responsibility of the financial management. At the end of 1973, the Porsche KG became a public company (*Aktiengesellschaft* = AG = joint stock company).

To keep in step with the considerably increased turnover, the Dr Ing hc F. Porsche AG Stuttgart extended its board of directors on November 8 1976. The directors responsible for finance, Heinz Branitzki, and for sales, Lars Schmidt, remained in office under the presidency of Dr Ing Ernst Fuhrmann, but three new vice-directors were nominated: Ing Helmut Bott, who had been with Porsche for many years, was made responsible for development, Karlernst Kalkbrenner was made responsible for the personnel and Hermann Kurtz for production.

About a quarter of the 4,000-odd employees of the company work on development in the most varied spheres of activity. Examples of these are engine development, design and emission control, metrology and vibrations, light metal processing, plastics, welding and bonding techniques, etc. This knowhow enables Porsche to carry out entire system developments, complete with the project studies, system analyses, calculations, general and production designs, advanced experiments, the construction of prototypes and testing, and reach the production stage and the production launch. They can also provide technical personnel and prepare time and cost plannings. With the opening of the Development Centre at Weissach, near Stuttgart, a new phase was opened in Porsche's activities. This new centre, which has its own proving ground for cars and cross-country vehicles, represents an investment of over DM 80 million. It enables Porsche to carry out almost any sort of development.

Much of the work taking place in the centre is ordered by governments, administrations and private companies which consult Porsche for advice or a decision as to the better qualification of various products or systems. Such confidence is the best reference for the technicians at Zuffenhausen. Large-scale research is currently being carried out to find the solution to topical problems, such as fighting atmospheric pollution and increasing the active and passive safety of motor cars.

On June 3 1977, the 250,000th sports car built by the Porsche company since the beginning of production in 1949, a 911 Coupé, left the assembly line. For a small company producing specialised cars, this is a remarkable record. That day, the breakdown of the production was the following: Type 356, 75,972 units; Types 911 and 912, 154,501; Type 924, 19,168; Type 928, 33; Others (racing cars), 326.

In the '70s, Japan became an important export market for Porsche. Masami Okumura, the owner and president of the Japanese import company, proudly celebrated in 1978 the 25th anniversary of his company, which in its first year of activity, 1953, sold eight 356 models. Even in 1970, only 97 Porsche sports cars were sold to Japanese customers. The abolition of the restrictions limiting imports of foreign cars into Japan allowed sales to progress considerably. Alone from 1973 to 1976, yearly sales soared from 122 to 495. In 1977, the figure rose to 663, while in the calendar year 1978, some 900 Porsches were sold and Okumura expected to reach his target of a thousand units the following year. This makes Japan a market as important today as the British or Swiss.

These figures are all the more remarkable considering that the costs of transport, sales expenditures and the adaptation of the cars to the specific Japanese laws raise the price of a Porsche in Japan to twice the level of the German prices. For example in 1980, a 930 Turbo cost over DM 148,000 in Japan, compared with DM 78,800 in Germany. However, this did not prevent 140 cars from being sold in Japan up to that date.

In the commercial year 1978-1979, Porsche AG continued to progress. The turnover rose by 20% from DM 1,123 million to DM 1,350 million. Car production turnover alone amounted to DM 1,191 million (966 million in the preceeding year), while car production rose to 39,500 units, an increase of 13%.

At the end of 1981, Prof Fuhrmann went into retirement and was replaced as the company's Managing Director by Peter W. Schutz, who had graduated in engineering in the United States and had previously been with the Caterpillar company as a development engineer. Dr Ferry Porsche remained as Chairman of the Board. At the end of the commercial year 1981-1982, ending on June 30 1982, the company's turnover had risen to DM 1,488 million with car production amounting to 1,289 million, even though the crisis had had its impact and had reduced production to 32,600 units, of which 32.5% were 911, 14% were 928 and 53.5% 924/944 models. Deliveries of the 944 only began around New Year, while the first 911 Cabriolets were delivered in the spring of 1982 and considerably boosted the production, which rose to over 200 cars per day. This fact is reflected in a rapid rise in the number of Porsche employees, which rose from 5,273 in June 1982 to 5,850 in May 1983.

Of the cars built during the 1981-1982 commercial year, 30% were sold in Germany and 70% were exported, the USA being the largest single export market accounting for 40% of the total sales.

14

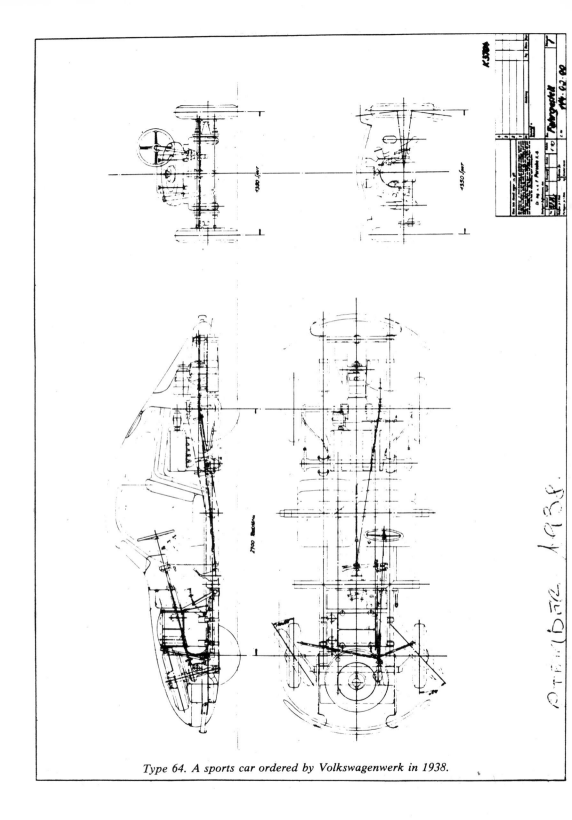

Type 64. A sports car ordered by Volkswagenwerk in 1938.

PRODUCTION CARS

Types 114/64/356 Aluminium (1938-1951)

Once more, the link between Porsche racing and production car design became obvious when, as early as 1937, development exercises to increase the output of the conservative VW engine laid the basis of what was to become the real Porsche car. At this time, the first pre-production series of the Volkswagen was being launched. With the help of twin carburettors, a Roots supercharger and later fuel injection, as well as using different cylinder heads and valves, the output of the engine was considerably increased. Porsche's idea was to build a sporting version of the utilitarian VW around one of those engines. Relentlessly, when it came to talks with the Deutsche Arbeitsfront—the official body to which Porsche was contracted—Professor Porsche came out with the request to be allowed to develop a more sporting version of the KdF car. With the same obstinacy, his request was rejected with the flat reply: 'A sports car is not a car for the people'.*

In spite of this negative attitude, plans for a sports car derivative continued to appear on the drawing boards of Ferdinand Porsche's closer collaborators. In a single week, between September 10 and 16 1938, the drawings were prepared for an aerodynamic sports coupé based on the VW. The drawings which bear the reference numbers 114, 114 K 1 and 114 K 2 differ only in details. A common feature was the location of the power unit: the modified VW unit was in front of the rear wheel centres—they were all midship-engined cars! The wheelbase was 2,750 mm (108 inches), the front and rear tracks 1,350 mm (53 inches), the turning circle was 10.5 metres (34.5 feet). The 5.50 × 17-inch tyres were fitted to Kronprinz disc wheels of the dimensions 3.25 × 17. The brakes were to be supplied by Ate and the shock absorbers by Boge.

The K 1 model was a three-seater. The third seat was for occasional use only and located transversely in the rear compartment. The K 2 model did not have a third seat. The two successors with the references 115 and 116 differed only in the power plant to be used. 115 was to be supercharged while the power unit for 116 was to be a VW engine bored out to 1.5 litres.

*The literal translation of 'Volkswagen' is 'people's car'.

15

In contrast to this range, the following Project 64 was ordered by the Volkswagenwerk in Fallersleben. At their request and in view of the miserable quality of the tyres available at the time, the VW sports car was to have two spare wheels located one behind the other under the front cover. All these plans seemed to be destined to be shelved indefinitely until a newly planned motoring event gave them a new impetus.

In the spring of 1939, the organisers of a large-scale international speed event from Berlin to Rome sent the rules of the contest to all likely competitors. Several well known manufacturers immediately started developing special vehicles or modifying existing production models to take part. As the first 600 km (approximately 375 miles) of this long-distance event were to be on the Autobahn linking Berlin to Munich, efficient streamlining seemed to be essential.

Prominent Arbeitsfront leaders insisted that Volkswagen should take part in the event, and some people remembered how strongly Professor Porsche had insisted, in previous years, that a sporting version of the KdF car should be developed. So, all of a sudden, he got the green light to build a KdF-based model to be competitive in the event planned for autumn 1939.

Needless to say this 'go ahead' message was received with much enthusiasm. The Porsche design office turned to the Type 114 drawings which had been shelved in September 1938. The first drawing for the new project, dated January 9 1939, was still based on a modified Type 114 chassis and bears the signature of draughtsman Karl Fröhlich. The three prototypes which were built used the chassis type 60 K 10 with an aerodynamic body and were known as Type 64. The chassis was little changed from original VW specification and exceeded 140 km/h (87 mph), powered by a four-cylinder VW engine tuned to produce 40 bhp!

The 64 was a pretty uncompromising racing car. The driver sat in the centreline of the car. If a passenger was to be carried, he could only be accommodated in a small, light bucket seat, offset to the rear of the driver's seat.

Unfortunately however, in September 1939 war was declared and prevented the Berlin-Rome trial from being staged. Of the three cars made, only one survived. Of the two others, one was probably destroyed by bombs and the other was cannibalised by the Americans when they marched into Germany, after the engine had been ruined by lack of oil. The surviving car was nursed through the war by Otto Mathé, an Austrian who drove it successfully in several races until 1951.

After the end of the war, the Porsche company which had emigrated to Gmünd in Kärnten (Austria) lived on, mainly from earnings accruing from repairing, modifying and servicing vehicles of all sorts. But the urge for productive action was still there and as early as summer 1946, the surviving members of the Porsche team were already working on sports and racing car projects, while Professor Porsche himself was still held in a French prison. Under the Chief Engineer of the period, Karl Rabe, and the chief of the body design office, Erwin Kommenda, they were busy designing and developing the Cisitalia Grand Prix car which had been ordered by the Italian industrialist Piero Dusio. Simultaneously, on July 17 1947 to be precise, again without any particular order, a 'VW Sports two-seater' appeared on a drawing board under the reference number 356.00.105!

The idea was to build a small series of an estimated maximum of 500 cars for a small circle of wealthy customers. But before Porsche went ahead with the project, Ferry Porsche Jr insisted on undertaking some market research. It seemed rather uncertain that so soon after a five-year long war, a significant market for such a vehicle existed in Europe.

Porsche explained his intentions in circles likely to be interested—mainly in Switzerland—and the answers he got were quite encouraging. Two Swiss, named Senger and Blank, agreed to raise the necessary money and production was started. At this point, Porsche No 1, an open two-seater based on a tubular frame (to the drawing of July 17 1947) was already a runner. The engine was located in front of the rear wheel centres, the gearbox being overhung at the rear. The power for this mid-engined sports car came from an 1,131 cc power plant which was quite obviously a close relative to the air-cooled VW unit. New cylinder heads with the valves arranged in V configuration and several other minor modifications had raised the power to 40 bhp at 4,000 rpm. Front and rear suspensions came straight from the 'Beetle', as did the steering and gearbox.

Weighing only 596 kg (1,314 lb) with a full tank, Porsche No 1 was good for an honest 135 km/h (84 mph) and even 5 km/h (3 mph) more if one bothered to cover up the passenger's seat. The car first took to the road in March 1948.

By this time, however, the drawing office was busy on drophead and fixed head coupé versions based on a pressed steel floor pan. Building the tubular-framed Porsche No 1 had indicated that this sort of construction was not economically justifiable. It also seemed essential to provide adequate room for luggage. From these considerations, Ferry Porsche drew the logical conclusions: the power plant was turned round again, back to the position it occupies in the 'Beetle', and a flat, pressed steel frame took the place of the space-consuming tubular frame. This created enough room behind the front seats to accommodate luggage as well as passengers in an emergency. The Porsche as we know it today was born.

Meanwhile, the tubular-frame Porsche had gone to its owner, R. von Senger, who lived in Zurich, and the Swiss magazine *Automobil Revue* had published a short test report on the car. The following extract is illuminating: 'Right in the atmosphere of the Grand Prix soon to take place [in those times there was still a Formula 1 Swiss Grand Prix], we extended the car around the Bremgarten Circuit and it soon inspired full confidence. This is how one imagines a modern car should handle, taking advantage of modern suspension to achieve good comfort together with the tenacious grips afforded by a modern, low-built and wieldy sports car.'

When this 001 open two-seater was granted its roadworthiness certificate from the Kärntner Landesbaudirektion, on June 8 1948, the first aluminium-bodied 356 coupé, built on a pressed steel platform, was already complete in Gmünd. Even before this car got its roadworthiness certificate, *Automobil Revue* showed interest in it. In the issue of July 7 1948, the following appreciation could be read: 'This car, which is derived from the Volkswagen, also incorporates the considerable experience gained by Porsche in the design of the Auto-Union racing car. Apart from minor modifications, the engine, the transmission and the front and rear suspensions are similar to those used in the VW. The frame however, which features box section side members and a continuous floor pan, is exceptionally stiff in torsion and carries an aerodynamically efficient two-seater coupé body.'

Nearly parallel to the coupé, a drophead was also produced with the main object of getting the roadworthiness certificate for that additional model, but it did not go into production for some time, which explains why its specification was somewhat different from the later production cars. Both cars got their certificate on August 7 1948, and only shortly after, in the following winter, small-scale production was started. Five hand-made cars left Gmünd every month. Every single aluminium body was hand-beaten by a Viennese master of the art, beating the metal over a wooden rig for hours on end.

At the beginning, the factory announced a weight of 680 kg (1,500 lb) for the complete car in running order. Only a short time later, when the first cars were supplied to customers, the weight had increased by a full 100 kg (220 lb). The alloy body had pivoted front quarter lights and twin leading shoe front brakes. Two years later, the Zuffenhausen-built all-steel Porsches were back to VW brake specifications. The bumpers were integral with the body and the V-shaped windscreen had a narrow centre pillar. The car could be bought with separate front seats, or with a bench seat! The measurement for wheelbase and front and rear track remained unchanged all through the 356 series. Maximum speed was just over 140 km/h (87 mph).

On March 20 1951, the Gmünd production was wound up. Altogether, 46 cars of the light alloy 356 series (Type 356-Alu), equally divided between drophead and fixed head coupés, were built in just under 2½ years. Only a few cars remained in the hands of the factory to be used as guinea pigs, but for many more years the alloy coupés were to make racing history.

114/64/356

Year	Body	Type	Chassis no	Engine no	Engine type	Gearbox	Cyl	Bore × stroke	Capacity	HP (DIN) at rpm	Torque (mkg) at rpm	Comp ratio	W.base (mm)	Track fr/rear (mm)	Length (mm)	Weight (kg)	No produced
1938 10.9	Coupé	114	Drawing[1]		VW 341-44	VW 539/40	4						2750	1350/1350			–
1938 14.9	Coupé	114 K1	Drawing[2]	–			4										–
1938 16.9	Coupé	114 K2	Drawing[3]	–			4										–
1938 16.9	Coupé	64	60 K 10[4]	–			4						2400	1284/1284			3
1947	Cabrio	356	Drawing[5,6]	–	VW 369	VW	4	73,5 × 64	1086	40/4200	7,0/2600	7:1	2100	1290/1250	3860	555 / 605	– / –
1948	Coupé	356	[7]	–	VW 369	VW	4	73,5 × 64	1086	40/4200	7,0/2600	7:1	2100	1290/1250	3870	765	–
	Cabrio	1100	356-001[9] [8]	356.2-034969	VW 369	VW	4	75,0 × 64	1131	40/4000	7,0/2600	7:1	2100	1290/1250	3860	600	–
	Cabrio			356.2-021343	VW 369	VW	4	73,5 × 64	1086	35/4000	7,0/2600	7:1	2150	1290/1250	3860	585	1
	Coupé		356.2-001-006		VW 369	VW	4	75,0 × 64	1131	40/4000	7,0/2600	7:1	2100	1290/1250	3860	780	6
			356.2-008														1
			356.2-010														1
			356.2-012-030														15
	Cabrio		356.2-007														1
			356.2-009														1
			356.2-011														1
			356.2-031-050														18
			356.2-052														1

Notes on Porsche 356 ancestors:
1) Central engine. Design No 114.0000-01. 2) Three-seater. 3) Two-seater.
4) Liège-Rome-Liège competition car, two spare wheels one behind the other under front lid. 5) Design No 356.000.105 dated 17.7.47, open two-seater with central engine. 6) Space frame. 7) Overhung rear engine, pressed steel frame.
8) Engine ahead of rear axle. The car to the indicated specifications was delivered to Herr von Senger in Zürich. 9) A car to these specifications was homologated individually on June 8 1948 by the Landesbaudirektion Kärnten in Sittal (Carinthia).

Porsche 356 models produced in Gmünd (Carinthia), Austria

Chassis	Engine	Body	Name of owner	Date	Notes
356.001	356-2-034969	Cabriolet	v. Senger, Zürich	8. 6. 48,	
356-2.001	356-6-028199	Coupé	v. Senger, Zürich	8. 6. 48	
356-2.002	356-6-021343	Coupé	v. Senger, Zürich	8. 6. 48	
356-2.003	356-6-014106	Coupé	v. Senger, Zürich	28. 10. 49	Assembled in Tatra workshops, Vienna
356-2.004	356-6-014109	Coupé	v. Senger, Zürich	–	Assembled by Kastenhofer, Vienna
356-2.006	356-6-063663	Coupé	Pekarek, Günther	7. 3. 49	Assembled by Tatra, Vienna
356-2.005	356-6-020896	Coupé	Walter, Helmuth	21.2.49	Assembled by Tatra, Vienna
356-2.007	356-7-037315	Cabriolet	Günther, Herbert	6. 2. 49	Assembled by Tatra, Vienna — demonstration car
356-2.008	356-1-000010	Coupé	v. Senger, Zürich	–	
356-2.009	356-2-040673	Cabriolet	Aschauer, Peter	7. 3. 49	
356-2.010	356-1-026857	Coupé	Porsche	12. 1. 49	Demonstration car
356-2.011	356-2-000029	Cabriolet	Pichler, Martin	17. 11. 49	
356-2.012	356-1-102845	Coupé	Walek, Franz	9. 3. 49	
356-2.013	356-1-000019	Coupé	Meyer's-Schruns	–	
356-2.014	356-1-000016	Coupé	Mayer, Robert	9. 3. 49	
356-2.015	356-1-000021	Coupé	Liewers - Wien	29. 3. 49	
356-2.016	356-1-000018	Coupé	Reisch, Fritz	22. 4. 49	Tatra-built
356-2.017	356-1-000030	Coupé	Henschel, Ernst	28. 6. 49	
356-2.018	356-1-000024	Coupé	Degerdon, Fritz	14. 6. 49	
356-2.019	356-1-000028	Coupé	Hruschka, Ing.	–	
356-2.020	356-1-000022	Coupé	Schindler-Paulus	12. 5. 49	Tatra-built
356-2.021	356-1-000023	Coupé	Müller, Dr. F.	14. 6. 49	
356-2.022	–	–			
356-2.023	356-1-000025	Coupé	Günther, Herbert	6. 5. 49	Tatra-built
356-2.024	–	–			
356-2.025	356-1-102835	Coupé	Jaeger, Rene Dr.	11. 2. 49	
356-2.026	356-1-000011	Coupé	Mautner, Markhoff	–	
356-2.027	356-1-000026	Coupé	Friedwagner, Franz	15. 6. 49	
356-2.028	–	–		–	
356-2.029	356-1-000020	Coupé	Müller, Josef	–	Tatra-built
356-2.030	–	–		–	
356-2.031	356-2-000027	Cabriolet	Scania Vabis/S	12. 6. 50	
356-2.032	356-2-000036	Cabriolet	Scania Vabis/S	12. 6. 50	
356-2.033	356-2-000032	Cabriolet	S. E. Mohamed Taher	–	President of the Egyptian Automobile Club (Tatra-built)
356-2.034	356-2-000037	Cabriolet	Scania Vabis/S	12. 6. 50	
356-2.035	356-2-000031	Cabriolet	Abdel Moneim	–	Delivered with unfinished body – finished outside
356-2.036	356-2-000034	Cabriolet	Autohaus Ebner	–	
356-2.037	356-2-000035	Cabriolet	Scania Vabis/S	18. 7. 50	
356-2.038	356-2-000038	Cabriolet	Scania Vabis/S	12. 6. 50	
356-2.039	356-2-000033	Cabriolet	Scania Vabis/S	18. 7. 50	
356-2.040	–	–		–	
356-2.041	356-2-000040	Cabriolet	Scania Vabis/S	12. 6. 50	
356-2.042	356-2-000039	Cabriolet	Scania Vabis/S	12. 6. 50	
356-2.043	356-2-000041	Cabriolet	Scania Vabis/S	18. 7. 50	
356-2.044	356-2-000042	Cabriolet	Scania Vabis/S	11. 5. 50	
356-2.045	356-2-000043	Cabriolet	Scania Vabis/S	18. 7. 50	
356-2.046	–	–		–	
356-2.047	356-2-000045	Cabriolet	Scania Vabis/S	18. 7. 50	
356-2.048	356-2-000044	Cabriolet	Scania Vabis/S	16. 11. 50	
356-2.049	356-2-000047	Cabriolet	Scania Vabis/S	15. 2. 51	
356-2.050	356-2-000046	Cabriolet	Scania Vabis/S	20. 3. 51	
356-2.052	356-2-000048	Cabriolet	Mathé, Otto	9. 2. 51	

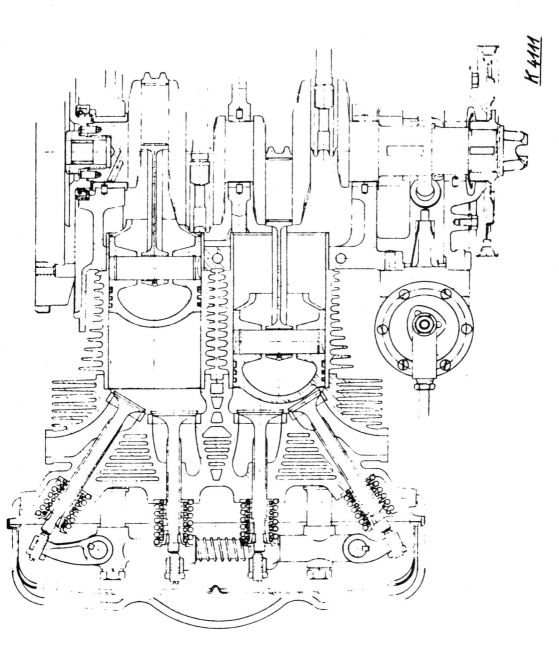

Longitudinal section through four-cylinder VW engine Type 369 for Porsche Type 356.

Overleaf: *Cross-section of engine Type 369:VW engine of 1,086 cc capacity developing 40 bhp (DIN).*

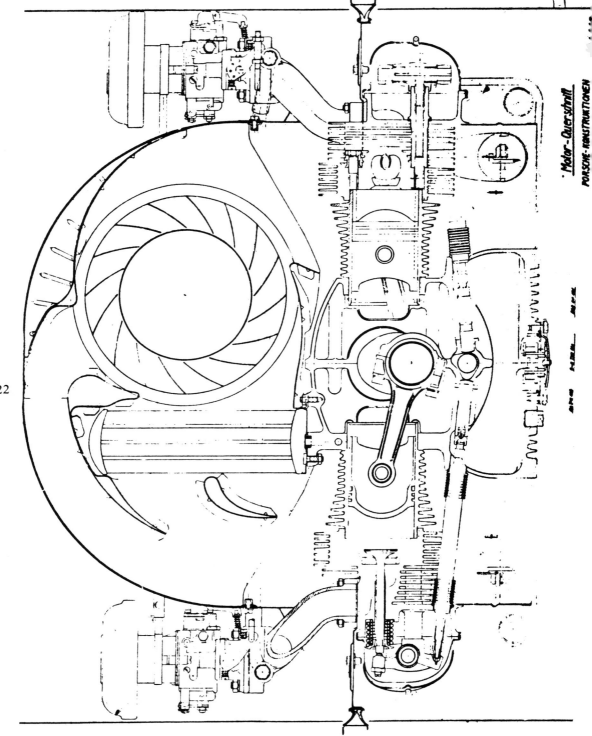

22

· Motor - Querschnitt
PORSCHE - KONSTRUKTIONEN

Wooden model of Type 114, made in 1938: study for a competition car based on the VW.

Porsche ancestor Type 64. Only three were built.

24

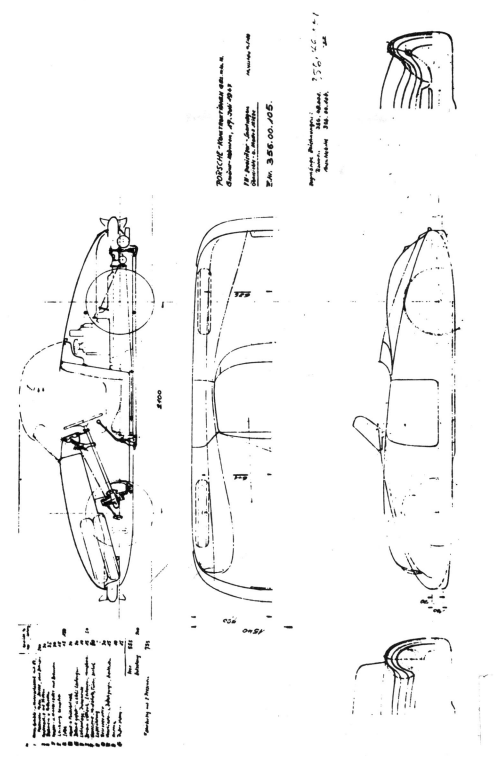

'VW two-seater sports car', drawing No 356.00.105 dated July 1947.

Porsche No 1 with separate frame, based on the July 1947 drawing.

26   *Next three pages: Extracts from the Certificate of Roadworthiness delivered to Porsche Konstruktionen GmbH by the Administration of Transport of Carinthia for 'Porsche Nr 1'.*

Einzelgenehmigung

Bescheid

An ___ P o r s c h e , Konstruktionen Ges.m.b.H. ___

G m ü n d ___

Zl. __28-30/48.__

Prüf.-Nr. __4328__

1. Das (Der) von Ihnen vorgeführte, nachstehend beschriebene Kraftfahrzeug (Anhänger) wurde am __8. Juni__ 194 8 gemäß dem Kraftfahrgesetz 1937, B. G. Bl. Nr. 29/1937, in der Fassung 1946, geprüft und genehmigt. Es (Er) entspricht (unter Berücksichtigung der in diesem Bescheid niedergelegten Einschränkungen)* den Vorschriften der Kraftfahrverordnung 1937 in der Fassung 1947. Gemäß § 29, Absatz 3, der Kraftfahrverordnung muß jede beabsichtige Änderung an diesem genehmigten Fahrzeuge der nach dem Standort des Fahrzeuges zuständigen Landesbehörde zur Entscheidung angezeigt werden.

2. Besondere Bedingungen:

k e i n e ___

3. Name und Wohnort des Erzeugers des Fahrgestelles und des Aufbaues:

___Porsche Konstruktionen Ges.m.b.H. Gmünd,Kärnten___

___Motor:Volkswagenwerke Fallersleben___

4. Firmenmäßige Typenbezeichnung des Fahrgestelles:

Sport 356/1 ___

Nichtzutreffendes streichen.

27

5. Technische Beschreibung des Fahrzeuges:

Art des Fahrzeuges		**Personenkraftwagen** **Sport-Zweisitzer,Motor im Heck**
Erzeugungsnummer sowie Jahr der Erzeugung des	a) Motors b) Fahrgestelles c) Aufbaues	a) Nr. 356-2-034969 ___ Jahr 1948 b) Nr. 356-001 ___ Jahr 1948 c) Nr. ___ Jahr ___
Eigengewicht des betriebsfertigen Fahrzeuges Zulässige Belastung Mithin zulässiges Gesamtgewicht		585 kg Nutzlast 200 kg 785 kg ___ kg
Kraftquelle		**Verbrennungskraftmaschine**
Bei Verbrennungs-kraftmaschinen Bauart des Motors	a) Arbeitsweise* b) Anzahl der Zylinder c) Hub d) Gesamthubraum e) Größte Nutzleistung des Motors	a) Vergaser, Viertakt b) Vier c) 64 mm (Bohrung 75 mm) d) 1.131 Liter e) 35 PS bei 4000 Umdrehungen i. d. Min.
Art des Schalldämpfers		Ovaler Resonanz-Schalldämpfer ohne Querwände mit seitlichen Einführungen u.fischschwanzförmigem Auspuff
Art der Kraftübertragung (Bei Anhängern: Hauptkupplung, Sicherheitskupplung)		Motor,Einscheiben-Trockenkupplung, Viergang-Schaltgetriebe u.1Rück-wärtsgang ,Hinterachse mit Ausgleichgetriebe.
Zahl und Art der Bremsvorrichtungen		Handbremse-mechanische Vierrad-Innenbackenbremse Fußbremse-mechanische Vierrad-Innenbackenbremse
Art und Ausmaß der Bereifung		Luft, 5,00 - 16
Bei Fahrzeugen, deren Gesamtgewicht 5 t übersteigt: Die Achsdrücke im beladenen Zustand		vorne ___ kg hinten ___ kg

Anzugeben ist nicht nur die Taktzahl, sondern auch Vergaser-, Diesel-, Gasmotor usw.

28

Bei nicht mit Luftreifen versehenen Fahrzeugen: Raddrücke auf 1 cm Reifenbreite im beladenen Zustand, bezogen auf die Breite der Auflagefläche des Reifens auf der Felge	vorne	_____ kg/cm
	hinten	_____ kg/cm
Radstand in Millimetern	2150	mm
Spurweite in Millimetern	a) vorne 1290 mm b) hinten 1250 mm	
Kleinster fahrbarer Kreis in Metern	10.2	m
Größte Länge	3860	mm
„ Breite	1670	mm
„ Höhe	1250	mm
Wesentliche Abweichung von den üblichen Bauarten	k e i n e	

6. Das in dem unten angeschlossenen Lichtbild dargestellte Kraftfahrzeug ist bei Einhaltung der in vorstehendem Bescheid unter Punkt 2 enthaltenen besonderen Bedingungen und bei Übereinstimmung mit den im Punkt 5 angeführten technischen Angaben für den Verkehr auf Straßen geeignet.

Rechtsmittelbelehrung:

Gegen diesen Bescheid kann binnen zwei Wochen nach Zustellung bei der Behörde, die ihn erlassen hat, Berufung eingebracht werden.

_____Klagenfurt_____, am __8. Juni_____ 194**8**

Für den Landeshauptmann:

Anlage: Lichtbild des Fahrzeuges 9 × 12 cm.

29

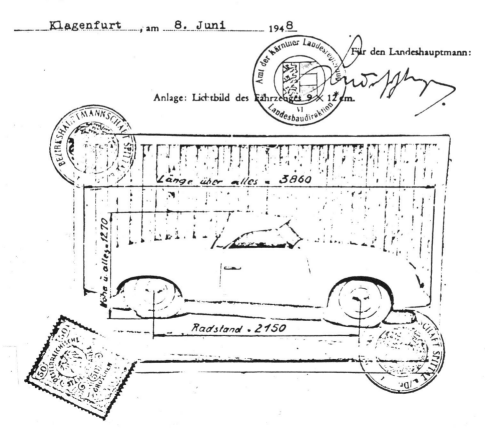

Bescheid.

Raum für
Stempelmarken.

An Fa.

....Porsche.Konstruktionen.G.m.b.H.,...............................

G m ü n d /Kärnten

Zahl 7512-30/48   Prüf-Nr. ....

1. Auf Grund der Prüfung vom ......13. Juli...... 194 8 wird die nachstehend beschriebene und in der beigegebenen Zeichnung wiedergegebene Type gemäß dem Kraftfahrgesetz, BGBl. Nr. 29/1937 in der Fassung des Jahres 1946, und der Kraftfahrverordnung, BGBl. Nr. 106/1937 in der Fassung des Jahres 1947, unter Berücksichtigung der im Bescheid, insbesondere in der technischen Beschreibung, festgelegten Einschränkungen genehmigt.

   Es wird darauf hingewiesen, daß zufolge § 28, Abs. 1, der Kraftfahrverordnung der Inhaber des Bescheides berechtigt und verpflichtet ist, für jedes der von ihm erzeugten oder in Handel gebrachten Fahrzeuge (Fahrgestelle) dieser Type Typenscheine, die eine getreue Abschrift dieses Bescheides enthalten, nach Anlage 2 der genannten Verordnung auszustellen, ferner daß gemäß § 28, Abs. 3, der Kraftfahrverordnung jede beabsichtigte Änderung an der Type bei der Behörde, die diesen Bescheid erlassen hat, zur Entscheidung anzuzeigen ist.

2. Besondere Bedingungen, Fristen:

                        k e i n e

30

3. Name und Wohnort des Erzeugers des Fahrgestelles und des Aufbaues:

    Porsche Konstruktionen Ges.m.b.H., Gmünd/Kärnten

4.

| Firmenmäßige Typenbezeichnung: | 356/2 |

5. Begründung .und Rechtsmittelbelehrung:
   Die Type entspricht unter den vom Prüfer im vorstehenden Bescheid gemachten Vorschriften den gesetzlichen Bestimmungen.
   Gegen diesen Bescheid steht binnen 2 Wochen nach Zustellung bei der Behörde, die ihn erlassen hat, die einzubringende Berufung offen.

   Klagenfurt , am 7. August 194 8

                                   Für den Landeshauptmann:

                                   Buschberger e.h.

Front and rear views of Porsche No 1, forerunner of all Porsche sports cars.

Facing page: Official homologation certificate for Porsche, Type 356/2 (Aluminium Coupé).

Porsche No 1 was a two-seater with folding emergency top. The engine was located directly behind the cockpit.

Wide sill dictated by the bulky tubular frame.

The instrumentation was rather spartan. Driver and passenger shared the bench seat.

33

Straight from the Porsche Museum: Porsche No 1, still original in most of its features.

Facing page: Test run of bodyless Porsche 356 watched by an interested crowd.

Dr Ferry Porsche (right) with the first Gmünd-built 356 aluminium coupé.

Rear view of early 356 aluminium coupé: already a typical Porsche.

Side view of 356 aluminium coupé produced in Gmünd.

Side and front views of aluminium coupé built in July 1948.

Allgemeine Betriebserlaubnis Nr. 625

für die Personenkraftwagen Typ : 356 der Firma
Dr.Ing. h.c. F. P o r s c h e KG in Stuttgart-Zuffenhausen

Auf Grund des anliegenden Gutachtens der Technischen Prüfstelle
für den Kraftfahrzeugverkehr beim Technischen Überwachungsverein
Stuttgart in Stuttgart vom 29. August 1950 wird für die reihen-
weise gefertigten Personenkraftwagen Typ 356 der Firma
Dr.Ing. h.c. F. Porsche KG in Stuttgart-Zuffenhausen widerruflich
die Allgemeine Betriebserlaubnis gemäß § 2o Abs. 1 der Verordnung über die Zulassung von Personen und Fahrzeugen zum Straßen-
verkehr vom 13. November 1937 (StVZO) erteilt.
Ferner wird versuchsweise und unter Vorbehalt jederzeitigen
Widerrufs der Abstand der Schlußlichter voneinander mit 89 Zenti-
meter genehmigt (§ 53,1 StVZO).
Der Hersteller hat für jedes dem Typ entsprechende Fahrzeug einen
Kraftfahrzeugbrief auszufüllen sowie die Richtigkeit der Angaben
über die Beschaffenheit des Fahrzeugs und dessen Übereinstimmung
mit dem genehmigten Typ zu bescheinigen. Die Vordrucke für die
Briefe sind von der Sammelstelle für Nachrichten über Kraft-
fahrzeuge und Kraftfahrzeugführer in Bielefeld, Herforder Stra-
ße 8, zu beziehen.

Im Falle einer Änderung des Typs ist ein entsprechender Nachtrag
zu der Allgemeinen Betriebserlaubnis zu beantragen.

Durch die Erteilung der Allgemeinen Betriebserlaubnis werden
Schutzrechte Dritter nicht berührt.

Die auf der Allgemeinen Betriebserlaubnis ruhenden Befugnisse
erlöschen mit Ablauf des 16. 11. 1953, wenn sie nicht nach
§ 2o Abs. 4 StVZO verlängert werden.

38

Offenbach (Main), den 17. November 1950

Der Bundesminister für Verkehr

Im Auftrag

(Schumann)

Anlage:
Gutachten d. Techn. Prüfstelle
f.d.Kraftfahrzeugverkehr beim
TÜV Stuttgart vom 29.8.1950
Nr. StV 7 - 1o7/716/5o

*General Certificate of Roadworthiness No 625 issued by the Ministry of Transport on
November 17 1950 for the Porsche Type 356. The (illegal) distance of 89 cm between the
tail lights is accepted provisionally.*

*Facing page: Drawing of 356 model with pressed steel platform, as built in Stuttgart from
late 1951.*

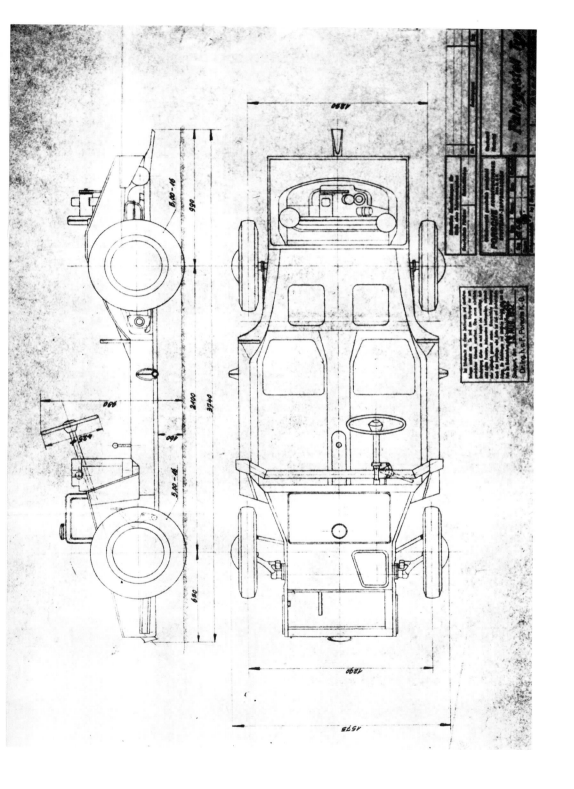

39

Type 356 (1949-1955)

In the summer of 1949, a handful of Porsche men began to prepare the transfer of the car production to Stuttgart in a workshop rented from the Reutter coach-building company in the Augustenstrasse. The company management had been informed that in summer 1950, the Americans were to move out of the Zuffenhausen factory and no time was to be lost in preparing the reconversion.

One year earlier, on September 17 1948, a contract had been signed by Volkswagenwerk and Porsche, of which the major outlines were to remain unchanged until mid-1974. An important point in the contract was that Porsche was to benefit from the VW service organisation. This promising agreement and the hope of soon being able to resume car production in Stuttgart, prompted Porsche to announce his sports car to the public. A Type 356 was exhibited at the Geneva motor show of 1949 and got an enthusiastic reception. Catalogues, illustrated only with drawings of the car, pointed convincingly to the advanced concept of the 356. In addition to the coupé on the stand, a drophead version was also offered, to be built by the Swiss coachbuilder Beutler, in Thun.

In view of the expected release of Porsche's own factory, production was started on a rather makeshift basis at the end of 1949. The executives directly under Dr Porsche were accommodated in a prefabricated house of about 100 square metres (119.6 square yards) which the company had bought for DM 19,000. Even the production had to be content with 500 square metres (598 square yards)—all that Reutters could provide—which had been rented for DM 1 per square metre per month. The premises consisted of wooden barracks and that is where the first 1,110 cc Porsches, powered by the 40 bhp modified VW engine, were built. They were offered at DM 9,950—quite a low price if one remembers that these cars were still almost entirely hand-made. They were real artists who formed chassis and body directly from a 1:1 drawing, practically without any mechanical aids. Only progressively, rigs were introduced to accelerate and facilitate the production, but nevertheless it took quite a long time before more than one single car left the barracks after a day's work. Neither was the period without its problems; once, for example, Professor Porsche put his body workers to shame when, just looking at a car, he maintained that it was not symmetrical. He had the car measured and this proved him right: the right-hand side was indeed two centimetres (nearly one inch) wider than the left-hand side.

But after some time, this pioneer period came to an end while everyone concentrated on increasing the production and extending the sales organisation. In spring 1950 Professor Prinzing, who jointly led the company with Dr Ferry

Porsche, took one of the Stuttgart-built cars to Volkswagen where VW main dealers and importers from Europe and overseas had a meeting. In a very short time he succeeded in getting firm orders for no fewer than 37 Porsche cars! The files reveal that, between themselves, Glöckler in Frankfurt, Kraus in Nürnberg, Islinger in Mannheim, Mahag in Munich, Hahn in Stuttgart and the Südbadische Automobilgesellschaft in Freiburg ordered the first 20 Porsche cars. The rest were dispatched to foreign companies, mainly Scania-Vabis in Sweden, Guerin in Portugal and Pon in Holland.

On the Thursday before Easter 1950 the first Stuttgart-built 356 was at long last complete and everyone came out to admire it in the factory forecourt in the Augustenstrasse. The grey coupé was run-in during the Easter period and was later used as a factory demonstrator.

Several factors contributed to the successful launch of the Porsche sports car. The list of Porsche customers included several prominent names from the worlds of film, radio and finance. The news spread quickly and consequently also aroused interest in wealthy circles outside Germany.

Sporting successes also helped establish the Porsche car's fame. Herbert Kaes, a cousin of Dr Porsche, must probably be given credit for the very first Porsche victory. He entered the tubular-frame two-seater for a race around the streets of Innsbruck which took place on July 11 1948 and easily won his class. But as early as 1950 the private owners took the initiative. Their innumerable successes took the fame of the reliable and fast air-cooled sports car from Stuttgart into the most remote corners of the world.

The first official works entry was made in 1951, using a slightly modified production car. The French importer Auguste Veuillet, a well known figure in French racing circles, had received his first Porsche—a bright blue coupé—only a few days before the Paris Salon of 1950. He was so enthusiastic about the car that he managed to persuade the 75-year-old Professor Porsche, who had visited him on his stand, that a good show in the Le Mans 24 Hours race would make the car known throughout the world if it could achieve any reasonable success. One year later this idea became reality. And one of the two drivers of the lone Porsche 1100 entered was Auguste Veuillet! Together with his co-driver Mouche, they won their class and the Porsche had reached the international scene.

When, on March 21 1951, the 500th Porsche was completed, only the manufacturers were surprised. When the 356 series was laid down none of the insiders had expected the production ever to reach such a figure. But when, hardly six months later, the 1,000th car was delivered, it suddenly seemed to be quite normal. The exercise closed with a turnover of DM 12,500,000 and 1,103 vehicles were built by a total staff of 214.

In August 1952 the first Porsche 356 built in Stuttgart met an undignified end. By that time, the coupé (familiarly called 'Cheetah') had done approximately 80,000 kilometres (50,000 miles) of testing, powered by a 1.5-litre engine and was heading for a total of a quarter of a million kilometres (156,000 miles). Unfortunately, a high speed accident on the motorway instantly turned it into a complete wreck. The driver was unhurt, but a few years later he was to be involved in an even more spectacular and much more publicised accident. He was the very gifted engine specialist Rolf Wütherich (who later achieved many successes as a co-driver in races and rallies) and he survived the accident in which he passengered the American film idol James Dean who drove his Porsche Spyder. While Dean was fatally injured, the doctors again managed to put Wütherich back into one piece.

Around the same period—near the end of 1952—came the first efforts to give the Porsche car an unmistakable trademark, symbol or heraldic sign. The initiative came mainly from foreign dealers and from customers. Overseas Porsche owners seemed particularly keen to have a sort of quality mark to adorn their car in addition to the Porsche script. Two symbols were considered: the native country of Professor Porsche and the city of Stuttgart where the cars were built. After some hard thinking and many discussions, the latter idea prevailed, mainly out of gratitude and satisfaction for the happy second start taken by the company in the capital of Württemberg. This is why the Porsche emblem includes both the arms of Stuttgart and those of Württemberg, together with the Porsche name. The design of the emblem was the responsibility of Dr Ferry Porsche under whose guidance the publicity chief of the period—Lepper—and a Porsche designer—Riemspiess—produced the final design.

A quarter of a century later it seems hardly credible that the proposed use of the arms of Württemberg should have created such a headache for everyone concerned. But in 1952, paper of the required quality was hard to get and so were printing matrixes. Getting gold for filling the negative print was also a real problem at the time. In addition came a considerable amount of correspondence with various authorities. The City of Stuttgart and the Ministry for Economic Affairs of the State of Württemburg had to give their approval to the use of their arms in the 'imaginary arms' of the Porsche company. Those responsible for the final design went to great pains to reproduce every particular of the arms they used, especially of the horse included in the arms of the City of Stuttgart. Not before 1953 did the Porsche emblem appear on the steering wheel hub of the 356. This Porsche trademark has remained unchanged from the beginning and is now registered in several countries.

General description: Type 356 (basic model)

Coachwork and chassis

The frame of the Stuttgart 356 was made of box section pressed steel and formed a single unit with the floor pan. Front and rear bumpers were integrated into the body. The toughened glass windscreen was made up of two panels joined in the car's longitudinal axis by a central runner. 3.00 D 16 rims carried by plain disc wheels were used. The direction indicator lights were small and circular, surrounded at the rear by rectangular tail lights. The number plate and stop lights were combined in a chromium-plated housing above the registration number. The engine cover had an air intake grille and the front cover carried a small chrome handle. The windscreen wipers parked to the left when seen from the driver's seat.

All wheels were independently sprung by torsion bars. The front dampers were single acting, the rear ones double acting. The steering required 2.4 turns from lock to lock. Steering was by worm and finger with a divided track rod, according to Porsche patents. The brakes were Bowden cable-operated and had leading and trailing shoes. Brake drum diameter was 230 mm (nine inches). The tyres were 4.75-16 or 5.00-16.

Engine

The air-cooled four-cylinder Porsche 356 engine was located in the back of the car. It was a development of the VW engine, with a power output of 40 bhp at

4,000 rpm. This power was obtained from 1,086 cc with a compression ratio of 7.0:1. The overhead valves were pushrod-operated from a central camshaft located below the crankshaft. The mixture was supplied by two Solex down-draught carburettors, Type 26 VFJ. The engine oil temperature was kept at a reasonable level by a finned tube cooler located in the airstream created by the cooling blower.

Transmission

The Fichtel & Sachs single-disc dry clutch transmitted the torque to a four-speed and reverse gearbox. Third and fourth had helical silent gears. The final drive was by a Palloid crown wheel and pinion assembly of 7:31 = 4.43:1 ratio and a bevel gear differential.

Equipment

Most cars were delivered with a bench front seat, but separate bucket seats could be supplied as an option. The height of the seat could be altered with the help of an additional cushion and (as was also the case with a bench seat) only the separate squabs could be folded forward. There were no 'emergency' rear seats, but an additional passenger could be carried over a short distance behind the front ones. The instrument panel was plain metal and carried two large dials. In its centre, a rectangular cutout was provided for the installation of a radio or a clock. The white steering wheel had three spokes—reduced to two on later cars. The door windows wound down and the interior trim colour was to the customer's choice.

Annual modifications

1951

A full year after the start of the Stuttgart production, the 1300 model (1,286 cc) was introduced. All models then had two leading shoe front brakes with finned drums. In October 1951 the 1,500 cc engine (60 bhp) was introduced. This engine had a more sporting camshaft and roller bearing big ends.

1952

The windscreen was now made in one piece, but was still folded in the centre. The bumpers were mounted slightly higher and at some distance from the body panels. The rectangular tail lights were replaced by circular ones of the same diameter as the directional lights. The perforated steel disc wheels, still of 406 mm (16-inch) diameter, could be supplied either sprayed or chromium-plated. The rear window of the drophead was increased in size. A folding, one-piece rear squab was added to the rear compartment. Moving the spare wheel to a position in front of the battery, where it was carried more or less upright, made it possible to accommodate some luggage in the front compartment. The 60 bhp version of the 1500 was replaced by a 55 bhp version, to be generally known as 'Dame' because of its refined manners. This was the first engine featuring the 'Alfinger' crankshaft (which got its name from the town of Wasseralfingen where it originated). This forged, plain bearing crankshaft had a stroke of 74 mm (three inches). A 1500 S power unit (70 bhp) rounded the programme up at the top end. A fully synchronised gearbox incorporating the patented Porsche split ring synchromesh system was a standard feature of all models. The diameter of the brake drums was increased to 280 mm (11 inches).

At the beginning of 1952 a suggestion from America led to the development of a new model based on the drophead coupé. The idea was to build a quick, light open car, known as 'Speedster' in overseas countries. Porsche built a first exclusive batch of 15 of which all but one went to America. This model, officially known as 'American Roadster', a direct ancestor of the 'Speedster' to be built two years later, was enthusiastically received. The Roadster was 60 kg (132 lb) lighter than the coupé: the normal seats were replaced by light buckets; the car had no wind-up windows; the instrument panel was rather spartan; the windscreen was light and low and the folding top would only be used in case of dire necessity. The engine was a 1500 S producing 70 bhp. Weighing no more than 605 kg (1,334 lb) complete (8.7 kg/bhp—116 bhp per ton), this 'American' Porsche made quite a few much larger-engined sports cars of the period look silly.

1953

The quality of the coachwork was constantly being improved. Soundproofing and the general equipment had made considerable progress. A new model appeared, the Porsche 356 with a 1300 S engine (1,290 cc—60 bhp) featuring a roller bearing crankshaft supplied by Hirth, but manufactured by Porsche in the following year.

An experiment to replace the VW trailing link front suspension by a MacPherson strut suspension was unsuccessful. W. Eyb designed a strut suspension which earned the experimental car the name 'Stork' because of its abnormally high ground clearance. The hub carriers of the 356 front suspension were reinforced and an anti-roll bar was added. The normal 1,300 cc engine now featured the Alfinger crankshaft. As this increased the stroke, the bore was reduced from 80 to 74.5 mm (3.14 to 2.93 inches) to avoid exceeding the 1,300 cc limit. The new model was called 1300 A. As from September 1954, all engines received a three-piece crankcase. Up to that date, Porsche had continued to use the old VW crankcase, even for the 1,500 cc engines, although these required some additional machining. At the end of 1954, the 1100 engine was phased out.

Modifications to the interior were the transfer of the heater control from the dashboard to the central tunnel and the addition of a windscreen washer. In September, the Type 540 'Speedster' was added to the programme, but to start with it was a US export-only model. The Speedster featured a wrap-round windscreen with narrow side pillars. The light all-weather top was distinctly lower and shorter than the former dropheads and folded away completely out of sight. The door waistline was 35 mm (1.4 inches) lower. The side windows were quickly removable. A chromium-plated protective strip ran along the side of the body at door handle height. The instrument panel was completely new with two large dials and a smaller one covered by a rounded shield facing the driver. The upper part of the dash was upholstered. The bucket seats with two long slots in their squab emphasised the sporting character of the 'Speedster'. Until the 356 A version appeared, the Speedster ran on 406 mm (16-inch) wheels and could be purchased with either the 55 bhp 1500 or the 70 bhp 1500 S engine. The basic model cost DM 12,200.

Discussions arose when the certificate of roadworthiness was applied for at the Stuttgart Technical Inspection Centre, which issued the following observations: 'With the top folded, there is no room for additional passengers on the emergency seats; if the top is raised, the emergency seats cannot be used by persons taller than 1.60 m [5 feet 4 inches], unless two holes are cut in the top to accommodate the passengers' heads.' The report also mentioned that getting into the car when the top was raised implied considerable acrobatic capabilities and that, when the seats had been reached, the passengers had to crouch to clear the top!

44

Year	Body	Model Type	Chassis no	Engine no	Engine type	Gearbox type	Cyl	Bore × stroke	Capacity	HP (DIN) at rpm	Torque (mkg) at rpm	Comp ratio	W'base (mm)	Track fr/rear (mm)	Length (mm)	Weight (kg)	No produced
1950	Coupé	1100	5001-5410	0101-0411	369	VW	4	73,5 × 64	1086	40/4200	7,15/2800	7:1	2100	1290/1250	3850	745	410
1951	Cabrio	1100	5132-5162	0412-0099	369	VW	4	73,5 × 64	1086	40/4200	7,15/2800	7:1	2100	1290/1250	3880	810	31
			5411-5600	10001-10137													190
	Coupé	1300	10001-10170	1001-1099	506	VW	4	80 × 64	1286	44/4200	8,3/2500	6,5:1					170
		1500	10350-10432	20001-20821	527	VW	4	80 × 74	1488	60/4400	10,4/3000	7:1				830	183
	Cabrio		10531-11125	30001-30737													595
1952	Coupé	1100	11126-12084	10138-10151	369	VW	4	73,5 × 64	1086	40/4200	7,15/2800	7:1	2100	1290/1250	3880	810	959
		1300	50001-50098	20822-21297	506	519-2	4	80 × 64	1286	44/4200	8,3/2500	6,5:1					98
	Cabrio	1500	10433-10469	30738-30750	527		4	80 × 74	1488	60/5000	10,8/2800	7:1				830	37
		1500	12301-12387	30751-31025	546		4	80 × 74	1488	55/4400	10,8/2800	6,8:1					87
		1500S	15001-15116	40001-40117	528		4	80 × 74	1488	70/5000	11,0/3600	8,2:1					116
1953	Coupé	1100	50099-51645	10152-10161	369	519-2	4	73,5 × 64	1086	40/4200	7,15/2800	7:1	2100	1290/1250	3950	810	1547
	Cabrio	1300	60001-60394	21298-21636	506		4	80 × 64	1286	44/4200	8,3/2500	6,5:1				830	394
		1500	–	31026-32569	546		4	80 × 74	1488	55/4400	10,8/2800	6,8:1					
		1500S	–	40118-40685	528		4	80 × 74	1488	70/5000	11,0/3600	8,2:1					
		1300S	–	50001-50017	589		4	74,5 × 74	1290	60/5500	9,0/3600	8,2:1					
1954	Coupé	1100	51646-53008	10162-10199	369	519-2	4	73,5 × 64	1086	40/4200	7,15/2800	7:1	2100	1290/1250	3950	830	1363
	Cabrio	1300	60395-60722	21637-21780	506		4	80 × 64	1286	44/4200	8,3/2500	6,5:1				830	328
	Speed.	1300S	80001-80200	50018-50099	589		4	74,5 × 74	1290	60/5500	9,0/3600	8,2:1				760	200
		1300A	–	21781-21999	506-1		4	74,5 × 74	1290		7,15/2800	7:1					
		1500	–	32570-33899	546		4	80 × 74	1488	55/4400	10,8/2800	6,8:1					
		1500S	–	40686-40999	528		4	80 × 74	1488	70/5000	11,0/3600	8,2:1					
		1300	–	22001-22021	506-2		4	74,5 × 74	1290	44/4200	8,3/2500	6,5:1					
		1300S	–	50101-	589-2		4	74,5 × 74	1290	60/5500	9,0/3600	8,2:1					
		1500	–	33901-34119	546-2		4	80 × 74	1488	55/4400	10,8/2800	6,5:1					
		1500S	–	41001-41048	528-2		4	80 × 74	1488	70/5000	11,0/3600	8,2:1					
1955	Coupé	1300	53009-55000	22022-22245	506-2	519-2	4	74,5 × 74	1290	44/4200	8,3/2500	6,5:1	2100	1290/1250	3950	830	1992
	Cabrio	1300S	60723-61000	-50127	589-2		4	74,5 × 74	1290	60/5500	9,0/3600	8,2:1				830	278
	Speed.	1500	80201-81900	34120-35790	546-2		4	80 × 74	1488	55/4400	10,8/2800	6,5:1				760	1700
		1500S		41049-41999	528-2		4	80 × 74	1488	70/5000	11,0/3600	8,2:1					

Notes:
Type 356: Standard VW gearbox (two-piece housing) from May 1950 to 1952.
No synchromesh. Central mounting.
Synchronised gearbox, Type 519 (two-piece housing) from June/July 1952. Central sandwich mounting.
Engine: Two-piece crankcase was replaced by three-piece design in November 1954.

45

Porsche 356 convertible, made in 1950. VW flat-four engine, 40 bhp (DIN) at 4,200 rpm.

46

Porsche 356 coupé with early two-piece V-windscreen.

Porsche 356 coupé, 1952 version. 1.3- and 1.5-litre engines were now available (44 and 60 bhp).

*Front and rear
views of 356
Speedster, pro-
duced from
September 1954
onwards.*

356 Speedster: fold-away top, modified instrument panel.

The 1950 convertible was less basic than earlier Porsches.

From the end of 1952, the Type 356 had separate bumpers, ventilated wheels and other minor changes.

Porsche 356 convertible, as from 1953 model: one piece V-shaped windscreen, improved instrumentation.

52   *Rear and side views of 40 bhp, 1,086 cc engine. Note single exhaust.*

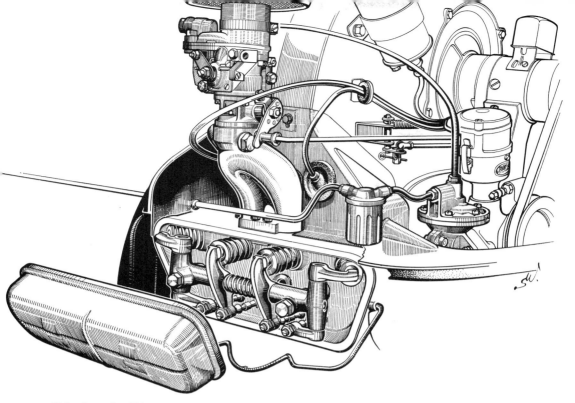

Side view of 1,300 cc engine: 1300 with 44 bhp, 1300 S with 60 bhp.

1300 Super engine: twin Solex carburettors, 60 bhp at 5,200 rpm. Roller bearing crankshaft.

Type 356 A (1955-1959)

A great celebration took place on March 12 1956. The Dr Ing hc F. Porsche GmbH company celebrated its Silver Jubilee, having been founded on March 16 1931. On this occasion the 10,000th Porsche car, a 356 A, was unveiled and driven out of the final assembly hall by Dr Porsche's youngest son, Wolfgang.

By this time the export quota of Porsche cars had reached 70 per cent of the total! Satisfied customers used their cars not only for everyday transport, but also for recreation and sporting activities. In the years 1954 to 1956 alone more than 400 international successes were achieved, which meant that, on average, every day of the year, there was somewhere a beaming Porsche driver getting the chequered flag. But this was not the only reason for satisfaction in Zuffenhausen: the company was then allowed to return to its own Factory No 1, released by the Americans. This immediately became the main administration building, housing the design office and the experimental, service and finance departments.

A car which had suffered accidental damage was used as an experimental guinea pig. Officially, it was Experimental Car No 35, but they called it 'Gottlieb', probably because a Daimler-Benz front suspension, complete with subframe and recirculating ball steering, was grafted to it. The Porsche rear suspension was modified to match. But 'Gottlieb', obviously ashamed of its many dents and of its primer finish, never appeared in public.

During the last year of the 356 A production run, Reutters produced 25 bodies per day at approximately DM 5,000 each! In spring 1959, the new building was at last completed and accommodated the car delivery and the spare parts departments. As part of the extension and rationalisation programme a second coachbuilder, Drauz in Heilbronn, was enrolled as a supplier. While Reutter continued to make the coupé, the hardtop and the convertible, Drauz built the D-type convertible which replaced the Speedster. The car was first exhibited in the Paris Salon of 1958 and deliveries began in August of the same year.

Deputising for the late Professor Porsche, his son Ferry received the Elmer A. Sperry Prize (awarded for an achievement of particular merit in the sphere of transport) on November 13 1958 in New York.

General description: Type 356 A (basic model)

Coachwork and chassis

The Porsche Type 356 A which superseded the 356 in autumn 1955 was also an all-steel vehicle in which the body was combined with the chassis frame and floorpan to make a single unit. The front springs consisted of two bundles of rectangular section leaves forming two torsion bars extending from one side of the chassis to the other. The rear wheels were sprung by a torsion bar of circular section on each side. The front wheels were located by short trailing links, while the rear wheels were carried by swinging half-axles located longitudinally by spring steel trailing arms. The suspension characteristics had been changed from the previous model and so had the damper settings. The torsion bar abuttments were adjustable as were the anti-roll bar links. The front trailing link bushes, which previously were of plastic material, were replaced by needle bearings to reduce friction. A two-spoke steering wheel operated the worm and finger mechanism (Porsche system) which provided a turning circle of 11 metres (36 feet) diameter. The four hydraulically operated Ate brakes had drums of 280 mm (11 inches) diameter. 4.50 J 15-inch rims replaced the former 16-inch diameter rims and 5.60 S 15 tyres were standard, except on the 1500 GS model.

Engine

Starting with the 356 A series, five different engines were offered: the 1300 producing 44 bhp, the 1300 S providing 60 bhp, the 1600 also yielding 60 bhp, the 1600 S producing 75 bhp and a new top model, the 1500 GS 'Carrera' with a resounding 100 bhp available. All engines had light alloy cylinder heads, crankcase and pistons. The cylinder walls were chromium-plated. In all engines except the 1500 GS, the overhead valves were operated by pushrods from a central camshaft and the crankshaft had plain bearings throughout, but roller bearings were used on the big ends of the 1300 S and 1600 S engines. The lubricant was fed under pressure to the bearings by a gear pump. The 1500 GS had four overhead camshafts and a built-up crankshaft on which the big ends and main bearings were rollers. In this engine a dry sump lubrication system featuring a pressure and a scavenge pump was used. The pushrod 1.5-litre engines were dropped.

Transmission

A single dry plate clutch separated the engine from the fully synchronised gearbox. The ratio of the spiral bevel and crown wheel final drive was 8:35.

Equipment

The V-type windscreen was replaced by a curved one. Door windows were made of toughened glass. The top of the dash was now padded and upholstered with imitation leather, and three large instruments were provided. An electric cigar lighter and an ashtray were standard and a cover for the radio opening was provided. A grab handle was added on the passenger's side, next to the glove box. The heater control was located on the central tunnel, behind the gear lever. The handbrake was of the umbrella type, next to the steering column. The direction indicator stalk was returned automatically by the steering and the windscreen washer was operated by a pedal. The amount of heated air admitted into the car could be adjusted by moving a sliding panel to more or less open the two outlets. The two separate front seats were now of the fully reclining type and the two rear 'emergency' seats had two separate squabs which could be folded flat to carry additional luggage. The car carried a gold-plated 'Porsche' script front and rear. Inside the passenger compartment the floor, the side runners and the rear compartment were covered with a Bouclé mat. The front indicator lights were new and combined with a small grille covering the twin horns. The Carrera (1500 GS) could be identified by the additional louvres cut into the engine cover.

Annual modifications

1956

Except for the gearbox production cars remained virtually unchanged. Instead of being split along its centre line, the new gearbox—Type 644—had a one-piece housing with an end cover through which the shafts were inserted from the front.

1957

On the occasion of the Frankfurt motor show, Porsche announced several improvements to the 356 A model. The worm and finger steering was replaced by a ZF worm and roller steering. The twin rear exhausts of the 1600 models were led through the bumper overriders to increase the ground clearance. Additional sporting appeal was provided by optional chrome-plated wheels with Rudge-type centre lock hubs. A towing eye was welded to the front part of the underpan. The floor pan was locally reinforced to take seat belts.

The doors were not only given new locks, but also an improved window winding mechanism. The coupé had two interior lights. Pivoting front quarter window panels improved the ventilation in the convertible. A door stop prevented the doors from closing by gravity on a slope. The directional, stop and tail lights were incorporated in a new, teardrop shaped bezel. The number plate light was now located under the plate. The coupé's rear light was spherically shaped and, in the case of the convertible, it had been further enlarged. Research work had led to the adoption of completely new seats in which the rear squab automatically conformed to the shape of the passenger's back. A one-piece, quickly removable hard top was offered for the convertible and the Speedster.

The 1300 models were phased out at the end of the year, but the Carrera was then offered in 'de Luxe' version (1,498 cc, 100 bhp) with an independent petrol heater instead of the engine-heated system. The engine in this car developed 10 hp less than in the 'Carrera GT' version. The pushrod engines got the same sort of Zenith twin-choke carburettors (Type 32 NDIX) as the Carrera. The 1600 S was quieter thanks to the use of a plain bearing crankshaft, and its power was 15 bhp higher than the normal 1600, though it was just as flexible.

A diaphragm spring single-plate clutch was now used, reducing the pedal effort, an improvement particularly appreciated by the ladies. A new crankcase improved the lubrication system and provided a better distribution of the oil, resulting in higher pressure at low engine speeds. A thermostat was provided to control the oil temperature automatically, and the oil pump was provided with two pick-ups, one on either side of the crankshaft axis. The pick-ups were controlled by an inertia valve closing one of them under the action of centrifugal force to avoid aspiration of air when the oil surged on bends taken at speed.

1958

The Speedster was dropped and replaced by the D-type convertible (D = Drauz, the coachbuilders). This model had a higher windscreen, a soft top with a larger rear window and winding windows. Normal Porsche seats replaced the light bucket seats. Some convertibles had two air intake grilles in the engine cover.

All models had further reinforced front stubaxles. The Carrera was still offered in two variants, but the engine capacity had been increased to 1,600 cc, raising the output by 5 bhp to 105 in the 'de Luxe' and 115 bhp in the 'GT' version. Both engines had a plain bearing, one-piece crankshaft. Thanks to the use of light alloy front and rear covers, as well as other weight-saving measures, Carrera models were notably lighter than the other production Porsches.

356A

Year	Body	Type	Chassis no	Engine no	Engine type	Gearbox type	Cyl	Bore × stroke	Capacity	HP (DIN) at rpm	Torque (mkg) at rpm	Comp ratio	W'base (mm)	Track fr/rear (mm)	Length (mm)	Weight (kg)	No produced
1955	Coupé	1300	55001-55390	22246-22273	506-2	519-2	4	74,5 x 74	1290	44/4200	8,25/2800	6,5:1	2100	1306/1272	3950	860	390
	Cabrio	1300S	61001-61069	50128-50135	589-2		4			60/5500	9,0/3600	8,2:1				880	69
	Speed.	1600	81901-82000	60001-60608	616-1		4	82,5 x 74	1582	60/4500	11,2/2800	7,5/1				815	100
		1600S	–	80001-80110	616-2		4			75/5000	11,9/3700	8,5:1					
1956	Coupé	1300	55391-58311	22274-22471	506-2	519-2	4	74,5 x 74	1290	44/4200	8,25/2800	6,5:1	2100	1306/1272	3950	880	2921
	Cabrio	1300S	61070-61499	50136-50155	589-2	644	4			60/5500	9,0/3600	8,2:1				900	430
	Speed.	1600	82001-82850	60609-63926	616-1		4	82,5 x 74	1582	60/4500	11,2/2800	7,5:1				835	850
		1600S	–	80111-80756	616-2		4			75/5000	11,9/3700	8,5:1					
1957	Coupé	1300	58312-59090	22472-22999	506-2	644	4	74,5 x 74	1290	44/4200	8,25/2800	6,5:1	2100	1306/1272	3950	930	779
		1300S	100001-101692	50156-50999	589-2		4			60/5500	9,0/3600	8,2:1					1692
		1600	101693-102504	63927-66999	616-1		4	82,5 x 74	1582	60/4500	11,2/2800	7,5:1					812
	Cabrio	1600S	61500- 61700	80757-81199	616-2		4			75/5000	11,9/3700	8,5:1				950	201
		1600	61701- 61892	67001-68216	616-1		4			60/4500	11,2/2800	7,5:1					192
		1600S	150001-150149	81201-81521	616-2		4			75/5000	11,9/3700	8,5:1					149
	Speed.		82851- 83691													885	841
			83792- 84366														575
1958	Coupé	1600	102505-106174	68217-72468	616-1	644	4	82,5 x 74	1582	60/4500	11,2/2800	7,5:1	2100	1306/1272	3950	885	3670
	Cabrio	1600S	150150-151531	81522-83145	616-2	716	4			75/5000	11,9/3700	8,5:1				905	1382
	Speed.		84367- 84922													815	556
	Convert.		85501- 85886													855	386
1959	Coupé	1600	106175-108917	72469-79999	616-1	716	4	82,5 x 74	1582	60/4500	11,2/2800	7,5:1	2100	1306/1272	3950	885	2743
	Cabrio	1600S	151532-152475	83146-84770	616-2		4			75/5000	11,9/3700	8,5:1				905	944
	Convert.		85887- 86830													855	944

Notes:
Type 356A: Synchromesh gearbox, Type 519 from June/July 1952.
Central sandwich mounting replaced in October 1955 by two outriggers, mounting Type 644.

Synchromesh gearbox Type 716 from September 1958. Mounting Type 644 with two outriggers.

57

The Porsche 356 A coupé replaced the 356 model in autumn 1955. Differences were mainly under the skin.

1956 model Carrera 356 A with twin exhaust.

Two views of 1956 model 356A convertible with 1600 engine.

60   *The D-convertible (D for Drauz) (above) appeared in 1958 as a replacement for the Speedster (below).*

The improved 1957 version of the Porsche 356 A convertible.

Porsche 356 A convertible. In contrast with the two-passenger Speedster, a true 2 + 2.

Carrera-engined 356 A hardtop with 1957 body modifications.

Type 356 A, 1957 model: exhaust pipes led through bumper overriders, new registration plate light.

Comprehensive instrument panel of 356 A coupé, as from 1957 model.

The trim of a late 1955 A-series Speedster was purposely kept light and functional.

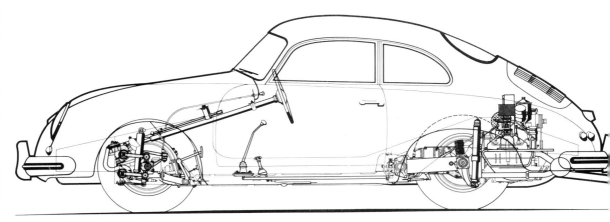

Top: Longitudinal section of an
early Porsche 356 A coupé.

Above: Porsche 356 A hardtop.
The last version of the A-series,
replaced by the 356 B in 1959.

Right: Top view of 1,500 cc flat-
four engine.

Type 356 B (1959-1963)

As production developed, so did the staff of the Porsche company which, at the beginning of 1960, had reached a figure around 1,250 workers and employees. Every effort was made to improve the quality control, as the company's now world-wide reputation was and still is based to a large extent on the high level of workmanship and reliability of its products. Nearly one in five of the workers concerned with production concentrated on quality control. Of the 255 men in the machining workshop and the production line, 56 performed quality checks. A total of 172 engineers and draughtsmen worked in the design office; 204 were engaged in experimental work and racing development, while the rest were otherwise employed in the company. On December 31 1960, 39,774 cars had left the factory. For every one of them, the Service Department had established four 'birth certificates': one for the engine, one for the transmission, one for a general vehicle check and an additional one for measurements.

On November 1 1960, the company moved into Factory Three, only a few yards away from Factory One. Here the sales department, the service shop, the spare centre and the car delivery were installed. The Porsche company then occupied 41,600 square metres (49,753 square yards) of which 28,800 (33,488) were actually inhabited. Orders were getting ever more numerous and as the production increased correspondingly, Porsche's turnover exceeded the 100 million Mark limit for the first time in 1960, when 108 million were turned over. A big step forward was taken in social matters in 1960, when the management decided that all workers paid on an hourly basis not only would be paid monthly, but would continue to be paid their full wage for a period of six weeks in case of illness.

The 356 B series continued to develop more and more from its ancestor, the VW Beetle. Only the two rear trailing arms and their bearings, the half shafts, the crown wheel and pinion assembly and the differential housing were still VW parts. The steering column flexible 'Hardy' joint and the cooling blower housing, still 'borrowed' from the Beetle at the beginning of the 356 B series, were soon to be replaced. In order to meet the ever-increasing demand for Porsche cars, two new suppliers appeared: the Wilhelm Karmann GmbH in Osnabrück and the Belgian Anciens Etablissements D'Ieteren frères in Brussels. In many years of cooperation with Volkswagen, both companies had given ample proof of their ability and in addition, D'Ieteren had been the sole importer for Porsche cars in Belgium for a long time. As Drauz, who had built the Roadster and convertible bodies, disappeared from the suppliers' list, the main supplier situation at the beginning of 1961 was as follows: Reutter building the coupé and convertible (to choice with soft or detachable hard top); Karmann building the hardtop coupé and D'Ieteren the Roadster.

During 1963, Porsche KG purchased the Reutter coachbuilding company. This increased the number of people occupied by Porsche by some 1,000 persons overnight, and the total ground surface of the body shop was more than doubled from 4,100 to 8,300 square metres (4,903 to 9,927 square yards).

General description: Type 356 B (basic model)

Coachwork and chassis

Important body modifications were introduced with the Porsche 356 B in 1959. The raised headlights gave the front wings (fenders) a different outline. The bumpers were raised to 95 mm (3.74 inches) and 105 mm (4.13 inches) above ground level, respectively front and rear, and were given more wrap-round. To match the higher front bumper, the lower part of the nose was more steeply raked rearward. The bumper overriders were redesigned. Better cooling for the new light alloy drum brakes was provided by two oval air intakes under the front bumper. The brake drums had transverse fins to create a centrifugal circulation of the cooling air. The luggage locker handle was wider, the hub caps were redesigned and both carried the Porsche emblem. The front directional indicator lights and their grille were also new. Two registration plate lights were carried by the rear bumper under which the reversing light was located. Under the front bumper, provision was made for adding fog lights. The rear suspension of the Super-90 and Carrera models featured a compensating transverse single leaf spring, centrally pivoted on the differential housing.

Engine

The pushrod engines had reinforced valve caps to match valve springs of different characteristics. The range of pushrod engines was extended by the addition of the S-90, producing 90 bhp.

Transmission

The pressure plate of the clutch was now integral with the diaphragm spring. The new Type 741 gearbox featured the latest developments in Porsche synchromesh which now incorporated a baulking system making it impossible for the driver to beat the synchromesh. This new gearbox also had lower mounted front supports. The gear lever and its console, the reverse gear selecting fork, the selector rods and the clutch release bearing were also new.

Equipment

The B-series coupé was given pivoted front window panels, similar to those of the convertible. A safer, tulip-shaped steering wheel was used on a shorter column. It had three assymetrical spokes and the central horn button was given small ears for easier manipulation. Special warm air outlets prevented the rear window from misting up. The gear lever was reduced in height from 330 to 290 mm (13 to 11.4 inches).

Special attention was given to ride comfort. In addition to improved front seats, the squab of the rear 'emergency' seat was now divided and the two parts could be folded forward separately—an improvement which required a modification to the central tunnel.

The convertible range was extended by the new 'Roadster' which could be purchased with either the 1600, the 1600 S or the S-90 engine. Compared with the convertible, the main difference was that the Roadster had only a light all-weather top, well in accordance with the taste of the younger sporting generation. In contrast to the old 'Speedster', which had been dropped from the range for some time, the Roadster had wind-up door windows and weighed only about 30 kg (66 lb) less than the coupé or convertible. The Roadster also had a slightly different instrument panel of a more sporting, functional character. Until February 1961, the Roadster was built by the Drauz coachbuilding company, but later cars were made by D'Ieteren in Brussels.

Annual modifications

1960

Karmann built fixed hardtop bodies of which the lower part was identical with the convertible. Abarth supplied a small series of 'Abarth-Carreras' for competition purposes. Early cars had a 1,600 cc, 135 bhp engine, later replaced by a 2-litre, 180 bhp unit.

1961

The 356 B was once more seriously revised (it was known internally as T6). The main visible modifications were the enlarged rear window of the coupé, a larger engine cover with two air intake grilles and a front luggage compartment lid of more nearly rectangular shape. The fuel tank was lower to increase the luggage space. The tank filler was now placed under a flap in the right-hand front wing (fender). Louvres were cut in front of the windscreen to improve ventilation. An electrically operated sliding roof was optional. Adjustable flaps allowed fresh air to be directed to the defroster outlets or on to the front passengers' feet. A lock held the front seat squabs in the upright position (except in the Roadster); the seat rails were improved for easier adjustment, a gear lever lock was fitted (only for Europe) and the windscreen washer reservoir was new. The windscreen wiper speed was made infinitely variable and the inside mirror was of the day/night variety. The air intake grille was deleted from the engine cooling blower, as was already the case in the S-90. The fuel lines of the 1600 engine and the supports of the carburettor operating linkage were modified. The 1600 S engine received four ring pistons (lead coated) together with cast iron cylinders, composite steel-and-light alloy pushrods to reduce valve clearance variation and a more efficient oil cooler. The S-90 was given a larger diaphragm spring and a correspondingly modified flywheel. The 'Carrera 2', featuring an engine enlarged to two litres and producing 130 bhp was announced in October 1961, but deliveries only began in spring 1962. An important feature was Porsche-designed disc brakes, notable for their outrigged disc with the caliper mounted inside the disc.

356B

Year	Body	Model Type	Chassis no	Engine no	Engine type	Gearbox type	Cyl	Bore × stroke	Cap-acity	HP (DIN) at rpm	Torque (mkg) at rpm	Comp ratio	W'base (mm)	Track fr/ rear (mm)	Length (mm)	Weight (kg)	No prod-uced
1959	Coupé	1600	108918-110237	600101-601500	616-1	741-1	4	82,5 x 74	1582	60/4500	11,2/2800	7,5:1	2100	1306/1272	4010	905	1320
	Cabrio	1600S	152476-152943	84771- 85550	616-2		4			75/5000	11,9/3700	8,5:1				925	468
	Roadster		86631- 87391													875	561
1960	Coupé	1600	110238-114650	601501-604700	616-1	741-2	4	82,5 x 74	1582	60/4500	11,2/2800	7,5:1	2100	1306/1272	4010	920	4413
	Cabrio	1600S	152944-154560	85551- 88320	616-2		4			75/5000	11,9/3700	8,5:1				940	1617
	Roadster	1600S-90	87392- 88920	800101-802000	616-7		4			90/5500	12,3/4300	9,0:1				890	1529
1961	Coupé	1600	114651-117476	604701-606799	616-1	741-2	4	82,5 x 74	1582	60/4500	11,2/2800	7,5:1	2100	1306/1272	4010	935	2826
	K-Hardt.	1600S	200001-201048	88321- 89999	616-2	741-A	4			75/5000	11,9/3700	8,5:1				955	1048
	Cabrio	1600S	154561-155569	085001-085670												955	1009
	Coupé	1600S-90	117601-118950	802001-803999	616-7		4			90/5500	12,3/4300	9,0:1				950	1350
	K-Hardt.	1600	201601-202200	606801-607760	616-1		4			60/4500	11,2/2800	7,5:1				970	600
	Cabrio	1600S	155601-156200	700001-701200	616-12		4			75/5000	11,9/3700	8,5:1				970	600
	Roadster	1600S-90	88921-89483 89601- 89849	804001-804630	616-7		4			90/5500	12,3/4300	9,0:1				905	563
1962	Coupé	1600	118951-121099	607751-608900	616-1	741-A	4	82,5 x 74	1582	60/4500	11,2/2800	7,5:1	2100	1306/1272	4010	950	2149
	K-Hardt.	1600S	202201-202299	701201-702800	616-2		4			75/5000	11,9/3700	8,5:1				970	99
	K-Coupé	1600S	210001-210899	804631-805600	616-7		4			90/5500	12,3/4300	9,0:1				950	899
	Cabrio	1600S-90	156201-156999												970	799
	Coupé	1600	121100-123042	608901-610000	616-1		4			60/4500	11,2/2800	7,5:1				950	1943
	K-Coupé	1600S	210900-212171	702801-705050	616-12		4			75/5000	11,9/3700	8,5:1				950	1272
	Cabrio	1600S-90	157000-157768	805601-806600	616-7		4			90/5500	12,3/4300	9,0:1				970	769

356B

Year	Body	Model Type	Chassis no	Engine no	Engine type	Gearbox type	Cyl	Bore × stroke	Cap-acity	HP (DIN) at rpm	Torque (mkg) at rpm	Comp ratio	W.base (mm)	Track fr/ rear (mm)	Length (mm)	Weight (kg)	No prod-uced
1963	Coupé	1600	123043-125239	610001-611000	616-1	741A	4	82,5 x 74	1582	60/4500	11,2/2800	7,5:1	2100	1306/1272	4010	950	2197
	K-Coupé		212172-214400	0600501-0600600												950	2229
	Cabrio		157769-158700	611001-611200												970	932
	Coupé	1600S	–	705051-706000	616-12	741A	4	82,5 x 74	1582	75/5000	11,9/3700	8,5:1	2100	1306/1272	4010	950	–
	K-Coupé		–	0700501-0701200												950	–
	Cabrio		–	706001-707200												970	–
	Coupé	1600S -90	–	806601-807000	616-7	741A	4	82,5 x 74	1582	90/5500	12,3/4300	9,0:1	2100	1306/1272	4010	950	–
	K-Coupé		–	0800501-0801000												950	–
	Cabrio		–	807001-807400												970	–

Notes:
Type 356B: Synchromesh gearbox, Type 741 (first model) from August 4 1959
to January 15 1960. Central 741 mounting.
Synchromesh gearbox, Type 741 (second model) from January 15 1960 to

September 1961. Twin outrigger, Type 644 mounting.
Synchromesh gearbox Type 741A from September 1961 to July 10 1963.
Mounting: 741 with twin outriggers. K-Coupé and K-Hardt (Hardtop) =
Karmann-built body.

69

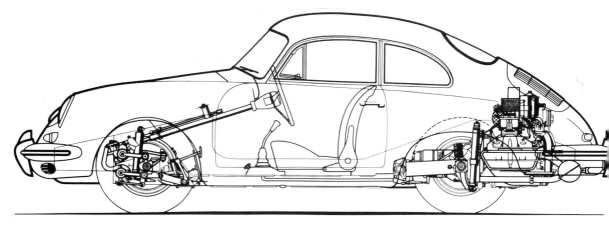

Longitudinal section of Porsche 356 B coupé showing the body modifications. Production began in autumn 1959.

70

Type 356 A (left) alongside Type 356 B. Note the latter's higher bumpers and lights.

Porsche 356 B convertible (above) and 356 B hardtop (below) with 1.6-litre engines.

72   *Coupé and convertible versions of Type 356 B. Available from 1961 with three engine variants.*

Type 356 B Carrera-2. Twin air grilles, larger rear window and other modifications.

The various Roadster
versions (more
sophisticated Speedsters)
were mainly built by
D'Ieteren in Belgium.

74

Porsche 356 B, 1,600 cc
'Super-90' with four-
cylinder engine
developing 90 bhp DIN.

Rear 'emergency' seats
of 356 B from 1951, with
separate folding backs.

Instrument panel of 356
B convertible and hard-
top (above left) and coupé
(left).

Cowled instrument panel of Porsche 356 B Roadster.

Front view of 2-litre, four-camshaft Carrera engine. 130 bhp DIN at 6,200 rpm.

Type 356 C (1963-1965)

On March 1 1964, all shares of the Reutter company were bought by the Porsche family. The production of reclining seat fittings and car seats however, was excluded from the takeover. These parts were to be made by the newly formed Recaro Group, production remaining in the former Reutter headquarters, in Stuttgart's Augustenstrasse. Recaro (who subsequently moved to Kirchheim/Teck—32 kilometres [20 miles] south of Stuttgart) supplied the standard seats for all Porsche models, as well as specially designed high-quality seats for almost any type of Porsche car.

Late in autumn 1964, production of the new 2-litre, six-cylinder Porsche started. To begin with the production of this new 911 model was approximately five cars per day. Parallel with the 911, the 356 C and 356 SC models continued to be made, the total daily production being around 40 cars.

Following the exceptional merits and successes of the Porsche company and its owners, the Porsche and Piëch families, honours poured in from everywhere. Late in summer 1964, the part-owner of Porsche KG, Kommerzialrat (Commercial Consultant) Louise Piëch, Dr Ferry Porsche's sister and sole proprietor of Porsche Konstruktionen KG in Salzburg (Austria), was awarded the 'Grosses Ehrenzeichen' (large distinction) by the Austrian Chancellor of the period, Dr Klaus, for her merits to the cause of the Austrian Republic.

One year later, on November 9 1965, on the occasion of the 150th anniversary of the foundation of the Vienna Technical High School, Ferry Porsche was given the title of Dr Honoris Causa for his contribution to the development of the motor car. After 17 years of extremely successful production the last car of the 356 series, a C-type convertible, left the production line in April 1965. Altogether 76,302 Porsche sports cars of the 356 series had made Porsche a worldwide trademark.

General description: Type 356 C (basic model)

Coachwork and chassis

Externally, the 356 C was almost identical with the final version of the 356 B. The only significant difference concerned the C-series' wheels, the securing bolts of which were closer together and covered by a different hub cap. ATE disc brakes (to Dunlop patents) dictated this modification. The 380 mm (15-inch) rims and the tyre dimensions remained the same as before. A one millimetre thicker anti-roll bar improved the handling, in conjunction with softer, pre-stressed rear torsion bars. The track rod joints were lubricated for life. The disc brakes required a modification to the shock absorber mountings. A supplementary rubber spring also served as a bump stop and prevented damage to the dampers. The C-models had Boge dampers, while adjustable Koni shock absorbers were standard on the SC. The rear compensating transverse leaf spring was deleted, as the newly tuned suspension made it virtually redundant, but it could still be obtained as an option by those wanting to be completely rid of final oversteer. The Hardy joint in the steering column was replaced by a Giubo 'doughnut' and the steering column was shortened on the same occasion.

Engine

The 1600, 1600 S and S-90 engines were replaced by the 1600 C (75 bhp) and the 1600 SC (95 bhp). The piston crown and the valve timing were modified, as were the inlet and exhaust ports, the valve spring cups, the crankcase ventilation, the main bearings and the machining of the crankshaft. Different size air and idle jets were used in the carburettors and the valve guides were now identical for inlet and outlet. The 2000 GS engine remained unchanged, while the 60 bhp pushrod unit was discontinued.

Transmission

The Fichtel & Sachs diaphragm clutch was replaced with a Häussermann clutch working on the same principle. The synchronising rings were reinforced for longer life. A limited slip differential could be obtained as an option.

Equipment

The central part of the instrument panel was deeper. The light and windscreen wiper switches were moved to the right of the steering column, together with the cigar lighter. The ventilation controls were modified. The coupé now had a map light for the passenger. A handbrake warning light was included in the combined instrument bezel. The heating system was controlled by a lever superseding the former knob, and two outlets were provided for rear window demisting. The gear lever was shortened to match the deeper instrument panel. The depth of the seat cushion was increased and the edge of the platform formed by the 'emergency' seat back was raised to prevent luggage from sliding forward. Straps were provided to secure the 'emergency' seat squab when upright. The armrest on the passenger side was shaped to facilitate door closing. The convertible top received a double zip fastener which could be opened and closed from the inside or outside. There were only two car keys; and the Roadster was dropped from the C-programme.

356C

Year	Body	Type	Chassis no	Engine no	Engine type	Gearbox type	Cyl	Bore × stroke	Cap-acity	HP (DIN) at rpm	Torque (mkg) at rpm	Comp ratio	W.base (mm)	Track fr/rear (mm)	Length (mm)	Weight (kg)	No prod-uced
1963	Coupé	1600C	126001-128104	710001-711870	616/15	741A	4	82,5 × 74	1582	75/5200	12,5/3600	8,5:1	2100	1306/1272	4010	935	2104
	K-Coupé		215001-216738	730001-731102		741C										935	1738
	Cabrio	1600SC	159001-159832	810001-811001	616/16		4			95/5800	12,6/4200	9,5:1				935	832
				820001-820522													
1964	Coupé	1600C	128105-131927	731103-733027	616/15		4	82,5 × 74	1582	75/5200	12,5/3600	8,5:1	2100	1306/1272	4010	935	3823
	K-Coupé		216739-221482	811002-813562												935	4744
	Cabrio	1600SC	159833-161577	820523-821701	616/16		4			95/5800	12,6/4200	9,5:1				935	1745
1965	Coupé	1600C	131928-131930	716805-	616/15		4	82,5 × 74	1582	75/5200	12,5/3600	8,5:1	2100	1306/1272	4010	935	3
	K-Coupé		221483-222579	733028-												935	1097
	Cabrio	1600SC	161578-162165	813563-	616/16		4			95/5800	12,6/4200	9,5:1				935	588
				821702-													

Notes:
Type 356C: Synchromesh gearbox, Type 741C from July 1963 to April 12 1965.
Mounting: 741 with twin outriggers.

Longitudinal section of Porsche 356 coupé with internal and external dimensions. From 1963.

80

In the C-series convertible, the rear window could be removed by undoing a zip fastener.

Hardtop (above) and coupé (below) versions of 356 C. Only two engine versions were provided.

The C-series is easily recognised from previous models by its larger rear window.

Additional identification of C-models is provided by twin rear grilles.

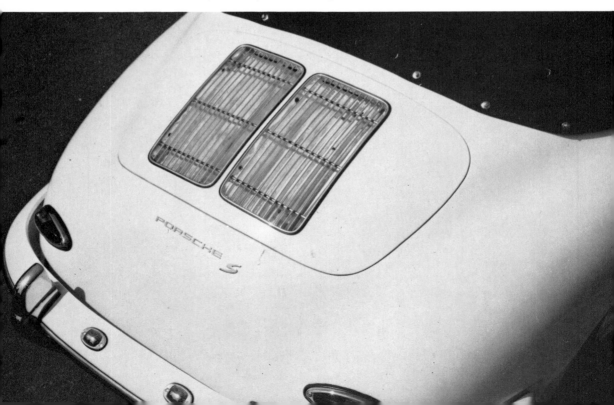

C-model dash panels were extended downwards.

Installed 1600 SC engine, 95 bhp at 5,800 rpm. (C series engines 75 bhp.) Oil-soaked air filters.

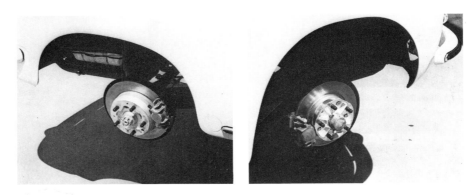

The 356 C was the first production Porsche with disc brakes on all four wheels.

After 17 years of production, the last 356, a C-convertible, left the assembly line in 1965.

Type 912 (1965-1968)/Type 912 E (1975-1976)

Although in September 1964 the Porsche 911 was put on the market as the 356's successor, it appeared that its price put it out of reach of some potential customers. A 1600 SC coupé cost DM 16,450 at the time, while the 911 cost DM 22,900. When in 1965 the 356 C-series was phased out, no Porsche was available in the price class of the former traditional models. The ever-increasing demand for a cheaper version of the 911, in which the high level of technology reached by the two models would not be sacrificed, was not ignored. It was met by a new model: the Type 912.

In the first days of April 1965, Porsche revealed its latest creation. To start with it was sold in Europe only, as its equipment and specification did not meet some British and overseas requirements. When these legal problems were solved the 912 became a bestseller, especially in the USA, and was built until the end of 1968, when the 2-litre 911 T replaced it.

The 912 was powered by a 1.6-litre pushrod engine, generally similar to the unit used in the 356 SC, but with its power reduced to 90 bhp. Outwardly, it was nearly identical to the Type 911. At the Frankfurt motor show of 1965, the range was extended by the 'Targa' model. In view of the characteristics of the four-cylinder engine, the five-speed gearbox developed for the 911 was offered as an option for the 912 and was specified by most buyers.

In their test reports, prominent writers described the 912 as a 'bread-and-butter car' at a price only just acceptable to most Porsche fans. Indeed, the 912 was never a car to which superlatives could apply, but in its time it could be considered a reasonable proposition on the sports car market. Even in 1965, though, it could not be called really fast and there were already some less flamboyant family cars which would out-accelerate it. But it was safe and fast enough to provide real driving pleasure.

More than ten years after the announcement of the original 912, the model was revived under the designation of 912 E. In contrast to its predecessor, this car was an overseas export model only. In Europe, its place was taken by the completely new 924, which was announced at the end of 1975. The new version of the 912 was just as difficult to distinguish externally from the contemporary 911. Its trim, both external and internal, was slightly simpler, but in the same class as the 911 series. The engine of this car was the 2-litre, air-cooled flat four unit, also used in the VW-Porsche 914-4. The engine had an electronically controlled fuel injection system with an airflow controlled metering unit (L-Jetronic) and an exhaust system featuring thermal reactors. It developed 90 bhp at 4,900 rpm. Top speed of the 912 E in fifth gear was 192 km/h (120 mph) and the car was offered in America for $3,000 less than a 911 S and $15,000 less than a Porsche Turbo. For this price the Americans could buy a real Porsche, cheaper to service and consuming less fuel than the 911, while incorporating all the advantages of a fully developed model. It was indeed a tough competitor for the VW-Porsche 914-4.

General description: Type 912 (basic model)

Coachwork and chassis

Particularly striking was the styling by Ferry Porsche Jr of the new body, incorporating the latest developments in body structure and design. The wheelbase was only 11 cm (4.3 inches) longer than in the 356 and the car was narrower, but the interior dimensions were quite a lot larger. An increase in window area of more than 50 per cent gave the 912 a brighter, less cramped-looking interior. The lengthened wheelbase had also improved the 'emergency' seating accommodation. The flat, 62-litre (13.6-gallon) tank formed the floor of the front luggage locker. The running gear too was completely new. The front wheels were suspended on a MacPherson-type damper strut located at its lower end by a triangular wishbone. The suspension function was entrusted to a longitudinal torsion bar. The steering was by rack-and-pinion. The rear suspension was of the semi-trailing link type in which each arm reacted on a transverse torsion bar.

The footbrake operated hydraulically on four discs with automatic adjustment for pad wear. A drum brake was incorporated within the rear disc and was operated by the hand lever. Tyre size and rim width were the same as for the early 911 models.

Engine

The 1,600 cc engine was developed from the 356 SC, 95 bhp unit, but with the output reduced to 90 bhp. It was a mixture between the reliable and refined 75 bhp unit and the former S-90 engine, and it can be said that the 912 engine combined the refinement of the 75 bhp engine with the urge of the more highly tuned version.

Compared with the old SC engine, the 912 gained in refinement by the use of an intake silencer suppressing the roar of the air rushing through the two twin-choke carburettors, a modification which, no doubt, cost a few horsepower. Flexibility had been improved by raising the maximum permitted engine speed from 5,500 to 6,000 rpm and modifying the shape of the torque curve.

Transmission

The car was fitted with a newly developed gearbox which could be purchased in four- and five-speed versions, the latter suiting the engine characteristics almost ideally. On the other hand more gear changing was required, especially in city driving and on narrow roads, including fairly frequent changes down into first gear—a rather tedious manoeuvre, as first had to be selected by pushing the lever against a spring to the left and then backwards. This newly developed gearbox had a further improved, more silent and more durable synchromesh, which also had a smoother action. The half-shafts incorporated two universal joints on each side.

Equipment

Wider and further developed Porsche seats provided even better seating comfort.

The entirely new instrument panel featured three large instruments combining all important functions. Two control stalks were to be found under the steering wheel, one operating the main and dipped lights, as well as the directional lights, and also allowing the headlights to be flashed; the other operating the windscreen washer and the three-speed wiper. The dashboard was padded both on its upper and its lower edge, and together with the three-piece offset steering column and the use of a laminated windscreen, notably contributed to the safety of the vehicle.

As in former models, the 'emergency' seat squab could be folded flat for extra luggage accommodation. The new front suspension also allowed a notable increase in the luggage capacity in the car's nose.

As in the 911 model, the battery was 12-volt (previous four-cylinder models had only 6-volt). The price of an early Porsche 912 with a four-speed gearbox was DM 16,250. The five-speed transmission cost an extra DM 340.

Annual modifications

1966
For the 1967 model, production of which began on August 1 1966 with chassis number 354.001 (Porsche body) and 458.101 (Karmann body), the engine and gearbox supports were modified. The track was widened with the use of thicker brake discs and several details were changed. These comprised new door locks, new instruments, modified fittings for opening the ashtray and the glove box, a different horn control, and a newly styled Porsche script.

1967
Several changes were made to the 912 and the three 911 models for 1968. After the works holiday, the 912 came off the assembly line with the following modifications: the wheelbase was lengthened by 57 mm (2.24 inches) to 2,268 mm (89.29 inches), and the front and rear wings (fenders) were slightly flared. The interior door panels were modified to increase the spare stowage capacity; the door handles were altered to pull-out levers recessed in the arm rests; the steering wheel was smaller and had a padded horn control. A push-down ashtray was fitted to the lower part of the dashboard and a new heating and ventilating system with a three-speed blower could be operated from the dash panel. A dipping mirror was bonded to the windscreen and the fuse box was moved to a position behind one of the headlights. Targa ventilation was improved by three long slots cut into the roll bar. A locking device was provided on the passenger side's rear squab. The rear brake pad area was increased in size. The electrically heated rear window, hazard lights, a glove box lamp and carpets to match the interior trim, replacing the former rubber mats, were also worthy of note. The rear reflectors were now mounted on the bumper. To special order, light alloy 5.5 × 14 or 6 × 15-inch wheels could be obtained, shod with 185 HR 14 or 185/70 VR 15 tyres respectively. The front anti-roll bar was deleted and US cars were fitted with exhaust emission control.

General description: Type 912 E (basic model)
Coachwork and chassis
The 912 E was based on the 911-2.7 body, but with fixed rear quarter windows (pivoted windows were an option) and other very minor differences.

The running gear was also nearly identical to that used in the 911, although there was a difference in the twin circuit braking system which did not feature internally ventilated discs.

Perforated pressed steel wheels were standard with 5.5 J × 15-inch wheels to which 165 HR 15 tyres were fitted.

Boge or Woodhead shock absorbers were used to damp the rear suspension movements and were identified accordingly. The 912 E had a fuel reservoir of 80 litre (17.6 gallon) capacity, incorporating a safety expansion chamber.

Engine

The crankcase and cylinders were those of the VW-Porsche 914-2.0 but the engine mountings were new. All moving parts were identical to those of the original engine. A secondary air pump was provided for exhaust emission control and was driven by a V-belt. The sheet metal ducting the cooling air around the engine was specially adapted for the 912 engine compartment. The fuel pump was mounted on the front cross member while the fuel filter was identical to that used in the 911's K-Jetronic injection system. Fuel was fed to the 912 engine by a Bosch L-Jetronic installation. The quantity of air aspirated by the engine was measured by a metering device, the signals of which were fed to an electronic control unit located by the right-hand rear wheel arch. The exhaust silencer and the heat exchanger for the exhaust emission control comprising secondary air injection, thermoreactors and exhaust gas recirculation were specially developed for the car. The operation of the exhaust gas recirculation had to be checked every 48,000 kilometres (30,000 miles). To ensure that this limit was not exceeded, the speedometer was fitted with a special counter triggering an 'EGR' warning light when this mileage was reached.

The VW-made engine had bore and stroke dimensions of 94 × 71 mm (3.7 × 2.8 inches), giving a total capacity of 1,971 cc. With a compression ratio of 7.6:1, it had an output of 90 bhp at 4,900 rpm. Its highest torque of 14 mkg (102 lb/ft) was reached at 4,000 rpm.

Transmission

The Type 923/02 five-speed gearbox was developed from the Type 915/44 transmission of the 911 and differed from it in the following details: clutch and clutch release mechanism, splines in the clutch disc hub, crown wheel and pinion ratio and fourth and fifth gear ratios. A limited slip differential with a 40 per cent locking factor was optional.

Equipment

Apart from the wheels, the only visible difference between a 912 E and a 911 was the script on the engine cover. Other differences were the following: the rear window heating resistance had only one heating position; the interior trim was simplified by the use of nylon velvet carpets and of imitation leather to frame the seats' upholstery. The loudspeaker perforations in the dash panel were deleted: if a radio was fitted, the loudspeakers were incorporated in the door panels. Both the door locking button and the bar connecting the door opening to the lock were modified.

Left: First public appearance of the 912 Targa was at the 1965 Frankfurt motor show.

Below: Early 912 Targa with short wheelbase.

Bottom: Early coupé version of 912.

Right: The 912 instrument panel was entirely different from that of the 356.

Below: Section drawing of Porsche 912 body shell (from April 1965).

Bottom: The 912 coupé was powered by a 1.6-litre, 90 bhp flat-four and cost approximately DM 16,000.

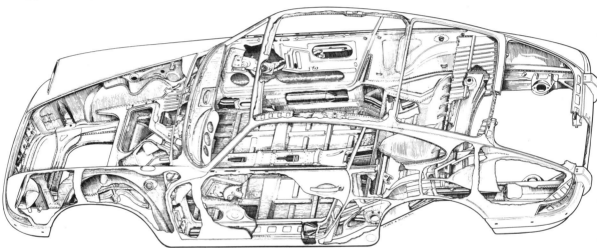

For the 912, the power of the four-cylinder engine was reduced to 90 bhp. There were versions with oil-soaked filters (above) and dry air filters (below).

*Rear running gear (above left) showing flexible longitudinal arm and diagonal hub carrier.
Front running gear (above right) showing wishbone, damper strut and disc brake.*

92

Porsche 912 E (1975-76). Equipment as 911-2.7. Engine 2-litre flat-four.

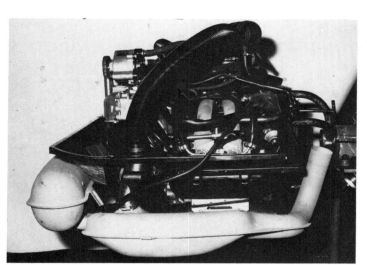

*The 2-litre engine of the
912 E (90 bhp) is almost
identical to the 914 engine.*

93

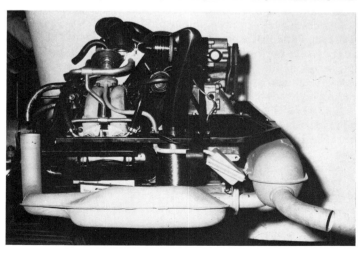

Types 914-4, 914-6 and 916
(1969-1976)

Extensive research had indicated that the central engine configuration might be the best solution for a real sports car intended to remain ahead of its time for many years. As Volkswagen's own research into the matter had led to similar conclusions, the decision was taken to embark on a joint development programme. This is how, in the frame of the already existing contract for mutual cooperation, the design of the VW-Porsche Type 914 was initiated.

Porsche's long racing experience had demonstrated that a central engine would be the best base for obtaining optimal handling and could be allied with reasonable accessibility. Installing the seats midway between the front and rear axles involved a compromise insofar as this position was actually ahead of the centre of gravity. But it was sufficiently far back that the wheel arches did not interfere with the feet of the occupants, while the engine was mounted as closely as possible to the rear wheel axis. This was reflected by the fact that 53 per cent of the total weight was carried by the rear wheels.

The improvement in handling, however, was dictated not only by the position of the engine, but also by the reduction of the polar moment of the vehicle around its vertical axis.

The addition of the length required by the passengers and the engine led to a longer wheelbase than the Porsche 911s. Comparatively short front and rear overhangs, however, resulted in a compact and wieldy vehicle.

While the 914-4 sold quite well, its more potent brother, the Type 914-6, was not a commercial success. Visually the two cars were practically identical, except for their wheels, although the performance of the 914-6 was in a completely different class. While owners of the four-cylinder 914 had to be content with the 80 bhp (later 100 bhp) developed by a mass-produced engine, the owner of a six-cylinder could point to a highly developed, high-efficiency engine. This was the 2-litre carburettor engine of the 911 T which provided the 914-6 with a top speed of nearly 130 mph and made it more than a match for its direct competitor from the Porsche stables, the 125 bhp 2.2-litre 911 T, when it came to 0 to 60 mph acceleration.

The small difference in price compared with the 911, however, brought Porsche an ever decreasing number of orders for the six-cylinder. Even competition successes—among others third place in the Rally Monte Carlo 1971—could not reverse the trend and the 914-6 was quietly phased out in the course of 1971.

In contrast to its more powerful brother, the 914-4 was progressively developed and in the model year 1976 it attained a really high level of refinement. But it could not compete with the roomier and more comfortable Porsche 924 announced at the end of 1975.

General description: Type 914 (basic model)

Coachwork and chassis

Even though the 914 was an open car, it was designed to equal the structural strength and torsional stiffness of the Porsche 911 coupé. The car had a two-door, all-steel construction, including a welded roll-over structure, the detachable roof panel being made of glass fibre. In addition to the front luggage compartment, there was a second locker of comparable capacity in the car's tail, adding up to a total capacity of 370,000 cc (13 cubic feet). The 62-litre (13.6-gallon) fuel tank was at the rear of the front luggage compartment, protected by a bulkhead. The two electric motors operating the pop-up headlights were mounted on the wheel arches, under the front cover. The roof had a four-point attachment. Provision was made to carry the roof panel, rattle free, in a rear locker when not in use. The engine bay was accessible through a grille between the passenger compartment and the rear locker. The door windows were guided by a box section frame running over plastic rollers, while the windscreen was bonded thermoelectrically to its frame. Much care was taken to give the body the lowest possible air drag, but a compromise had to be accepted for the front, where the front edge of the luggage locker had to be high enough to provide sufficient capacity. Thanks to its low build, however (1.24 metres/49 inches) the 914 achieved the same total drag as the 911. Maximum speed was reduced by 2 km/h (1.3 mph) when the headlights were raised. In several aspects, the car exceeded the requirements of most safety standards. Some examples are the flush-fitting door handles, the safety interior mirror, the supplementary protection of the fuel tank, the recessed steering wheel hub protected by a large pad, and the polyurethane mouldings carried by the bumpers.

The body structure was divided and reinforced by four transverse walls. All 914 models had ZF rack-and-pinion safety steering. The pinion shaft was offset from the steering column, the two being joined by an intermediate shaft with splined universals at either end, requiring no attention. In addition to the handbrake, the lever of which was sited between the driver's seat and the door, the VW-Porsche had four disc brakes with automatic adjustment for wear. The rear hydraulic circuit incorporated a pressure limiting valve to prevent premature locking of the rear wheels. In view of its higher performance, the 914-6 had ventilated front discs.

The front suspension was by twin-acting damper struts of which the upper end was located in the body structure, while the lower end swivelled on a wishbone pivoted on a transverse member to which the rack-and-pinion steering was also bolted. The suspension medium consisted of two longitudinal torsion bars of 17.9 mm (0.7 inch) diameter, acting on the wishbones. A progressive acting, hollow rubber spring incorporated in the damper acted as a bump stop.

The rear wheels were guided by semi-trailing arms providing the toe-in and camber changes required to obtain optimal handling. The suspension itself was by spring units combining a damper and a coil spring.

Engine

The 914 came with the choice of two engines. One was the four-cylinder, fuel injection (Bosch electronic) engine used in the VW 411 E (80 bhp at 4,900 rpm, 13.6 mkg—100 lb/ft—at 2,700 rpm), the other well-known Porsche six-cylinder carburettor engine of the 911 T yielding 110 bhp at 5,800 rpm and 16 mkg (116 lb/ft) at 4,200 rpm. As the six-cylinder engine is described elsewhere in this book, we shall limit ourselves here to recalling only the main data of the four-cylinder VW unit. The flat four-cylinder engine had each pair of finned cast iron cylinders bolted to a common light alloy cylinder head. This carried parallel valves operated by pushrods and rockers from a central camshaft. The latter was driven from the crankshaft by spur gears. The forged crankshaft had four bearings. A gear pump, driven from the camshaft, circulated the lubricant under pressure through the engine. A radial blower, bolted to the crankshaft, provided the air flow required to cool the engine. The compression ratio of 8.2:1 enabled the 914 engine to digest fuels of comparatively poor quality.

Transmission
Both models used the Porsche five-speed gearbox and from the beginning of 1970, the Sportomatic transmission was also made available. All transmissions were modified because, in this case, the engine lay in front of the rear wheel axis, while the gearbox was overhung. Operation of the single disc dry clutch was by a Bowden cable. The drive-shafts each incorporated two homokinetic universals.

Equipment
The interior width made it possible to accommodate three abreast—at least for short distances. The driver's seat was a bucket with incorporated headrest and could be adjusted longitudinally over a range of approximately six inches. It could also be inclined to a choice of three positions. The somewhat wider, non-adjustable passenger seat, also made of plastic material, had a removable cushion. Leg room adjustment was provided for by a rectangular section foot-cushion which could be turned appropriately and was popularly known as the 'dog's bone'. On the driver's side, the door padding included a pocket; on the opposite side, it was supplemented by an armrest serving also as a door-pull. The floor was covered with needle felt, while the roll-over structure and the roof's front edge were padded. Stale air was extracted from the passenger compartment through two ducts having their opening behind the seat squabs.

The front 160,000 cc (5.6 cubic feet) and rear 210,000 cc (7.4 cubic feet) luggage compartments were covered with plain needle felt. The instrument panel carried three combined instruments, a cigar lighter, an ash tray, a glove box and the controls for the infinitely adjustable heating and ventilating system. The heater control lever and the hand throttle were carried on the central tunnel.

Annual modifications

1971
In order to meet certain revised European emission standards, the following parts of the electronic fuel injection system were changed: the vacuum sensor, the ignition distributor, the throttle valve housing and the electronic control unit.

Alloy or steel 5.5 × 15-inch wheels shod with 165 HR 15 tyres were available at extra cost. The shorter rear skirt was slotted to increase the air circulation around the exhaust silencer. An extra coat hook was fitted to the right-hand side of the roll-over structure. Windscreen demisting was improved by the addition of a central air outlet in the centre of the dash. The headlight control was modified so that the lights could be wound down only if the ignition key was in the zero position. This also involved the use of a new ignition lock.

1972

The modifications to the 1972 model mostly applied to the engine and its injection system, though there were changes to the interior trim and some of the controls. The cockpit ventilation was improved by the addition of air outlets on either side of the instrument panel, so that the door windows were kept free from mist. The interior door trim was woven. The passenger seat was adjustable for reach and for height. Windscreen wiper and washer were operated by a single stalk under the steering wheel. The steering column was also modified.

The VW-Porsche 914-6 was dropped from the programme, because it clashed with the Porsche 911 T and was not competitive in terms of value for money.

1973

Starting from the well-proven 1.7-litre fuel injection engine, the Porsche engineers developed a new 2-litre engine. It featured electronic fuel injection, developed 100 bhp and was capable of accelerating the 914-2.0 in only 10.5 seconds from rest to 100 km/h (equivalent to just under ten seconds from 0 to 60 mph). The maximum speed of over 190 km/h (118 mph) could be sustained indefinitely.

The new engine developed its maximum torque of 16 mkg (116 lb/ft) as low as 3,500 rpm. The overtaking times were reduced correspondingly: from 80 to 140 km/h (50 to 80 mph) the car required only 13 seconds. The vehicle was made quieter by new engine supports, a new dry air filter and a sound insulating mat glued to the bulkhead separating the engine from the passenger compartment. Softer springing increased the ride comfort and as a result of this the rear skirt was shortened to avoid scraping the ground on full bump on undulating roads. The heat in the rear luggage compartment was reduced by the use of a new insulating material. The new 914 models were easily recognised by their dull black bumpers and the black script on the rear panel.

There were several improvements in the passenger compartment too: in connection with the fore-and-aft passenger seat adjustment, a fixed foot rest was fitted, while the roof panel was trimmed in the same cloth as the seats. The door handle recesses and window cranking handles were finished in dull black. The gate guiding the gear lever was modified to improve the lever's location in the different channels and the lever itself was shortened. The speedometer now read to 250 km/h.

A comfort kit was offered, including vinyl covering of the roll-over structure, framed by chromium-plated mouldings, twin matched horns, a central console with clock, voltmeter and oil thermometer, a leather sleeve around the gear lever and a more resistant velvet carpet on the floor. An additionally available sports kit offered forged light alloy wheels, front and rear anti-roll bars and quartz-halogen main beam lamps.

1974

There were only minor modifications to the 914-2.0 engine, which did not affect the general technical data. The throttle linkage of the US engine got an additional return spring near the throttle housing. Large rubber buffers were added to the overseas models' rear bumper. All cars received newly styled wheels. An additional towing eye was welded to the front underpan. The symbols on the instrument panel were partly modified and, for safety reasons, the travel of the fore-and-aft seat adjustment was reduced, compared with the previous model. All cars had automatic three-point inertia reel seat belts. The 1.7-litre engine with electronic fuel injection was replaced by a 1.8 version in which the mixture was supplied by a twin-carburettor installation for European cars, while the US and Canadian models got the new Bosch L-Jetronic injection system. The carburettor engine had a maximum power of 85 bhp at 5,000 rpm with a maximum torque of 13.8 mkg (101 lb/ft) at 3,400 rpm. The L-Jetronic US version had an output of 76 bhp at 4,800 rpm and a maximum torque of 13 mkg (95 lb/ft) at 3,400 rpm. The main modifications to the 1.8-litre engine, compared with its predecessor, were an increased bore (from 90 to 93 mm), modified combustion chambers and intake and exhaust ports. The valves were enlarged and the rockers were of a modified design. The clutch acquired a reinforced pressure plate.

1975
Front and rear impact-resistant bumpers were the main identification items of the 1975 models. Strong pressed steel profiles covered with a resilient material resisted collisions up to 8 km/h (5 mph). Rectangular auxiliary headlights or foglights, if required, were deeply recessed in the front bumper. The horns were located externally on either side of the front underpanel. As in the latest Porsche models, the rear number plate was illuminated from the sides.

The 1.8-litre carburettor and the 2.0-litre L-Jetronic engines in European versions remained unchanged, but there were alterations to the engines sold in the USA and in California, where stricter emission norms are enforced. For California, the exhaust system included a reactor and heat exchangers and was divided in a primary silencer, a catalyser and a secondary silencer. USA engines were similar, except that the catalyser was deleted and replaced by a straight-through pipe. Additionally, the California version featured exhaust gas recirculation. The fuel pump was moved forward under the fuel tank; the expansion chamber of the tank changed shape and material.

A glass fibre front spoiler was made available as special equipment. The 1975 colour programme comprised five new colours and four additional ones were available at extra cost. There was a choice of nine different tartan materials for the central part of the seat upholstery.

General description: Type 916

The happy few who managed to secure one of the 11 prototypes of the Porsche 916 can be assured of having one of the most exclusive cars in the world. Officially a Porsche 916 never existed, but insiders have known this car since 1972, when it was submitted to the costing department and flatly refused. Only the 11 prototypes remain, of which the Porsche and Piëch families preserve five for themselves. One 916 was shipped to America, the other five were sold under the counter in Germany to faithful Porsche friends.

In this car, the 914's detachable plastic roof was replaced by a steel roof welded to the body to improve its torsional rigidity. The longitudinal members of the floor structure were reinforced and additionally wrapped in plastic material.

The suspension was similar to that of the 914-6, but 185/70 tyres on 178 mm (seven-inch) wide light alloy wheels took care of the required adhesion and cornering power. To accommodate this running gear, the wings (fenders) were widened, making the 916 9 cm (just over 3.5 inches) wider than the 914. A newly designed front air dam combatted front end lift at high speed and the rear skirt was also redesigned. The air intake for the front oil cooler and the recesses for the auxiliary headlights were cleverly integrated in the air dam. The engine was the most powerful available in the Porsche range at the time: the 2.4-litre 911 S. This provided 190 bhp at 6,500 rpm, but some 916 owners later swopped this for the 2.7-litre Carrera engine (210 bhp) when it was put on the market.

Bilstein dampers were used throughout and anti-roll bars were provided front and rear. Four ventilated 911 S disc brakes stopped this 230 km/h (143 mph) car, capable of reaching 100 km/h (60 mph) from rest in less than seven seconds.

Even if a bend was entered at an apparently impossible speed, it was most likely to be still well within the 916's limits. Without apparent side slip, the car followed the line dictated by the driver in a slightly understeering attitude, up to cornering speeds far exceeding those of normal closed cars. But if the accelerator was released in such a situation, the driver had to get pretty busy: suddenly the 916 would tuck into the curve and immediate correction with steering and accelerator would be called for. The 916 was at its best in a succession of fast curves through which it could be driven tremendously fast, providing immediate response to directional changes was imposed by a competent driver.

The 916 was and remains an exotic car. Externally its styling makes this immediately apparent, while the technical specification does not lag behind. Even if the 916 was never officially announced, it remains an interesting link in the development story of the Stuttgart factory.

912/914.4/914.6/916

Year	Body	Model Type	Chassis no	Engine no	Engine type	Gearbox type	Cyl	Bore × stroke	Capacity	HP (DIN) at rpm	Torque (mkg) at rpm	Comp ratio	W.base (mm)	Track fr/rear (mm)	Length (mm)	Weight (kg)	No produced
1965	K-Coupé	912	450001-454470	830001-832090	616/36	902/0	4	82,5 x 74	1582	90/5800	12,4/3500	9,3:1	2211	1337/1317	4163	970	4470
	Coupé	912	350001-351970	740001-744210		902/1											1970
1966	K-Coupé	912	454470-458100	832091-836000	616/36	902/0	4	82,5 x 74	1582	90/5800	12,4/3500	9,3:1	2211	1337/1317 1353/1321	4163	995	3630
		912	458101-461140	744211-750001										1337/1317 1353/1321			3040
	Coupé	912	351971-354000 354001-354970														2030
1967	K-Coupé	912	461141-463204	836001-836610	616/36	902/0	4	82,5 x 74	1582	90/5800	12,4/3500	9,3:1	2211	1337/1317	4163	995	2064
	Coupé	912	354971-355601	750001-753430													631
	Targa	912	550001-550544	836611-837070 753431-756195													544
1968	K-Coupé	912	12800001-12805598	1080001-1080351	616/36	902/50	4	82,5 x 74	1582	90/5800	12,4/3500	9,3:1	2211	1337/1317	4163	995	5598
	Coupé	912	12820001-12820427			902/02											427
	Targa	912	12870001-12871217	1085001-1086115		902/01											1217
	Coupé	912	12900001-12900428		616/39	902/04											428
	K-Coupé	912	129020001-129023450	1280001-1285847		902/06											3450
	Targa	912	129010001-129010801			902/05											801
1969	Coupé	914.4	4702900001-4702913312	W0000001-0013312	W80	914/11	4	90 x 66	1679	80/4900	13,6/2700	8,2:1	2450	1337/1374	3985	900	13312
	Coupé	914.6	9140430001-9140432668	6400001-6400889 6404001-6405781	901/36 901/38	914/01	6	80 x 66	1991	110/5800	16,0/4200	8,6:1	2450	1361/1382	3985	940	2668

100

912/914.4/914.6/916

Year	Body	Type	Chassis no	Engine no	Engine type	Gearbox type	Cyl	Bore × stroke	Capacity	HP (DIN) at rpm	Torque (mkg) at rpm	Comp ratio	W.base (mm)	Track fr/rear (mm)	Length (mm)	Weight (kg)	No produced
1969	Coupé	916	9142300010-9142330020	6325001-6325002 6325021-6325027	911/86	923/01	6 6	84 × 70,4 90 × 70,4	2341 2687	190/6500 210/6300	22,0/5200 26,0/5100	8,5:1 8,5:1	2450 2450	1386/1480 1386/1480	3985 3985	910 1080	11
1970	Coupé	914.4	4712900001-4712916231	W1000001-1016231	W80	914/11	4	90 × 66	1679	80/4900	13,6/2700	8,2:1	2450	1337/1374	3985	900	16231
	Coupé	914.6	9141430001-9141430443	6410011-6410268 6414001-6414163	901/36 901/38	914/01	6	80 × 66	1991	110/5800	16,0/4200	8,6:1	2450	1361/1382	3985	940	443
1971	Coupé	914.4	4722900140-4722921580	W2000001-2021580	W80 EA 80	914/11	4	90 × 66	1679	80/4900	13,6/2700	8,2:1	2450	1337/1374	3985	900	21440
	Coupé	914.6	9142430001-9142430240	6420001-6420270	901/38	914/01	6	80 × 66	1991	110/5800	16,0/4200	8,6:1	2450	1361/1382	3985	940	240
1972	Coupé	914.4	4732900001-4732927660	W3000001-	W80	914/12	4	90 × 66	1679	80/4900	13,6/2700	8,2:1	2450	1343/1383	3985	950	27660
				EA3000001- EB3000001- GB3000001- GA3000001-	EA 80 EB72 GB100 GA95		4 4 4	90 × 66 94 × 71,1 94 × 71,1	1679 1971 1971	72/4900 100/5000 95/4900	13,6/2700 16,0/3500 16,0/3500	7,3:1 8,0:1 7,6:1	2450 2450 2450	1343/1383 1343/1383 1343/1383	3985 3985 3985	970 950 970	
1973	Coupé	914.4	4742900001-47429…	AN4000001-	AN85	914/12	4	93 × 66	1795	85/5000	13,8/3400	8,6:1	2450	1343/1383	3985	950	
				EC4000001- GB4000001- GA4000001-	EC76 GB100 GA95		4 4 4	93 × 66 94 × 71,1 94 × 71,1	1795 1971 1971	76/4800 100/4900 95/4900	13,8/3400 16,0/3500 16,0/3500	7,5:1 8,0:1 7,6:1	2450	1343/1383	4050 3985 4050	970 950 970	
1975	Coupé	912E	9126000001-9126002099	-	-	923/02	4	94 × 71,1	1971	90/4900	14,0/4000	7,6:1	2271	1360/1330	4291	1160	2099

Notes:
Type 912: Synchromesh gearbox 902/1 (five-speed) until 1965 model, except USA. One-piece gearbox and differential housing.
Synchromesh gearbox 902/0 USA (five-speed): 1966 and 1967 models. Housing as 902/1.
Synchromesh gearbox 902/02 (five-speed) for Europe as from 1968 model. Housing: as 902/1.

Synchromesh gearbox 902/01 (four-speed) for USA and domestic models from 1968 model. Housing as 902/1.
Type 914: Engine type W80: 1.7 litre, 80 bhp (DIN) at 4900 rpm. EC or EC-a: US version, 76 bhp. EC-b: California version, 76 bhp. AN: 85 bhp. GC-a: US version, 88 bhp. GC-b: California version, 88 bhp. GB: 100 bhp.
Gearbox 914/11 (five-speed) until 1971. From 1972 gearbox 914/12 (five-speed), Type 901.
914-6 gearbox is from Porsche 911, Type 901, five speeds.

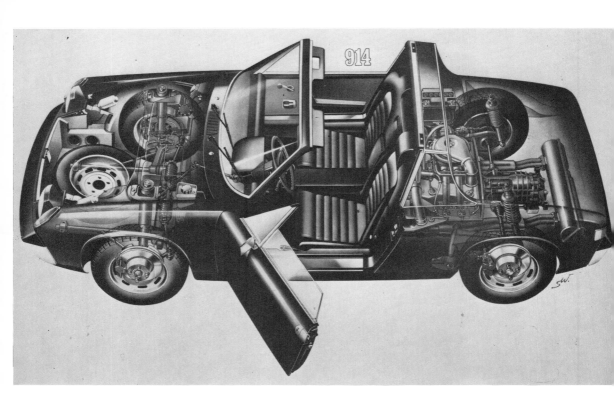

Cutaway views of VW-Porsche 914-4 and 914-6.

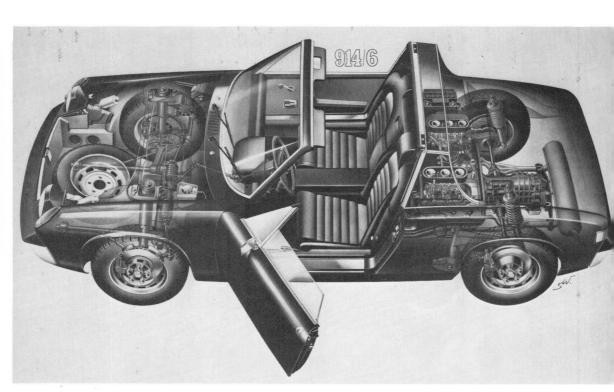

Externally the Types 914-4 and 914-6 differed mainly in their wheels; the 914-6 had wider rims.

The 914 types had two luggage compartments of almost equal capacity, front (right) and rear (below right).

104

There was no space between the squabs of the 914 and the engine compartment.

914 headlights popped up automatically when switched on.

The 914-6 had a 2-litre, six-cylinder Porsche engine.

105

The cockpit was essentially functional and nearly identical for the four- and six-cylinder models.

106   *From the 1975 model on, the 914-4 had reinforced front and rear bumpers.*

With the 2-litre, four-cylinder engine, the 914 of 1975-76 had reached a high degree of refinement.

Only 11 Porsche 916s were built. It was a high performance version of the 914 featuring a 2.4-litre, six-cylinder, 190 bhp engine.

The 916's running gear was basically similar to the 914-6, but 17.8 cm (7-inch) rims were fitted.

The 916's front spoiler improved high-speed wheel adhesion.

Flared arches covering the wide wheels made the 916 9 cm (3½ inches) wider than the 914.

916 internal trim was to customer's choice.

Type 901/911-2.0 (1963-1969)

Not often is a car born so naturally as the first Porsche, Type 356. It was a nice little sports car, made up of VW parts, without any research into the market, just as its creators felt it should be. There had been no intention to build many of them, but for nearly 15 years this 'toy car' for enthusiasts remained on the scene, being constantly developed and endowed with more power. But some day there had to be a new Porsche, a completely new car, designed from scratch and which would not have to rely on parts from some mass-produced, bread-and-butter car. Out of many conversations, a concept of which the first drawings date back to 1956 slowly crystallised—again smooth and essentially functional.

Ferdinand 'Butzi' Porsche did not take his task lightly: 'It is easier and somehow also simpler to work for outside customers than for one's own company.' There were notch-back prototypes in an attempt to make the new Porsche a real four-seater, but finally the decision was taken to stick to a real sports car concept, a classic two-seater with two additional occasional seats. One reason for this was also that the typical Porsche shape was now known all over the world and that the new car should be immediately recognisable. In the final 901/911 design, the similarity to the 356 was particularly obvious in the shape of the front and rear parts of the body.

Large glass areas and a low waistline made the car more elegant and improved the visibility, but whatever the proposed changes, the wheelbase of 2.20 m (87 inches) was a fixed parameter from the start: Ferry Porsche himself was adamant about it.

The first Porsche had been built to suit simply personal tastes, just as the available components would allow it. The 901/911 was in complete contrast to this. Both its shape and its technical specification were the results of intense thinking. In spite of friendly Cassandras' prophecies, the engine remained overhung in the back. In this case, as in many others, the suitability of the car for sporting events were taken in serious consideration. Ferry Porsche, for instance, thought that front-engined cars could not remain competitive in the long run and that for serious competition, a central-engined car would be required. But both from an image and a production point of view, it is hardly feasible to have a front-engined production car and to race a central-engined car based on similar mechanical components. This was an important factor in the decision to retain an overhung rear engine.

There were three types of engine to choose from. In any case, it had to be a six-cylinder because of its higher refinement. Finally an air-cooled flat-six was preferred because neither a V-6 nor a straight-six were really suitable for installation in the car's tail.

An important factor in the choice of that type of engine was Porsche's great experience of air-cooled flat engines. Overheating problems were not feared and it was hoped that the noise problem, which is obviously more acute where there are no water jackets to absorb mechanical noises, could be mastered. Several new ideas were adopted in the running gear design. In order to obtain the maximum possible luggage capacity in the nose of the car, the 901 received a MacPherson suspension with damper struts and lower wishbones. Great care was taken in the detail design to keep the locker as roomy as possible. The rear swinging half-axles were modified to a semi-trailing link design providing a more favourable geometry.

A safety steering column incorporating two universals was used and further safety provided by the dished steering wheel with four near-horizontal spokes. Originally it was even intended to fit dull black instrument surrounds and windscreen wiper arms and blades, but the dealers were so ferociously opposed to the idea that it was abandoned, chrome still being a sort of status symbol at the time. Times have certainly changed! Today chrome is used most sparingly and it is hard to find any trace of it on any Porsche model.

From the start, the new Porsche pointed to the orientation taken by the company towards ever more comfortable cars, progressively refined over the years. For a car of such short wheelbase, the ride was generally acclaimed as astonishingly good. The suspension was decidedly softer than that of the Carrera or the 356 C models. The tail-happiness of the early models was soon effectively combated, as was the effort required to operate the pedal of the otherwise excellent Ate four-wheel disc braking system.

At the end of autumn 1964, a French manufacturer protested against the use of the type number 901 because the combination of three figures, of which the middle one is a zero, had been registered by him as a trademark. This is why the new Porsche became commercially known as the Type 911. Its list price in Germany was DM 21,900.

General description: Type 901/911-2.0 (basic model)

Coachwork and chassis

The usable volume of the 901/911 was very large, considering its outside dimensions. The location of all mechanical units and accessories, as well as the design of its structure, were all aimed at making the best of the car's dimensions. The front luggage locker was particularly clever and could take bags of quite large dimensions. The front seats were located exactly midway between the two axles, coinciding with the axis of the fore-and-aft oscillations. Behind them were two 'emergency' seats which formed an additional luggage platform after their squabs had been folded forward. Design features aimed at increasing the car's capacity were manifold. The fuel tank was located very low and the spare wheel lay flat in the car's nose, only slightly above the floor pan. The rack-and-pinion steering gear was in a similar position and for this reason, the steering column was of three piece design with the central part at an angle—an expensive layout, but also an important safety factor. The pinion of the steering gear was in the car's central axis, which permitted the use of the same steering gear for right- and left-hand drive cars.

The front suspension was of the MacPherson type, using damper struts slightly inclined inward. In order to reduce the diameter of the strut unit, the coil springs usually associated with the MacPherson system were replaced by longitudinal torsion bars, running through the tubular base of the lower wishbones. This was pivoted in Flanblocs and Silentblocs requiring no service. Each torsion bar was anchored to the front end of the wishbone and reacted against the tubular front cross member at its rear end, where an adjustment screw was provided. A hollow rubber auxiliary spring steeply increased the suspension rate in the last third of the bump travel. An anti-roll bar was additionally provided. The front end geometry was such that the main running gear data, such as track, camber, caster and king pin inclination varied by only a negligible amount with suspension movements. Left- and right-hand front suspensions were linked by the transverse tube locating the rear end of the wishbones and torsion bars.

The rear wheels were carried by longitudinal arms pivoted in service-free rubber bushes. The use of longitudinal arms made it possible to give the wheels some negative camber, increasing the cornering force that could be generated and varying little with the suspension movements. The weight of the vehicle was carried by transverse torsion bars, progressive additional stiffness being provided in the last third of the bump travel by auxiliary rubber springs. The dampers were pivoted on long levers, so that their stroke was longer than the wheel movements. All wheels were provided with disc brakes totalling a friction area of 185 cm^2 (28.67 square inches).

Engine

The new six-cylinder engine with its cooling blower, its exhaust system and the heat exchangers for the cockpit heating system were grouped into a very compact unit. Salient features were the robust eight-bearing crankshaft and the dry sump lubrication. The latter notably simplified the crankcase ventilation and reduced oil frothing and oil consuming splash. The axial cooling air blower was belt-driven from the crankshaft and co-axial with the generator. The latter was an alternator providing a high output at low engine speeds. The carburation was by six Solex overflow carburettors, Type 40 PJ, with one overflow chamber for each group of three carburettors. The exhaust system comprised, on each side, one manifold leading into one primary expansion chamber from which a pipe led to the main exhaust silencer. Thanks to such features as the eight-bearing crankshaft, the dry-sump lubrication and the overhead cam valve gear, this comparatively small six-cylinder unit had a great development potential.

The flat-six engine had a single overhead camshaft for each group of three cylinders. The drive was taken from the crankshaft to an intermediate gear and was transmitted to the camshafts by chains. These required no adjustment: they were kept under tension by a hydraulic tensioner and guided by three rubber-lined shoes. The camshaft and the six rockers were contained in a cambox covering three cylinder heads. The valves were in V formation and the combustion chamber was hemispherical, allowing large valve diameters. Large cooling fins were provided and there was ample space between the cylinders for air circulation. The fins extended to near the hot combustion chamber walls. Each cylinder had its own head. All cast parts of the engine were of light alloy, while the cylinders were 'Biral' (cast iron sleeve with a finned aluminium jacket cast around it).

Transmission

The Type 901 five-speed gearbox was a new Porsche design featuring a rigid, finned alloy barrel housing. All forward gears were synchronised by the well-known Porsche split ring synchronisation system. The differential was carried in the same housing. A multi-disc limited slip differential, made by ZF to American patents, was available. The half shafts had two universals each; while on the outer end the univeral was of the normal Hooke type, a Nadella universal was used on the inner (differential) end. This incorporated a swivelling centre piece allowing axial movements. The drive was taken from the engine to the gearbox by a single disc diaphragm spring clutch.

Equipment

Standard equipment comprised: an electric windscreen washer operating the wipers automatically, a three-speed windscreen wiper, pivoted quarter windows front and rear (with thief-proof lock), a laminated glass windscreen and a heated rear window. Also to be noted were: asymetrically dipping lights, two reversing lights, adjustable instrument lighting, two fog lights and a luggage locker light, twin horns, a headlight flasher control, five large instruments (speedometer, tachometer, combined oil and fuel level indicator, oil thermometer and oil pressure gauge), various warning lights and an electric clock. Both doors could be locked from outside, the glove box lid was lockable, the flap giving access to the fuel tank filler could be opened only from inside the car, and there was a combined steering and ignition lock.

The interior equipment was very comprehensive, including a pull-out ashtray, upper and lower padding of the dashboard, a cigar lighter, a grab handle on the passenger's door, armrests shaped to facilitate closing the door, anchorage points for seat belts, two coat hooks, two padded sun visors—with a make-up mirror on the passenger's side—two door pockets, fully reclining squabs, heater and fresh air ducts and a velour mat with a long-wearing rubber pad on the driver's side. The car was also equipped with an independent petrol-electric heater by Webasto and a towing eye at the front end. A special retouching pencil came with the car.

Annual modifications

1965

The 'Targa' model announced by Porsche at the beginning of September 1965 was the first production safety convertible in the world. The roll-over structure pioneered a completely new concept of the convertible car: not only did it provide the occupants of an open car with very effective protection, but it also permitted completely new variations on the open car theme. In its press releases, Porsche proposed four Targa combinations called Spyder, Hard-Top, Voyage and Bel-Air, all in one single convertible car. Deliveries of the Targa, available in 911 and 912 forms, started in spring 1966.

1966

In the second half of 1966 the Type 911 S was announced for the model year 1967. The chassis numbers had the same combinations of figures as for the normal 911 models, with the letter 'S' added. The main differences, compared with the normal 911, were: 160 bhp at 6,600 rpm, soft-nitrided connecting rods, forged pistons, modified cylinder heads, larger intake and exhaust valves and modified valve timing. The carburettors (Weber) were identical to those introduced on the normal 911 in February 1966, except for differences in jet and choke sizes. The Bosch sparking plugs were 'harder', the cooling air blower had a 5 mm (0.2 inch) smaller diameter and the clutch release bearing revolved constantly. The 911 S was equipped with Koni shock absorbers, had an anti-roll bar at the rear as well as at the front, and ventilated brake discs. As in the normal 911, the wheels had a 127 mm (5-inch)-wide rim, but they were made of forged aluminium alloy. The thicker brake discs had widened the front track by 16 mm (0.63 inch) and the rear track by 8.4 mm (0.33 inch), while the weight in running order of 1,030 kg (2,272 lb) was exactly 50 kg (110 lb) lower than for the normal car. Maximum speed was raised from 210 to 225 km/h (from 131 to 140 mph). For the first time an engine speed limiter was fitted.

In the cockpit, the leather-covered steering wheel and the move of the tachometer red zone to the 7,200-7,400 rpm range were immediately obvious, as was the leather covering of the dashboard. The ashtray and the glove box received new handles, and typescript was silver coloured, the gear change pattern was engraved in the lever knob and the rubber mats were replaced by carpets. The bumper overriders had a rubber protection, the bumpers and the moulding under the door got a thicker rubber strip.

1967

As from August 1 1967, the Porsche programme was extended with the 911 T. The range then comprised the 912 (90 bhp, four cylinders), the 911 T (110 bhp, T standing for 'Touring'), the 911 L (130 bhp) and 911 S (160 bhp).

Changes were as follows:

Type 911 L (successor to the normal 911 with an interior trim and equipment very similar to the 911S: the diameter of the front anti-roll bar was reduced from 13 to 11 mm [0.51 to 0.43 inch]).

Type 911 S: remained substantially unchanged.

Type 911 T: replaced the 911 of the previous model year and was similar to the 912 in its equipment and chassis specifications.

For the enthusiastic driver who likes to decide for himself when he wants to change gear, but does not want to bother about a clutch pedal, Porsche offered the four-speed 'Sportomatic' transmission at DM 990 on all six-cylinder models.

All cars had several new safety features: recessed external door opening push-buttons, dull black windscreen wiper arms and blades, anchorage points for front seat belts, a larger external mirror, a rubber ashtray handle, an anti-glare and deformable instrument panel, quartz-halogen fog lights, wider wheel rims (137.5 mm = 5.5 inches) and a twin-circuit braking system.

1968

The B-Programme for 1969 featured several important modifications. All 911 T, E and S models had an extensively revised heating and ventilating system with a three-speed blower, the pivoted front quarter windows being retained on the Targa only. The wheelbase was lengthened by 57 mm to 2,268 mm (2.24 inches to 89.3 inches). In view of the wider wheels and tyres offered, the front and rear wheel openings were slightly flared. The generator was more powerful (770 watt), the single battery was replaced by twin batteries of 35 Amp/hr each, located in front of the front wheel arches, quartz-halogen main lights were standard and so was an electrically heated rear window. Hazard lights were fitted, there was a lamp in the glove box, the fuse box was moved to the front luggage locker, there was a hand throttle between the seats, the mirror was of the dipping type, the door trim incorporated larger pockets, the inside door opening trigger was recessed into the arm rest, the steering wheel was smaller and had a padded horn push, there was a push-down ashtray under the instrument panel, the front seat squabs had a locking device, the Targa had air extractor openings each side of the roll-over structure and the reversing lights were modified.

The 'T' could be obtained with a 'comfort kit' bringing its equipment up to the other models' standard. It comprised hydro-pneumatic front struts, air horns, velvet carpets, an oil pressure and level indicator, a leather-covered steering wheel, rubber protected bumper overriders, a chromium-plated moulding under the doors and a larger 'Porsche' script. Last but not least came the 137.5 mm (5.5-inch)-wide alloy wheels shod with 185/70 HR 14 tyres.

This equipment was standard on the 911 E and 911 S models, except that the hydro-pneumatic struts were optional only on the 911 S and that the standard alloy wheels were 381 mm (15 inches) in diameter and had a 152.4 mm (6-inch)-wide rim with 185/70 HR 15 tyres, save for the 'Sportomatic' 911 E which had the same wheels and tyres as included in the comfort kit. The quartz-halogen fog lights and the petrol-electric independent heating system were dropped from the 911 S equipment.

Of primary importance was the equipment of the 911 E (successor to the 911 L) and of the 911 S with mechanical fuel injection, which raised the power of the 911 E to 140 bhp at 6,500 rpm, and of the 911 S to 170 bhp at 6,800 rpm. Both these engines also received an electronic high capacity discharge ignition system.

All models got larger rear brake calipers and the 911 S was also fitted with larger front brake calipers made of light alloy. E and S models were fitted with ventilated discs all round. In addition to the self-levelling hydro-pneumatic front suspension struts, standard on the E and optional on the T and S models, there were various other front end modifications: the stub-axle and steering arm were welded to the suspension strut; the wishbones were in one piece and a simplified rack-and-pinion steering gear was used. The ventilated discs increased the track dimensions by approximately 10 mm (0.4 inch) and the 6-inch wheels by another 10 mm. This and the increased wheelbase resulted in a 20 cm (7.87-inch) larger turning circle. No front anti-roll bar was fitted to cars using self-levelling struts.

The increase in wheelbase from 2,211 to 2,268 mm (87 to 89.3 inches) was obtained by moving back the rear wheels without moving the power unit from its original position. This was done by increasing the length of the semi-trailing arms and replacing the Nadella shafts with new 'Löbro' half-shafts incorporating Rzeppa constant velocity universals. In order to retain the same flexibility of the rear suspension, stronger torsion bars were used in connection with the longer semi-trailing arms.

In the 911 S, the mean effective radius and the friction surface of the brake pads was increased.

901/911-2.0

Year	Body	Model Type	Chassis no	Engine no	Engine type	Gearbox type	Cyl	Bore × stroke	Capacity	HP (DIN) at rpm	Torque (mkg) at rpm	Comp ratio	W.base (mm)	Track fr/rear (mm)	Length (mm)	Weight (kg)	No produced
1963	Coupé	901	–	–	901	901	6	80 × 66	1991	130/6200	16,5/4600	9,0:1	2204	1332/1312	4135	1000	–
1964	Coupé	911	300001-300235	900001-900360	901/01	901/0	6	80 × 66	1991	130/6100	17,8/4200	9,0:1	2211	1337/1317	4163	1080	235
1965	Coupé	911	300236-303390 303391-305100	900361-903550 903551-907000	901/01	902/1	6	80 × 66	1991	130/6100	17,8/4200	9,0:1	2211	1337/1317	4163	1080	3155 1710
1966	Coupé	911	305101-307350 307351-308522	907001-911000 911001-911190	901/05 901/06	902/1 902/0	6	80 × 66	1991	130/6100	17,8/4200	9,0:1	2211	1353/1325	4163	1030	2250 1172
	Targa	911	500001-500718	911191-912050													718
	Coupé	911S	305101S-308523S	960001-961144 961145-962178	901/02	901/02	6	80 × 66	1991	160/6600	18,2/5200	9,8:1	2211	1367/1339	4163	1030	523
	Targa	911S	500001S-500718S														718
1967	Coupé	911US	11830001-11830473	3280001-3281606 3380001-3380463	901/14 901/17	902/0 902/1	6	80 × 66	1991	130/6100	17,8/4200	9,0:1	2211	1353/1325	4163	1080	473
	K-Coupé	911	11835001-11835742			905/00											742
	Targa	911	11880001-11880268														268
	Coupé	911L	11810001-11810720	3080001-3080655 3180001-3180347 3880001-3880028	901/06 901/07 901/30	902/1	6	80 × 66	1991	130/6100	17,8/4200	9,0:1	2211	1353/1325	4163	1080	720
	Targa	911L	11860001-11860307														307
	Coupé	911T	11820001-11820928	2080001-2081754	901/03	901/10	6	80 × 66	1991	110/5800	16,0/4200	8,6:1	2211	1353/1325	4163	1080	928
	K-Coupé	911T	11825001-11825683														683
	Targa	911T	11870001-11870521														521
	Coupé	911S	11800001-11801267	4080001-4081549	901/02	901/02	6	80 × 66	1991	160/6600	18,2/5200	9,8:1	2211	1367/1335	4163	1080	1267
	K-Coupé	911S		4180001-4180227	901/08	905/01											
	Targa	911S	118500001-11850442														442

116

901/911–2.0

Year	Body	Type	Chassis no	Engine no	Engine type	Gearbox type	Cyl	Bore × stroke	Capacity	HP (DIN) at rpm	Torque (mkg) at rpm	Comp ratio	W.base (mm)	Track fr/ rear (mm)	Length (mm)	Weight (kg)	No produced
1967	Coupé	911L-US	11805001-118055449	3280001-3281606 3380001-3380464	901/14 901/17	902/0 902/1	6	80 × 66	1991	130/6100	17,8/4200	9,0:1	2211	1353/1325	4163	1080	5449
	Targa	911L-US	11855001-118555134			905/00											5134
1968	Coupé	911T	11900001-11900343	6190001-6192455 6193001-6193297	901/03 901/13	901/06 901/12	6	80 × 66	1991	110/5800	16,0/4200	8,6:1	2268	1367/1335	4163	1020	343
	K-Coupé	911T	119120001-119123561	6195001-6197292	901/16	905/13								1364/1345			3561
	Targa	911T	119100001-119111282	6198001-6198184	901/19												282
	Coupé	911E	119200001-119200954	6290001-6292270 6298001-6298583	901/09 901/11	901/07 901/13	6	80 × 66	1991	140/6500	17,8/4500	9,1:1	2268	1374/1355	4163	1020	954
1968	K-Coupé	911E	119220001-119221014			901/06 901/12	6	80 × 66	1991	140/6500	17,8/4500	9,1:1	2268	1374/1355	4163	1020	1014
	Targa	911E	119210001-119210858			905/13								1364/1345			858
	Coupé	911S	119300001-119301492	6390001-6392126	901/10	901/07	6	80 × 66	1991	170/6800	18,5/5500	9,9:1	2268	1374/1355	4163	995	1492
	Targa	911S	119310001-119310614			901/13											614

Notes:

Type 911-2.0: Synchromesh gearbox 901/0 (five-speed, one-piece housing for gearbox and differential). 1965 model up to July 26 1965.
Synchromesh gearbox 902/1: 1966 and 1967 models, except USA. Specs as 901/0.
Synchromesh gearbox 902/0 USA (four-speed): 1966 and 1967 models. Housing as 901/0.
Synchromesh gearbox 901/02 (five-speed): 1967 models, except USA. Housing as 901/0.
Synchromesh gearbox 901/10 (four-speed): Domestic and European models from 1968 (not USA). Housing as 901/0.
Sportomatic 905/00 (four-speed): Option from 1968 models for 911 USA.
911 L-USA, 911 L-domestic and Europe. Housing as 901/0.
Sportomatic 905/01 (four-speed): Option from 1968 models for domestic and European 911 S and 911 T. Housing as 901/0.

Engines: 901/01: Standard engine with Solex carburettors (from September 1964).
901/02: Engine for 911 S (from July 1966).
901/03: Engine for four-speed gearbox (from July 1966).
901/05: As 901/01, but with Weber carburettors (from February 1966).
901/06: As 901/05, but with different heat exchangers and camshafts (from November 1966). With Sportomatic from July 1967.
901/07: As 901/05, but with Sportomatic fittings (from July 1967).
901/08: With Sportomatic (from July 1967).
901/13: With Sportomatic (from July 1967).
901/14: As 901/06, but with US emission control (from July 1967).
901/17: As 901/06, but with US emission control and Sportomatic fittings (from July 1967).

901 coupé, as it was announced. A few details were changed before production began.

Porsche 911-2.0. First series with transverse '911' script.

Side view of Porsche 911 with 2-litre, six-cylinder engine. 1965 model.

Porsche 911 T Targa with fixed rear window, new door handles and Sportomatic.

120   *For 1968, the programme included three models: 911 T, L and S.*

The 1968 models were equipped with laminated windscreen and twin brake circuits.

Instrument panel of Porsche 911. It has remained substantially unaltered.

Additional luggage room is provided by the folding 'emergency' seat squabs.

Section drawings of Type 901 Porsche six-cylinder engine (first version).

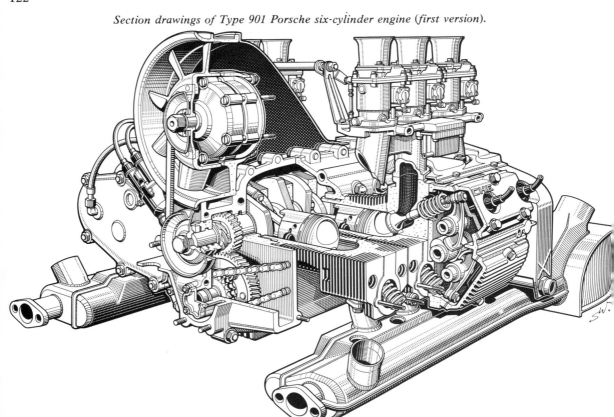

130 bhp 911 with Weber carburettors (above). Early experimental 901 engine (below). 123

Type 911-2.2 (1969-1971)

The 911 development programme was by no means interrupted by the launch of the 914. In September 1969, the 2.2 versions of the 911 were announced in Zuffenhausen. If the enlarged engines are the main points of interest of these 'C-Programme' cars, several other modifications are also worthy of note.

In addition to the power increase from which the Types 911 T, E and S benefitted, there was also a very welcome increase in torque, making the engines more flexible and city driving more pleasant.

No higher maximum speeds were claimed, although in fact all models became slightly faster. Neither was there any significant increase in fuel consumption.

The critical tendency of the 2-litre models to oversteer had already been notably reduced in the B-series (1969 models) by increasing the wheelbase, improving the weight distribution and fitting wider rims and tyres. There was further improvement in the C-series, the best model on that score being a specially trimmed 911 T fitted with the optional front and rear anti-roll bars. In contrast, the 911 E on which the controversial hydro-pneumatic struts were standard, was tuned more specially for comfort. Porsche customers did not seem to be very attracted by this set-up and the self-levelling struts soon disappeared.

In view of the increased power of its engine, the 911 T now also featured four ventilated brake discs. They required a fairly strong push on the pedal, which did not please the ladies too much.

General description: Type 911-2.2 (basic model)

Coachwork and chassis

All 1970 models (production of which began in September 1969) had the capacity of their six-cylinder engine increased to 2.2 litres. This was obtained by increasing the cylinder bore from 80 to 84 mm (3.15 to 3.3 inches).

Apart from this major modification, several details were improved. Among the detail modifications, the upper anchorage point of the front suspension struts was moved forward by approximately 14 mm (0.55 inch) to reduce the front wheel trail. The entire platform, including the floor, the longitudinal members, the wheel arches and the seat pans were galvanised for better rust protection.

To reduce the weight, the engine bay cover and the central part of the 911 E and S bumpers were made of aluminium. An inconspicuous but important modification to the instrument panel was that the instruments were now inserted (and could be removed) from the cockpit side of the facia. They were secured by a rubber ring.

The external door handles were new, the push-button being replaced by a trigger behind the handle: this was not only safer in the case of an accident, but also made door opening more natural by avoiding the simultaneous pushing (the button) and pulling (the door) necessary with the older arrangement. The Targa models were fitted with a new, lighter folding top. All models were protected by a PVC undercoat.

The front suspension of the 911 E was tuned to suit the hydro-pneumatic struts. In the other cars, the abutment screws of the front torsion bars were modified for easier adjustment of the ride height. To start with, the ZF rack-and-pinion steering gear was retained for all types, but at a later date, the 911 T received the simplified steering gear used in the 914. The reduced front wheel trail adopted for all models made the steering lighter and reduced the reactions through the steering wheel.

All 2.2 911 models had a twin-circuit braking system with ventilated discs all round. The 911 T had cast iron calipers all round, while light alloy calipers were fitted to the front wheels of the 911 E and S.

Engine
The substitution of aluminium with magnesium alloy as a crankcase material made a new bearing necessary for the intermediate shaft which previously ran directly in the aluminium housing. The connecting rods were reinforced and had longer big end bolts. The number of cooling fins on the cylinders was increased and the cylinders were slightly shortened at their bottom ends to clear the reinforced connecting rods. The cylinder head joint face was modified where it bore on the gasket. The inlet and exhaust valve diameter was increased and now the same for all engines, but the port sizes varied according to the engine types.

All 911 T engines now drew the mixture from two Zenith Type 40 TIN carburettors. These had three chokes and two float chambers in one unit.

All 911 models exported to the USA were equipped with a fuel tank venting system meeting the American requirements.

Transmission
All new models received a larger diameter diaphragm clutch with an inverted release system, designed to reduce the operating forces. The new clutch involved the use of a different Bowden cable arrangement.

A five-speed gearbox, Type 911/01, was standard on the 911 E and 911 S. The 911 T had the Type 911/00 four-speed box. A Sportomatic transmission was an option, except for the 911 S, and all models could be obtained with a ZF limited slip differential with a 40 or 80 per cent locking factor.

Equipment
The interior and dashboard of the 2.2-litre models provided an easy control and an excellent view of all instruments. Two stalks carried by the steering column (windscreen wiper/washer and directional lights/headlight flasher) could be operated without moving the hands from the steering wheel. The instruments were circular, non-reflecting and directly in front of the driver. They included a tachometer, a speedometer, an oil thermometer and oil pressure gauge, a fuel level gauge and a clock.

The ventilating system was of the through-flow type. A separately adjustable heating and ventilating system included a three-speed fan. An electrically heated rear window, an electric windscreen washer, headlights with a quartz-halogen main beam, reversing lights and hazard lights were standard equipment. New were an illuminated ashtray and a four-position ignition and steering lock. A two-stage electrically heated windscreen was an option. US export cars were equipped with a buzzer reminding the driver to remove the ignition key before leaving the vehicle.

Annual modifications

1971
Modified emission laws in some European countries necessitated minor modifications to the fuel injection and ignition systems: the vacuum sensor of the injection system, the ignition distributor, the throttle valve housing and the fuel metering unit in the injection pump were modified. In addition, the electric fuel pump, previously mounted on the front suspension cross member, was moved to the rear of the car, between the main cross member and the left-hand semi-trailing arm.

Better torque was the main improvement brought by the capacity increase to 2.2 litres in 1969.

Year	Body	Type	Chassis no	Engine no	Engine type	Gearbox type	Cyl	Bore × stroke	Capacity	HP (DIN) at rpm	Torque (mkg) at rpm	Comp ratio	W.base (mm)	Track fr/ rear (mm)	Length (mm)	Weight (kg)	No produced
1969	Coupé	911T	911010001-9110102418	6100001-6103000	911/03	911/00	6	84 × 66	2195	125/5800	18,0/4200	8,6:1	2268	1362/1343	4163	1020	2418
	K-Coupé	911T	919120001-9110124126	6103501-6104547	911/07												4126
	Targa	911T	9110110001-9110112545	6103001-6103230	911/06												2545
	S-Matic	911T		6105001-6107999	911/08	905/20											
	Coupé	911E	9110200001-9110201304	6108501-6109955	911/01	911/01	6	84 × 66	2195	155/6200	19,5/4500	9,1:1	2268	1374/1355	4163	1020	1304
	K-Coupé	911E	9110220001-9110220667	6108001-6108374	911/04												667
	Targa	911E	9110210001-9110210933	6200001-6202476													933
	S-Matic	911E		6208001-6208434		905/20											
	Coupé	911S	9110300001-9110301744	6300001-6302480	911/02	911/01	6	84 × 66	2195	180/6500	20,3/5200	9,8:1	2268	1374/1355	4163	1020	1744
	Targa	911S	9110310001-9110310729														729
1970	Coupé	911T	9111100001-911110583	6110001-6113475	911/03	911/00	6	84 × 66	2195	125/5800	18,0/4200	8,6:1	2268	1362/1343	4163	1020	583
	K-Coupé	911T	9111120001-9111121934	6114001-6118119	911/07												1934
	Targa	911T	9111110001-9111113476	6119001-6119190	911/06												3476
	S-Matic	911T		6119501-619728	911/08	905/20											
	Coupé	911E	9111200001-9111201088	6210001-6211767	911/01	911/01	6	84 × 66	2195	155/6200	19,5/4500	9,1:1	2268	1374/1355	4163	1020	1088
	Targa	911E	9111210001-9111210935														935
	S-Matic	911E		6218001-6218260	911/04	905/20									2268		1020	
	Coupé	911S	9111300001-9111301430	6310001-6311959	911/02	911/01	6	84 × 66	2195	180/6500	20,3/5200	9,8:1	2268	1374/1355	4163	1020	1430
	Targa	911S	9111310001-9111310788														788

127

Notes:
Type 911-2.2: Engine 911/01: 155 bhp, fuel injection, manual gearbox. 911/02: 180 bhp fuel injection engine for 911 S. 911/03: 125 bhp carburettor engine for Europe. 911/04: 155 bhp, fuel injection, Sportomatic. 911/06: 125 bhp, carburettors, Sportomatic. 911/07: 125 bhp carburettor USA engine, manual gearbox. 911/08: 125 bhp carburettor USA engine, Sportomatic. Gearbox 911/01: Five-speed for 911 E and 911 S. 911/00: Four-speed for 911 T. 905/20: Optional Sportomatic transmission for 911 T and 911 E.

The Porsche 911-2.2 (from autumn 1969) had a more luxurious interior than its predecessors.

The 2.2-litre was built in three variants: T (125 hp), E (155 hp) and S (180 hp).

Porsche 911 T-2.2 with thin rubber protection strip on front bumper and no overriders.

911 S, USA version, with thick rubber strips, bumper overriders and US lights.

Type 911-2.4 (1971-1973)

After seven years of production, the 911 series acquired its second engine capacity increase. Further progress was made in refinement and performance. Under the pressure of the strict US emission norms (the USA still being Porsche's No 1 export market), the engine experts developed a 2.4-litre power plant running on regular grade fuel.

Far from adversely affecting performance, the reduced octane requirement—which for a long time left filling station attendants sceptical—went hand-in-hand with further increased performance as well as much better flexibility. The new 2.4-litre 911 S gained 10 bhp compared with its forerunner, making it a total of 190, the push of which was really felt above 5,000 rpm, some 500 rpm lower than in the case of the 2.2. You can't get something for nothing, however, and all cars used more fuel than they used to, a representative figure for the 911 S being between five and 7.5 kilometres per litre (14 to 21 miles per gallon) according to the owner's driving habits. The increased power required a new gearbox. For the driver, the main difference was the gear change pattern in which first and second gears were in line. The ever-increasing top speed (a new 911 S could do over 230 km/h (147 mph) made the problem of straight line stability more and more acute. By a clever arrangement of various accessories, a front/rear weight distribution of 42/58 had already been obtained in the previous C and D series. Now modified rear shock absorber mountings and a front air dam improved the high speed behaviour of the 2.4-litre models. To start with, only the 911 S was fitted with the front air dam, but there was such a demand for it from 911 T and E owners, that it finally became standard equipment on all models.

Apart from the 911 S air dam, all 2.4-litre models could be easily distinguished from their predecessors by their matt black air intake grille and the matt black rear Porsche script. Another identification mark was the oil filler flap located just behind the right-hand door, the oil tank having been moved to this position forward of the rear wheels to further improve the weight distribution. To open the flap, however, the door had to be opened and service station attendants so often mistook the oil tank filler for the fuel tank filler that this arrangement was quickly abandoned. Both oil tank and filler were put back into the engine compartment.

General description: Type 911-2.4 (basic model)

Coachwork and chassis

As from September 1 1971 all Porsche cars were modified, either as part of the normal development programme or in order to meet modified European emission laws.

The E-Programme 2.4 model could be unmistakably identified by the oil filler flap on the right-hand side of the body, following the move of the tank forward of the wheel. The tank was opened by a push button accessible after opening the right-hand door. The tank was secured by a metallic strap. The oil pipes between the tank and the engine were of a larger diameter than before.

The comfort of these 1972 models was improved by the use of softer dampers front and rear. All cars were normally equipped with Boge front damper struts, but Bilstein or Koni dampers could be obtained to special order. The 911 T and E models were supplied without anti-roll bars, but the 911 S had 15 mm (0.59 inch) diameter anti-roll bars front and rear. The front strut ball bearing console was modified. As the differential was approximately 10 mm (0.39 inch) farther back than before, and the dampers were of a different design, the damper mounting brackets were also modified.

The 911 E came with enamelled steel wheels of 6 J × 15 dimensions shod with 185/70 VR 15 tyres, but light alloy wheels of the same dimensions were optional. The 911 T continued on 5.5 J × 15 steel wheels and 165 HR 15 tyres, but 185 tyres on the same wheels or the same wheels and tyres as on the 911 E were optional. On the 911 S, 6 J × 15 alloy wheels, shod with 185/70 VR 15 tyres, were standard equipment.

Black eloxided scripts and air intake grille underlined the sporting character of the cars. For reasons of appearance too, the front bumper overriders were deleted on the 911 T and E, while the 911 S came with its bumper integral with the air dam which improved the high speed stability of the car. The same bumper/air dam combination was optional on the other models. The basic equipment of the 911 E was now the same as in the 911 T. The new gearbox required a modification to the rear emergency seat pans, the squabs of which were moved back. The upper part of the rear bulkhead was now identical for the coupé and Targa models. The luggage compartment was fitted with its own lamp and with the introduction of the air dam, the optional foglights were moved to the front horn grilles. The 911 E received the same instruments as the 911 T, and the instruments themselves were identical for all models.

Engine

All Porsche six-cylinder engines now had a capacity of 2,341 cc. The capacity increase was obtained in this case by lengthening the stroke from 66 to 70.4 mm (2.6 to 2.77 inches). The 911 T engine retained its Solex-Zenith 40 TIN carburettors for the European markets, but with a supplementary control for closed throttle operation. Its power was 130 bhp at 5,600 rpm. For the US market, the T was equipped with a mechanical fuel injection system raising the power to 140 bhp at 5,600 rpm. The 911 E and S produced 165 bhp at 6,200 rpm and 190 bhp at 6,500 rpm respectively.

The compression ratio of all three engine types was reduced to enable them to run on regular fuel. The crankcase was reinforced with additional webs, and there were additional oil jets directing oil into the pistons for internal cooling. The ignition distributor mounting was modified, the distributor now being flange mounted on the crankcase. The longer stroke crankshaft also had slightly retouched connecting rod journals and modified bearings. The pistons were shorter and flatter. The entire induction system was new, with plastic intake pipes. Plastic was also used for the air filter housing and the intake air pre-heating system was modified. The ignition distributor was of either Marelli or Bosch manufacture.

Transmission
The increased power and torque of the 2.4-litre engines required a new, reinforced transmission, known as the Type 915. A four-speed version was standard on all models, but a five-speed box was also available. The gear change pattern was modified: first and second gears were in one plane and so were third and fourth gears. To engage fifth or reverse gear, the lever had to be pushed to the right against a spring. Moving the lever forward engaged fifth, while reverse was obtained by moving it back. The barrel-type gearbox housing was abandoned in favour of three-piece housing consisting of the differential housing, the gearbox housing and the gearbox end cover. The differential housing was more deeply ribbed than ever before.

The gearbox support was wider than before and the composite rubber and metal bearings were bolted on, so as to be easily replaceable. The clutch release mechanism was also modified. There was an optional 85-litre (18.7-gallon) fuel tank available. In order to retain the original luggage capacity when the tank was mounted, a space saver spare tyre was fitted together with an air bottle for its inflation.

Annual modifications

1973
The external flap giving access to the oil filler was deleted. The oil tank was moved back to its original position behind the right-hand rear wheel with its filler inside the engine compartment. The front oil cooler was replaced by a simpler and less fragile finned serpentine. The baffles directing the cooling air around the engine were modified to divide the air stream over the oil cooler. The intake air preheating was made adjustable on the carburettor engines. The oil tank was made of stainless steel and was of increased capacity. This allowed the oil change intervals to be doubled from 6,000 to 12,000 miles. The crankcase of all 911 engines was reinforced in the main bearing area. A cast gear lever support improved the precision of the movements and the positiveness of the reverse stop. The rear trailing arm brackets were modified to allow the arms to be removed without first having to remove the entire power unit from the car.

The 911 E was fitted with new ATS pressure cast wheels, also offered optionally on the 911 T. An 85-litre fuel tank, space-saver tyre and an electric compressor for its inflation were made standard equipment on all models. The front horn grilles and the front and rear light surrounds were made of black plastic. The combined bumper and air dam was standard equipment on all models. The front seat anchorage was modified to meet new legal requirements. The new exhaust silencer was entirely made of stainless steel and remained unpainted.

911-2.4

Year	Body	Type	Chassis no	Engine no	Engine type	Gearbox type	Cyl	Bore × stroke	Cap-acity	HP (DIN) at rpm	Torque (mkg) at rpm	Comp ratio	W base (mm)	Track fr/ rear (mm)	Length (mm)	Weight (kg)	No prod-uced
1971	Coupé	911T	9112500001-9112501963	6520001-6523284	911/57	915/12	6	84 x 70,4	2341	130/5600	20/4000	7,5:1	2271	1360/1342	4147	1050	1963
	Targa	911T	9112510001-9112511523			915/02											1523
	S-Matic	911T		6529001-6529224	911/67	905/21								1372/1354			
	Coupé	911T-US	9112100001-9112102931	6120001-6124478	911/51		6	84 x 70,4	2341	140/5600	20/4000	7,5:1	2271	1360/1342	4147	1050	2931
	Targa	911T-US	9112110001-9112111821														1821
	S-Matic	911T-US		6129001-6129293	911/61	925/00								1372/1354			
	Coupé	911E	9112200001-9112201124	6220001-6221765	911/52	915/12	6	84 x 70,4	2341	165/6200	21/4500	8,0:1	2271	1372/1354	4147	1050	1124
	Targa	911E	9112210001-9112210861														861
	S-Matic	911E		6629001-6229248	911/62	925/00											
	Coupé	911S	9112300001-9112301750	6320001-6322586	911/53	915/12	6	84 x 70,4	2341	190/6500	22/5200	8,5:1	2271	1372/1354	4147	1050	1750
	Targa	911S	9112310001-9112310989														989
	S-Matic	911S		6329001-6329147	911/63	925/01											
1972	Coupé	911T	9113500001-9113501875	6530001-6533239	911/57	915/12	6	84 x 70,4	2341	130/5600	20/4000	7,5:1	2271	1360/1342	4127	1050	1875
	Targa	911T	9113510001-9113511541														1541
	S-Matic	911T		6539001-6539197	911/67	905/21											
	Coupé	911T-US	9113100001-9113101252	6130001-6131926	911/51	915/12	6	84 x 70,4	2341	140/5600	20/4000	7,5:1	2271	1360/1342	4127	1050	1252

133

911-2.4

Year	Body	Type	Chassis no	Engine no	Engine type	Gearbox type	Cyl	Bore × stroke	Capacity	HP (DIN) at rpm	Torque (mkg) at rpm	Comp ratio	W'base (mm)	Track fr/rear (mm)	Length (mm)	Weight (kg)	No produced
1972	Targa	911T-US	9113110001-9113110781		911/51		6	84 x 70,4	2341	140/5600	20/4000	7,5:1	2271	1360/1342	4127	1050	781
	S-Matic	911T-US		6139001-6139149	911/61	925/00											
	Coupé	911T-C	9113101501-9113103444	6133001-6136092	911/91	915/12	6	84 x 70,4	2341	140/5600	20/4000		2271	1360/1342	4127	1050	1944
	Targa	911T-C	9113111001-9113112302														1302
	S-Matic	911T-C		6139301-6139502	911/96	925/00											
	Coupé	911E	9113200001-9113201366	6230001-6232125	911/52	915/12	6	84 x 70,4	2341	165/6200	21/4500	8:1	2271	1372/1354	4127	1075	1366
	Targa	911E	9113210001-9113211055														1055
	S-Matic	911E		6239001-6239319	911/62	925/00											
	Coupé	911S	9113300001-9113301430	6330001-6332231	911/53	915/12	6	84 x 70,4	2341	190/6500	22/5200	8,5:1	2271	1372/1354	4147	1075	1430
	Targa	911S	9113310001-9113310925														925
	S-Matic	911S		6339001-6339136	911/63	925/01											
	Coupé	911SC	9113600001-9113601590	6630001-6631551	911/83	915/08	6	84 x 70,4	2341	210/6300	26/5100	8,5:1	2271	1372/1394	4147	1075	1590

Notes:

Type 911-2.4: 911/51: Fuel injection engine (140 bhp) for 911 T exported to Australia, Canada, Japan and USA. 911/61: as 911/51, but with Sportomatic fittings. 911/57: 130 bhp carburettor engine for 911 T. 911/67: As 911/57, but with Sportomatic fittings. 911/52: 165 bhp fuel injection engine for 911 E. 911/62: As 911/52, but with Sportomatic fittings. 911/53: 190 bhp fuel injection engine for 911 S. 911/63: As 911/53, but with Sportomatic fittings. Gearbox 915/12: Four-speed for 911 T, E and S. 915/02: Five-speed for 911 T, E and S. 925/00: Four-speed Sportomatic for 911 T-USA and 911 E. 905/21: Four-speed Sportomatic for 911 T-Europe. 925/01: Four-speed Sportomatic for 911 S.

134

Top: Porsche 911 S-2.4 (190 bhp). Note front air dam.

Above: 2.4-litre Targa. The external oil filler cap was a feature of 1972 models only.

Left: Instrument panel with five circular dials remains essentially unaltered to the present day.

136 *External oil filler was not featured on 1973 models which had new wheels and stainless steel exhaust.*

Type Carrera RS 2.7 (1972-1973)

After being almost ten years without a 'Carrera'—the last Porsche officially called 'Carrera' was a 356 C—Porsche dug up the name for a car worthy of it.

In order to keep the 911 competitive in the GT class of motor sport, it had become necessary to extend the range by a new model providing the base for deriving a successful competition model within the frame of the regulations. In order to be homologated in the GT group, 500 identical units had to be made. For the comparatively very modest price of DM 33,000, Porsche offered a very special 911 weighing a mere 900 kg and powered by a 2.7-litre engine developing 210 bhp and capable of 240 km/h (149 mph).

Its enthusiastic reception puzzled even the makers. In November 1972, after only three months of production, the initial batch was sold out and a second batch of 500 cars went almost as quickly. Quite obviously, the prestige of the 'Carrera' name had been underrated. But those who acquired the car were not disappointed as it really lived up to its name, derived from the Mexican road race named 'Carrera Panamericana' in which Porsche scored many successes. It formed the base for a racing model which was to score innumerable successes continuing well into the '80s.

Neither efforts nor money were spared to reduce the weight by over 100 kg, compared to the 2.4-litre 911 S, but customers with no competition ambitions could buy the sports kit for about DM 700 or the touring kit (some DM 2,500 extra) to bring the Carrera at least optically and in its interior accommodation up to the standards of the other 911 models.

The main exterior feature of the Carrera was its 'duck's tail' rear spoiler which could be exchanged for the standard engine cover only under the customer's responsibility. Combined with the front air dam, the spoiler increased the maximum speed and reduced the tendency to oversteer at high speeds. Such was the prestige of the 'Carrera' that many owners of lesser 911 models gave their car the 'Carrera look' by exchanging their standard engine cover for the 'duck's tail' cover. Giving them Carrera performance was not so easy, as the 2.7-litre engine was an exclusive Carrera feature, obtained by an increase in the bore size. Though this increased the power, the Carrera's specific power was slightly lower than in the 911 S. In return, the engine was very flexible and could easily be driven at 2,000 rpm in fifth gear. The fuel consumption too was a good surprise: an Imperial gallon of regular (yes!) fuel would take the Carrera over a distance of anything between 14 and 18 miles, making full use of its performance.

The running gear, uncompromisingly tuned for fast cornering, enabled the car to reach very high cornering speeds and the knowledge that even the driver of a Ferrari GTB-4 had to take them seriously was worth DM 53,000 to the 1,036 drivers who bought a Carrera 2.7 RS.

General description: Type Carrera 2.7 RS (basic model)

Coachwork and chassis

All the Carrera RS's were fitted with Bilstein front struts using a rather stiff damper setting. The front anti-roll bar diameter was 15 mm, as in other 911 models. The rear support of the front wishbones was an aluminium forging. The rear diagonal suspension arms were reinforced and so were the rear wheel bearing housings. Increased rigidity of the rear tubular transverse member carrying the suspension was obtained by a central support linking it to the floor pan. Forged aluminium wheels were standard, with 6J × 15 front rims carrying 185/70 VR 15 tyres and 7J × 15 rear rims carrying 215/60 VR 15 tyres. Seven millimetre distance pieces further increased the rear track.

Engine

The capacity increase from 2.4 to 2.7 litres (exactly 2,687 cc) was achieved by increasing the bore from 84 to 90 mm. Maximum power was 210 bhp DIN at 6,300 rpm and Nikasil-coated aluminium cylinders were used for the first time in a production model, the number of fins being reduced from 15 to 11. The forged pistons were flatter than in the 911 S, but most of the other engine components, as crankshafts, camshafts, valves, cylinder heads were common to both engines, as was the valve timing.

Transmission

The Carrera RS 2.7's type 915 gearbox was fitted with an oil pump incorporated in the front cover and driven by the gearbox output shaft.

Equipment

The specific Carrera colour was called 'Grand Prix White', but all the other standard and optional colour schemes were available, though the 'Carrera' script on the body side panels and the enamelled wheels could only be had in combination with red, blue and green finishes. All cars were delivered with a fibreglass engine cover incorporating the 'duck's tail' spoiler. The car could be ordered in one of the three trim options: Sport, Touring or Racing. In the 'Sport' version, only one 12-volt battery was fitted and a single tone horn replaced the twin air horns. While the front bumper was the standard steel component in the Touring version, it was made of fibreglass in the other two versions. While the interior trim of the 'Touring' version was similar to the 911 S, the RS 'Sport' was more spartan; there was no clock or glovebox door and all sound-proofing material was deleted, except for the mats applied to either side of the wall separating the cockpit from the engine. The rear emergency seats were deleted and the rear quarter windows were fixed. The front seats were lightweight Recaro shells, thinly trimmed with adjustable squabs. The door trim panels were much simplified, the armrest and oddment box being deleted and only a leather grip being provided to pull the door shut. The engine cover lock and operating cable were replaced by simple rubber fasteners.

Top: Porsche Carrera RS 2.7. 210 bhp and 240 km/h (149 mph) costing DM 33,000.

Above: The 'duck's tail' spoiler was a distinctive external feature of the Carrera RS.

Left: This piece of moulded plastic was soon seen on many non-Carrera models.

Type 911-2.7 (1973-1977)

Few of the world's cars which retain their body shape for ten years have reached such a high degree of development as the Porsche models. In autumn 1963, the first 911 was revealed with a 2-litre engine at the Frankfurt Motor Show. In autumn 1973, the G-series appeared, this 8th series differing in detail from its predecessor. The company's desire to constantly improve the safety, the comfort and to reduce the typical nuisances of automobiles, in other words to be always a step ahead of the latest technical developments, was particularly obvious in the 1974 models of which production started in September 1973. If the character of the 911 range remained intact, the new models were clearly different from their predecessors. With the appearance of the new series, the model designation was changed and the labels 'T' and 'E' disappeared. The basic model was now the Porsche 911 (without any suffix), boasting no less than 150 bhp. The next step was the 911 S (175 bhp), while the Carrera mustering 210 bhp was introduced as the top model of the range. The general increase in cubic capacity to nearly 2.7 litres and the new Bosch K-Jetronic fuel injection system of the 911 and 911 S engines allowed them to meet the ever stricter emission laws and to improve the engine flexibility for more relaxed driving in heavy traffic.

The Carrera, which still featured mechanical fuel injection to get the highest possible power out of its engine, was taken into the regular programme after the tremendous commercial success of the previous year's limited pilot series. Externally, the main difference of the G-Programme cars compared with their predecessors was the larger and higher aluminium bumpers, meeting the main body structure through an accordion-like rubber joint. The interior was also extensively revised: the door trim panels had more rigid pockets and new, lighter seats had an incorporated headrest. Also new was a small filler under the fuel tank filler flap, feeding the windscreen washer reservoir of nearly nine litres (two gallons) capacity! First class workmanship was evident in both the coupé and the Targa versions of all three models. They were more than ever cars from which driver and passenger could derive immense pleasure. The capacity increase notably changed the characteristics of the 911 and 911 S models, compared with their predecessors. Their higher torque, delivered at lower engine speeds, allowed a more fluid and relaxed driving style. The Carrera, which was now sold without rear spoiler and with full de luxe equipment, was more in the old Porsche tradition. It was also quite at ease in city traffic, but when the engine speed rose over 4,000 rpm, tremendous power was suddenly unleashed. From a standing start, 100 km/h (60 mph) could be reached in under six seconds and top speed was 240 km/h (149 mph). The improvement in fuel consumption was quite surprising too. All cars used regular grade fuel and the normal 911 achieved anything between 7.7 and 9 km per litre (21.5 and 25.5 mpg), the 911 S from 6.6 to 7.7 km per litre (18.5 to 21.5 mpg) and even the Carrera seldom did worse than 5.9 km/l (16.5 mpg) (911: 17.6-20.9; 911 S: 15.2-17.6; Carrera: 13.6 miles per US gallon).

The general comfort was well above average for a sports car, even if the steering remained rather sensitive to irregularities in the road surface. The brakes were above reproach and remained fade-free, even if submitted to the wildest driving techniques. The international motoring press praised the new Porsche models for their very high standards of quality and workmanship, as well as for their reliability, matched only by their less flamboyant cousin, the VW Beetle.

On June 3 1977, the 250,000th Porsche sports car made since production started in 1948/49, a 911 coupé, left the assembly line. In a world in which success stories have become commonplace, this does not sound very much to boast about, but for a comparatively small factory specialising in the production of exclusive sports cars, it was an event to be proud of. According to Porsche's files, a total of 75,972 of the various Types 356 were built and the 250,000th Porsche was also the 154,501st of the 911/912 series. At the same date, 19,168 Porsche 924, 33 Porsche 928 and no less than 326 racing models had been built.

General description: Type 911-2.7 (basic model)

Coachwork and chassis
All 1974 Porsche models received a new simplified, one-piece front anti-roll bar, doing away with the former links. The diameter was 16 mm (0.6 inch) in the 911 and 911 S and 20 mm (0.78 inch) in the Carrera which also had an 18 mm (0.7 inch) diameter rear anti-roll bar of the same design as before. The front anti-roll bar was rubber jointed to the wishbones and pivoted in rubber bushes carried in the front cross member. The wishbones were modified accordingly. To special order, the 911 and 911 S models could be ordered with the same anti-roll bar combination as the Carrera. The front towing eye was welded to the right-hand side front wishbone support.

The front wheels were now centred on the front hub, avoiding any possibility of mounting the wheel off-centre. While the Carrera retained the alloy 'S' front brake calipers, the 911 and 911 S used the smaller M-type cast iron caliper. The rear semi-trailing arms were made of light alloy and carried a larger wheel bearing. The effort required to release the clutch was reduced by an auxiliary over-centre spring acting on the pedal. To reduce the force required for braking, the length of the brake pedal lever was increased from 232 to 250 mm (9.1 to 9.8 inches).

Engine
All three types had a new 2.7-litre engine. In the 911 and 911 S the former fuel injection system was replaced by the Bosch K-Jetronic system, although the Carrera engine continued with the well-proven mechanical system, better suited to high specific power outputs. As this engine did not meet the ever stricter American exhaust emission standards, only the two K-Jetronic engines were fitted to the US models, the 911 S and the Carrera differing only in their equipment. The 911 and 911 S engines now used the same 90 mm (3.5 inch) bore Nikasil light alloy cylinders, already fitted to the Carrera, but these were soon to be replaced by Alusil cylinders. Instead of being forged, the pistons of the two less

powerful engines were cast. Intake and exhaust valves, rockers and camshaft drive remained unchanged. Only the camshafts themselves were modified in the 911 and 911 S to provide a 'softer' timing. The front oil cooler was now rigidly connected to the oil pipes and secured to the body shell by a single support.

The K-Jetronic injection system of the 911 and 911 S had already been fitted to the 911 T exported to the United States from the beginning of 1973. In this installation, the quantity of fuel delivered continuously to the engine by a high pressure electric pump was governed by the quantity of air drawn through the intake system.

The new bumpers dictated for all three engine types a new silencer with a different tail pipe location. The heat exchangers for the cockpit heating system were made of aluminised sheet steel providing better resistance to corrosion.

Transmission
All 1974 cars were equipped with the Type 915 four-speed gearbox, a five-speed version, or the Sportomatic transmission was available, although there was no Sportomatic Carrera. Only the gear ratios were changed, compared with previous models. The transmission oil pump which had been fitted to early Carrera RS models was removed.

Equipment
The general outline of the body was modified by the new bumpers. Generally speaking, special attention was given both to the exterior and interior equipment to enhance safety. The Targa was now made available in the Carrera line.

The bumpers were made of aluminium and were carried on special crushable tubes allowing the bumper to move back, so that up to a collision speed of 8 km/h (5 mph) no important part of the vehicle would be damaged. All cars were fitted with a front air dam reducing front end lift and improving high speed stability. Except for the main lights, all the front lights were integrated into the bumper. They were protected by a prominent rubber guard extending along the full length of the bumper. The front wings (fenders) were modified for better integration of the bumper into the body lines. The rear bumper was also protected by a rubber strip and in addition carried two thick rubber overriders on which the number plate lights were mounted. Crushable tubes, similar to the front ones, carried the real bumper and allowed an inward movement of approximately 50 mm (2 inches). Special hydraulic impact dampers could be fitted in place of the crushable tubes on special request. In this case, the energy was absorbed hydraulically and the bumper returned to its original position after the impact. Accordion joints between bumper and body allowed for bumper displacements. The new bumper arrangement made it necessary to replace the two separate batteries with one larger battery, located at the front end, on the left-hand side of the luggage compartment.

Targa models now had a one-piece roof, although the folding top remained as an option. It now had an additional central locating peg. All three models got a steel fuel tank of approximately 80-litre (17.6-gallon) capacity into which the space saver spare wheel was recessed.

The most obvious modification to the interior was the new lightweight seats with integral headrest. All models were fitted with inertia reel seat belts as standard equipment. On the dashboard, adjustable demisting vents for the side windows were added. The directional indicator light stalk was modified in shape. The steering wheel (400 mm [15.75 inches] for the 911 and 911 S, 380 mm [14.96 inches] for the Carrera) was covered with a large protective pad. The door trim panels were new and incorporated rigid pockets with a hinged cover. Carreras were equipped with electric window switches as standard equipment. There were several minor modifications to the electrical equipment, mainly to the front auxiliary lights, number plate lights, reversing lights, battery, position of some relays and fuses, clock (now quartz-electric) and tachometer, which was now electronic. Cars for export to Sweden were equipped with headlight washers, optional on other models, while the US models had an ignition interlock system. All instruments, switches and control knobs were padded and so arranged that they could not create injuries in the case of an accident.

Annual modifications

1975

Most of the details identifying the 1975 models were aimed at further improving the comfort. The heating system was thoroughly revised for better adjustability and consistency. The aluminised heat exhangers were made smaller. In the 911 and 911 S models, the heater output at low engine speeds was increased by an additional electric fan. There were now two heater control levers, making it possible to adjust the output into the right-hand and left-hand sides of the cockpit. In order to meet the increased current requirement of the installation, the output of the alternator was raised to 980 watts.

There were slight modifications to the 911 S gear ratios. Third and fourth gears of the four-speed gearbox and fourth and fifth of the five-speed were slightly higher geared. The sound insulation of the body was improved and the rear anti-roll bar brackets were made a standard fitting to facilitate adding the optional rear bar.

The equipment was improved both in volume and in quality. The basic 911 came with 6J × 15 cast alloy wheels and the same 185/70 VR 15 tyres as the 911 S. The Carrera top model was distinguished by new visible differences: the external mirror and the headlight surrounds were sprayed in the same colour as the car and the Targa had a matt black roll-over structure.

1976

Externally the cars remained practically unchanged, but only one 2.7-litre model was kept in the range, the 911, which now developed 165 bhp. The other models in the range were the Carrera (3 litres-200 bhp) and the Turbo (3 litres-260 bhp).

The visible modifications were limited to details, but a very important step forward was the use of high-temperature zinc-coated sheet steel for the manufacture of the entire body structure (except for the coupé's roof on early production cars). Coated on both sides, this made the structure virtually immune from rust and corrosion attacks and enabled Porsche to issue a six-year warranty against the formation of rust on cars not involved in serious accidents. Improved door locks and an improved locking system for the Targa's pivoted front quarter windows were typical of 1976 model modifications. The external mirror was heated, sprayed in the same colour as the car and was electrically adjustable from inside.

The rear bulkhead was more thickly padded and there was a one-piece carpet floor covering. The door trim panels were covered with leather or imitation leather featuring an oblique motif, and were padded. Provision was made for mounting loudspeakers in the doors of which the pockets were upholstered.

A new option was the thermostatic heater control, which was made standard equipment in the Carrera and Turbo models. The installation comprised an electric governor located over the handbrake bracket and carrying an infinitely adjustable rotating switch on which the required temperature could be preselected. The control unit received signals from two heat sensors, one located near the left-hand heat exchanger control, the other between the sun visors in the cockpit, and adjusted the cockpit temperature as preselected.

Another option on the 911 was the 'Tempostat' automatic speed control. This device controlled the accelerator to a preselected speed, adjusting the throttle opening as required by slopes and wind conditions, as long as the power requirements remained within the engine's capabilities. The speed at which the car was travelling when the Tempostat was put into operation was electronically memorised by the control unit which then kept it constant. The selected speed could always be increased or decreased by operating the small stalk under the wiper/washer stalk.

The 165 bhp 911 engine was very similar to the previous year's 911 S and had unlinered Alusil cylinders—both the 911 and the Carrera now used the same camshaft housing as the Turbo. A wider oil pressure pump increased the oil flow through the engine. The engine cooling blower had only five blades instead of 11 and was driven at a higher speed, the object of the modification being to increase the alternator speed. The 80-litre (17.6-gallon) fuel tank was internally lead-coated to prevent corrosion and the fuel pump was moved to the front of the car, in order to combat vapour lock.

Better hot starting was obtained in the 911 by the addition of a supplementary air slide located between the intake pipes of No 5 and 6 cylinders controlled by an electrically heated bi-metallic spiral.

The 911 came with the Type 915/49 four-speed gearbox. The Type 915/44 or the three-speed Sportomatic transmission, Type 925/09/12/13, were optional. The latter replaced the previous four-speed Sportomatic. A limited slip differential with a 40 or 80 per cent locking factor was available on request.

All cars were equipped with an electronic speedometer. It was governed by a disc mounted on the differential cage and incorporating a triggering magnet. The front suspension struts of the 911 2.7 were slightly more inclined inward than before to facilitate the camber adjustment. The car also received the new 'A'-Type cast iron front brake calipers, providing the same pad area as the 'S'-Type alloy calipers still used on the Turbo.

1977

The Bosch fuel pump was modified both internally and externally, the pressurised fuel accumulator now being provided with a return circuit, as in the Turbo. The fuel filter was also modified and had a finer mesh. The airflow meter lever of the K-Jetronic injection system carried a new riveted leaf spring bearing on the carbon monoxide adjusting screw and its closed position stop was modified. A vacuum connection for the new brake servo was added to the throttle valve housing.

An electrically heated thermo-valve was added in the warm running regulator circuit. Cars delivered with the 'Comfort Kit M 470' (which included 185 HR 14 tyres) were fitted with an automatic speed governor preventing the car from exceeding 210 km/h (130 mph)—the limit set by the tyre rating. When this speed was reached, the fuel supply to the engine was cut momentarily and only after the speed had dropped by about 5 mph was the pump energised again.

All cars destined for the US (including California), Canadian and Japanese markets had an engine with an additional air pump, twin thermal reactors and exhaust gas recirculation (EGR).

The Type 915 gearbox fitted to both the 911 and the Carrera was improved in several ways. First and second gears were fitted with twin baulking segments and the first gear dogs were cut asymetrically to facilitate engagement from rest. The first gear synchronising ring was smaller, but the first and second gear selecting muff was reinforced.

As a special option, the 911 could, as before, be equipped with Carrera-type anti-roll bars: front 20 mm diameter, rear 18 mm (0.79 and 0.7 inch), and in order to simplify the rear ride height adjustment, without having to remove the torsion bars, the trailing arms were made in two pieces with an eccentric screw adjustment.

All 911s equipped with Sportomatic were fitted with a Type T 52 brake servo. The cars were made more thief-proof by the use of shortened push buttons which, in the locked position, disappeared completely in the window-moulding. They could only be raised by turning a knob recessed in the door trim panel. To make the thieves' lives even harder, the pivoting window panels were omitted from the Targa models.

A central console with shelf was offered as an option. It was designed to accommodate, as required, the air conditioning controls, a traffic decoder,* an automatic radio selector, stereo-cassettes and a microphone, etc. The blower and fresh air controls were now separate and hot weather ventilation was considerably improved by the provision of two large cold air outlets in the central part of the dashboard.

The 911 could be purchased, at no extra cost, with a five-speed gearbox or with a three-speed Sportomatic in place of the standard four-speed box, the previous speed Sportomatic being replaced by the three-speed Sportomatic. This is technically a mechanical three-speed box combined with a hydraulic torque converter. The servo-operated clutch is disengaged as soon as the driver tries to move the gear-lever.

1978

The new basic six-cylinder model is the Porsche 911 SC which replaces both the 911 and the Carrera 3.0. Its 3-litre engine, which has a new, stronger crankshaft and larger diameter main and connecting rod bearings, develops 180 bhp at 5,500 rpm and has a maximum torque of 27 mkg (197 lb/ft) which even exceeds that of the Carrera 3.0. Consequently, its performance approaches that of the Carrera 3.0 from which it inherits the widened rear fenders and the 178 mm (7-inch) wide rear wheel rims. A return to an 11-bladed cooling air blower has been made, the exhaust has been modified for improved silencing and an air pump is fitted even to European specification engines, in order to meet future emission norms without excessively detuning the engine. A capacity discharge ignition system without contact breaker is now used.

The interior trim is also strongly reminiscent of the Carrera 3.0 and a five-speed gearbox, a brake servo and an auxiliary over-centre spring for reduced declutching effort are all part of the standard specification. Another important refinement is a completely new, Porsche-designed clutch disc hub providing much increased elasticity which completely eliminates the low speed gear chatter which has been a 911 characteristic from the beginning.

The 911 SC is also made in the Targa version.

*An ingenious German device which automatically tunes in to any traffic warnings being broadcast.

911-2.7

Year	Body	Type	Chassis no	Engine no	Engine type	Gearbox type	Cyl	Bore × stroke	Cap-acity	HP (DIN) at rpm	Torque (mkg) at rpm	Comp ratio	W'base (mm)	Track fr/ rear (mm)	Length (mm)	Weight (kg)	No prod-uced
1973	Coupé	RS	9113600001-9113601036	6630001-6631551	911/83	915/08	6	90 x 70,4	2687	210/6300	26/5100	8,5:1	2271	1372/1372	4147	1075	1036
	Coupé	SC	9113601590-											1394/1394			
1974	Coupé	911	9114100001-9114104014	6140001-6146625	911/92	911/16	6	90 x 70,4	2687	150/5700	24/3800	8,0:1	2271	1360/1342	4291	1075	4014
	Targa	911	9114110001-9114113110			915/06									1372/1354			3110
	S-Matic	911		6149001-6149517	911/97	925/02									1372/1380		1090	
	Coupé	911S	9114300001-9114301359	6340001-6342804	911/93	915/16	6	90 x 70,4	2687	175/5800	24/4000	8,5:1	2271	1360/1342	4291	1075	1359
	Targa	911S	9114310001-9114310898			915/16									1372/1354			898
	S-Matic	911S		6349001-6349236	911/98	925/02									1372/1380		1090	
	Coupé	Carrera	9114600001-9114601036	6640001-6641456	911/83	915/16	6	90 x 70,4	2687	210/6300	26/5100	8,5:1	2271	1372/1354	4291	1075	1036
	Targa	Carrera	9114610001-9114610433			915/06									1372/1380			433
	Coupé	Carrera -US	9114400001-9114400528	6340001-6840169	911/93	915/16	6	90 x 70,4	2687	175/5800	24/4000	8,5:1	2271	1360/1342	4291	1075	528
	Targa		9114410001-9114410246			915/06									1372/1354			246
	S-Matic					925/02									1372/1380		1090	
1975	Coupé	911	9115100001-9115101238	6150001-6152007	911/41	915/48	6	90 x 70,4	2687	150/5700	24/3800	8,0:1	2271	1372/1354	4291	1075	1238
	Targa	911	9115110001-9115110998			915/43									1372/1380			998
	S-Matic	911		6159001-6159252	911/46	925/02									1372/1380		1090	

146

911-2.7

Year	Body	Type	Chassis no	Engine no	Engine type	Gearbox type	Cyl	Bore × stroke	Cap-acity	HP (DIN) at rpm	Torque (mkg) at rpm	Comp ratio	W'base (mm)	Track fr/ rear (mm)	Length (mm)	Weight (kg)	No prod-uced
1975	Coupé	911S-US	9115200001-9115202310	6450001-6452440	911/43	915/45	6	90 x 70,4	2687	165/5800	23/4000	8,5:1	2271	1372/1342	4291	1100	2310
	Targa	911S-US	9115210001-9115211517			915/40								1372/1368			1517
	S-Matic	911S-US		6459001-6459135	911/48	925/10										1115	
	Coupé	911S	9115300001-9115300385	6350001-6350567	911/42	915/45	6	90 x 70,4	2687	175/5800	24/4000	8,5:1	2271	1372/1354	4291	1075	385
	Targa	911S	9115310001-9115310266			915/40								1372/1380			266
	S-Matic	911S		6359001-6359105	911/47	925/02										1090	
	Coupé	Carrera	9115600001-9115600518	6650021-6650712	911/83	915/16	6	90 x 70,4	2687	210/6300	26/5100	8,5:1	2271	1372/1354	4291	1075	518
	Targa	Carrera	9115610001-9115610197			915/06								1372/1380			197
	Coupé -US	Carrera	9115400001-9115400395	6450001-6452440	911/43	915/4	6	90 x 70,4	2687	165/5800	23/4000	8,5:1	2271	1372/1342	4291	1100	395
	Targa		9115410001-9115410174											1372/1368			
	S-Matic			6459001-6459135	911/48	925/10											
1976	Coupé	911	9116300001-9116301868	6360001-6363029	911/81	915/49	6	90 x 70,4	2687	165/5800	24/4000	8,5:1	2271	1372/1354	4291	1075	1868
	Targa	911	9116310001-9116311576			915/44								1372/1380			1576
	S-Matic	911		6369001-6369435	911/86	925/09											1090	
	Coupé-US	911S	9116200001-9116202079	6460001-6462305	911/82	915/44	6	90 x 70,4	2687	165/5800	24/4000	8,5:1	2271	1372/1342	4291	1100	2079
	Targa-US	911S	9116210001-9116212175	6560001-6561837	911/84												2175

911-2.7

Year	Body	Type	Chassis no	Engine no	Engine type	Gearbox type	Cyl	HP (DIN) at rpm	Cap-acity	Bore × stroke	Torque (mkg) at rpm	Comp ratio	W'base (mm)	Track fr/ rear (mm)	Length (mm)	Weight (kg)	No prod-uced
	S-Matic-US	911S	9116100001-9116100130	6569001-6569160	911/89	925/12	6	165/5800	2687	90 x 70,4	24/4000	8,5:1	2271	1372/1354	4291	1115	130
	Coupé-Japan	911	9116609001-9116609123	6160001-6160140	911/41	915/44	6	165/5800	2687	90 x 70,4	24/4000	8,5:1	2271		4291	1075	123
1)	Coupé	911	9116609001-9116609030	6668001-6668155	911/83	915/49	6	210/6300	2687	90 x 70,4	26/5100	8,5:1	2271	1369/1380	4291	1100	30
1)	Targa	911															
1977	Coupé	911	9117300001-9117302449	6370001-6373531	911/81	915/60	6	165/5800	2687	90 x 70,4	24/4000	8,5:1	2271	1369/1354	4291	1120	2449
	Targa	911	9117310001-9117311724	6379001-6379322		915/65											1724
	S-Matic	911			911/86	925/15											
	Coupé-US	911S	9117200001-9117203388	6270001-6276041	911/85	915/61	6	165/5800	2687	90 x 70,4	24/4000	8,5:1	2271	1369/1354	4291	1120	3388
	Targa-US	911S	9117210001-9117212747										2271				2747
	S-Matic-US	911S		6279001-6279113	911/90	925/17											
	Coupé-Japan	911S		6170001-6170273	911/94	915/66											
	S-Matic-Japan	911S		6179001-6179110	911/99	925/17											

Notes:

Type 911 2.7: RS/SC Coupé with Type 911/83 engine, 2.7-litre, 210 bhp, manual gearbox. Five-speed gearbox, Type 915/08 with oil pump.
911/98: 2.7/175 bhp for 911 S/Carrera Sportomatic for USA.
Gearbox 915/06: Five speeds (option). 915/16: Four speeds. 925/02: Sportomatic (option).
Engine 911/41: 2.7/150 bhp for Porsche 911. 911/42: 2.7/175 bhp for Porsche 911 S. 911/43: 2.7/165 bhp for Porsche 911 S and Carrera, USA. 911/44: 2.7/160 bhp for Porsche 911 S and Carrera, California. 911/46: 2.7/150 bhp for 911 Sportomatic. 911/47: 2.7/175 bhp for 911 S Sportomatic. USA. 911/48: 2.7/160 bhp for 911 S and Carrera Sportomatic, California. 911/83: 2.7/210 bhp for Carrera. Gearbox 915/48: Four-speed for 911. 915/43: Five-speed for 911. 925/04: Four-speed Sportomatic for 911 and 911 S.

Engine 911/92: 2.7/150 bhp for 911. 911/93: 2.7/175 bhp for 911 S and Carrera, USA. 911/83: 2.7/210 bhp for Carrera. 911/97: 2.7/150 bhp for 911 Sportomatic.
Gearbox 915/45: Four-speed for 911 S, USA. 915/40: Five-speed for 911 S, 911 S, USA. 915/16: Four-speed for Carrera. 915/06: Five-speed for Carrera. 925/10: Three-speed Sportomatic for 911 S, USA and Carrera, USA.
Engine 911/81: 2.7/165 bhp for 911. 911/86: 2.7/165 bhp for 911 Sportomatic. 911/82: 2.7/165 bhp for 911 S, USA. 911/84: 2.7/165 bhp for 911 S, California. 911/89: 2.7/165 bhp for 911 S, USA and California Sportomatic.
Gearbox 925/09: Three-speed Sportomatic for 911. 915/44: Five-speed for 911 and 911 S, USA. 925/12: Three-speed Sportomatic for 911 and 911 S, USA.
1) Special model: 210 bhp engine.

Front and rear views of second Carrera series with full de luxe equipment. 149

150 *The American version of the Carrera (from 1974 model) had normal 2.7-litre, 175 bhp 911 S engine.*

1975 Porsche 911: from that year on, alloy wheels became standard on the basic model.

The 911 basic models for 1974: 150 bhp and steel wheels. Above: Targa. Below: Coupé.

Basic 911 models for 1975 had better equipment. Alloy wheels were standard.

Basic 1975 Porsche 911 had supplementary blower in heating system.

The Carrera 2.7 model had better equipment in addition to more power.

Carrera 2.7 with optional large tail spoiler and (mandatory) extended front air dam.

A limited special 911 series was made on the occasion of the company's 25th anniversary.

The 500 cars of the limited series were exclusively equipped.

From the G-Series (1974 models), seats with integral headrest were adopted.

1975 model modifications: improved door locks, cloth door trims.

External mirror was electrically adjustable, heated and the housing painted to match the body.

Revised dashboard of 1975 models. Note large padded knobs.

2.7-litre engine with K-Jetronic injection. Above: European version. Below: USA version.

158   *911 Targa, 1977 model. Visible modifications to the interior trim only.*

1977 model 911/2.7 Targa: a well-balanced, mature design.

The 250,000th Porsche, a 911/2.7 coupé, came off the line on June 3 1977.

Turning knob door lock release improves thief-proofing.

Face-level air outlets in the central part of the dash panel improved the ventilation of 1977 models.

*Central console with
provision for storing
stereo-cassettes and
for fitting additional
radio equipment.*

*1978 Porsche 911 SC
combines features of
previous 911/2.7
and Carrera 3.0
models.*

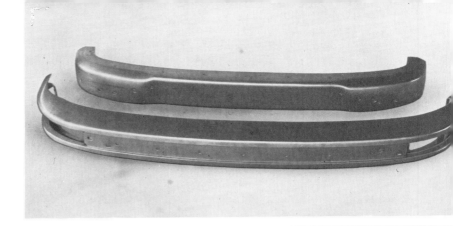

Aluminium is used by Porsche in ever-increasing quantities. Here the bumpers and semi-trailing arms (Turbo left, 911 right).

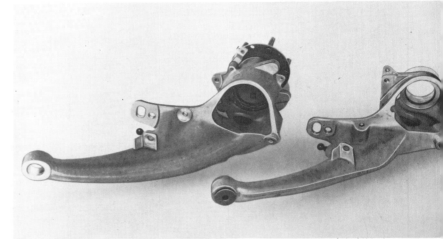

Front brakes: left Carrera 2.7, right normal 911 (1974-75).

Aluminium semi-trailing link of 911-2.7 (above) and corresponding fabricated steel part of earlier 911 (below).

Right: 911 S-2.4 front running gear. Below right: Same for 2.7.

164

Type 915 transmission used for all rear-engined Porsches from 2.4 models, except for Turbo.

Type Carrera 3.0 (1975-1977)

The Carrera 3.0 continued the tradition of one of the most famous Porsches in the history of motor sport. The 3-litre model provided a very high performance and magnificent handling and safety in a more relaxed way, with less noise and better comfort, than all its predecessors. The capacity increase from 2.7 to 3 litres notably improved the engine's flexibility and mid-range performance, the maximum torque of 190 lb/ft now being developed at 4,200 rpm instead of 5,100 rpm. While the Carrera 2.7 RS required 34.2 seconds to accelerate from 40 to 160 km/h (25 to 100 mph) in top gear, the 3-litre took only 30.9 seconds. The maximum power of the 200 bhp engine was obtained at only 6,000 rpm. Acceleration and maximum speed, however, were identical with those of its predecessor. And, not to be scorned, the latest Carrera consumed less fuel, thanks to its K-Jetronic injection system.

The Carrera 3.0 came with lavish standard equipment. The automatic heater control, the electrically adjustable and heated external mirror, the headlight washers and the electric window switches merit special mention.

All 1976 models were guaranteed for a full year with no mileage limitation. With the introduction of zinc-coated sheet metal for the body shell—a complete innovation in the motor industry—Porsche gave an additional full six-year warranty on the floorpan and the entire stressed structure.

External identification of the Carrera 3.0 from its immediate predecessors was easier than in the case of the other 911 models. All previously chromium-plated parts were finished in matt black and wider rear wings (fenders) allowed fat high-speed radial tyres to be used. Forged alloy wheels, the front ones 152 mm (6 inches) the rear ones 178 mm (7 inches) wide were standard equipment, but 152 mm and 203 mm (8 inch) wide wheels respectively were available at extra cost.

General description: Type Carrera 3.0 (basic model)

Coachwork and chassis

The basically unmodified Type 911 body was changed only in details but, as already mentioned, incorporated high-temperature zinc-coated sheet steel. The decision to use this material was taken only after many years of experimentation, and after the pros and cons of this and other solutions had been thoroughly analysed. The introduction of the zinc-coated sheet metal was Porsche's latest step in a programme aiming at increasing the life and the overall economy of its vehicles. The previously applied anti-corrosion protection, including the permanent sealing of all box sections, the underpan protection and the high quality finish applied over a primer layer obtained by the electrophoretic process, was retained.

In addition to this, the use of rust-resistant aluminium components was extended. They now included the bumpers, the wheels, the rear semi-trailing arms, the front suspension cross member, the engine crankcase, cylinders and pistons, the gearbox housing and the steering gear housing. The stainless steel Targa roll-over structure was also fully corrosion resistant.

Modifications to the running gear were very few. As in the other 911 models, the front suspension struts of the Carrera were slightly more inclined inwards to facilitate camber adjustment. The front brakes got new cast iron calipers, providing a friction area identical with that of the light alloy calipers. The front suspension torsion bars had a diameter of 19 mm (0.75 inch) while the anti-roll bar was 20 mm (0.79 inch) thick. The rear torsion bars were 23 mm (0.9 inch) in diameter and the anti-roll bar was of 18 mm (0.7 inch) diameter. The rear wings (fenders) were wider than those of the 911 in order to accommodate the 215/60 VR 15 high speed tyres.

Engine

The capacity increase to 2,993 cc was obtained by increasing the cylinder bore from 90 to 95 mm (3.5 to 3.75 inches). The cast aluminium pistons were obviously new too but the cylinder material was still Nikasil. The compression ratio of 8.5:1 allowed the use of regular grade fuel. The Carrera was fitted with the camshaft housing of the Porsche Turbo, and the camshaft itself was also new. The intake valves were now of 49 mm (1.9 inches) diameter; the exhaust valves were similar to those of the Turbo engine, but were not sodium filled. Engine lubrication was improved by a larger capacity oil pressure pump. The engine cooling blower had only five blades as mentioned. The fuel tank and pump were modified as in the 911-2.7 and the Bosch six-plunger injection pump was replaced by the Bosch K-Jetronic continuous flow injection system, basically similar to the 911-2.7 installation, but of different dimensions.

Transmission

The Carrera 3.0 was equipped with the Type 915/49 four-speed gearbox. A five-speed version and the three-speed Sportomatic were optional. A stronger clutch release cable was used and the cable guiding nipple was screwed to the gearbox housing. In Sportomatic cars, the clutch release governor valve was modified to suit the different intake vacuum resulting from the change from mechanical to K-Jetronic injection. Both the clutch servo and the torque converter housing were modified to suit the higher engine torque.

Equipment

The Carrera 3.0 was exceptionally well equipped. A leather-covered steering wheel, leather-covered seats and interior trim were standard, but cloth and imitation leather were also available. The floor was covered with thick carpets, the door trim panels and the rear cockpit panel were beaded, the rigid door pockets were lined with cloth and the thermostatic heater control was also standard equipment. The coupé had electric window switches. Further standard equipment of both coupé and Targa models was an electrically adjustable and heated external mirror, a door and ignition key incorporating a small light, matt black exterior trim, headlight surrounds and external mirror sprayed in the same colour as the body, and headlight washers.

Annual modifications

1977

As the 911, the Carrera 3.0 had an improved Bosch fuel pump. The pressurised fuel accumulator was provided with a return circuit and the fuel filter was new, with a finer mesh.

The K-Jetronic injection system received an improved air flow meter and a modified flow meter lever stop. A vacuum connection was added to the throttle valve housing to operate the new brake servo. An electrically heated thermostatic valve was incorporated in the warm running regulator circuit.

All cars delivered to the US (including California), Canada and Japan were fitted with an air pump for exhaust manifold air injection, with twin thermal reactors and with exhaust gas recirculation (EGR). In addition to the over-centre spring acting on the pedal, a second auxiliary spring was provided on the clutch release lever to reduce the effort required for declutching. The operating lever on the pedal shaft was modified accordingly.

Modifications were also made to the first and second speed synchromesh of the Type 915 gearbox. The rear trailing arms were made in two pieces with an eccentric screw adjustment to facilitate ride height adjustment. A brake servo, Type T 52 was added. It was located inside the front luggage compartment.

Thief-proofing was improved by the use of shortened locking push-buttons which, in the locked position, completely disappeared into the window moulding, so that they could not be manually pulled open. To unlock the door, it was necessary to turn a knob incorporated in the door casing. The pivoting window panels which had been fitted to Targa models were deleted—again to improve thief-proofing.

A central console with shelf was offered as an option. The blower and fresh air controls were now separate and hot weather ventilation much improved by the provision of two large cold air outlets in the central region of the dash panel. In cars fitted with air conditioning, these outlets carried refrigerated air.

Instead of the standard four-speed gearbox, the customer could specify a five-speed box or a three-speed Sportomatic without having to pay any extra.

The Carrera's equipment was quite unusually comprehensive, even by luxury car standards: the thermostatic heater control, the electrically operated and heated external mirror, the electric window switches, the headlight washing installation and the choice of three different transmissions, without extra cost, are surely worth mentioning.

With the introduction of the 1978 models, the Carrera 3.0 disappeared from the Porsche programme, but the new 911 SC model which replaced both the 911 and the Carrera 3.0 owed much to the latter, including a 3-litre engine (restricted to 180 bhp) and the Carrera's body shell with wide rear fenders.

1976 Carrera had unchanged appearance, but 3-litre engine.

Since 1976 bodies have been made of zinc-coated steel and carry a six-year warranty for corrosion on all structural parts.

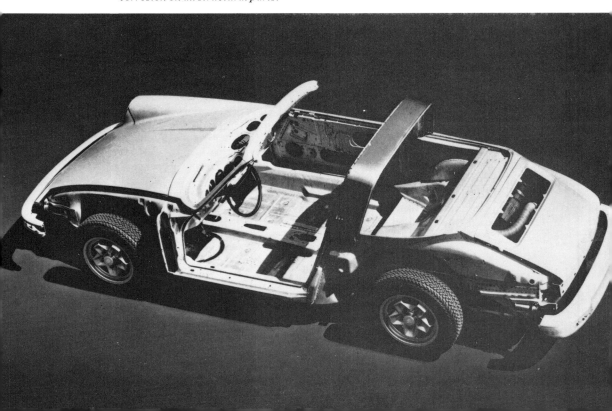

Carrera 3.0, 1977 model: 200 bhp from 3 litres, top speed over 230 km/h (143 mph).

Type 911 SC 3.0 (from 1978)

The classic 911 remains the basis of Porsche production. The Carrera is deleted and the 911 is up-rated to become the 911 SC, which has nearly the same performance as the Carrera.

With a capacity of 2,994 cc, the six-cylinder engine develops 180 bhp at 5,500 rpm, providing a maximum torque of 27 mkg (195 lb/ft) at 4,100 rpm. This engine enables the car to reach a speed of 225 km/h (140 mph) and to accelerate from 0 to 100 km/h (62 mph) in seven seconds. The breaker-less ignition system requires no maintenance. An air pump is added to reduce exhaust emissions. Further modifications include an aluminium alloy (instead of magnesium) housing and a reinforced differential for the five-speed gearbox. A three-speed Sportomatic transmission remains as an option. The running gear includes front and rear anti-roll bars and 380 mm (15 inch) diameter wheels with 152 mm (six inch) rims front and 178 mm (seven inch) rims rear, as in the former Carrera. Sixteen-inch wheels with 50 series tyre are an option. The brakes are servo-operated while the clutch action is assisted by an over-centre spring.

The body and running gear of the new 911 SC are also similar to the Carrera's with wider rear fenders to accommodate the seven-inch wide wheels. The suffix SC means that the car lies somewhere between the 911 S and the Carrera. New colour schemes were introduced while fixed quarter-windows made the car more thiefproof. Both the Coupé and the Targa were retained in the 911 SC series.

Annual modifications

1979
In the 1979 models, the comfort of the 911 SC was further improved by the automatic control of the heater output.

1980
Several improvements make the Porsche 911, now in its 16th production year, more attractive than ever. The air cooled 3-litre, six-cylinder engine now produces 188 bhp. The comparatively modest power increase compared to its predecessor is a result of detail improvements, mainly to the ignition system, to reduce the fuel consumption. The nominal performance figures remain, however, unchanged: maximum speed 225 km/h (140 mph); acceleration from 0 to 100 km/h (62 mph) in seven seconds. The 911 SC is still the only Porsche built as a

Coupé and as a Targa. A new interior and black window frames further improve the car's appearance. The 911 SC also becomes even more practical and comfortable, thanks mainly to the electric window lifters, the central console and the 380 mm (15 inch) diameter three-spoke steering wheel. A further refinement is the illumination of the engine compartment.

1980 model 911 SCs get the same oil radiator as the 911 Turbo, replacing the oil cooling serpentine to reduce the engine oil temperature under extreme conditions. 24 mm instead of 23 mm diameter torsion bars are used in the rear suspension.

1981

In this model year, the classic 911 probably became the most fuel efficient 3-litre car in the world, while performance was further improved.

In its seventeenth production year the official (DIN 70030) fuel consumption figures are as follows: at a steady 90 km/h (55 mph), 35.2 mpg (29.3 miles per US gallon); 120 km/h (75 mph), 29.1 mpg (24.2 miles per US gallon); urban cycle, 21 mpg (17.5 miles per US gallon). These are figures which would be very creditable even for a medium-class saloon car, which the 911SC, *certainly is not*. The engine now develops 204 bhp, the car has a maximum speed of 235 km/h (146 mph) and reaches 100 km/h (62 mph) from rest in 6.9 seconds.

The apparently irreconcilable targets of increasing power and reducing fuel consumption at the same time were achieved through careful optimisation of the horizontally opposed six-cylinder engine. The compression ratio was raised from 8.6 to 9.8:1, which made premium fuel mandatory for the 911 SC, as it already was for all other Porsche cars. The new pistons incorporating a squish area and a combustion recess near the sparking plug create a high turbulence for quicker combustion of the air fuel mixture. The valve timing diagram is also modified. These modifications in turn required a revision of the ignition and fuel injection systems. Several details were improved to increase the car's general comfort. In spite of considerably stricter emission norms, the engine's power output was now raised back to slightly above the level of the Carrera 3.0.

Externally, only the additional directional lights on the body side and new colour schemes differentiate the 1980 model 911 SC from its predecessors. In the car's interior, berber cloth is a new option, and so are special sports seats and leather upholsteries in new colours and patterns. The durability of the 911 SC Coupé and Targa is further emphasised by the extension of the warranty against rust damage from six to seven years now applying not just to the pan but to the entire body.

1982 and 1983

Except for changes in colour schemes and interior trim, the 911 SC remains unchanged, but a convertible is added to the body range in spring 1982. Maximum load allowed on the Coupé's roof is increased to 75 kg (165 lb) for 1982.

172   *Only external identification of 1981 model 911 SC is the direction indicators on the side panels. Above: Coupé. Below: Targa.*

An oil cooler replaces the serpentine from 1978 models on.

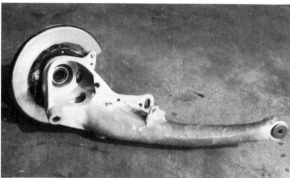

Rear suspension arm with brake disc.

Front wishbones of 911 SC.

Side view of 3-litre, six-cylinder engine.

The Porsche 911 SC convertible, 1982.

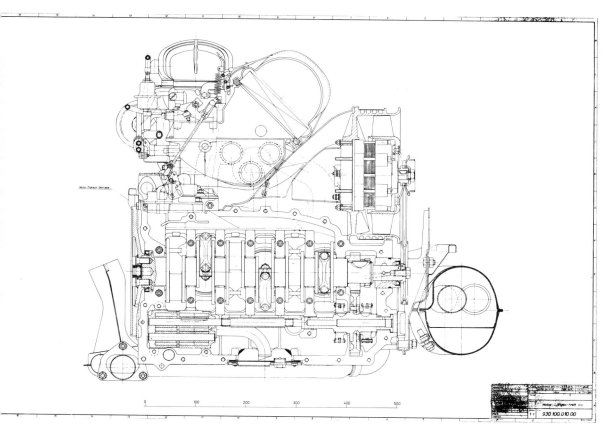

Motor - Längsschnitt (911)

930.100.010.00

Longitudinal section of 911 SC engine—1981 model—204 bhp.

Type 930 Turbo (1974-1977)

To top the Porsche range with a real prestige car, the Turbo was announced at the Paris Motor Show in October 1974, at a time when the entire German motor industry was still badly suffering from the economic recession. This, however, had not affected the determination of the Porsche management and engineers to develop the 911 model to compete in equipment, appearance and performance with the most glamorous of the Italian 'exotics'.

There is no doubt that their aim was achieved. The Turbo's enormously wide tyres, its drastically widened fenders, the standard front air dam and above all the striking rear spoiler could not fail to attract immediate attention. The body was completely devoid of chrome plating: even the rear view mirror and the headlight surrounds were either dull black or finished in the same scheme as the body itself.

The equipment in particular emphasised the efforts to make the car as perfect as possible. The thermostatic heater installation, which is part of the standard equipment, aimed at providing in this sphere a comfort in accordance with the price of the vehicle—a difficult task with an air-cooled engine. The well-known heat control lever was and is still to be found on the central tube, between the front seats, but it is moved by an electric motor. All the driver (or passenger) has to do is turn a knob to select the desired temperature and the electric motor is energised by a governor according to signals received from two heat sensors, one above the windscreen, the other near the left-hand heater control valve, at the heat exchanger outlet. Otherwise, the interior was little different from that of other 911 series Porsches.

The flat-six engine (as used in the Carrera 3.0) had reached the end of its development potential for a road car, in unsupercharged form. Only supercharging gave any promise of achieving the required power, while retaining good tractability and keeping within legal noise and emission limits, not to mention the prestige and exclusivity attached to such technical novelty. The Bosch K-Jetronic fuel injection system also contributes to low exhaust emissions and keeps the consumption down to a very reasonable figure, while the contact breaker-less capacity discharge ignition system keeps the plugs clean.

The 6.5:1 compression ratio seems rather low, but the turbo engine nevertheless requires premium grade fuel: this is because, at the maximum boost pressure of 0.8 bar (12 psi), the theoretical overall compression is as high as 11.7:1.

Naturally, the much increased power (260 bhp at 5,500 rpm) necessitated some modifications to the body, the running gear and the transmission. A large front air dam and a striking rear spoiler combatted front and rear aerodynamic lift and thus provided notably improved stability. The front suspension geometry was modified to provide some anti-dive, while the rear diagonal suspension arms were more rigid and pivoted around the same fulcrum points as in the Carrera RSR (racing version). The Turbo's track is noticeably wider than in other 911 models. This resulted not only from the wider alloy wheels (178 mm/7-inch rims front, 203 mm/8-inch rims rear), but also from added distance pieces. The dampers (Bilstein) are harder and the rear torsion bars are also stiffer than in other models, their diameter being increased from 23 to 26 mm (0.9 to 1 inch). Standard tyre equipment is 185/70 VR 15 front and 215/60 VR 15 rear, but an extra DM 800 would buy 50 series Pirelli P.7 radials.

The 254 lb/ft torque of the turbocharged engine was also more than the Type 915 gearbox could cope with durably and a new transmission had to be developed. In order to retain the existing main dimensions, the new Type 930 gearbox had only four speeds, of which the gears were wider and made of more resistant material. The clutch diameter was also increased from 220 to 240 mm (8.66 to 9.45 inches). In fact, the modifications were so manifold that Porsche gave the Turbo a new Type number: 930.

No car is more docile than the Porsche Turbo, which will happily potter at 2,000 rpm in top gear. But push the throttle pedal hard down, use the gears to the full and the docile town carriage leaps forward like a full-blooded racing car: in only 3.6 seconds it sprints to 80 km/h (50 mph), reaches the 160 km/h (100 mph) mark in 11.8 seconds and is up to 200 km/h (125 mph) in less than 20 seconds. Maximum speed is around 250 km/h (155 mph) at 6,000 rpm.

The delayed throttle response characteristic of turbo charged engines has been reduced to a minimum, thanks to a special turbocharger output recirculation, and the delay is so short that it is easily taken into account by any driver of some experience—and surely it takes some experience to safely use all that power!

The brakes, of course, have a hard time and unfortunately the originally planned ventilated *and* perforated brake discs had not been sufficiently developed for series production when the car was marketed. Only when the 3.3-litre version was announced, in September 1977, did the Turbo get brakes allowing it to make consistent use of its full performance potential.

General description: Type 930 Turbo (basic model)

Coachwork and chassis

Except for the wider fenders, only minor features differentiate the 930 Turbo externally from the Porsche 911. The wider rear fenders are protected by a plastic skirt.

The front suspension is by struts and transverse wishbones, while the rear suspension is taken care of by semi-trailing links, the geometry of which was developed from the Carrera's racing version. The rear semi-trailing arms are cast in aluminium while the wheel bearings are identical with those of the type 917 racing car. The diameter of the torsion bars is 19 mm at the front and 26 mm at the rear. Bilstein gas filled dampers are used all round. The anti-roll bars have a diameter of 18 mm front and rear while the rack and pinion steering has a 17.8:1 ratio. The brake pedal operates the four ventilated but not perforated disc brakes. The handbrake operates rear drums mechanically. The 380 mm (15 inch) diameter wheels have a rim width of seven inches front and eight inches. They carry 185/70 VR 15 and 215/60 VR 15 tyres respectively, but 205/50 VR 15 and 225/50 VR 15 tyres are optional.

With a weight of 1,150 kilos, the Porsche Turbo (known internally as type 930) has a power-to-weight ratio of 228 bhp/ton, but is unsuitable for pulling a caravan. Front and rear spoilers developed from the Carrera racing versions virtually eliminate the aerodynamic lift, improving braking and road holding while reducing the sensitivity to side winds.

Engine

The power unit of the Porsche Turbo is the well proven engine of the Porsche 911, to which an exhaust turbocharger providing an exceptionally high power output is added. Having a capacity of 3 litres, this engine is no monster, but successfully competes in terms of output and refinement with the best sports car engines to be found anywhere. The experience gained in motor racing helped Porsche produce a turbocharged road going car providing hereto unknown refinement.

Thanks to the turbocharger, the volumetric efficiency and the brake mean effective pressure reaches levels inaccessible to normal atmospheric engines. The blower is driven by the turbine wheel which itself is energised by the exhaust gases, thus making use of energy which would otherwise be lost. Turbocharging is, in fact, a very economical way of supercharging. It is also a quiet way of increasing an engine's power as the turbocharger silences the exhaust. This is why Porsche's turbocharged racing cars are so comparatively quiet and why the road going Porsche Turbo fulfills the noise regulations with a distinctly smaller tail silencer than its atmospheric counterparts.

By combining turbocharging with the K-Jetronic fuel injection system Porsche was the first company to combine turbocharging and continuous injection. The turbocharger itself consists of a turbine and a compressor wheel mounted on a common shaft and running in an appropriate housing. The turbine is driven by the engine's exhaust gases and runs up to 90,000 rpm. The compressor wheel which turns at the same velocity sucks air through the air filter and the metering unit of the injection system, compresses it to 0.8 bar (approximately 11 psi) above atmospheric pressure and feeds the cylinders through the intake pipe, the throttle valve and the intake manifold. The K-Jetronic injection system is larger when compared with the installation in the atmospheric engines and it incorporates a starter valve which momentarily increases the quantity of fuel injected when the engine is hot, so as to ensure a secure start. In addition, the breakerless ignition system, originally developed for motor racing, does not require any maintenance.

Further technical details include as in the Carrera 3.0, a cast aluminium crankcase. The pistons and cylinders are aluminium and Nikasil respectively. The intake valve material is highly heat resistant while the exhaust valves are sodium cooled. The oil pressure pump is larger than in the atmospheric engine, while an adequate fuel feed is ensured by two electric pumps instead of a single one.

Gearbox

A special version of the gearbox used in the 911 series was developed for the Turbo. Wider gears made of a more resistant material take care of the much higher torque of the engine. For the same reason, the gearbox housing is cast in aluminium alloy instead of magnesium. This gearbox has only four speeds, the elasticity and high torque of the turbocharged engine making a fifth gear unnecessary. The diameter of the single plate clutch is increased in order to reliably transmit the engine's 35 mkg (253 lb/ft) torque.

Equipment

The turbo is made only as a Coupé. Black mouldings and window frames emphasise the exclusive character of the car, as do headlight surrounds and an external rear view mirror matching the distinguished colour schemes, while the interior appointments are of the highest quality.

Tempered glass all round ensures that the interior remains pleasantly cool in summer without impairing the visibility in winter. A rather exceptional feature is the electrically heated windscreen, while two-stage heating is provided for the rear window. Electric window lifters, headlight washers, a rear window wiper, intermittent windscreen wiper operation, fog lights and automatic heater control are all part of the standard equipment.

Here are a few further details concerning the standard equipment: the upholstery is a combination of leather and cloth with a Scottish pattern. A 'Turbo' script decorates the back rest of the left rear seat. A small lamp is incorporated in the door key to facilitate locating the key hole. Optimum reception can be expected from the fully automatic radio set, energising four loudspeakers in the car's interior. The telescopic antenna is electrically operated. If any customer does not like the standard metallic finish, he can have any special finish applied without having to pay a supplement.

Annual modifications

1976

All Porsche cars from model year 1976 on are provided with a full one-year guarantee without mileage limitation. In addition, a special six-year warranty covers the car against corrosion of the entire floor pan. This is unique in the automobile industry and is made possible by the use of hot dipped, zinc coated sheet metal.

The very extensive standard equipment of Porsche's top model is further extended by some useful additions, in the shape of, for instance, a heated and electrically adjustable exterior mirror, while 50 series tyres of the dimensions 205/50 VR 15 front and 225/50 VR 15 rear are now standard equipment.

1977

A number of useful additions and improvements make the Porsche Turbo even more desirable. New colour schemes for exterior and interior, plus further improved equipment underline the exclusive character of Porsche cars.

Important improvements are the face level ventilation and the recessed interior door locking knobs. To unlock the doors, a small hand wheel must be turned, making breaking into the car with the help of wire or hooks virtually impossible. Driving is made more comfortable by the addition of a brake-servo and of an over-centre spring helping to depress the clutch pedal. Further improvements are the illumination of the ventilation and heater controls, twin ventilation levers, a twin warning light for handbrake and safety belt, the addition of a rear window wiper, the two-stage heated and tinted rear window, a new central console, 50 series tyres on 16 inch instead of 15 inch rims and a turbocharger pressure gauge. Technical improvements for the 1977 model include: improved twin fuel pumps, a modified pressurised fuel accumulator and an improved fuel filter. The electrical boost pressure gauge incorporated in the revolution counter is additional to the excess pressure safety switch. It is electrically operated by a pressure switch mounted on the pressure line.

The throttle valve housing now incorporates a connection to the brake servo. Only engines to USA or Japanese specifications are fitted with a thermostatic control valve. Additionally, cars bound for the USA, California, Canada and Japan are equipped with an air pump, an exhaust system incorporating two reactors and exhaust gas recirculation (egr).

The synchronisation of the Type 930 gearbox is improved in detail, the Turbo gets the simplified 20 mm front anti-roll bar (without separate links) of the normal Type 911. Standard tyre equipment is now 205/55 VR on 7J × 16 front wheels and 225/50 VR 16 on 8J × 16 wheels.

To facilitate adjustment of the rear ride height, the flexible trailing links are made in two pieces to incorporate eccentric adjustment bolts. The brake servo type T52 is added to the standard equipment.

Turbo prototype was first exhibited at the Paris motor show of 1974.

Ready to leap forward: the Porsche Turbo, 1975 model.

Porsche 930 Turbo, 1975 model. 3 litres, 260 bhp, 250 km/h (155 mph).

Tail and front view of standard Porsche Turbo.

For 1976, the Turbo had an electrically adjustable outside mirror and 50-series tyres.

From the 1977 model onwards, the Turbo had 41 cm (16 inch) diameter wheels.

The chosen cockpit temperature is automatically maintained by two sensors. One of them is shown below right.

184

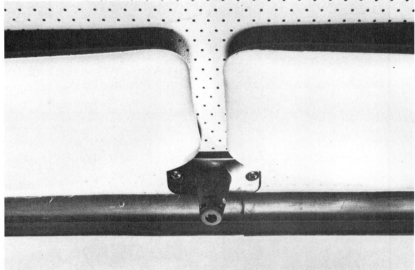

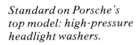

Standard on Porsche's top model: high-pressure headlight washers.

The European exhaust system (left) is less complicated than the US version (below left).

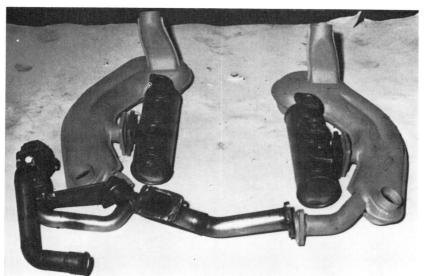

185

The turbocharger provides charged filling for the cylinders.

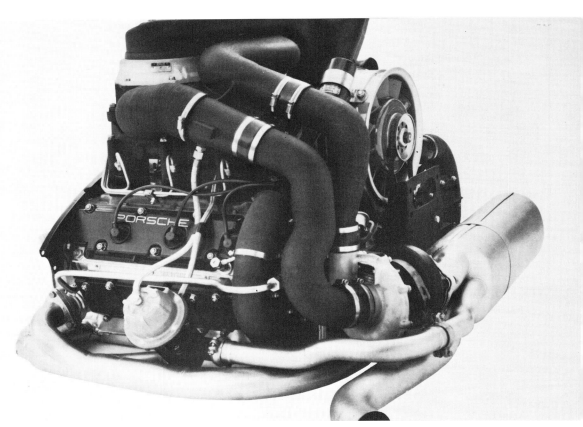

Above: Turbo engine, Type 930/50: 260 bhp for Europe, 245 bhp for USA.

Above right: Side view of transmission Types 930/ 30 and 32 of the Turbo. Right: The Turbo's rear spoiler contains the cooler of the air conditioning plant.

Type 930 Turbo 3.3 (from 1977)

Since January 1975, when Porsche began to produce the first Turbos, the caution displayed by the press and the public towards turbocharged vehicles was quickly proved unfounded. The car aroused enormous enthusiasm and a large number of car manufacturers began development of turbocharged engines. Porsche had proved that a turbocharged car could fulfill all the requirements of exacting sports car enthusiasts.

The well known deficiences of turbocharged engines, such as slow throttle response and insufficient torque in the lower revolution range were solved by Porsche by the use of a wastegate, a system up until then only used in racing cars. This made it possible to obtain a noticeable increase of the torque from low engine speeds onwards.

At the same time, the turbocharger allows a more complete combustion of the exhaust gases and a corresponding reduction of exhaust emissions. Turbocharging allowed Porsche to simultaneously improve performance and reduce the air pollution.

However, not only the engine came in for improvement. The gearbox, for example, was completely redesigned to take the immense torque of the engine, while front and rear suspensions were modified in the light of racing experience. Aerodynamic aids, such as the front air dam and rear spoiler were improved. In and outside, the equipment was uprated to match the performance and luxury image of the car.

When the Porsche Turbo 3.0 was announced, nobody thought that there would be demands for even higher performance. But the demand arose. It was met by the decision taken in Spring 1976 to develop an even more potent car, the Turbo 3.3, of which the production began in Autumn 1977.

General description: Type 930 Turbo 3.3 (basic model)

Coachwork and chassis

The new rear spoiler developed for the Turbo 3.3 is a result of extensive wind tunnel tests in which the shape, the angle of incidence and the shape of the air intake louvres were finalised. The result is further reduced lift without any increase in drag. The higher air pressure acting on the upper surface of the spoiler also increases the air flow into the engine compartment and the intercooler which is a major feature of the 3.3. The raised position of the spoiler also makes room for the intercooler and for the optional large compressor of the air conditioning plant.

The spoiler contains the ducts leading air to the engine-mounted intercooler and the optional air-conditioning condenser. As in the previous model, the front suspension is by 19 mm diameter longitudinal torsion bars and a 20 mm diameter anti-roll bar. The rear semi-trailing links are controlled by transverse mounted 26 mm torsion bars and an 18 mm anti-roll bar. Gas filled Bilstein hydraulic dampers are used front and rear. The twin circuit braking system incorporates a vacuum servo and all four brake discs are both ventilated and perforated. Standard tyres are 205/55 VR 16 on the 7J × 16 front wheels and 225/50 VR 16 on the rear 8J × 16 wheels. The official performance figures are: maximum speed 260 km/h (161 mph); 0 to 100 km/h (62 mph) in 5.4 seconds and a standing start kilometre (0.62 mile) in 24 seconds.

The increase in maximum speed and acceleration made more powerful brakes necessary. Here again Porsche took advantage of the experience gained in many years of racing: the cast iron discs of the 3.3 are thicker than before, incorporating larger section ventilation channels and are additionally perforated, which also improves the response when the discs are exposed to water splashes. The mounting of the brake disc on the hub required a lot of development because the considerable variation in the disc temperature makes it prone to cracking. The problem, which is particularly acute at the front, was solved by mounting the disc on splines which compensate for the difference in expansions of the disc and the hub. The aluminium calipers are a development of those of the 917 racing car. They are heavily finned to improve both the cooling and the rigidity. Every caliper contains 4 pistons, the front ones having a larger diameter than the rear ones in order to obtain the correct front/rear distribution of the braking force.

The braking area is 48 cm², while the thickness of the pads is 13.5 mm all round. The brake master cylinder was increased in size and the servo was modified to meet the requirements of the new installation. The parking brake was also improved.

Engine

The exact capacity of the Turbo 3.3 is 3,298 cc, resulting from a 97 mm bore and a 74.4 mm stroke. As both bore and stroke were increased, several components had to be redesigned, such as the crankshaft, connecting rods, the pistons and cylinders and also the oil pump. The general layout of the engine, however, remained unaffected. Neither were any modifications required to be made to the exhaust system, including the turbocharger turbine. This does not apply to the compressor and its housing which were increased in size to meet the higher demands of the larger engine.

The power required to drive the turbocharger reaches a peak of approximately 41 bhp = 13% of the engine's maximum power. The exhaust gas driven turbine and the compressor share a common shaft rotating at approximately 90,000 rpm. The compressed air leaves the compressor at temperatures which can be as high as 130°C.

To reduce this temperature, the Porsche Turbo 3.3 is the first production car to have an intercooler. This reduces the temperature of the air before it reaches the throttle valve and the six cylinders. Ambient air circulating through the spoiler and the intercooler into the engine compartment is used to cool the intake charge. It is aspirated by the engine cooling fan and proceeds from there to cool the cylinders and cylinder heads.

Lower intake air temperature means a higher density of the charge. This in turn means that the same filling of the cylinders can be obtained for a lower boost pressure. The intercooler reduces the temperature of the relevant engine components, which is particularly important in the case of the pistons and cylinders. It also reduces the final compression temperature, and in case advantage is taken of the higher density of the charge to reduce the boost pressure, it also reduces the exhaust back pressure. The lower compression temperature in turn allows the use of a higher compression ratio in the engine. In the case of the Turbo 3.3 it was raised to 7.0:1, (6.5:1 in the Turbo 3.0) which results in better fuel efficiency.

Two variants of the engine were produced: one for USA, Canada and Japan producing 265 bhp and one for the rest of the world producing 300 bhp. This power is obtained with the same boost pressure as the 260 bhp of the obsolete Turbo 3.0 and the specific output of 91 bhp/litre is almost 5% higher than for the previous 3-litre unit.

Gearbox

Since the maximum engine power was obtained at 5,500 rpm, as in the previous engine, the fourth gear ratio was made slightly taller. The maximum speed of 260 km/h (161 mph) is now obtained at 5,750 rpm.

The clutch was revised in two respects: to take care of the increased engine torque and to reduce the gear chatter. The chatter is produced by the irregular rotational speed of any piston engine. This induces a vibration of the idle gears in the gearbox. To eliminate this, the clutch hub was completely redesigned to take a rubber vibration damper. This being thicker than the previous type, the bell housing had to be lengthened by 30 mm and the engine to be relocated by the same amount towards the rear.

189

Equipment

As its predecessor, the Turbo 3.3 is made exclusively in the Coupé version. The interior appointments are worthy of the exclusive character of this fastest model in the Porsche sports car range.

Annual modifications

1979

Porsche's top model remains completely unchanged for 1979. This 300 hp sports car is unique in combining complete tractability with racing car performance. The use of the otherwise wasted energy contained in the exhaust gases to drive the turbocharger contributes to the reduction of atmospheric pollution. But the turbocharger also reduces noise, both by silencing the exhaust and by enabling the engine to provide a very high output at comparatively low revolution speeds.

1980

Development has produced a new silencing system with twin exhaust pipes which reduces the noise emission from 82 dBA by 2.5% to 79 dBA without any loss of power. A proper oil radiator is now used in place of the oil cooling serpentine to keep the engine oil temperature at a reasonable level even under the hardest conditions.

The performance is unaltered and the use of zinc coated sheet steel for the entire car makes it immune to rust.

1981
The Porsche 930 Turbo 3.3 remains one of the most respected sports cars in the world. For 1981, the technical specification and appearance have remained virtually unaltered.

After five years' experience, Porsche have extended the anti-rust warranty to the entire car and to seven years without any intermediate treatment.

1982
The Turbo is continued without any major modifications, except for new colour schemes and interior trims. The maximum load allowed to be carried on the roof is increased to 75 kg.

1983
A revised K-Jetronic injection system and a waste gate dump pipe bypassing the exhaust silencer increase the maximum torque from 42 to 44 mkg (304 to 318 lb/ft) at unaltered 4,000 rpm and considerably reduce the fuel consumption.

911 SC-3.0 / 930 Turbo 3.0 / 930 Turbo 3.3

Year	Model Body	Type	Chassis no	Motor	Gearbox type	Cyl	Bore × stroke	Cap-acity	HP (DIN) at rpm	Torque (mkg) at rpm	Comp ratio	W'base (mm)	Track fr/ rear (mm)	Length (mm)	Weight (kg)	No prod-uced
1975	Coupé	911-3.0	9116600001- 9116601093	930/02	915/44 915/49	6	95×70,4	2994	200/6000	26/4200	8,5:1	2271	1372/1380	4291	1120	1093
	Targa	911-3.0 911-3.0 Sporto-matic	9116610001- 91166110479	930/12	925/13											479
1977	Coupé	911-3.0	9117600001- 9117601473	930/02	915/61	6	95×70,4	2994	200/6000	26/4200	8,5:1	2271	1372/1380	4291	1120	1473
	Targa	911-3.0 911-3.0 Sporto-matic	911761001- 9117610646	930/12	925/16											646
1978	Coupé	911SC-3.0	9118300001- 9118302438	930/03	915/61	6	95×70,4	2994	180/5500	27/4200	8,5:1	2272	1369/1379	4291	1160	2438
	Targa	911SC-3.0 911SC-3.0 Sporto-matic	9118310001- 9118311729	930/13	925/16											1729
	Coupé-US California	911SC-3.0	9118200001- 9118202436	930/04 930/06	915/61	6	95×70,4	2994	180/5500	27/4200	8,5:1	2272	1361/1367	4291	1160	2436
	Targa-US	911SC-3.0 911SC-3.0 Sporto-matic	9118210001- 9118212579	930/14	925/16											2579

911 SC-3.0 / 930 Turbo 3.0 / 930 Turbo 3.3

Year	Body	Type	Chassis no	Motor	Gearbox type	Cyl	Bore × stroke	Capacity	HP (DIN) at rpm	Torque (mkg) at rpm	Comp ratio	W base (mm)	Track fr/rear (mm)	Length (mm)	Weight (kg)	No produced
	Coupé-Japan Targa-Japan		WPO22291ZBS 129500- WPO22291ZBS 169500-	930/17	915/63	6	95×70,4	2994	180/5500	25/4200	9,3:1	2272	1369/1379	4291	1250	
1975	Coupé	930-3.0	9305700001- 9305700284	930/50	930/30	6	95×70,4	2994	260/5500	35/4000	6,5:1	2272	1432/1501	4291	1140	284
1976	Coupé	930-3.0	9306700001- 9306700644	930/50 930/52	930/30 930/32	6	95×70,4	2994	260/5500	35/4000	6,5:1	2272	1431/1501	4291	1140	644
	Coupé-US	930-3.0	9306800001- 9306800530	930/51	930/30	6	95×70,4	2994	245/5500	35/4000	6,5:1	2272	1431/1501	4291	1140	530
1977	Coupé	930-3.0	9307700001- 9307700695	930/52	930/33	6	95×70,4	2994	260/5500	35/4000	6,5:1	2272	1438/1511	4291	1195	695
	Coupé-US	930-3.0	9307800001- 9307800727	930/54 930/53		6	95×70,4	2994	245/5500	35/4000	6,5:1	2272	1431/1501	4291	1195	727
1978	Coupé	930-3.3	9308700001- 9308700735	930/60	930/34	6	97×74,4	3299	300/5500	42/4000	7,0:1	2272	1432/1501	4291	1300	735
	Coupé-US	930-3.3	9308800001- 9308800461	930/61		6	97×74,4	3299	265/5500	40,3/4000	7,0:1	2272	1432/1501	4291	1300	461
	Coupé-Japan	930-3.3	9308709501- 9308709561	930/62		6	97×74,4	3299	265/5500	40,3/4000	7,0:1	2272	1432/1501	4291	1300	61
1979	Coupé	930-3.3	9309700001- 9309700820	930/60	930/34	6	97×74,4	3299	300/5500	42/4000	7,0:1	2272	1432/1501	4291	1300	820
	Coupé-US	930-3.3	9309800001- 9309801200	930/61		6	97×74,4	3299	265/5500	40,3/4000	7,0:1	2272	1432/1501	4291	1300	1200
	Coupé Japan	930-3.3	9309709501- 9309709532	930/62		6	97×74,4	3299	265/5500	40,3/4000	7,0:1	2272	1432/1501	4291	1300	32
1980	Coupé	930-3.3	93A0070001- 93A0070840	930/60	930/34	6	97×74,4	3299	300/5500	42/4000	7,0:1	2272	1432/1501	4291	1295	840

192

911 SC-3.0 / 930 Turbo 3.0 / 930 Turbo 3.3

Year	Model Body	Type	Chassis no	Motor	Gearbox type	Cyl	Bore × stroke	Cap-acity	HP (DIN) at rpm	Torque (mkg) at rpm	Comp ratio	W'base (mm)	Track fr/rear (mm)	Length (mm)	Weight (kg)	No prod-uced
1978	Coupé-Japan	911	9118309501-9118309804	930/05 930/15	915/61	6	95×70,4	2994	180/5500	27/4200	8,5:1	2272	1361/1367	4291	1160	304
1979	Coupé	911SC-3.0	9119300001-9119303319	930/03	915/62	6	95×70,4	2994	188/5500	27/4200	8,6:1	2272	1369/1379	4291	1160	3319
1979	Targa	911SC-3.0	9119310001-9119313319													3319
	Coupé-US-California	911SC-3.0	9119200001-9119202013	930/04 930/06	915/63	6	95×70,4	2994	180/5500	25/4200	9,3:1	2272	1369/1379	4291	1160	2013
	Targa-US California	911SC-3.0	9119210001-9119211965	930/04 930/06												1965
	Coupé-Japan	911SC-3.0	9119309501-9119309873													373
1980	Coupé	911SC-3.0	91A0130001-91A0134831	930/09 930/08	915/62	6	95×70,4	2994	188/5500	27/4300	9,8:1	2272	1369/1379	4291	1160	4831
	Targa	911SC-3.0														
	Coupé-US	911SC-3.0	91A0140001-91A0144272	930/07		6	95×70,4	2994	180/5500	25/4200	9,3:1	2272	1369/1379	4291	1250	4272
	Targa-US	911SC-3.0														
1981	Coupé	911SC-3.0	WPO22291ZBS 100001- WPO22291ZBS 140001-	930/10	915/62	6	95×70,4	2994	204/5900	27/4300	9,8:1	2272	1369/1379	4291	1160	
	Targa	911SC-3.0														
	Coupé-US	911SC-3.0	WPOAA091-BS 120001- WPOEA091-BS 160001-	930/16	915/63	6	95×70,4	2994	180/5500	25/4200	9,3:1	2272	1369/1379	4291	1250	
	Targa-US	911SC-3.0														
1981	Coupé	930-3.3	WPO22293ZBS 000001-													
	Coupé-Canada	930-3.3	WPOJA093-BS 050001-													

Notes: **Type 911 SC-3.0:** Engine 930/02:3.0/200 bhp for Carrera. 930/12:3.0/200 bhp for Carrera Sportomatic. Gearbox 915/44: Five-speed manual. 915/49: Four-speed manual. 925/13: Three-speed Sportomatic. From model year 1980 no differenciation between Coupé and Targa chassis numbers. **Type 930:** Engine 930/50:3.0/260 bhp for Turbo. 930/51:3.0/245 bhp for Turbo, USA. Gearbox 930/30: Four-speed manual. 930/32: Four-speed for 50-series tyres.

193

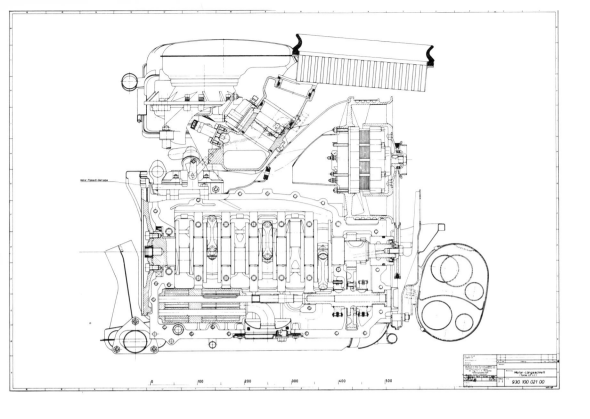

194   *Prominent feature of the 3.3-litre Turbo engine is the large intercooler. 300 bhp raises the top speed to 260 km/h (161 mph).*

Since 1974, the fastest German sports car: Porsche 930 Turbo, here in its latest 3.3 litre version.

Porsche 930 Turbo 3.3: 300 bhp and 0-100 km/h in 5.4 seconds.

From 1980 model on, quieter twin tail-pipe exhaust.

Ventilated and perforated front brake disc.

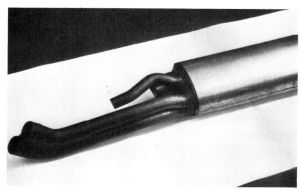
Twin tail-pipe exhaust from 1980 model on.

197

Rear suspension and ventilated and perforated brake disc.

Waste gate limiting the boost pressure.

Type 924 (from 1975)

Few cars have had such an erratic gestation as the Porsche Type 924. When Volkswagenwerk entrusted Porsche with the development order EA 425, back in 1970, its object was a successor for the VW-Porsche 914. It was to be a pure VW until Volkswagen's new Managing Director, Toni Schmücker, was appointed and promptly cancelled the sports car project. As the car was by then nearly fully developed, Porsche decided to take it into their own programme and to have it built in the Audi-NSU factory in Neckarsulm. Unlike most of the mechanical components, the 2 + 2 coupé body was a completely new development. It featured a large rear opening, a sloping bonnet (hood), long range and directional indicator lights recessed in the front bumper, pop-up main headlights and an integral front air dam.

The body shell had deliberately been designed for low drag and actually has a drag coefficient of 0.36, providing a high top speed and a low fuel consumption. The completely transparent rear hatch allows easy access to the smoothly contoured, large luggage compartment, the capacity of which can be further extended by folding the rear squabs forward.

The front seats were borrowed from the 911 range and are beyond reproach. But, whereas the front compartment is quite spacious, the rear one is rather cramped and the two recesses padded to form the 'emergency' seats, separated by the high central tunnel, are hardly suitable for anything but small children. The layout of the instruments and controls is beyond criticism. In addition to the three circular instruments located in front of the driver, an oil thermometer, oil pressure gauge and a clock are carried on the central console, but only as optional extras. The sheet metal body is zinc-coated by the hot dip process and carries Porsche's six-year warranty—as with the 911 series.

An important feature of the 924 is its transaxle transmission: the water-cooled engine and the clutch are in the front of the car, but the gearbox is combined to a transaxle unit with the final drive. This transaxle is rigidly connected with the engine by means of a tube nearly two metres (79 inches) long bolted to the bell housing. In this tube runs a propeller shaft a mere 20 mm in diameter acting as a torsion bar to smoothen the drive, carried in four bearings.

The 2-litre, four-cylinder engine, inclined at an angle of 40 degrees, is a development of the single overhead camshaft Audi 100 engine. It is fed by a Bosch K-Jetronic injection system and develops 125 bhp at 5,800 rpm. A detuned version of this engine is, incidentally, to be found in a VW light van.

Such an engine cannot provide electrifying performance, but the factory claims

0 to 60 mph acceleration in ten seconds and a maximum speed of 124 mph. The ratios of the unmodified Audi four-speed gearbox are not ideally suitable for a sports car. This is why Porsche introduced their own five-speed gearbox which became optionally available in the 1978 models. In the five-speed gearbox, fifth is an overdrive gear, but with the lower final gearing used, the overall gearing in top gear is practically identical with that of the four-speed gearbox. It is on the high side, providing the advantage of allowing effortless 115 mph cruising together with a very low fuel consumption. The car has to be driven very hard indeed to get worse than 23 mpg (Imperial—19 miles per US gallon).

The MacPherson front suspension and semi-trailing links rear suspension are also borrowed from the VW model range. They provide the base for good, unproblematic handling. They make high cornering speeds possible, with the car assuming a neutral or slightly understeering attitude, unless it is pushed to the limit, when it changes to slight, easily controlled oversteer. Good rear wheel grip and excellent straight line stability complete the satisfactory overall picture, especially if the optional front and rear anti-roll bars are specified.

The rack-and-pinion steering is accurate, sufficiently high geared and nevertheless pleasantly light when the car is on the move. The mixed braking system—floating caliper front disc brakes and drum rear brakes—adequately matches the car's performance. The comfort offered by the suspension is quite good by sports car standards and copes very well with even the worst surfaces.

Judging by the development from which other Porsche models have benefited, a bright future might have been expected for the 924, but even in its 1977 version, it was already the best-selling sports car in the world.

Annual modifications

1977

To meet a request expressed by many customers, a roll-up cover was added to hide the luggage contained in the rear compartment. The fully automatic transmission announced when the 924 was introduced became available in October 1976. In addition an oil pressure gauge and a voltmeter were mounted on the central console and included in the standard equipment, while hard rubber rubbing strips were added on the body sides. At the beginning of January 1977, a special series of Porsche 924 was produced to celebrate the two world championships won by Porsche during 1976. The cars were finished in white and carried blue and red side stripes matching the colours of the Porsche-Martini factory team. The front and rear seats were also finished in red with blue surrounds. The floor mats were also red and so was the luggage compartment upholstery. This special edition was fitted with anti-roll bars front and rear, white enamelled light alloy wheels, 185/70 HR 14 steel-belted tyres and a leather-covered steering wheel. A special plaque recalled the two world championships won by Porsche.

1978

In the third year of production, few modifications were introduced. The most significant was the redesign of the rear suspension, which now incorporated rubber bushes which greatly improved the ride quality and reduced the noise level, thus obviating the main criticism of the 924.

A five-speed gearbox, requested by many customers, is now offered at extra cost, together with the fully automatic transmission, but the four-speed box remains standard equipment. In addition, new colour schemes and new, higher quality seat upholstery extend the available colour combinations. The colour of the luggage cover now matches the colour of the interior. Further improvements are an optically and acoustically improved exhaust system, of which the oval tail pipe is easily recognised, while up-rated suspension dampers, electric window lifters and stove enamelled black alloy wheels are optional. After only 26 months of production, the 50,000th Porsche 924 left the assembly line and the 100,000th was produced on February 4 1981. Up to 100 cars a day are assembled in cooperation with AUDI-NSU in their Neckarsulm factory and the model goes virtually unchanged into the 1979 model year.

1980
An Audi five-speed gearbox becomes standard on the Porsche 924, the best selling Porsche model ever. It differs from the previous five-speed gearbox by being located aft of the differential instead of ahead of it and by its gear change pattern: the gears one to four are arranged in the usual 'H' pattern, while fifth is dog-legged to the right and forward, opposite reverse. The gear change pattern has become the same as that of the Porsche 911 SC and a requirement of many 924 customers is met by this modification.

The diameter of the brake servo is increased from seven to nine inches, noticeably reducing the effort required to operate the pedal. An exterior mirror manually operated from inside the car becomes standard while the luggage compartment is automatically illuminated as it is opened. A small refinement is a flap over the tank filler cap.

Externally too, the Porsche 924 has become more attractive. In addition to new colours, two-tone colour schemes and new interior appointments, it is easily identified by its black side window frames.

The technical specification remains unaltered. The 2-litre, four-cylinder engine of the 200 km/h (125 mph) Porsche 924 develops 125 bhp at 5,800 rpm. It is rigidly linked to the rear transaxle by a large diameter tube containing the propeller-shaft. This lay-out provides a weight distribution of almost ideal 50% front and rear. The car's popularity is based both on its six years' warranty against rust damage and the 12,500 miles inspection intervals, but also on its fuel economy: according to the new European standards it will do 43 mpg at a steady 90 km/h (55 mph), 35 mpg at a steady 120 km/h (75 mph) and 23 mpg in the urban cycle. US data: 35.8 mpg at 90 km/h; 29 mpg at 120 km/h, 19 mpg urban.

1981
Only minor modifications differentiate the Porsche 924 from its predecessors. The car is now in its seventh production year and the anti-rust warranty is extended to seven years and to the entire body instead of the floor pan only, underlining the car's durability. The 1981 model is identified by its additional directional lights on the sides of the front fenders and a fog tail light has been added. Comfort is enhanced by additional sound damping material.

A front anti-roll bar is now standard equipment, matched by stiffer rear torsion bars, reducing roll in corners and further improving the handling. New colour schemes and interiors, also Porsche scripts on the door trim panels, distinguish the new 924 externally. The new car has also inherited the air horns of the 924 Turbo. Among the new options are a cassette console, seats entirely upholstered in cloth, or special sports seats. The 924 can also be obtained with multi-spoke alloy wheels and 60 series tyres.

To commemorate the successful debut of the 924 at Le Mans, a special series called '924 Le Mans' was offered until Autumn 1980. Finished in Alpine white, and with three coloured stripes, these cars have a black leather interior set off by white stripes. Technically, the Le Mans differs from the normal 924, mainly by its even more sporting running gear. Its $6J \times 15$ light metal wheels are finished in black and white and carry 205/60 VR 15 tyres. Up-rated dampers and anti-roll bars front and rear are standard. So is the small 36 cm diameter four-spoke leather covered steering wheel, normally available only as an extra-cost option. The rear spoiler which normally adorns the 924 Turbo reduces its drag coefficient to 0.33, probably the lowest of any production sports Coupé.

1982

The 924 continues virtually unchanged into the 1982 model year. The previously optional three-spoke steering wheel becomes standard and a Porsche badge over the glove box identifies the 1982 series. The maximum load allowed to be carried on the roof is increased from 35 to 75 kg.

1983

With the demise of the 924 Turbo (now only built to order for Italy), the Porsche 924 has inherited the 924 Turbo's rear spoiler which reduces its drag coefficient from 0.36 to 0.33. As the 924 has a frontal area of only 1.79 sq m, the total drag surface is only 0.59, the lowest of any production car. Also inherited from the 924 Turbo is the improved sound proofing, while the interior trim is up-rated to 944 level. Eleven new colour schemes are available.

Experimental cars

During the summer of 1979, ten Porsche experimental cars were produced to take part in a large scale experiment, together with 800 other cars, in which new sources of energy are to be investigated as to their suitability for road transport. One of the aims of the operation is to find out the effects of methanol, either pure or added to petrol, in an internal combustion engine and to measure consumption and emission characteristics.

In the case of the Porsche experimental cars, 15% methanol was added to the petrol. The lean mixture engine of the methanol Porsche 924 had its compression raised to 12.5:1 compared to 9.3 of the normal car. Thanks to the high compression ratio and the leaner mixtures with which the engine can operate, the emissions are very clean while the energy saving lies between 5% and 15% in spite of a power output raised by 5 bhp to 130 bhp.

One of the modifications required to make the 924 engine suitable for methanol was the removal of some plastic components of the fuel system likely to be attacked by methanol. These were replaced by components made of different materials. Some other modifications were made to improve the thermodynamic efficiency of the engine: along with the higher compression ratio came reshaped combustion chambers and a fully electronic ignition system with programmed advanced curve. The standard Bosch K-Jetronic injection system of the 924 had also to be adapted to the different fuel.

These experimental Porsche 924s will not only run on methanol produced from coal or from natural gas, but also on aethanol, provided the engine settings are modified accordingly. Aethanol can be biologically produced from such natural products as beetroots, manioc roots, sugar cane or cereals. In some parts of Brazil, 25% aethanol has already been added to petrol for several years. In the American state of Nebraska, some filling stations offer gasonol, consisting of 90% petrol and 10% aethanol produced from cereals.

Weight distribution of various types of design

Conventional Design

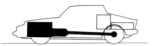

− Unloaded: Little weight on rear axle = bad traction of driving wheels (especially in winter and on bad roads)

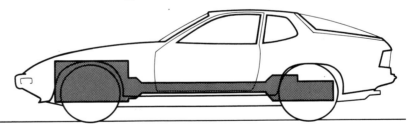

+ Loaded: Heavy weight on rear axle = good traction of driving wheels
+ Large, variable luggage compartment

Rear Engine

+ Unloaded: Heavy weight on rear axle good traction of driving wheels

+ Loaded: Heavy weight on rear axle good traction of driving wheels
− Split luggage compartment

Front-Wheel Drive

+ Unloaded: Heavy weight on front axle = good traction of driving wheels

− Loaded: Little weight on front axle = bad traction of driving wheels (winter and bad roads)
+ Large, variable luggage compartment

202

Transaxle Design – Porsche 924

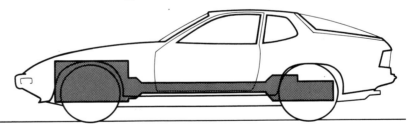

+ Unloaded: Heavy weight on rear axle (through transmission in rear), thus good traction of driving wheels.

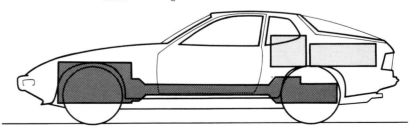

+ Loaded: Heavy weight on rear axle (through transmission in rear + part of load), thus good traction of driving wheels.
+ Large, variable luggage compartment.

Side, front and rear views of the Porsche 924.

The 924's interior and instruments are fully up to Porsche standards.

Transaxle system: a plain shaft of only 20 mm (¾ inch) diameter connects engine and transmission.

204

Water-cooled, 2-litre, four-cylinder engine with K-Jetronic fuel injection develops 125 bhp.

From the 1977 series, the Porsche 924 was provided with a protective rubber moulding on its sides. The alloy wheels are an option.

An easy to handle roller blind covers the luggage compartment of the Porsche 924. This was introduced, together with luggage straps, in 1977.

Martini-Porsche 924: a special series on the occasion of Porsche's victory in two World Championships.

Above: Porsche five-speed gearbox used from 1980 models on. Above right: The 924's functional cockpit.
Below: Side views of four-cylinder Audi engine fitted to Porsche 924: 125 bhp from 2 litres swept volume.

Front (left) and rear (right) suspensions of Porsche 924, from 1981 model on.

208   *A 125 bhp Porsche 924 with special 'Emergency doctor's' equipment.*

Porsche 924, 1981 model. Externally only the lateral direction indicators marked it out from its predecessors.

Type 924 Turbo (1978-1982)

Not surprisingly, shortly after the 924 had established itself, a demand arose for more power. This could not be ignored, especially as the means to provide it existed and had already been applied to other Porsche models to fulfill the requirement: the turbocharger.

However, in the case of the 924, the problem was different. While the 911 Turbo was never intended to be built in large quantities, the 924 Turbo was conceived as a more powerful production version of the 924. A high output was to be combined with complete tractability and the car was to provide the same sort of comfort as the normal 924. In other words: it was to fill the gap between the 924 and the 911 SC. A lot of work went into the engine to ensure the same reliability and durability as that of the unsupercharged version. The 924 Turbo engines are not made by Audi: they are assembled in the Zuffenhausen factory where they are also submitted to all the tests Porsche engines undergo before they are sent to the final car assembly line, which is, in this case, in Neckarsulm.

The main difference between the unturbocharged and the turbocharged 924 engine, which originally developed 170 hp, is the completely new cylinder head featuring much modified combustion chambers. To meet the special requirements of turbocharging, the valves are made of a special heat resistant alloy and those on the exhaust side have their diameter increased by 3 mm, while the sparking plugs are moved to the intake side of the head. This allows their temperature to be kept comparatively low in spite of a 36% increase in power output. A mechanical ignition cut-out incorporated in the distributor of the breakerless transistor ignition system prevents overrevving.

A lot of attention was devoted to obtaining a progressive transition of the unsupercharged to the supercharged operating range of the engine. Among the measures taken, are the comparatively high geometrical compression ratio of 7.5:1 and the characteristics of the turbocharger which becomes effective at comparatively low revolutions. From approximately 2,800 rpm on, the maximum boost of 0.7 bar (approximately 10 psi) increases the effective compression ratio to approximately 10.8:1.

The 930 Turbo was the first production car in which the turbocharger pressure was controlled by a wastegate and the 924 Turbo followed in its footsteps. If the boost pressure exceeds the predetermined maximum figure, a bypass valve (wastegate) leads part of the exhaust gases through a silencer into the atmosphere, bypassing the turbine.

The Bosch K-Jetronic injection system was naturally adapted to the higher output. The 924 Turbo also requires more cooling: a separate full-flow oil cooler dispels the additional heat produced by the greater amount of energy processed by the engine. Additional air intakes ventilate the rather crowded engine room. A so-called NACA intake on the right hand side of the bonnet circulates the air without increasing the drag. A rubber air dam under the engine underpan creates a depression under the car, helping to ventilate both the engine and the brakes.

The more than 50% higher torque output made a larger clutch and a stronger propeller shaft necessary. Thanks to its greater rigidity, this shaft requires only three instead of four bearings in the transaxle tube. The drive shafts were also reinforced and the spacing of the ratios in the Porsche five-speed gearbox was modified. The slightly larger rolling radius of the 15 inch wheels slightly increases the effective gearing.

General description: Type 924 Turbo (basic model)

Coachwork and chassis

No effort was made to produce a spectacular 924 Turbo set apart from the normal model. Most of the external modifications are functional: the additional openings in the bonnet meet the more exacting cooling requirements, the five-stud, 15 inch aluminium wheels of multispoke design are required to accommodate the up-rated brakes and the high speed tyres while the rear polyurethane spoiler reduces both lift and drag.

Further optical differences are limited to a different rocker panel, black window frames and optional two-tone colour finishes. In the cockpit, the leather covered three-spoke steering wheel borrowed from the 930 Turbo is immediately recognisable (though a four-spoke wheel is an option); the gear lever gaiter is made of leather and the sides of the centre console are covered with cloth. The tartan seat upholstery is also a special 924 Turbo feature.

The instruments are a different colour while in the tail of the car the space-saving spare wheel leaves more room for luggage. A small electric compressor is provided to inflate it in case of necessity but can also be useful for other purposes. The 924 is well known for having a chassis that is faster than its engine, however, this does not mean that the 25 km/h (15 mph) higher top speed could be accommodated without any modifications. The fact that the turbo-charged engine, complete with all accessories, weighs 29 kg more than the normal engine required a revision of the spring and damper rates. This was effected in keeping with the sporting, but nevertheless comfortable, basic character of the car. Anti-roll bars are to be found front and rear while special sports dampers are optional. In order to reduce the effort required for parking, the ratio of the rack and pinion steering was increased by 5% without ill-effects under other driving conditions. The noticeably higher power developed by the engine was matched by changes in the running gear which incorporates some components of both the 911 and 928 models. The main points of difference are the larger wheel bearings, the five instead of four studs holding the wheels and the four internally ventilated disc brakes operated by the twin circuit hydraulic system. The up-rated brakes required a change from 14- to 15-inch wheels, the latter shod with 185/70 VR 15 tyres. The brake servo was also increased in size from seven to nine inch diameter, while the hand brake now operates drums located in the rear wheels. As a result of using discs all round, the rear track was increased by 20 mm. All other characteristics of the 924 are retained, among them the well balanced weight distribution which remains almost unaffected by the load carried.

Engine

The engine is based on the 924 four-cylinder unit of 1,984 cc, but the turbocharger increases its power to 170 bhp at 5,500 rpm—300 rpm less than for the normal 924 engine. The maximum torque of 24.5 mkg (181 lb/ft) is produced as low as 3,500 rpm.

The turbocharger consists of a turbine and a compressor wheel mounted on a common shaft. The exhaust gases drive the turbine wheel which, at full throttle, reaches a velocity of 90,000 rpm. The compressor wheel it drives revolves at the same speed and sucks in air which is fed to the combustion chambers at a pressure of 0.7 bar (approximately 10 psi). This ensures that the cylinders are filled with a greater quantity of air than the pistons can normally draw in.

In common with the 930 Turbo, the Porsche 924 Turbo is fitted with an additional full flow oil cooler, platinum pointed sparking plugs and a breakerless transistor ignition system requiring no servicing. Such specifications go a long way to make the 924 Turbo completely untemperamental in spite of its very high specific power.

A special engine assembly line was installed in Zuffenhausen for the 924 Turbo. Each individual engine is carefully tested before being sent to the car assembly line in Neckarsulm. The 225 mm diameter clutch is operated by a self-adjusting hydraulic mechanism.

Considerable care was taken to reduce the noise level of the 924 Turbo which is even quieter than the normal 924, in spite of its much higher power. The turbocharger itself contributes to a reduction of the exhaust noise: as it absorbs a part of the calorific and dynamic energy of the exhaust gases, it acts as a supplementary silencer.

Gearbox

In common with other front-engined Porsche models, the 924 Turbo has its gearbox combined with the differential and rigidly linked to the engine by a thick tube. This ensures a very small but desirable rear weight bias. The 25 mm diameter propeller-shaft is 5 mm thicker than in the normal 924.

The standard Porsche five-speed gearbox and the half shafts were reinforced to accommodate the higher engine torque and the higher top speed of the car.

Equipment

The functional and aerodynamically efficient body is generally similar to that of the 924. The additional rear spoiler, however, improves the adhesion of the rear driving wheels, while reducing the air drag. The drag coefficient of 0.33 is very low for a production car. Other typical features of the Porsche 924 Turbo are the additional air intakes and the so called NACA intake on the right hand side of the bonnet. They improve the circulation of air in the engine compartment. Additional openings in the front air dam take care of the requirements of the oil-cooler and of the front brakes.

While the front seats are designed to suit sporting drivers, the rear ones have basically been designed for children, though they can accommodate adults over short distances. The large luggage compartment is accessible through the pivoted rear window. The locker capacity of 340 litres can be increased to 540 by folding the rear squabs of the back seats forward. A 'space saver' spare wheel is standard equipment in the 924 Turbo. A roll-up cover hides any luggage carried in the locker and also protects it from sun.

Annual modifications

1980
The 924 Turbo is continued virtually unaltered for 1980. In common with the normal 924, new colour schemes in single and two tones and new interior finishes distinguish the new models. Together with its more modest brother, the 924 Turbo gains an external mirror with manual remote control and a door over the tank filler cap. Electric window lifters and a rear fog light are now standard equipment.

1981
The Porsche 924 has proven that turbocharging an internal combustion engine can produce a high specific power along with a low fuel consumption. But a new electronic ignition system goes a step further in exploiting these possibilities: though the power output is now 177 bhp (over 4% higher than before), a reduction in fuel consumption of approx 13% is obtained.

This was achieved by two specific measures: one is the new digitally controlled ignition advance control, which adjusts the ignition to obtain the highest power and the lowest consumption for any operating conditions of the engine. In turn, this very precise ignition advance control made it possible to raise the compression ratio from 7.5:1 to 8.5:1—very high indeed for a turbocharged engine especially for one with no help from an intercooler.

The heart of the installation, known as DZV (digitalelekronische Zündzeit-punktverstellung), is an electronic calculator which, from such data as engine speed, boost pressure and compressed air temperature, computes the optimum advance requirement and provides it. As electronics do not wear, the precise settings of the installation remain unaltered over the entire life of the engine, without requiring any service.

The idling consumption, which is important mainly when the car is used in urban districts, was reduced by the use of an idle speed stabiliser incorporated in the electronic ignition system. This adjusts the ignition timing in such a way that the idling speed remains constant, even if such accessories as air conditioning or lights are switched on. Lower consumption and higher power point to higher engine efficiency. The energy contained in the fuel is used more efficiently and less energy is dispelled by the cooling system and the exhaust. The lower thermal stress under which the engine operates has made it possible to use a smaller turbine, resulting in better engine flexibility in the lower speed ranges. This is also a merit of the raised geometrical compression ratio which also has had the effect of raising the maximum torque to 184.5 lb/ft at 3,500 rpm.

The 924 Turbo has not only become one of the most economical and fastest sports cars, it is probably the most economical in its class, as the following fuel consumption figures indicate: at a steady 90 km/h (55 mph), 42 miles per imperial gallon (35 miles per US gallon); at a steady 120 km/h (75 mph), 33 mpg (27.5 miles per US gallon) and in the urban cycle, 25 mpg (21 miles per US gallon). While the fuel consumption was reduced by some 13%, the tank capacity of the European version of the 924 Turbo was increased to 84 litres (22.2 gallons). New colour schemes and interior appointments, Porsche scripts on the door trim panels and additional directional lights on the front fender side panels identify the new models. Options are a central console for music cassettes, seats upholstered entirely in cloth, or sports seats, as well as a new digital radio and cassette player.

Porsche are also setting new standards in matters of car value preservation: the anti-rust warranty is extended from six to seven years and now applies to the entire body instead of only the floor pan.

1982

Only new colour schemes and a Porsche badge above the glove box distinguish the 1982 model from its predecessors, though the load allowed to be carried on the roof is increased to 75 kg. Except for a few cars for the Italian market (where cars over 2 litres are heavily taxed), the production of the 924 Turbo is discontinued from summer 1982 on.

Porsche 924 Turbo. It was launched in Spring 1979 with 170 bhp, increased to 177 bhp in 1981 model. Fuel consumption is exceptionally low.

Top left: Ventilated rear brake disc. Top right: 924 Turbo engine—177 bhp at 5,500 rpm. Above left: Front suspension. Above right: Porsche five-speed gearbox. Below left: Ventilated front brake disc. Below right: Complete transaxle. Bottom left: Rear suspension with drive shafts. Bottom right: Turbocharger—maximum revs, 90,000 rpm.

Turbocharged Audi engine as modified by Porsche.

Porsche 924 Turbo. It fills the gap between the 924 and the 911 SC. From 1981 model on with digital ignition timing control and five per cent more power.

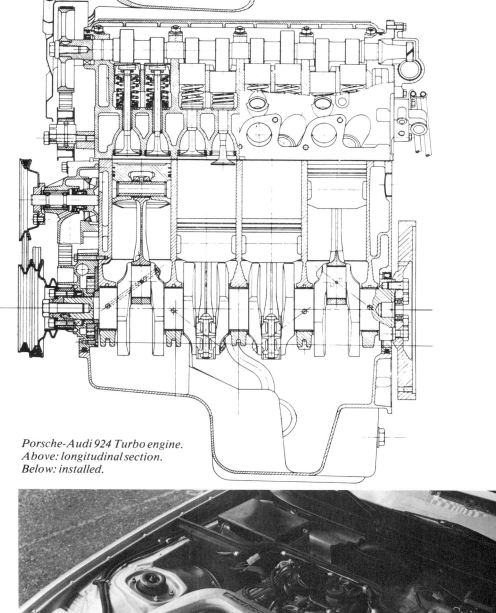

Porsche-Audi 924 Turbo engine.
Above: longitudinal section.
Below: installed.

Type 924 Carrera GT
(1979–1980)

It is Porsche tradition to include serious high performance competition cars in its production programme. Famous examples are the Spyder RS, the Carrera 6, the 917 or the 935. Some of them were suitable for road use, such as the Abarth Carrera, the Carrera 904 GTS and the Carrera RS. All these cars were basically developed from the classic rear-engined models 356 and 911.

The first competition car derived from the new generation of front-engined Porsche models appeared as an experimental study derived from the 924 Turbo on the occasion of the Frankfurt Motor Show of 1979. Its name 'Carrera GT' clearly indicated that this car was to continue the series of high performance road going Porsche sports cars requiring only comparatively minor modifications to be competitive in rallies and racing.

Compared to the normal 924 Turbo, the 924 Carrera GT offers less comfort but more performance. More spartan and lighter interior appointments contribute to the weight reduction of the vehicle by some 150 kg. Modifications to the body allow the use of wider competition tyres and improve its aerodynamic efficiency.

Improved traction and handling result from the use of larger brakes and tyres, up-rated springs and dampers and a limited slip differential. The study was mainly intended to test the reaction of the public. This was necessary because if a competition car based on the 924 Turbo was to be homologated in Group 4, it would be necessary to build 400 identical cars in a period of 12 months. The response exceeded all expectations and the Weissach team immediately got down to work. As had been the case with the 911 Turbo several years before, it again became evident that there is a considerable demand for very high performance competition cars, suitable for road use.

The distinctly sporting appearance of the study car resulted mainly from the necessity to find room for the wider competition tyres. The front air dam and the larger tail spoiler were dictated by both the necessity to increase the aerodynamic down-force and to reduce the drag.

Compared with the normal 924 Turbo, the running gear of the study car was not modified extensively. The official power claim was 210 bhp at 6,000 rpm, part of the power increase being obtained by the addition of an intercooler. The crankshaft and the cylinder head were adapted accordingly. Weight was saved in the interior appointments, on the transaxle tube, on the rear suspension and on the body shell itself. Further weight amounting to a total of 150 kg was saved by using thinner sheet steel for unstressed body parts, aluminium for the doors and the bonnet and plastic material for the front air dam, the front fenders and the rear fender extensions. Only one year after its presentation as an experiment, the 924 Carrera GT became reality: 400 units were made in only a few months and 200 of them were sold in Germany only.

General description

Coachwork and chassis

In spite of the added parts and the enlarged air intakes, optimisation in the wind tunnel made it possible to retain the very low drag coefficient of 0.33 of the standard 924 Turbo. The modified fenders made necessary by the wider tyres and the wider track, are made of glass fibre reinforced polyurethane. Like their counterparts fitted to the type 928, they resist small blows, are insensitive to stone chipping and corrosion and are, to a certain extent, flexible. In the case of major damage, they can easily be replaced.

The 1980 Carrera GT developed from the 924 Turbo, is a fully road going automobile: it is reasonably comfortable, spacious, and quiet. But it requires only minor modifications to become a competitive racing car as was the 924 Le Mans, which was unveiled to the international sporting press in Weissach, in June 1980.

The standard Carrera weighs 1,180 kg and features McPherson front suspension with coil springs and Bilstein struts. At the rear, the semi-trailing link suspension also uses Bilstein dampers but in this case with torsion bars.

In view of the 240 km/h (150 mph) maximum speed, the internally ventilated disc brakes, operated through a vacuum servo and twin hydraulic circuits are additionally cooled by special air ducts. The car accelerates from rest to 100 km/h (62 mph) in only 6.9 seconds. The 7J × 15 forged aluminium wheels carry 215/60 VR 15 tyres front and rear. As a special option, similar wheels of 16 inch diameter can be supplied: seven inches wide with 205/55 VR tyres at the front and 8 inches wide with 225/50 VR tyres at the rear.

Engine

The main interest focuses on the new electronic ignition system featuring digital control of the advance setting (DZV). Not only does it enable Porsche to extract 210 bhp at 6,000 rpm from a turbocharged 2-litre engine, but it also increases the torque in the lower revolution ranges. Thanks to the electronic circuits, the ignition setting matches the requirements of the engine, with only an extremely small tolerance, and this has made it possible to increase the compression ratio from 7.5 to 8.5:1. This makes the increase in power when the boost pressure starts to rise, very much more progressive.

The second important feature of this digital ignition control is a very low fuel consumption. According to the new DIN norms, the Carrera GT is very nearly as economical as the 924 Turbo: the average of the 3 conventional figures is a remarkable 31 miles per imperial gallon (25.8 miles per US gallon).

With bore and stroke dimensions of 86.5 by 84.4 mm, and a total capacity of 1,984 cc, the straight-four, water cooled engine is fed from the turbocharger through an intercooler. Its maximum torque of 28 mkg (202.5 lb/ft) is obtained at 3,500 rpm.

Gearbox

The transmission is largely identical with that of the 924 Turbo; the engine which, as in other 924 models, carries the single plate clutch, is rigidly linked to the five-speed rear transaxle by a tube through which the propeller shaft runs.

Equipment
The equipment is very similar to that of the 924 Turbo but is adapted to the more sporting character of the car.

The 924 Carrera GT (here in its prototype study form) derived its sporting appeal from its fat tyres, widened fenders and front and rear spoilers.

924 / 924 Turbo / 924 Carrera GT

Year	Model Type	Body	Chassis no	Engine type	Gearbox type	Cyl	Bore × stroke	Cap-acity	HP (DIN) at rpm	Torque (mkg) at rpm	Comp ratio	W base (mm)	Track fr/ rear (mm)	Length (mm)	Weight (kg)	No prod-uced
1976	924	Coupé	9246100001- 9246105145	924XK	924YR	4	86,5x84,4	1984	125/5800	16,8/3500	9,3:1	2400	1418/1372	4213	1080	5145
1977	924	Coupé- Autom.	9247100001- 9247108512	047/8 047/9	088/6 087/3	4	86,5x84,4	1984	125/5800	16,8/3500	9,3:1	2400	1418/1372	4213	1080	8512
	924	Coupé- US- Autom.	9247230001- 9247235789	047/9 047/6	087/6	4	86,5x84,4	1984	115/5750	16,8/3500	8,5:1	2400	1418/1372	4320	1190	5789
	924	Coupé	9247200001- 9247209163	047/8	088/A	4	86,5x84,4	1984	100/5500	15,6/3000	8,0:1	2400	1418/1372	4320	1190	9163
	924	Coupé- Japan	9247300001- 9247300261	047/4		4	86,5x84,4	1984	100/5500	15,6/3000	8,0:1	2400	1418/1372	4320	1190	261
	924	Coupé- Japan Autom.	9247330001- 9247330164	047/5		4	86,5x84,4	1984	115/5750	15,9/3500	8,5:1	2400	1418/1372	4320	1190	164
	924	Coupé- US- Autom.	9247210001- 9247211707			4	86,5x84,4	1984	115/5750	15,9/3500	8,5:1	2400	1418/1372	4320	1190	1707
1978	924 Rechts- lenker	Coupé Autom.	9248100001- 9248109474	924XK 924XJ	YR VA RK VB	4 4	86,5x84,4 86,5x84,4	1984 1984	125/5800 125/5800	16,8/3500 16,8/3500	9,3:1 9,3:1	2400	1418/1372	4213	1130	9474
	924	Coupé- US- Californ. Autom.	9248200001- 9248211638	924XG 924XE	RL VB	4 4	86,5x84,4 86,5x84,4	1984 1984	115/5750 115/5750	15,9/3500 15,9/3500	8,5:1 8,5:1	2400	1418/1372	4320	1190	11638
	924	Coupé- Japan Autom.	9248330001- 9248330450	924XG	RL	4	86,5x84,4	1984	115/5750	15,9/3500	8,5:1	2400	1418/1372	4320	1190	450

221

222

924 / 924 Turbo / 924 Carrera GT

Year	Model Body	Type	Chassis no	Engine type	Gearbox type	Cyl	Bore × stroke	Capacity	HP (DIN) at rpm	Torque (mkg) at rpm	Comp ratio	W'base (mm)	Track fr/rear (mm)	Length (mm)	Weight (kg)	No produced
1979	Coupé	924	9249100001-	924XK	YR	4	86,5x84,4	1984	125/5800	16,8/3500	9,3:1	2400	1418/1372	4212	1130	10475
	Autom.	(rhd*)	9249110475	924XJ	VA/RK	4	86,5x84,4	1984	125/5800	16,8/3500	9,3:1	2400	1418/1372	4212	1130	
	Coupé-US-Californ.	924	9249200001-	924XG	VB	4	86,5x84,4	1984	115/5750	15,9/3500	8,5:1	2400	1418/1372	4320	1190	9636
	Autom.		9249209636	924XE	RL	4	86,5x84,4	1984	115/5750	15,9/3500	8,5:1	2400	1418/1372	4320	1190	
	Coupé-Japan	924	9249330001-	924XG	VB	4	86,5x84,4	1984	115/5750	15,9/3500	8,5:1	2400	1418/1372	4320	1190	508
	Autom.		9249330508		RL				115/5750	159/3500	8,5:1	2400	1418/1372	4320	1190	
1980	Coupé	924	92A0410001-	924XK	016/8-VQ	4	86,5x84,4	1984	125/5800	16,8/3500	9,3:1	2400	1418/1372	4212	1130	9094
	Autom.	(rhd*)	92A0419094	924XJ		4	86,5x84,4	1984	125/5800	16,8/3500	9,3:1	2400	1418/1372	4212	1130	
	Coupé-US-Californ.	924	92A0430001-	924XG	RK 016/9-VR	4	86,5x84,4	1984	115/5750	15,9/3500	8,5:1	2400	1418/1372	4320	1190	3700
	Autom.		92A0433700	924XE	VR	4	86,5x84,4	1984	115/5750	15,9/3500	8,5:1	2400	1418/1372	4320	1190	
	Coupé-Japan Autom.	924	92A0440001-92AO	924XG	RL 016/9-VR RL	4	86,5x84,4	1984	115/5750	15,9/3500	8,5:1	2400	1418/1372	4320	1190	
1981	Coupé	924 (rhd*)		924XK	016/8-VQ	4	86,5x84,4	1984	125/5800	16,8/3500	9,3:1	2400	1418/1372	4212	1130	
				924XJ	VQ	4			125/5800	16,8/3500	9,3:1	2400	1418/1372	4212	1130	
	Autom.				RK											

*Right-hand drive

924 / 924 Turbo / 924 Carrera GT / 924 GTS

Year	Model Body	Type	Chassis no	Engine type	Gearbox type	Cyl	Bore × stroke	Cap-acity	HP (DIN) at rpm	Torque (mkg) at rpm	Comp ratio	W'base (mm)	Track fr/ rear (mm)	Length (mm)	Weight (kg)	No prod-uced
1981	Coupé-US-Californ. Autom.	924		924XG 924XE	016/9-VR RL	4 4	86,5x84,4 86,5x84,4	1984 1984	115/5750 115/5750	15,9/3500 15,9/3500	8,5:1 8,5:1	2400 2400	1418/1372 1418/1372	4320 4320	1190 1190	
	Coupé-Japan Autom.	924		924XG	016/9-VR RL	4	86,5x84,4	1984	115/5750	15,9/3500	8,5:1	2400	1418/1372	4320	1190	
1979	Coupé	924 Turbo	9249400001-9249401982	M 31/01	G 31/01	4	86,5x84,4	1984	170/5500	25/3500	7,5:1	2400	1418/1392	4212	1180	1982
	Coupé-US	924 Turbo	9249500001-924950	M 31/02	G 31/01	4	86,5x84,4	1984	150/5500	21/3500	7,5:1	2400	1418/1392	4320	1280	
1980	Coupé	924 Turbo	93A0140001-93A0141803	M 31/01	G 31/01	4	86,5x84,4	1984	170/5500	25/3500	7,5:1	2400	1418/1392	4212	1180	1803
	Coupé-US	924 Turbo	93A0150001-93A0153440	M 31/02	G 31/01	4	86,5x84,4	1984	150/5500	21/3500	7,5:1	2400	1418/1392	4320	1280	3440
1981	Coupé	924 Turbo		M 31/03	G 31/01	4	86,5x84,4	1984	177/5500	25,5/3500	8,5:1	2400	1418/1392	4212	1180	
	Coupé-US-Japan	924 Turbo		M 31/04	G 31/02 016 GMX	4	86,5x84,4	1984	150/5750	21,4/3500	8,0:1	2400	1418/1375	4300	1260	
1980	Coupé	924 Carrera GT	93BN700001-00006 93BN700051-00450	M 31/50	G 31/03	4	86,5x84,4	1984	210/6000	28,5/3500	8,5:1	2400	1477/1476	4320	1180	406
1981	Coupé	924 Carrera GTS	93BN710001-0050	924GTS	937/50	4	86,5/84,4	1984	245/6250	34/3000	8,0:1	2400	1475/1481	4240	1121	50

Porsche 924 Carrera study, as exhibited at the Frankfurt Motor Show in 1979. The public's reaction exceeded all expectations.

Less than a year after the study had been shown, the 924 Carrera GT was made available to the public.

The widened fenders housing the fat tyres are of polyurethane.

Under the bonnet, a 210 bhp 2-litre engine.

1,200 kg, 150 mph and DM50,000: that is the 924 Carrera GT.

Type 928 (1977-1982)

Around 1968, as the 911 became more and more popular, Porsche's design and styling departments began to think about a new generation of models. At that time, the company was working overtime on a very important commitment to develop a new model for Volkswagen, known as VW EA 266, which was later to be abandoned when it had almost reached the production stage. This and other factors delayed the decision, especially as the 911 proved especially responsive to development and had become a real favourite, in all its versions, a position which it has not relinquished to this day. But there was another, perhaps more important reason for waiting: at the end of the '60s, it became clear that the technical development of the car had reached a crossroads. An air cooled rear engine? A mid-engine? Or perhaps even a water cooled front engine? Where was the future to be? The air cooled rear engine, for years Porsche's solution, seemed to be least promising, while the central engine was soon rejected for taking up too much space, except in pure two-seater cars which were not very popular in Europe. This was later clearly confirmed by the comparative failure of the VW-Porsche 914.

In 1970, it was then decided to develop a sports car from the EA 266 project which was nearly finalised. This was a quite unconventional machine of which the water cooled horizontal engine was lying flat under the rear seat. It looked as if history was to repeat itself: Porsche designing a mass producton car for Volkswagen and deriving its own sports model from it—just as in the case of the 356. This would have put an end to any plans for building a larger Porsche.

However, in autumn 1971 everything happened at once. Dr Ernst Fuhrman was appointed Technical Director of Porsche and the new Volkswagen chief, Rudolf Leiding, cancelled the whole EA 266 project which had reached a very advanced stage of development. In a matter of days Porsche was back where it had been two years earlier.

Plans drawn up by the development team under Helmuth Bott which had been shelved in summer 1970 went back on to the drawing boards.

Taking into account current and expected legal requirements, as well as such basic requirements as handling, performance, comfort, luggage capacity, safety, aerodynamics, easy maintenance, etc, the basic concept featured a front engine but with a rear mounted gearbox to improve the weight distribution. The two units were rigidly linked by a tube in which ran the propeller shaft. Porsche called this the Transaxle system.

The project was submitted for approval on October 21 1971, Dr Fuhrmann's birthday. On the following November 8 a note records a most important decision: '. . . the proposed car featuring a front engine and a rear gearbox linked by a central tube . . . may be developed . . .'. The creative phase had thus begun. Dipl Ing Wolfhelm Gorissen Chief of Chassis Design, was put in charge of the project. He gave up his position in 1975 to be replaced by both Dipl Ing Peter Falk and Dipl Ing Helmuth Flegl, two leading members of the Experimental Department. The operation was supervised by the Chief of Design, Ing Wolfgang Eyb.

Before Christmas 1971, all the main features of the new car were finalised. The engine was to be a particularly low 90° V-8 of nearly 5 litres capacity. It was to be water cooled and to have one overhead camshaft per bank, driven by cog belts. A maximum power of approximately 300 bhp was aimed at.

While work was proceeding on the new car, a new contract was signed with the Volkswagen company of which the object was the design and development of a successor to the VW-Porsche 914. The subject of this project known as EA 425, was a sports car incorporating as many mass production parts as possible. The production was to start at the end of 1975.

But again, this was not to be: Volkswagen had run into serious difficulties and Toni Schmücker who had taken the succession of Rudolf Leiding decided that a sports car did not belong into the program of Volkswagen. This was a serious blow, but rather than abandon the project and scrap the almost fully developed prototype, Porsche bought the rights to produce the car, and the already ordered machine tools to build the model and entrusted Volkswagen with the production of the new model in its Audi-NSU factory at Neckarsulm. This is how the Volkswagen prototype EA 245 became the Porsche 924, of which the production began early in 1976.

But back to the Porsche 928. At the end of January 1972, the styling studio had prepared promising designs. In February, several 1:5 scale models were tested in the wind tunnel and at the beginning of June, the lay-out of the interior had been completed. Immediately after the decision was taken to adopt the transaxle system, several experimental models were built to be tried on rigs and in a specially prepared vehicle. This was a Mercedes-Benz 350 SL, known internally as V1. As early as May 15 it had been modified to incorporate a gearbox (from the type 908/03) just ahead of the differential casing.

Intensive investigations about the vibration characteristics of the transaxle system were made, serious problems being expected in this area. The 65 page report on this problem was submitted on October 6. Its conclusions resulted in quite amazing progress: in December 1972, the vibration characteristics had been modified to the extent that the noise in the experimental V1 car was reduced by 50% compared with the beginning of the experiments.

On June 26 1973, the preliminary experiments regarding the transaxle system were completed. The next step was to be the development of the actual engine and transmission of the 928.

The first rig tests took place in August. The complete engine and transmission were then mounted into V3, an Audi 100 Coupé body grafted to the floor pan of the future 928. The car was completed on September 19 1973 and for the first time the complete power unit of the 928, including the engine, the central tube and the transaxle could be tried out on the road. It brilliantly survived the first large scale endurance tests which took place in Algeria in November 1973.

Back in 1972, work on the engine had been proceeding very satisfactorily; the first prototype parts were expected for October. In August a cog belt rig test was made and after completion of a 100 hours' endurance test, the assembly of the first complete engine could begin shortly before Christmas 1972. On January 16 1973, the first 928 engine, a 5-litre with carburettors, was running on a test bed in Weissach. But only a few minutes later water came streaming out of the crankcase, requiring an immediate stop. On March 5 the engine was running again and passed its second test run with noticeably better results. A week later an endurance test carried out under full load was stopped after 25 hours, after a crack appeared in the crankcase.

The insufficiently stiff bottom end was reinforced and, on March 21, another endurance test was initiated. This time, the target of 250 hours was achieved, of which 209 under full load. On May 11 the engine ran for the first time with the Bosch K-electronic injection system.

The latest styling modifications had been approved by the company owners and a final meeting was arranged for November 19 1973.

But meanwhile, the soaring oil prices following the fourth war between the Arab countries and Israel came as a hard blow for Porsche, and on the day on which the 928 body was to be finally approved, the advisory board and the board of directors agreed to postpone the launch of the car and investigate other possibilities such as redesigning the 928 to make it a four-seater, applying some of the 928 technical solutions to the 911, redesigning the 911 both in shape and mechanical design, or even powering the 928 with a smaller engine based on the 911.

The project stood still until November 15 1974, when, following a long discussion, it was decided to go ahead with the 928 as originally planned, and to produce it along with the 911. In January 1975, its engine capacity was finally settled at 4.5 litres.

The development of the running gear had been pursued as intensively as had been the case for the body, transaxle and engine. The main data had been settled at the beginning of 1972 and the first road tests began in the spring of the same year to continue through the summer. For these tests, the experimental parts were built into modified cars from other manufacturers.

It soon emerged that any problem concerning the front suspension could be easily solved. Not so where the rear suspension was concerned. Many high performance cars capable of high cornering speeds suffer from the lift-off reaction—the tendency for the car to suddenly turn into a corner when the accelerator pedal is lifted or when the brakes are applied, a problem which could not be overcome.

Many experiments were carried out on the experimental car V2, an Opel Admiral, on to which the suspension layout intended for the 928 had been grafted. It took one year to achieve success, as related by a report dated October 1973, which concluded: 'The lift-off reaction can be minimised by programmed toe-in variation of the rear wheels'.

Due to pressure of time, it was decided to continue the development of the originally planned double wish bone suspension. This, however, proved to intrude excessively into the rear parts of the car, which led to the replacement of the coil springs by twin torsion bars located behind the rear seats. The design was terminated in January 1974 and built into the first prototype bearing the designation 928 V1 of which the road tests began on May 16 1974. These tests showed that the lift-off reaction was still excessive. As a result of many experiments, it was decided at the end of October 1974 to completely redesign the rear suspension to meet the requirements set out two years before.

Two teams in direct competition with each other developed two different solutions from which the final design, now known as Weissach axle, emerged at the beginning of 1975. In autumn 1973, as the first prototype of the 928 were nearing completion, it appeared that it would not be easy to meet the targets the development engineers had set themselves for comfort and safety without exceeding the weight limit originally set. Extensive use of aluminium body panels, providing a 50% saving in weight, whilst retaining the same resistance, provided the answer. However, aluminium was also attractive because of its resistance to corrosion.

On January 24 1974, despite the difficulties expected in welding and pressing aluminium, it was decided to fabricate two fenders and one bonnet in this material. Later the decision was taken to extend the use of aluminium to the doors including their interior structure and to the hatch door. The calculated weight saving was 42.5 kg (93.7 lb). For reasons of cost, the hatch door was finally made in steel, which reduced the saving by a few kilos.

The first aluminium parts were used in prototype 928 W2, which took to the road in June 1974. The final weight saving compared to steel sheet is 30.7 kg (67.7 lb) = 43%.

The testing activities reached their climax between 1974 and 1976. These included seven accelerated destruction tests, each over 5,000 miles of the aggravated Weissach rough road circuit, each the equivalent of 155,000 miles on the road. The engines too were subjected to spectacular endurance tests on the test beds. They included 300 hours at full load and five endurance tests of 600 hours each.

At the same time, other prototypes covered 50,000 miles each under mixed driving conditions in town, country and motorways. Maximum speed tests took place on the Volkswagen proving ground. In addition to the exhaust emission endurance tests, the 928 prototypes were taken four times to North Africa for high speed road tests in the Algerian hinterland. These runs in Algeria, which are part of every Porsche development programme, stress men and material to the limit of their possibilities.

Tests under extreme winter conditions on the Turracher-Höhe pass in Austria and as far north as the Polar circle in Finland put the cars to test in radically different conditions.

Finally, the cars had to be submitted to the various tests relating to the safety of their occupants, as prescribed by the authorities of a large number of nations. In addition to the large variety of tests related to internal safety, three cars were destroyed in barrier tests, one frontal, and two (one either side) with an angle of 30° to the barrier. All in all, the safety tests on complete cars and on individual units ran into the hundreds.

A large part of the experimental and development work was done on so called V-cars used from 1972 to the beginning of 1977. V-1 was the already mentioned Mercedes-Benz 350 SL which served from July 1972 for transaxle developments. At the beginning of 1974, it ran with the Daimler-Benz three-speed automatic transmission, as planned for use in the 928. At this stage, V-1 still had its original engine which was later replaced by a Porsche 928 engine, complete with the 928 front suspension.

V-2 was an Opel Admiral, which took up its duty in October 1972, mainly for running gear experiments. It retained its original engine and transmission, but was fitted with prototype 928 running gear. It was also weighted to simulate the expected weight distribution of the 928. In October 1973, investigations began on programmed rear wheel toe-in to reduce the lift-off reaction.

V-3 was an Audi 100 Coupé, which was used from September 1973 to develop the transmission, the floor pan and the front end of the car, including the wheel arches and the suspension pick-up points. Early in 1975, it was fitted with an automatic transmission.

V-4 was also an Audi 100 Coupé, but its body was soon sawed along its longitudinal axis and widened by 110 mm. This car had the final 928 floor pan, a 5-litre K-Jetronic engine and the 928 manual gearbox and transaxle. It was used from July 1974 on for running gear and engine developments.

V-5 was also an Audi 100 Coupé, generally similar to V-4 and was used from 1974 on for running gear developments. It had the almost finalised 928 rear end, but without the toe-in variation link.

A 'Munga' was built up in 1973 to serve as a mobile engine test bed. This strange vehicle which had some resemblance to the Auto-Union Munga (a Jeep-like vehicle used by the German army), was only just roadworthy. It was powered by a 5-litre carburettor engine and had a transaxle tube to which a racing gearbox of the Porsche 908/03 was bolted.

From 1974 on 13 real 928 prototypes were successively built to conclude the development programme. The first 928 prototype—928 K1—had plastic external panels and was not fully roadworthy. It was used for body development and experiments on the heating and ventilation systems, on electricity and for exhaust emission tests.

928 W-1, built in April 1974, was the first fully roadworthy prototype with a steel body. It was used for running gear development, powered by the first K-Jetronic injected 4.5-litre engine and used for tests on the snowbound roads around the Turracher-Höhe pass. 928 W-2 was technically identical to W-1 and was used from June 1974 on.

928 W-3, built in November 1974 was probably the most important prototype in the development phase of the 928. It was completed in time for the decisive joint meeting of the board of directors and the main share-holders of the company at which it was decided to produce the model, a decision in which the remarkable handling of W-3 played a decisive part. This prototype was powered by a 5 litre K-Jetronic engine. It was fitted with a manual gearbox and the already improved version of the Weissach rear suspension. In summer 1974, W-3 was taken to Algeria and was later used for road tests in Germany for which the car was appropriately camouflaged. The final design of the Weissach rear suspension was reached on this car whose floor pan was also modified to the final specifications. It was on this car too, that the settings of the suspension, as later used on production cars, were arrived at.

928 W-4, used from October 1974, had a 5-litre K-Jetronic engine and manual gearbox. It was used for two accelerated endurance runs on Weissach's destruction tracks before being handed over to the engine development engineers.

928 W-5 was used from May 1975 on and was the last prototype of the first batch. It had a 4.5-litre K-Jetronic engine and 3-speed automatic transmission. It was used for several detail developments.

928 W-6 followed in July 1976 and was the first car of the second batch of prototypes. Both in its appearance and technical specifications it was nearly identical with future production cars. It was used on the occasion of the public presentation of the 928 and was later written off in a barrier crash test in Weissach.

928 W-7 was largely identical to W-6 and was used from September 1976 for experiments to determine running gear settings, body developments, performance tests, demonstrations inside the company and to dealers. It was also present at the press launch which took place near Nice in January 1977.

928 W-8 was identical to the first batch of production cars. It was completed in November 1976 and was destroyed in a crash test in Weissach. 928 W-9 was used from November 1976 for endurance tests on the road and was technically identical to W-8.

928 W-10 was also identical to W-8 and was used from January 1977 as a guinea pig for experiments on vibration and noise. 928 W-11 was also identical to production models, but had automatic transmission. It was first used in January 1977.

928 W-12 which was completed in March 1977 was the last 928 prototype and was identical with the O-series which was already on the production line. It was used for general testing purposes.

In addition to the 19 experimental cars and prototypes, six cars were built for crash tests, but some of them were never fully completed. Many stationary rig tests were performed on separate units and valuable preliminary work was done on modified Porsche 911 models into which experimental components were integrated.

General description: Type 928 (basic model)

Coachwork and chassis
Lightweight is the key word which dominated the design of the 928 body. The structure is a monocoque construction of which all the stressed parts are made of steel sheet, zinc-coated on both sides, as in the types 911 and 924.

In order to save weight, the doors, the fenders and the bonnet of the 928 are pressed in aluminium. This made it possible to reduce their weight by up to 50%.

Relating the weight of the body structure to the weight of the entire car, it appears that the body structure amounts to only 18% of the total weight in the 928, while the corresponding figure for the 911 is 23%. This was achieved without reducing in any way the beam and torsional rigidity of the body which both have a decisive influence on comfort and handling. Chiefly responsible for this is a rigid structure integrated into the body and forming a protective cage around the occupants. In connection with the crushable zones protecting the occupants from all directions and directly resulting from the car's shape, this protective cage makes the 928 a particularly safe car in the unfortunate case of an accident. In the cases of a frontal or rear crash, additional protection is provided by the rigidity of the entire engine and transaxle unit.

The large rear window, hinged at its upper end and balanced by two gas filled struts, gives access to the 200-litre luggage compartment. Folding the rear seat squabs flat increases the capacity to 400 litres. Even large objects of up to . 90 cm (35.4 inches) width, 36 cm (14.2 inches) height and 1.4 m (55.1 inches)· length can be accommodated inside the compartment without difficulty. The hatch door can be opened only with its key. When it is turned, the door opens automatically. A tool kit and jack are situated in a special recess and provision is also made to accommodate the warning triangle.

The aluminium bumpers, designed to resist an 8 km/h (5 mph) impact without damage, are integrated into the body and are connected to the longitudinal members of the shell by energy absorbing tubes. The parking lights are recessed in the bumpers which, at the front, also carry the standard quartz-iodine fog and driving lights.

The pop-up headlights recline uncovered in the front fenders as long as they are not in use. An electric motor raises them as soon as the light switch is operated. The headlights can be adjusted from the driver's seat to adapt the beam to the load carried in the car. Headlight washers are standard. Difficult to remove insects can be washed away from the windscreen by a special cleaning compound sprayed on to the screen before it is rinsed with the normal screen washer. A rear wiper is standard as is the 2-stage heating of the toughened glass rear window. The quarter windows are fixed since the ventilating system is adequate on its own. Laminated glass is used for the windscreen.

The 12-volt battery and the 86-litre (18.9 Imperial gallon) fuel tank are located behind the gear box since the transaxle system leaves no room for them elsewhere. The tank is made of polyethylene and designed to deform under pressure. Thanks to appropriate reinforcements of the body structure, the severe US safety regulations and crash tests are met without difficulties.

The location of the easy-maintenance 25 kg (55 lb) battery carried in a container bolted to the gear box was specially chosen to assist the damping of the transaxle, consequently reducing noise, and to additionally improve rear wheel adhesion.

An electric sliding roof is optional. Its rear edge can be raised ensuring draft-free and reasonably quiet ventilation even at high speeds.

Maximum total vehicle weight is 1,870 kg (4,122 lb), curb weight being 1,450 to 1,540 kg (3,197 to 3,395 lb), according to the equipment. Unbraked trailers up to 750 kg (1,653 lb) and braked trailers up to 1,600 kg (3,527 lb) may be towed, so that 928 owners should have no problem towing a boat or a comparatively large caravan. The maximum permissible roof load is 35 kg (77 lb). Provision is made to attach ski-carriers and their is ample clearance for snow chains. The transverse, unequal wishbone front suspension provides a negative scrub radius, making the steering insensitive to forces likely to deviate the car from its line, such as a blow-out or unequal front wheel grip when braking.

The elasticity of the steering gear is designed to provide good feel, especially when cornering fast. Particular care was taken to ensure good straight line stability and clean response to quick changes of direction, such as in S bends or when overtaking. The servo assistance decreases with increasing engine speed. This allows easy parking while retaining good feel at high speeds. Extremely rigid cast aluminium wishbones ensure a correct geometry and immediate response to suspension movements.

Anti-dive front suspension geometry reduces brake dive by 30%. Similar characteristics of the rear suspension limit total brake dive to a minimum.

Mainly responsible for the unproblematic handling of the 928, however, is the novel rear suspension. Two major characteristics stand out:

The diagonally pivoted lower wishbone is connected at its front end to the car's main structure by a special link which counteracts any dangerous lift-off reaction. When cornered at high speed, most cars tend to turn into the curve if the accelerator is suddenly lifted. In extreme cases, this can even provoke a spin. The reaction becomes particularly sharp in comparatively light, high powered cars. Experiments carried out by Porsche indicate that the driver must react within less than 0.3 seconds to avoid dangerous consequences. As this is asking too much from a normal driver, the rear suspension was designed to counteract the reaction by increasing the rear wheel toe-in.

The solution is completely novel and an important contribution to the active safety of the car. Anti-roll bars are provided front and rear. They reduce body roll under fast cornering and provide quicker response to steering movements. In connection with transverse wishbone suspensions front and rear, allowing a perfect control of the camber variations, sporting road behaviour can be combined with low tyre wear.

The anti-squat and anti-dive geometry reduces by approximately 60% the squat caused by weight transfer when the car is accelerated and keeps the rear end down when braking.

Though it is now an established fact that the real driving comfort contributes to safety, a widespread opinion still associates soft suspension with comfort. The 928 clearly shows that comfort in the car is mainly the result of vice free road behaviour allowing relaxed driving.

Ventilated disc brakes front and rear are operated by a twin circuit diagonal system. The rear floating caliper brakes are combined with the duo-servo drum brake operated by the hand lever. Tests made in Weissach have indicated that in floating caliper brakes, the temperature of the brake fluid remains much lower than in the case of fixed caliper brakes. Any risk of brake failure caused by boiling fluid is thus eliminated because much better ventilation of the brake cylinders can be arranged.

The 928 rolls on 7J × 16 cast alloy wheels, shod with 225/50 VR 16 tubeless tyres. The space saver spare wheel is recessed in the luggage compartment floor.

Engine

Length, width and height of 860 by 750 by 710 mm respectively are very compact dimensions for a water-cooled 4.5-litre V-8 engine. At 0.98 kg/hp it is also very light for a production engine. The low weight of 236 kg (520.3 lb), without radiator, clutch, starter motor and oil, but complete with the exhaust manifold and all accessories, results from the widespread use of light alloys (108 kg) and plastic materials (6.4 kg).

The compact build of the engine results from the use of liquid cooling. The light alloy cylinder block and heads accelerate heat transfer while water-cooling also has the advantage of good sound damping and simplifying the car heater installation. Special aluminium alloy pistons, coated with a thin iron layer run directly in the specially treated aluminium cylinder bores. They form a low friction, high wear resistant combination.

Toothed belts drive one camshaft per head, silently operating the valves by means of hydraulic tappets. The sump is designed to prevent starvation under any conditions and all oil lines are cast into the block. The crankshaft is forged and the connecting rods are forged from sintered metal.

The K-Jetronic continuous flow fuel injection system is a joint development by Porsche and Bosch. The compression ratio of 8.5:1 allows the use of regular fuel. The oil change intervals of 12,500 miles are characteristic of the easy maintenance of the engine whose breakerless ignition system, hydraulically operated valves and closed circuit cooling system require no maintenance whatsoever.

The circulation of air through the radiator is assisted by a fan driven by a viscous coupling. This incorporates a thermostat which allows the fan to run very slowly as long as the water temperature is low, with resulting low noise and low power absorption. As the temperature of the cooling water rises, the fan is driven at engine speed up to approximately 3,500 rpm, then its speed remains about constant. This ensures good cooling together with low noise and a reasonable absorption of power.

The drive is taken through a twin disc clutch, especially developed for the 928. As in many other technical details, 928 owners benefit from Porsche's racing experience. If a single disc clutch had been used to transmit the very high torque of the 4.5-litre engine, the clutch would have been very heavy to operate and would have required a very large disc, the inertia of which would have caused problems with the gearbox synchromesh. To avoid these problems, Porsche adopted a hydraulically operated twin disc clutch as used in many successful Porsche racing cars.

The engine develops 240 bhp at 5,500 rpm and a maximum torque of 35.5 mkg (260 lb/ft) at 3,600 rpm. Maximum permissible engine speed is 6,300 rpm. The car has a maximum speed exceeding 230 km/h (143 mph) and accelerates from rest to 100 km/h (62 mph) in less than seven seconds.

Gearbox

The engine and gearbox are rigidly linked together by the transaxle tube. The Porsche five-speed synchromesh gearbox is located ahead of the differential and has been especially designed to ensure silence. For this reason a three-shaft box is used in which fifth gear is direct. The rigid and precise gear change mechanism insulates the lever from vibrations. The drive shafts have twin homokinetic universals with provision for length variations. From autumn 1977 on, the car became obtainable with a Daimler-Benz three-speed automatic transmission whose shift programme was modified to suit a sports car. A 40% limited slip differential as offered for the 911, is another option.

Equipment

The spacious 2 + 2 body is lavishly equipped. The main guide lines in the design of the interior were functionality, easy operation and high passive safety.

An example of the thought given to details is the adjustment for height of the steering column, which simultaneously moves the entire instrument board, so that the instruments are never hidden by the steering wheel. All important switches and controls are located in immediate proximity of the steering wheel and clearly identified.

The pedals can also be adjusted for reach. The armrests carried by the doors are adjustable and electrically adjustable front seats are optional. They can be adjusted vertically, horizontally and for squab angle.

The external mirror is electrically adjustable from inside the car and is heated whenever the rear window defroster is switched on. The door windows and the optional sliding roof are also electrically operated. The two doors are locked and unlocked when the key is turned in the driver's door. Large adjustable sun visors are provided. A vanity mirror is recessed in the roof on the passenger's side. When in use, it is illuminated by two lights which automatically light up.

The inclination of the main headlights can be adjusted hydraulically from the driver's seat. A special windscreen washing compound is contained in an 0.7-litre (1.2 pint) tank to dissolve silicones and insects which can then be washed away with water contained in a 9-litre (15.8 pint) tank which also supplies the main headlights. To special order a special parallel link rear window wiper can be obtained. It is driven by an electric motor mounted on the main body structure by means of a special clutch which disconnects the drive when the hatch door is opened. A two-stage rear window defroster is provided.

The new Porsche radio cassette installation is standard. It includes four large speakers, two recessed in the doors and two in the rear of the body. The Tempomat is also part of the standard equipment. A kind of cruise control, it allows the car to be driven steadily at any selected speed between 50 and 200 km/h (30 and 125 mph). The car maintains the speed automatically eliminating the need for the driver to constantly operate the accelerator or watch the speedometer.

A central warning system comprising a large light located between the speedometer and the revolution counter informs the driver of any possible trouble. The system controls 12 different functions in two stages. In the first stage, a persistent bright light indicates a major fault. Less important faults are indicated in the second stage.

The two separate, thickly upholstered rear seats each have a hinged squab which can be folded flat to increase the luggage capacity. A lockable glove box separates the seats. Inertia reel rear seat belts underline the care given to passive safety.

The luggage compartment is accessible both from inside and outside the car. An elastic net is provided to keep small items in place while a cover can be installed to hide any luggage contained in the compartment.

The space saving spare wheel is kept in a recess of the luggage compartment floor together with an electric compressor and the jack, while the tools are kept in a covered recess in the rear wall of the compartment.

Customers have a wide choice of upholsteries and can order their car partially or entirely trimmed in leather. Roof and interior trim panels are large and treated to create a soft effect.

Cockpit temperature is adjusted by blending ambient and heated air. The blended air output is controlled by a five-speed fan which runs continuously. An air conditioning installation comprising a wobble plate compressor is optional. In this case, even the glove box is incorporated in the circuit, so that drinks and sweets can be kept cool. Stale air is aspirated below the door windows and fed through the door sills to the front door pillar from where is escapes through the front door joint. Both with or without air conditioning provision is made for defrosting and demisting the windscreen.

Annual modifications

1979

The Porsche 928 is elected 'Car of the Year 1978' by a jury of 51 leading European motoring journalists. The award has existed since 1963 and this is the first time it goes to a sports car.

The car goes unmodified into its second production year and the demand still exceeds the production capacity of the factory.

1980

Performance and handling characteristics of the Porsche 928 remain unchanged, but considerable work has gone into the engine in order to optimise its fuel consumption.

According to the new, more realistic DIN norm 70.030 adopted by all West European countries, the fuel economy of the Porsche 928 is improved to 29 mpg

(24 miles per US gallon) at a steady speeed of 90 km/h (55 mph); 23.7 mpg (19.7 miles per US gallon) at 120 km/h (75 mph); and 16 mpg (13.3 miles per US gallon) in the urban cycle. This is mainly a result of raising the compression ratio from 8.5:1 to 10:1, a modification which makes premium fuel mandatory. The output of the 4.5-litre V-8 engine remains unaltered at 240 bhp, now at 5,250 rpm, but maximum torque is increased from 260 to 280 lb/ft, still at 3,600 rpm. The entire body structure is made of zinc coated steel and carries a six-year anti-rust warranty.

Road tests confirm the much reduced fuel consumption of the modifed version. Porsche has thus already fulfilled the promise made by the German automobile industry on April 30 1979 to the German Minister for Economy: to reduce the average fuel consumption of its vehicles, as it was in 1977, by 10% to 12% before 1985.

1981

For the new model year, the 928 gets a rear fog light. The rear wiper and the headlight washers are now standard. Other options are seats with berber upholstery or leather covered sports seats. Additionally, Porsche has extended its anti-rust warranty from six to seven years without any intermediate treatment and from the floor pan to the entire body.

1982

An addition to the instrumentation is a fuel consumption meter giving a very accurate reading of the instantaneous fuel consumption and enabling the driver to adjust accordingly. The ventilation is also improved by a 10% increase in the air flow and there is an additional shelf on the driver's side. The 928 also inherits the four-spoke steering wheel and the larger battery of the 928 S. The permissible roof load is increased from 35 to 75 kg (77 to 165 lb).

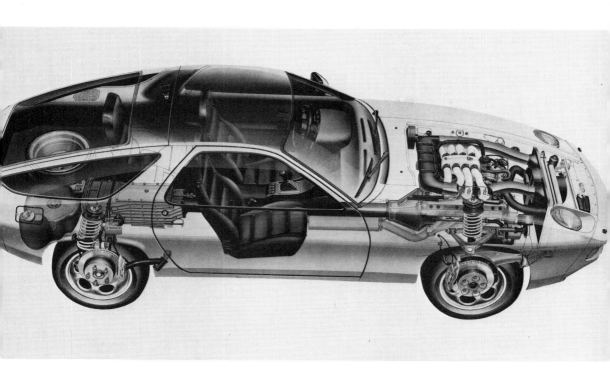

Cutaway and side views of the V8-engined Porsche 928.

238   *When not in use, the headlights retract into the streamlined, sloping front.*

Rounded shapes are a feature of the 928's functional styling.

The instrument panel moves with the adjustable steering column. Pedals and seats are adjustable as well.

240

Luggage room can be extended by folding emergency seat backs.

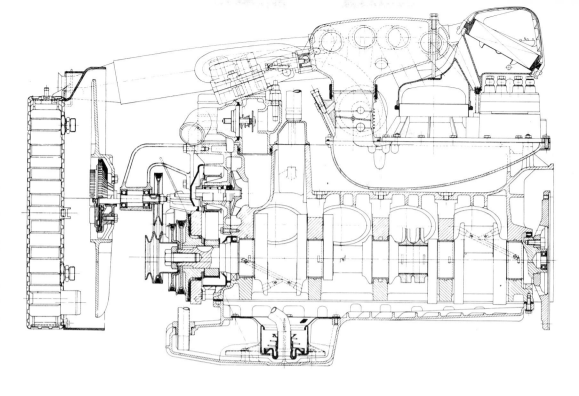

Longitudinal and cross-sectional drawings of the 928 engine: a 4.5-litre V8 producing 240 bhp.

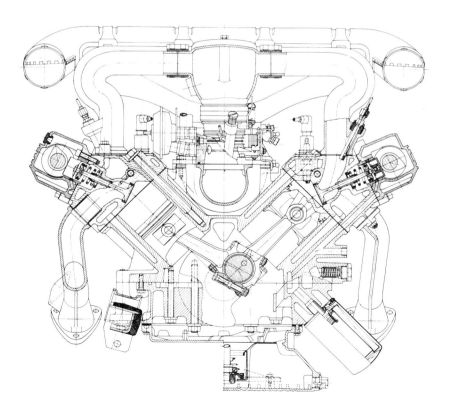

Side views of the all-aluminium, water-cooled V8 engine.

Like all contemporary production Porsches, the 928 engine is fed by a Bosch K-Jetronic injection system.

Front view of the compact 90° V8 engine.

Top: A rigid tube links the engine bell housing to the rear transaxle unit. Above: The engine and transaxle also carry a large part of the running gear, thus damping out road noise.

The 'Weissach' independent rear suspension automatically compensates for any toe-in variations induced by driving and braking forces.

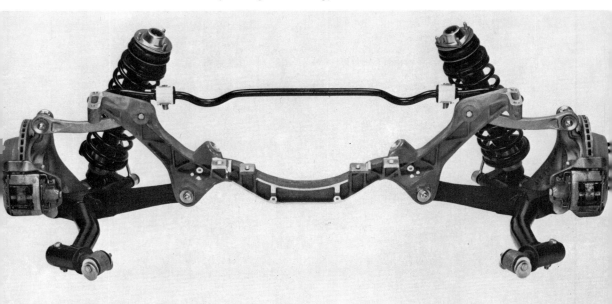

Rear fog light and wiper
became standard in 1980
for 1981 models.

Externally hardly changed:
Porsche 928 with 240 bhp,
4.5-litre V-8 engine.

From 1980 model on, fuel
consumption was much
reduced.

The body shell is made of
zinc-coated steel and
carries a seven-year
warranty.

Floating brake calipers help avoid overheating of brake fluid.

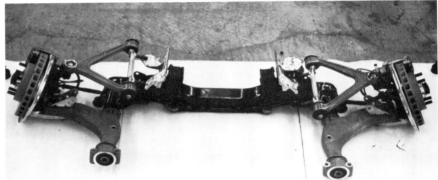

Type 928 front suspension: the wishbones are aluminium castings.

246

The instrument panel lies directly in front of the driver and moves up and down with the adjustable steering column.

Type 928 S (from 1979)

It is a Porsche tradition to offer any basic model with engines in different states of tune. Typical examples were the normal and super versions of the 356 with engines of 60 and 75 bhp and the 911 which, for a long period, could be had in T (110 bhp) L (130 bhp) and S (160 bhp) versions.

Initially the power of the 928 engine was deliberately kept below the designed possibilities of the V-8. The modest compression ratio of 8.5:1 made it possible to use regular fuel. For the 928 S, it was raised to 10:1, a similar step being taken simultaneously for the normal 928 engine. It resulted in improved thermal efficiency and a corresponding reduction of the fuel consumption, though the higher compression ratio now used requires the use of premium fuel.

The 928 S engine has its bore increased from 95 to 97 mm to raise the capacity to 4,664 cc. Higher compression, larger valves, different cams and a twin straight through exhaust system result in higher power and a faster running engine: the maximum power of the 928 S is 300 bhp at 5,900 rpm. The torque curve too is characteristic of the more sporting character of the engine: while the normal 928 engine reaches it maximum torque of 38.8 mkg (280 lb/ft) at 3,600 rpm, the 928 S produces 38.9 mkg (284 lb/ft) at 4,500 rpm. The maximum permissible engine speed of 6,500 rpm is limited by an ignition cut out. In the lower revolution ranges, the 928 S displays the same impressive pulling power as the 928. But while the driver of a 928 feels tempted to change up rather early as the engine gets out of breath in the higher ranges, the revving ability of the 928 S, coupled with the engine's increasing power, is a constant source of fascination.

There is never any doubt about the additional 60 bhp. In this form the big V-8 displays its full potential and justifies the overhead camshaft design backed by a long racing experience.

The higher power naturally puts higher requirements on the running gear. This is well up to its task, in part thanks to the transaxle lay-out which ensures good adhesion of the driving wheels. Fast cornering is made both safe and enjoyable by the well controlled excess power available and the stabilising characteristics of the Weissach suspension.

When the 928 was conceived, the problem of the lead content of the fuel available in Germany was still under discussion. For this reason, the engine was designed to operate on regular petrol, even though a higher consumption was known to result. But meanwhile, the main concern had become the fuel consumption which also became the most important item in the American legislation.

While the increased compression ratio takes care of this requirement where the engine is concerned, the body provides its own contribution to the solution of the consumption problem by a reduction of the air drag. An additional front air dam and a rear spoiler reduce the drag coefficient to 0.38. The result of these measures are fuel consumption figures of anything between 15 and 20 mpg (12.5 and 16.5 miles per US gallon) according to how the car is driven.

A four spoke steering wheel, standard part-leather upholstery, a large choice of interior cloths and a wide choice of metallic colour finishes are all standard in the 928 S, in addition to the normal equipment of the 928, such as automatic speed control, electronic warning system, additional windscreen washing system, headlight washers, sun visors in the rear compartment, four loud-speakers, a rear window wiper and many other details.

The radio is also new, not only for the 928 S. It incorporates additional functions and an additional amplifier can be fitted, increasing the output to 4 × 15 watt. Provision is made for storing cassette tapes in the central console. The automatically controlled air conditioning system is completely new. Once set, it keeps the interior at a constant temperature. This is achieved by an electronic box which receives signals from two sensors and operates flaps and the blower accordingly. Several programmes are provided which operate independantly from the inside and outside temperature: normal; cool weather (the compressor is put out of use) and damp weather (keeps the windscreen free from mist). The fan control can be overriden and the central air outlet can be fed with cold or warm air.

The front air dam, the rear spoiler and the new design of the light alloy disc wheels are the main identification marks of the new 928 S. The forged wheels with aloxided surface are of exclusive design and also reduce weight. Thicker brake discs and larger brake pads take care of the increased power. The running gear remains otherwise unaltered. In comfort and handling, the 928 and 928 S are identical.

As the 928, the S version is available with a five-speed manual or a fully automatic transmission. The power steering provides good road feel and the assistance is reduced as the car speed increases.

The 928 S has a maximum speed of a generous 250 km/h (155 mph) and accelerates from 0 to 100 km/h (62 mph) in only 6.6 seconds. 160 km/h (100 mph) is reached in only 14.6 seconds. The official fuel consumption figures are as follows: 25 mpg (20.8 miles per US gallon) at a constant 90 km/h (55 mph); 22 mpg (18.3 miles per US gallon) at a constant 120 km/h (75 mph) and 14.3 mpg (11.9 miles per US gallon) in the urban cycle.

The steel structure is entirely zinc coated and carries a six year warranty against rust. Many components of body and running gear are made of aluminium with the main object of reducing weight, but also because of their good resistance to the elements.

Annual modifications

1981
The headlight washers, the rear screenwiper and the fog tail light are now part of the standard equipment. New options are the seats upholstered in berber fabric and the leather covered sports seats. A Blaupunkt QTS radio can be specified in place of the Porsche radio. There are also new colour schemes.

1982

The instrumentation is complemented by a fuel consumption meter giving a very accurate and instantaneous reading enabling the driver to adjust his driving accordingly. The ventilation is improved by a 10% increase of the air flow and there is an additional shelf on the driver's side. The electric adjustment of the driver's seat becomes standard and the permissible roof load is increased to 75 kg (165 lb).

1983

The characteristic oval holed light alloy wheels of the discontinued 928 are now standard wear for the 928 S. Hydraulically damped engine mountings and a new hydraulic tensioner of the cog-belt driving the camshafts have brought further refinement and further reduced the service requirements. The seat edges are covered in real leather and the colour of the instrument nacelle matches the rest of the interior.

Front air dam, rear spoiler and a special wheel design are the identification marks of the 155 mph Porsche 928 S. Acceleration from 0 to 100 km/h in 6.6 seconds.

249

The aerodynamic aids drop the C_d to 0.38—the fuel consumption oscillates between 15 and 20 mpg (12.5 and 16.5 miles per US gallon).

The 4.6-litre V-8 engine develops 300 bhp at 5,900 rpm, 60 bhp more than the 928.

928 / 928S

Year	Model Body	Type	Chassis no	Engine type	Gearbox type	Cyl	Bore × stroke	Cap-acity	HP (DIN) at rpm	Torque (mkg) at rpm	Comp ratio	W'base (mm)	Track fr/ rear (mm)	Length (mm)	Weight (kg)	No prod-uced
1978	Coupé	928	9288100001- 2646	M 28/01	G 28/03	8	95×78,9	4474	240/5500	35,6/3600	8,5:1	2500	1551/1530	4447	1490	2646
		928 Autom.	9288100001- 2646	M 28/02	A 22/01											
		928 USA	9288200001- 1139	M 28/03	G 28/03	8	95×78,9	4474	230/5250	35,0/3600	8,5:1	2500	1551/1530	4462		139
		928 Japan	9288209501- 9575	M 28/03	G 28/03											75
		928 USA Autom.	9288209001- 1139	M 28/04	A 22/01											
		928 Japan Autom.	9288209501- 9575	M 28/04	A 22/02											
1979	Coupé	928	9288100001- 3059	M 28/01	G 28/03	8	95×78,9	4474	240/5500	35,6/3600	8,5:1	2500	1551/1530	4447	1520	3059
		928 Autom.	929100001- 3059	M 28/02	A 22/01											
		928 USA	9289200001- 2285	M 28/03	G 28/03	8	95×78,9	4474	230/5250	35,0/3600	8,5:1	2500	1551/1530	4462		2285
		928 Japan	9289209501- 9623	M 28/03	G 28/03											123
		928 USA Autom.	9289200001- 2285	M 28/04	A 22/02											
		928 Japan Autom.	9289209501- 9623	M 28/04	A 22/02											

928 / 928 S

Year	Body	Model Type	Chassis no	Engine type	Gearbox type	Cyl	Bore × stroke	Cap-acity	HP (DIN) at rpm	Torque (mkg) at rpm	Comp ratio	W'base (mm)	Track fr/rear (mm)	Length (mm)	Weight (kg)	No prod-uced
1980	Coupé	928	92A0800001-1192	M 28/09	G 28/03	8	95×78,9	4474	240/5250	38,7/3600	10:1	2500	1552/1529	4447	1520	1192
		928 Autom.	92A0800001-1192	M 28/10	A 22/01											
		928 USA	92A0810001-1649	M 28/13	G 28/03	8	95×78,9	4474	231/5500	36,7/4000	9:1	2500	1552/1529	4462		1649
		928 Japan	92A0800001-1192	M 28/14	G 28/03											
		928 USA Autom.	92A0810001-1649	M 28/13	A 22/01											
		928 Japan Autom.	92A0800001-1192	M 28/14	A 22/01											
1981	Coupé	928	WPO222922 BS800001-	M 28/09	G 28/05	8	95×78,9	4474	240/5250	38,7/3600	10:1	2500	1552/1529	4447	1450	
		928 Autom.		M 28/10	A 22/01											
		928 USA	WPOJAO92 BS820001-	M 28/15	G 28/05	8	95×78,9	4474	231/5500	36,7/4000	9:1	2500	1552/1529	4447	1450	
		928 USA Autom.		M 28/16	A 22/01											
		928 Japan		M 28/17	G 28/05	8	95×78,9	4474	231/5500	36,7/4000	9:1	2500	1552/1529	4462	1450	
		928 Japan Autom.		M 28/18	A 22/01											
		928 S	WPO222922ZBS 840001-	M 28/11	G 28/05	8	97×78,9	4664	300/5900	39,2/4500	10:1	2500		4462	1450	
		928 S-Autom.		M 28/12	A 22/04											

251

Type 944 (from 1981)

Following the successful performance of the so-called 924 GTP-Le Mans in the famous 24 Hours Race, the Porsche 944 was officially announced in autumn 1981.

Its body shell is basically similar to that of the Porsche 924 and, in appearance, the 944 is a very close relative of the 924 Carrera GT. But though the frontal appearance of the 944 is very similar, the front fenders are made of zinc coated steel, as used for the entire body, and similarly shaped fenders are used at the rear, giving the car a distinctive appearance while preserving the very low air drag coefficient characteristic of the 924 body. A deep front air dam and a neat rear spoiler reduce the lift and keep the large rear window, which opens to give access to the luggage compartment, free from dirt. A rear wiper remains however an option, as it facilitates the removal of snow or rain drops when the car has been left standing.

Coachwork and chassis

The 944's running gear is basically similar to the 924's. It features McPherson coil spring front suspension with wide base wishbones pivoted on the cast alloy transverse member, and an anti-roll bar. At the rear, semi-trailing links are used in conjunction with transverse torsion bars running in a cross tube carrying the entire suspension. This tube is itself carried by the body shell by means of rubber mounted light alloy supports reducing the intrusion of road noise into the passenger compartment. The 7J × 15 cast alloy wheels are shod with 185/70 VR 15 tubless tyres. The now famous Porsche forged alloy wheels are optional in the dimension 7J × 16 in conjunction with 205/55 VR 16 ultra-low profile tyres which are best used with the optional 'sports' suspension featuring stiffer dampers, a rear anti-roll bar and a stronger front anti-roll bar to match. In all cases, the spare wheel is a 165-15 Space Saver with which an electric compressor and a pressure gauge are provided.

At 2.4 m, the wheelbase is the same as the 924's, but the front and rear tracks are noticeably wider. Internally ventilated disc brakes are used all-round, their floating calipers being operated via a large vacuum servo and a twin hydraulic circuit with front/rear split. The fuel tank contains 66 litres (14.5 Imperial gallons or 17.4 US gallons), including a 6-litre reserve.

The basic features and internal dimensions of the coupé body, providing rear accommodation for children, are the same as for the 924. The large luggage compartment, easily accessible by lifting the large, counter-balanced rear window can be further increased in size by pivoting the rear squabs forward. In addition, up to 75 kg (165 lb) can be carried on the roof. There is a choice of two leather covered steering wheels of 38 and 36 cm diameter. A precise fuel consumption indicator, sensing the actual fuel flow, is incorporated in the tachometer dial and operates in any gear.

The heating and ventilating installation is new and incorporates vacuum operated flap valves. Full air conditioning is available as an option. The weight of the complete car, with full tanks, is 1,180 kg. In common with every other Porsche, the use of hot zinc-dipped steel sheet for the entire body structure allows Porsche to give its customers a seven year anti-rust warranty without any intermediate treatment and of which the validity is retained in the case of a change of owner.

Engine

The most remarkable feature of the 944 is its TOP (Thermodynamically Optimised Porsche) engine installed at a 45 degree angle to the right. With a capacity of 2,479 cc, it is one of the largest four-cylinders on the market. As in the special Le Mans engine, from which it differs essentially by being unsupercharged and by its single overhead camshaft cylinder head, the water cooled cylinder block is cast in a special aluminium alloy in which the iron coated pistons run directly. Bore and stroke are 100 × 78.9 mm. In such a large straight-four engine, the unbalanced forces of the second order would normally create considerable roughness. This is avoided by the use of twin balance shafts, counter-rotating at twice the crankshaft speed and driven by a cog-belt. These shafts are set at different heights from the crankshaft and also partly compensate for the engine's torque reaction, thus reducing the impulses to be absorbed by the rubber engine mountings. Another cog-belt drives the camshaft which operates two valves per cylinder by means of self-adjusting hydraulic tappets. Shaped to produce a high turbulence, the combustion chambers allow the very high compression ratio of 10.6:1 conducive to very high thermal efficiency and resultant low fuel consumption.

Such a high compression ratio would not be usable, however, without the help of the Digital Electronic Control of the engine which rules both the ignition advance and the fuel injected by the timed L-Jetronic fuel injection system. It ensures that, at all times, the ignition advance very closely follows the requirements of the engine and that ignition advance and fuel injector output combine to achieve the lowest fuel economy compatible with top performance under all conditions, including cold starting, the warming-up period and hot starting.

The comparatively low stressed engine produces 163 bhp DIN at 5,800 rpm— a specific output of just over 65 bhp/litre—but it can be run up to 6,500 rpm, the limit set by the electronic ignition cut-out. Rather than on sheer power, the accent was set on flexibility, as indicated by the engine speed of only 3,000 rpm where the maximum torque of 151 lb/ft is obtained. This in turn allows high gearing to be used, providing relaxed high speed cruising and good fuel economy. This and the engine's high thermal efficiency combine to produce quite outstanding fuel consumption figures for a high performance, 2.5-litre sports car. The official steady speed figures are 40.4 mpg (33.7 miles per US gallon) at 90 km/h (55 mph), 32.5 mpg (27.1 miles per US gallon) at 120 km/h (75 mph), with an urban cycle consumption of 24.8 mpg (20.7 miles per US gallon).

253

Transmission

Quite naturally, the proven transaxle system is retained for the Porsche 944. A rigid tube in which the propeller shaft is supported in four bearings, links the bell housing containing the clutch to the rear mounted gearbox and differential unit, ensuring a front/rear weight distribution of around 50/50, varying but little with the weight carried and forming an ideal basis for safe and predictable handling. A fully synchronised (including reverse) five-speed gearbox of Audi manufacture, but fitted with specific Porsche gear ratios is standard equipment. The ratios have been chosen essentially with high performance in view and the car's maximum speed of 137 mph is obtained at 5,950 rpm. 100 km/h (62 mph) is reached from rest in 8.4 seconds—a conservative claim if independent road tests are anything to go by. A VW-made three-speed automatic transmission, well suited to the engine's torque characteristics, is available as an option.

The entire engine and transaxle unit is carried in four rubber mountings which, thanks to their wide spacing, can be very soft without causing any undesirable movement. The front supports, which rest on the sturdy light alloy transverse member, feature hydraulic internal damping to avoid disturbing low frequency bounce of the engine on certain rough road surfaces.

The combination of an exceptionally smooth-running and silent engine, good sound proofing and low aerodynamic noises resulting from the smooth body shape result in remarkable silence, right up to the highest speed ranges.

Equipment

A central console carries the heating and ventilation controls, a cigar lighter and three additional instruments: an oil pressure gauge, a voltmeter and an analog quartz clock. It also contains an ashtray and space is provided for the installation of a radio. The adjustable front seat squabs extend upwards to form a headrest and fold forward to give access to the emergency rear seats. While the more exposed sides of the seats and squabs are upholstered in artificial leather, the central parts are covered with high quality velvet material providing both good grip and good ventilation.

The counterbalanced lift-up rear window provides easy access to the luggage compartment which can be extended by folding the rear squabs forward. A roll-up cover keeps the contents of the luggage room out of sight. Lights are provided in the cockpit, in the luggage compartment, in the glove box and to illuminate the ashtray.

Among the many extras available are the sun roof, the electric window mechanism, the automatic speed control, the rear window wiper and washer and air conditioning. The electrically adjustable outside rear view mirror, originally an option, became standard in the 1983 model.

The Porsche 944's long range lights are recessed in the bumper. They can also be used for flashing.

The 944 has become the most popular model in the Porsche range. It allies 137 mph top speed with very low fuel consumption.

The 2.5-litre, four-cylinder Porsche 944 aluminium engine is inclined 45 degrees to the left. It develops 163 bhp at 5,800 rpm.

256

Cutaway model of the Porsche 944.

PRODUCTION SPORTS CARS

Types 356/356 C

It took quite some time in Germany for motor sport to get back into its stride after the Second World War. New cars were non-existent. Spares and fuel were only to be found in the most unlikely places. Of necessity, all competition cars used were of pre-war vintage or home-built from parts of various origins. To limit the cost, most home-built cars used engines of anything between 1,100 and 1,500 cc, most of them based on the VW. The 1,086 cc VW engine of which a small series had been built (normal engines were of 1,131 cc capacity) was particularly popular. The engine lent itself well to tuning, in many cases the compression ratio was considerably increased to run on alcohol fuel, while some were fitted with special cylinder heads in which the valves were arranged in V-formation, and some engines even used four carburettors. VW chassis were lightened by what was often more enthusiastic than scientific drilling, but however clumsily some of these cars were built, their builders had the merit of reviving motor sport in post-war Germany.

Slowly the assembly lines of the automobile factories started moving. Motor sport enthusiasts were happy to see any suitable new model. Porsche's first Stuttgart-built 1,100 cc 356 was soon part of the sporting scene. Of the legendary Gmünd-built aluminium coupés, Porsche had kept all remaining examples for their own use. It was with one of those cars that the company made its first official entry into the international sporting scene. One of them was put at the disposal of a French crew for the Le Mans 24 Hours race of 1951. One of the drivers was Auguste Veuillet, the Porsche importer in France, who, with his co-driver Mouche, succeeded in winning the 1,100 cc class. This enormously boosted the young company's prestige and started a success story which is still continuing.

On the occasion of the Le Mans race, the 'aluminium box' (as the mechanics called it) was equipped with rear wheel covers to increase the maximum speed by further reducing drag, and the slightly tuned engine produced 4 bhp more than in standard form. The car weighed only 640 kg (1,410 lb) and it achieved just over 160 km/h (100 mph) on only 44 bhp.

In the same year, Huschke von Hanstein and Peter-Max Müller finished second in the 1,100 cc class of the gruelling Liège-Rome-Liège long-distance rally. On that occasion, another aluminium coupé was fitted with a prototype

1,500 cc engine producing 60 bhp. Driving this hybrid, Paul von Guilleaume and Count von der Mühle finished first in their class and third overall in the same event.

In the period from September 29 to October 2 1951, Peter-Max Müller, Walter Glöckler, Richard von Frankenberg, Huschke von Hanstein and Hermann Ramelow obtained several international records driving an aluminium coupé fitted with a 1,500 cc engine on Montlhéry track, near Paris. In 72 hours, the car covered 10,968 km (6,815 miles) at an average of 152.35 km/h (94.66 mph).

Private owners driving the all-steel 356 with an 1,100 cc, 40 bhp engine were mainly active in rallies. Even the 1300 and 1500 were no bombs until the 1300 S and 1500 S versions, with 60 and 75 bhp respectively, arrived. But Porsche soon recognised that a specially built car was really necessary to provide private owners with competitive machinery. Such a model was the 'Carrera' which appeared in 1955 in the 356 A series. This '1500 GS' model, as it was known internally, had a 1,500 cc engine boasting no less than 100 bhp, which would be increased to 110 two years later.

Its successor, which appeared in 1958, was offered in two different versions. One was the 'Carrera de Luxe' for discriminating drivers who had no intention of entering their car for competitions (the 1.6-litre engine developed 105 bhp), while the 1600 GS 'Carrera GT' was a lighter version trimmed for racing and rallying, with an engine developing 115 bhp.

Starting with the 356 B series in 1959, the 'Super 90' was offered as a less costly high-performance model, but the Carrera series continued as 1600 GS with 115 bhp and, from 1961, as 2000 GS with 130 bhp. The 1600 GS had a Reutter-built lightweight body and was called 'Carrera GT'. Except for the body lightening and the twin ohc engine, the car was very similar to the Super 90 in its specification. Some 40 Carrera GTs were built and sold for DM 21,500.

At the end of 1959 a series of 20 lightweight 'Carrera GTL's were ordered from Carlo Abarth in Italy, to whom all mechanical units, the floor pan and the running gear were supplied and who built them into a specially made body. The car became known as the 'Abarth-Carrera' and was intended to meet the ever stronger opposition from the 1,300 cc class which, on many occasions, had given even the 1,600 cc Porsches something to think about.

The Abarth coupé weighed 780 kg (1,719 lb), only 20 kg (44 lb) less than the Reutter-built GT, but its better aerodynamic shape made it faster: it did 230 km/h (143 mph) on no more than 135 bhp.

With the first Abarth-built Carrera, Herbert Linge and Hans-Joachim Walter won their class in the 1960 Le Mans 24 Hours race. Later cars were slightly modified by Porsche who offered them in three different versions: one had the standard 82 db exhaust system and developed 115 bhp at 6,500 rpm; a so-called rally exhaust increased this to 128 bhp at 6,700 rpm, while the 'Sebring' racing exhaust system brought the power up to at least 135 bhp at 7,400 rpm. With the standard exhaust, the Abarth accelerated from 0 to 100 km/h (60 mph) in 9.6 seconds and reached 210 km/h (131 mph). The racing version of the Carrera GTL reached 60 mph in 8.5 seconds, took 26.5 seconds to reach 180 km/h (113 mph) and covered a kilometre (0.62 mile) from a standing start in only 29.6 seconds.

Though the workmanship on the body was rather unsatisfactory, the GTL was very competitive and the 21 cars built were sold very quickly at a price of DM 25,000.

Even the 2,000 cc 'Carrera 2' in its 1961 and 1963 versions, based respectively on the 356 B and 356 C, could not compete with the Abarth-Carrera. The 130 bhp delivered by its four ohc engine was just not enough to make the 1,020 kg (2,249 lb) car, essentially intended as a fast road car, competitive against the smaller-engined but very much lighter Abarth-Carrera GTL. Neither were those other models in the 356 C line offered with engines of 75 and 95 bhp very competitive, so the Abarth-Carrera must be regarded as the last and most highly developed model of the sporting 356 series. Nevertheless, 107 Carrera 2s of the 356 B and 85 of the 356 C series were sold.

For serious competition at private owner level, the Abarth-Carrera had no successor until the six-cylinder 911 appeared on the market.

General description: Type 356 aluminium coupé

Coachwork and chassis

The steel floorpan, built up from box section members, and the aluminium sheet body formed a unit exceptionally resistant to flexion and torsion. The two-door coupé had two seats with some room, but no proper seats behind them. The V-shaped windscreen was in two pieces and the equipment was similar to that of the later 356 series.

The front suspension was by parallel trailing links acting on transverse torsion bars enclosed in the tubular front members. At the rear, there were swinging half-axles located by torsionally flexible trailing links controlled by transverse torsion bars. The all-round drum brakes were operated by Bowden cables (the installation was later modified to hydraulic brakes). The fuel tank had a capacity of 50 litres (11 gallons), providing a range of 650 kilometres (400 miles-plus) under normal conditions.

Engine

The engine was a flat-four located behind the rear axle and with its cylinders across the car. Bore and stroke were 73.5×64 mm $(2.9 \times 2.5$ inches) respectively, giving a capacity of 1,086 cc and a power of 40 bhp at 4,000 rpm. The overhead valves were operated by pushrods from a central camshaft. Fuel feed was by a diaphragm pump. Two downdraught carburettors were topped by dry air filters. The engine was air-cooled by a centrifugal blower and there was a separate finned tube oil cooler. The lubrication was by forced feed and the ignition energised by a 6-volt battery.

Transmission

The drive was taken by a single dry plate clutch to a constant mesh four-speed and reverse gearbox.

General description: Type 356-1100

Coachwork and chassis

The all-steel body was welded to the floorpan. The two-door coupé (later also convertible) had two rear seats and two 'emergency' seats. The windscreen was V-shaped, but in one piece with slightly rounded sides. The coupé had four side windows, the convertible only two. The headlights were built into the mudguards. While the convertible had a notchback, the coupé was of fastback shape. The front wheels were located by twin trailing links acting upon two transverse torsion bars of square cross section, made up of several steel leaves. At the rear, the swinging half-axles were located by torsionally deformable trailing links each acting on one cylindrical transverse torsion bar. The hydraulic drum brakes had two leading shoes, each operated by its own cylinder at the front, and a leading and trailing shoe operated by a single cylinder at the rear. The wheels were offered in two dimensions: 3.25 and 3.50 D × 16, and there was a choice of three different tyre dimensions: 4.50/5.00/5.25 × 16.

Engine

The 1,100 cc engine, Type 369, was a four-stroke flat-four located in the back of the vehicle. Individual cast iron cylinders were used. The crankcase, pistons and cylinder heads were of light metal, as were the four main bearings, while the big end bearings were steel-backed lead bronze. The air cooling was activated by a centrifugal blower. Two downdraught Solex carburettors, Type 32 PBI of 32 mm (1.26 inches) diameter, were fitted.

Transmission

In addition to the standard four-speed constant mesh gearbox, there were two sets of alternative gear pairs for second, third and top available.

General description: Type 356 A-1300 S

Coachwork and chassis

All-steel 2+2 two-door body, welded to the floor structure incorporating box section members. One-piece, rounded windscreen. The coupé had four side windows, the convertible two. The headlights were integrated into the front mudguards. The coupé had a 'fastback'.

The front suspension comprised two pairs of trailing links acting directly on two square-section torsion bars made up of a bundle of leaves. It was completed by an anti-roll bar. At the rear, two cylindrical torsion bars were directly connected to trailing arms controlling the half-axles. The hydraulic drum brakes had two leading shoes at the front, and a leading and a trailing shoe at the rear. The wheels were 4.50 J × 15 and tyres were available in the dimensions 5.60 × 15 and 5.90 × 15.

Engine

The 1300 S (1600 S) engine had four individual light alloy cylinders with chromium-plated bores. The crankcase, pistons and cylinder heads were of light alloy. The four main bearings were light alloy lined while the connecting rod big ends ran in roller bearings. A vertical blower provided the cooling air. Two Solex downdraught carburettors were fitted, Type 32 PBIC in the 1300 S engine and Type 40 PBIC in the 1600 S. They differed only by their internal diameter of 32 and 40 mm respectively (1.26 and 1.57 inches).

Transmission

In addition to the standard four-speed gearbox, two sets of second, third and fourth gear pinions were available, and two alternatives to the standard final drive were also offered.

Additional equipment

An electric fuel pump and ventilated brake back plates were available from the factory.

The Type 356 aluminium coupés, built in Austria, were well adapted to competition work.

Front and rear views of 356 aluminium coupé. These cars were competitive to the end of 1950.

261

Record breaking in Montlhéry in 1951: 10,968 km (6,815 miles) in 72 hours.

262

The aluminium cars were successful in all branches of the sport, even dirt-track racing. This is the famous one-armed driver Otto Mathé's unique right-hand drive car.

Side view of 1,100 cc-engined 356 coupé: a much-favoured rally car.

Front and rear views of the 356-1100. The competition models of the time were very close to standard.

263

264   *Even the interior of the 356 remained unaltered for competition work.*

Twin-carburettor, four-cylinder engine: 40 bhp from 1,086 cc.

Side view of Type 369 engine with transmission and single exhaust tail pipe.

Front running gear: 100 per cent VW with twin trailing links and torsion bars.

French-owned Type 356 in the 1953 Monte Carlo Rally.

The 356 scored many successes in long-distance rallies.

266

Porsche 356 A with 1300 S engine. This 60 bhp version was made until the end of 1955.

Front and rear views of 356 A-1300 S: suitable for competition work without extra preparation.

267

Interior and instruments, as standard.

The 1300 S engine had roller-mounted big ends and light-alloy main bearings.

*Power train of 356 A-1300 S.
Note twin tail pipes.*

*Front axle: trailing arms,
two transverse torsion
bars, centrally clamped,
anti-roll bar and steering
damper.*

269

*Mille Miglia 1955. Richard
von Frankenberg, first in
class, driving a 1300 S.*

General description: Type 356-1500 GS (Carrera)

Except for the engine, the 1.5-litre A-series Carrera was nearly identical to the basic model 356 A-1300 S. The main difference lay in the engine which was a completely new design, not in any way related to the other, VW-derived Porsche engines. It had a light alloy crankcase, light alloy cylinder heads and pistons, and light alloy individual cylinders of which the bores were chromium-plated. The built-up Hirth crankshaft ran in four roller bearings and so did the connecting rod bearings. The 85×66 mm (3.3×2.6 inch) bore and stroke dimensions were decidedly oversquare, resulting in a comparatively low piston speed. In each of the cylinder heads, slave arm tappets were interposed between the twin overhead camshafts and the valves, arranged in V-formation. Camshaft drive was by shaft and bevel gears. Each combustion chamber had twin plugs fired by two distributors, driven from the intake camshafts. The engine drew its mixture from twin Solex, twin-choke carburettors, Type 40 PJJ-4. Lubrication was by the dry sump system: the oil was aspirated in the sump by a scavenge pump which fed it to a separate tank. The vertical cooling fan was belt-driven at crankshaft speed and was co-axial with the dynamo. With a compression ratio of 9:1, this 1.5-litre engine had an output of 100 bhp at 6,200 rpm. The car's timed maximum speed was just under 200 km/h (125 mph), while the 0 to 60 mph acceleration took 11.3 seconds. The kilometre mark was reached in 31.3 seconds. Under normal conditions, the fuel consumption was 7.7 kilometres per litre (21.5 miles per gallon), premium grade being required.

The gearbox, featuring Porsche split ring synchromesh, was similar to the standard model, except for its slightly higher geared upper two ratios, but two additional gear sets were available for competition use. An exhaust system without connection for interior heating was available. The 5.90-15 tyres of the GS were slightly larger than those of the other models. Another difference was the slightly larger wood-rimmed steering wheel, while instruments were adapted to the higher performance, with readings up to 8,000 rpm and 250 km/h. Proper bucket seats were provided for both driver and co-driver.

Below left: Carrera 1500 GS in action, with bumpers, hub covers, rubber mouldings, etc removed. Below right: Rear view of 1500 GS as normally delivered.

Porsche 356 A-1500 GS
Carrera. Almost
indistinguishable from the
356 A-1300 S.

1500 GS engine: 1,498 cc,
twin ignition, 100 bhp at
6,200 rpm, nearly
200 km/h (124 mph).

Bucket seats for driver
and co-driver of 1500 GS.
The wood-rimmed
steering wheel and the
instrument calibration
differed from other 356 A
models.

Power train of 1500 GS. Wide choice of gearbox ratios.

Front axle was the same as that used on the 356 A-1300 S.

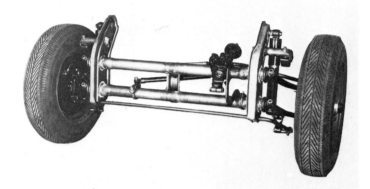

272

A Carrera in action in the famous Liège-Rome-Liège endurance rally of 1955.

General description: Type 356 A-1600 GS (Carrera)

Technically speaking, the 1.6-litre Carrera was almost identical to its 1,500 cc predecessor. Externally, it could be identified by the lack of bumper overriders and by the replacement of the twin stop and tail lights by a single dual-purpose, drop-shaped unit. The number plate was now illuminated from below instead of from above. Right and left of the rear air intake grille, six additional louvres were provided. Weight had been saved by replacing the window winding mechanism by simple leather straps. Only the most essential instruments were provided on the dashboard. Interior mats were reduced to their simplest expression (needle felt or Skai). Driver and co-driver sat in light bucket seats. Except for its slightly larger bore, the main difference between the 1500 and the 1600 GS engines was the use on the latter of a one-piece forged crankshaft with plain bearings throughout. The twin ignition system and the two twin-choke Solex carburettors (Type 40 DJJ-4) were retained, although some cars were fitted with Weber 40 DCM-1 carburettors. Alternative second, third and fourth gear ratios were available for the four-speed gearbox, while the final drive remained unchanged. Competition options were a limited slip differential, an electrically heated windscreen, a free-flow exhaust system, Rudge centre-lock hubs and air intake trumpets to replace the air filters.

Supreme in the 1,600 cc GT class: Porsche 356 A Carrera in action. 273

Porsche 356 A-1600 GS Carrera.
Technically little different from
1500 GS.

Body modifications: lights,
louvered rear cover, no bumper
overriders.

Karl Federhofer driving his
Porsche Carrera 1600 GS. He
scored many successes in the
production GT class.

1600 GS engine: plain bearing crankshaft, 115 bhp at 6,500 rpm.

Spartan interior: leather strap-operated side windows, fewer instruments.

275

1600 GS power train. Limited slip differential and straight-through exhaust optional.

1.6-litre Carrera front axle was similar to 1300 S.

General description: Type 356 B-1600

Coachwork and chassis

Two-door, 2+2 all-steel body welded to a platform reinforced by box section members. One-piece, curved windscreen. The coupé had four side windows, the roadster only two. Pivoted rear quarter windows were provided in the coupé and the hardtop. The headlights were recessed into the front mudguards. The coupé had a 'fastback' tail.

The front suspension had twin trailing arms on each side and two torsion bars consisting of a bundle of spring leaves. The suspension was controlled by an anti-roll bar. At the rear, the swinging half-axles were located by a trailing arm, each acting on a transverse, cylindrical torsion bar. An additional, centrally pivoted transverse single leaf spring was provided to reduce rear roll resistance. The hydraulically operated four-wheel drum brakes had two leading shoes in the front drums. Wheel dimensions were 4.50 S-15 with 5.90-15 or 165-15 tyres. The coupé and the convertible weighed 870 kg (1,918 lb), the roadster 30 kg (66 lb) less.

Several accessories were offered for competition use, among others an 80-litre (17.6-gallon) fuel tank, an electrically heated windscreen, centre lock hubs, bucket seats, a limited slip differential, a free-flow exhaust system and air trumpets to replace the air filters.

Engine

The rear-mounted four-stroke, flat-four engine was air-cooled. The crankcase was of light alloy and two types of individual cylinders were used: Ferral, with cast iron bore surfaces, or Chromal with chromium-plated bores. The pistons and cylinder heads were also of aluminium alloy. The two twin-choke carburettors were either Weber or Solex. The valves were in V-formation and operated from a gear-driven central camshaft by means of pushrods and rockers. The forged crankshaft ran in four tri-metal bearings held in the light alloy crankcase. The cooling air was activated by a centrifugal blower and the engine was lubricated under pressure. Bore and stroke were 82.5×74 mm (3.24×2.9 inches), giving a capacity of 1,582 cc and a power of 90 bhp at 5,500 rpm.

Transmission

The single dry plate clutch transmitted the drive to the four-speed gearbox for which several different gear sets were available, as well as two non-standard final drives.

277

Porsche 356 B-1600: the car for the less ambitious competitor.

278

Front and rear views of 356 B-1600. Competition equipment included large fuel tank, free-flow exhaust and limited slip differential.

Standard interior. For competition, reclining bucket seats and a heated windscreen were available.

The engine remained standard, but it was permissible to replace the air filters with trumpets.

Power train. Note standard alloy radially finned brake drum.

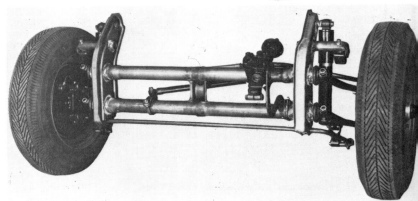

The semi-trailing link front axle remained unchanged.

356 B-1600 with sports equipment in the 1960 Tour de France.

General description: Type 356 B-1600 GS

Coachwork and chassis

The structure composed of the body welded to the platform was similar to the standard 356 B series, but both doors and the front and rear covers were aluminium alloy, which was also used for the structure of the two bucket seats. The rear swinging half-axles were located by torsionally deformable trailing links acting upon transverse, cylindrical torsion bars. A vernier adjustment allowed a very accurate setting of the ride height. The suspension movements were controlled by hydraulic, telescopic dampers while a single leaf, centrally pivoted transverse spring combated oversteer by reducing the rear roll-resistance.

The front wheels were located by two pairs of trailing links connected to two transverse, rectangular section torsion bars, built up from a bundle of spring leaves. An anti-roll bar was fitted.

Hydraulic disc brakes replaced the drum brakes, still available as an option.

The coupé and convertible were made by Reutter, the roadster by D'Ieteren in Belgium and the production of a small series of (drum-braked) competition coupés was entrusted to Carlo Abarth in Turin.

Light alloy 4.5 J-15 rims were riveted to the steel wheel centres. They were shod with 165-15 tyres. The ZF worm and roller steering had a ratio of 16:1; 2½ steering wheel turns were required from lock to lock. The fuel tank took 80 litres (17.6 gallons). Maximum speed was approximately 200 km/h (125 mph).

For competition use, the 1600 GS could be obtained with the following extras: 127 mm (5-inch) wide rims shod with 185-15 or 5.50-15 tyres, special camshafts, Weber 46 JDM carburettors with intake trumpets, a free-flow exhaust system, a more powerful dynamo, an electrically heated windscreen, a roll-over bar, safety belts, centre-lock hubs and camshaft balance weights. Furthermore, a 50- or 100-litre tank (11- or 22-gallon), an independent petrol-electric heater, a non-limited slip differential, Type 356 B drum brakes in normal or GT version, oil bath air filters and light alloy hubcaps could be obtained.

Engine

The 1,587.5 cc engine had bore and stroke dimensions of 87.5 × 66 mm (3.4 × 2.6 inches) and produced 115 bhp at 6,500 rpm. Lubrication was by a dry sump circuit.

The crankcase, cylinder heads, pistons and individual cylinders were of aluminium alloy. The compression ratio was 9.8:1. The crankshaft and big end bearings were tri-metal shells. Four shaft and bevel gear driven overhead camshafts operated two valves per cylinder. Mixture was provided by two Solex downdraught twin-choke carburettors, Type 44 PII-4, fed by two Bendix electric pumps. The engine had a 12-volt twin ignition system.

Transmission

The 200 mm diameter (7.87 inch) Häussermann single dry plate clutch was cable-operated. A wide choice of ratios was available for the four-speed gearbox. The final drive ratio was 7:31. From here the drive was transmitted to the wheels through universally jointed halfshafts.

356 A-1600 GS driven by Huschke von Hanstein in a hill climb.

Below: 1600 GS-GT with bumpers removed in a race on an airfield in 1961. Bottom: The GT version of the 1600 GS produced 115 bhp and was an excellent rally car.

General description: Types 356 B-2000 GS/ 2000 GS/GT (Carrera 2)

Body, chassis and running gear as well as the general equipment were identical with the 1600 GS, but the engine capacity was increased to 1,966 cc. Thanks to the capacity increase, the four-camshaft engine developed 130 bhp at 6,200 rpm in the standard version, and 140 or 155 bhp at 6,200 and 6,600 rpm respectively in the GT versions, according to the type of event for which they were to be used. Compression ratio was 9.5:1 for the standard model and 9.8:1 for the competition version. The standard car had two 40 PII-4 Solex carburettors, while the competition car was fitted with 46 IDM-2 Weber instruments, both of twin-choke specification. The racing engine had steeper cams and soft nitrided connecting rods. All engines had a 12-volt ignition system, but the installation was of higher efficiency in the GT model which also had to use 'harder' Bosch spark plugs.

In the interest of luggage locker capacity, the fuel tank of the GS was limited to 50 litres (11 gallons), but the GT had a 110-litre (24.2-gallon) tank with the large filler cap protruding through the front cover.

While the 2000 GS only came with the standard and the US gear ratios, four different sets were available for the 2000 GT, although in every case the 7:31 final drive was retained. A limited slip differential was standard on the GT and optional on the GS.

In the GT version, the doors and front and rear covers were aluminium-panelled. The frames of the Plexiglas door windows were also of aluminium alloy and the rear quarter windows were fixed. Both these and the rear window were Plexiglas. The decorative windscreen surround was deleted, and so were the rear 'emergency' seats. The steering wheel was wood rimmed and the front and rear bumper overriders were removed, the rear number plate lights now being carried by the bumper itself.

General description: Type 356 B-Carrera GTL-Abarth

Technically, the car was generally similar to the 356 B GS models. It differed mainly as regards its body, designed and manufactured by Carlo Abarth in Turin with the main object of achieving a low air drag. The general appearance was longer and lower. The window area was slightly larger than in the standard model, providing the driver with a better view of the road. All non-essential equipment was eradicated from the interior, but the two bucket seats were both comfortable and functional. Most of the sound-deadening material was deleted. The car weighed approximately 140 kg (309 lb) less than a standard 356 B.

The standard engine had a capacity of 1,588 cc (bore and stroke 87.5 × 66 mm as on the 1600 GS) and produced 115 bhp at 6,500 rpm. There was a twin ignition system and the valves, set in V-formation in the cylinder heads, were operated by twin overhead camshafts. The camshaft drive was by shafts and bevel pinions. The forged crankshaft ran in four plain bearings while lubrication was by the dry sump system incorporating an 8-litre (1.76-gallon) tank. In contrast to normal 356 B models, there was a 12-volt battery providing the energy required by the twin ignition system.

The ratios of the four-speed gearbox were optional. The dry single-plate clutch was a Häussermann unit and a limited slip differential was standard, as was an

80-litre (17.6-gallon) fuel tank. Optional extras were a free-flow exhaust system, intake trumpets, safety belts, a roll-over bar and centre lock hubs. Later, a modified distributor drive (from the crankshaft instead of the camshafts) was made available.

General description: Type 356 C-1600 SC

Coachwork and chassis

The body and the pressed steel box-section platform were welded to a single unit. Front suspension was by twin trailing links connected to transverse spring leaf bundles of rectangular section, each forming a torsion bar. An anti-roll bar was also fitted. Rear suspension was by swinging half-axles located by trailing arms, each connected to a transverse, cylindrical torsion bar. Double-acting telescopic shock absorbers were fitted front and rear. The foot brake hydraulically operated the four disc brakes, while the hand lever operated the rear brakes mechanically. The 4.5 J × 15-inch rims were fitted with 165-15 radial tyres. Tank capacity was 50 litres (11 gallons).

Options: 70- or 90-litre tank (15.4- or 19.8-gallon), petrol-electric heater, intake trumpets, fresh air ventilator, roll-over bar, under-shield for engine and transmission, bucket seats, electrically heated windscreen, light alloy 127 mm (5-inch) wide rims, pivoted compensating transverse single leaf rear spring and a Fichtel & Sachs clutch.

Engine

The 1600 SC engine had a three-piece cast aluminium crankcase. Bore and stroke of 82.5 × 74 mm (3.24 × 2.95 inches) gave a capacity of 1,582 cc. With a compression ratio of 9.5:1, the four-cylinder engine yielded 95 bhp at 5,500 rpm. A forged crankshaft ran in four plain bearings. Bearings 1 and 4 were made of special light alloy, while bearings 2 and 3 were steel-backed thin shell bearings. Thin shell tri-metal bearings were used on the big ends. The small ends carried a bronze bush. The cylinders were Ferral (light alloy with iron-lined bores). Each pair of cylinders carried a single deeply finned light alloy head, with pressed-in valve seats and guides. The plugs were screwed into 'Heli-Coil' inserts. The three-bearing camshaft was located centrally in the crankcase and driven by helical spur gears. From the camshafts, the valves were operated through inverted cup tappets, pushrods and rockers. The exhaust valves were protected by a layer of chrome-nickel steel and were filled with sodium for better cooling.

Two Solex twin choke 40 PII-4 carburettors supplied the mixture. Cooling was by a radial blower, driven from the crankshaft by a V-belt.

Engine lubrication was by forced feed with a full flow cooler to which cooling air was directed from the blower.

There was also a 75 bhp engine available. This had a non-counterweighted crankshaft, cast iron cylinders with pistons giving a compression ratio of 8.5:1, two Zenith twin choke carburettors, Type 32 NDIX, an intake silencer and a 'softer' camshaft.

Transmission

Dry single-plate clutch, cable operated. Central gear lever controlling the Porsche-synchronised four-speed gearbox. There was a choice of two first gear sets and three sets of all other gears. There was also a choice of two final drive ratios. A limited slip differential was not available.

Porsche 356 B-2000 GS-GT. It had a larger rear window and front cover than the 1600, but running gear was unchanged.

Rear and front views of 2000 GS-GT: covers and doors were aluminium, side windows Plexiglas.

285

Power train of 2000 GS-GT with Porsche's own disc brakes.

Front suspension as 1600 GS: twin trailing arms, centrally clamped transverse torsion bars, anti-roll bar.

286

2000 GS-GT engine had four overhead camshafts and was available in three states of tune: 130, 140 and 155 bhp.

The 2000 GT scored class wins in the Monte Carlo Rally in 1963 and in the Midnight Sun Rally.

Porsche Abarth-Carrera GTL. Abarth-built body on 356 B chassis.

288

The Carrera GTL's interior was purely functional.

Characteristic rear view showing large louvered areas and additional air intake.

Front and rear ends were those of the 356 B, with drum brakes.

289

The better body shape and lighter weight gave the Carrera-Abarth an advantage.

The 2000 GS-GT car was developed from the Porsche 356B chassis.

290

Insiders called the
Porsche 2000 GS-
GT 'the wedge', for
obvious reasons.

European GT hill-
climb champion
Herbert Müller
driving a 356 B
with special body.

291

The normal Porsche
356 C with 1600 SC
(95 bhp) engine was
seldom used for
racing, for it stood
little chance.

Type 914-6

The Porsche 914-6 had a comparatively short international sporting life, but it would be unfair to say that it did not put up a good show. It certainly did not achieve such spectacular successes as the contemporary 911 models, but it was an excellent car for long-distance racing, where its comparative lack of power (220 bhp from 2-litres capacity) was made up for by excellent reliability.

The sixth place overall and victory in the GT class obtained by the French drivers Guy Chasseuil and Claude Ballot-Léna in the 1970 Le Mans 24 Hours race was an excellent start to the 914-6's international career. It was followed up by other notable results as fifth and sixth places in the GT class of the Nürburgring 1,000 Km race, fifth place in the GT class in the 6-Hours of Watkins Glen (USA), and first, second and third places in the Marathon de la Route, an 86-hour speed event on the Nürburgring.

An ever-increasing number of private owners, however, preferred the competition version of the 911 S, offered at the same price of DM 49,680 as the 914-6 in competition version. The reason was that the extra half-litre of the 911 S gave it an advantage of more than 50 bhp and a much better chance of an overall GT victory. Most races were run without a separate 2,000 cc GT class anyway, and if one wanted to win the class, being overshadowed by bigger-engined cars was not particularly attractive.

Porsche soon became aware of this problem and as the sales of the production model also stagnated, it was decided to put all eggs into one basket and to enter three factory-prepared 914-6s for the 1971 Monte Carlo Rally. Of these, two retired and only Waldegaard, who had previously won two 'Montes' in a row, driving 911s, reached the finish in third position. To all intents this was the death knell for the 914-6 in international motor sport, although it continued to achieve occasional successes up to 1976.

General description: Type 914-6

Coachwork and chassis
Racing and rally versions of the 914-6 differed from the standard version in the following points: the front and rear covers, front and rear bumpers as well as the rocker panels were of plastic material. The rear window was Plexiglas. The engine compartment cover was lightened and the mudguards were all widened. The interior equipment was much simplified and the upholstery was reduced to a

minimum. While the driver had a fully padded and upholstered bucket seat, the passenger's was bare plastic. There was an engine oil cooler in the nose of the car and the front cover gave access to a 100-litre (22-gallon) steel fuel tank of which the quick action filler cap protruded through the cover. The Targa top, normally removable, was reinforced by a special frame and firmly screwed to the body. The front suspension was of the MacPherson type with triangulated lower links controlled by longitudinal torsion bars. At the rear, the semi-trailing arms, which were reinforced compared with the standard type, were controlled by coil spring and damper struts. Anti-roll bars were fitted front and rear. The rack-and-pinion steering had an overall ratio of 17.1:1. The four radially cooled disc brakes were operated by twin hydraulic circuits. The front calipers were from the 908 racing model, the rear ones those of the Porsche 911. Rim widths were 152 mm (six inches) at the front and 178 mm (seven inches) at the rear, suitable for racing tyres of the dimensions 4.00 M-15 or 4.75/10.00-15 front and 4.75/10.00 or 4.75/11.30-15 rear.

Engine

The racing engine, Type 901/25 retained the bore and stroke dimensions of 80 × 66 mm (3 × 2.6 inches) of the standard flat-six, giving a capacity of 1,991 cc. Compared with the standard engine, the following items were modified: light alloy cylinders with chromium-plated bores were used instead of cast iron cylinders; racing pistons were fitted and the cylinder heads had specially machined intake and exhaust ports. The crankshaft and the connecting rods remained as standard. The two 46 IDA three-choke Weber carburettors were bolted on to special intake manifolds. Racing camshafts, transistor twin ignition and a racing exhaust system contributed to the engine's power output of 220 bhp at 8,000 rpm.

Transmission

The five-speed gearbox, Type 901, was similar to the standard box, but a wide choice of ratios was available for all gears. Final drive was 7:31 with a limited slip differential. The clutch was reinforced in view of the engine's extra power.

356/914-6

Year	Body	Model Type	Chassis no	Engine type	Gearbox type	Cyl	Bore × stroke	Cap-acity	HP (DIN) at rpm	Torque (mkg) at rpm	Comp ratio	W.base (mm)	Track fr/ rear (mm)	Length (mm)	Weight (kg)
1949	Coupé	356-Alu	356/2.053-055	369	VW	4 4	73,5 x 64 75 x 64	1086 1131	40/4200 40/4000	7,15/2800 7,2/2700	7:1 7:1	2100	1250/1290	3870	600
1950	Coupé	356-1100	5001- 5600 10531-12387 50001-51570	369	519	4	73,5 x 64	1086	40/4200	7,15/2800	7:1	2100	1290/1250	3950	790
1955	Coupé Cabriolet	356A-1300S	55001-55390 61001-61892	589/2	644	4	74,5 x 74	1290	60/5500	9,0/3600	7,5:1	2100	1306/1272	3950	845
1955	Coupé Cabriolet	356A-1600S	55001-55390 61001-61892	616/2	716/0 716/2 644	4	82,5 x 74	1582	75/5000	11,9/3700	8,5:1	2100	1306/1272	3950	845
1955	Coupé Cabriolet	356A-1500GS	12235-12387 53456-59090 55001-55390 61001-61892	547/1	716/5 644 716/1 716/4	4	85 x 66	1498	100/6500	12,0/5200	9:1	2100	1306/1272	3950	835
1957	Coupé	356A-1500GS de luxe	58312-59090	547/1	741/1	4	85 x 66	1498	100/6200	12,1/5200	9:1	2100	1306/1272	3950	950
1957	Coupé	356A-1500 GS-GT	58312-59090	547/1	741/1	4	85 x 66	1498	110/6400	12,6/5200	9:1	2100	1306/1272	3950	835
1958	Coupé Cabriolet Speed.	356A-1600GS de luxe	150001-153334 104524-106174 84938- 85886	692/2	741/3	4	87,5 x 66	1588	105/6500	12,3/5000	9,5:1	2100	1306/1272	3950	840

294

356/914-6

Year	Body	Model Type	Chassis no	Engine type	Gearbox type	Cyl	Bore × stroke	Cap-acity	HP (DIN) at rpm	Torque (mkg) at rpm	Comp ratio	W.base (mm)	Track fr/ rear (mm)	Length (mm)	Weight (kg)
1959	Coupé Cabriolet Speed.	356A-1600 GS-GT	150001- 15334 104524-106174 84938- 85886	692/3	741/1	4	87,5 x 66	1588	115/6500	12,8/5500	9,8:1	2100	1306/1272	3950	880
1960	Coupé 'Abarth'	356B-1600 GTL	11001-1021	692/3A	741/5 741/6 741/7 741/8	4	87,5 x 66	1588	115/6500	12,8/5500	9,8:1	2100	1306/1272	3980	778
1960	Coupé	356B-1600 GS-GT	104524-106174	692/3	741/1 741/3 741/4	4	87,5 x 66	1588	115/6500	12,8/5500	9,8:1	2100	1306/1272	4010	900
1961	Coupé	356B-2000GS	119289-121099	587/1	741/9A 741/20A	4	92 x 74	1966	130/6200	16,5/4600	9,5:1	2100	1306/1272	4010	1020
1963	Coupé	356C-2000GS	119289-125239 156566-158700	587/2	741/9A	4	92 x 74	1966	130/6200	16,5/4600	9,5:1	2100	1306/1272	4010	1020
1971	Coupé	914-6	9141430139-0141	901/25	914	6	80 x 66	1991	220/7800	20,5/6500	10,3:1	2450	1377/1427	3985	880

First version of VW-Porsche 914-6. The wheel arches were not yet finalised.

Front and rear views of 914-6 as prepared for the endurance event Marathon de la Route.

296

Front and rear
covers, bumpers
and rocker panels
were made of
glass fibre.

100-litre (22-
gallon) fuel tank,
reinforced damper
mountings, hand-
operated pop-up
lights.

*VW-Porsche 914-6
in racing trim:
220 bhp from the
2-litre, six-cylinder
engine.*

*Lightened interior,
simplified trim and
racing bucket
seats.*

298

*Swedish driver
Aake Andersson
practising for the
1971 Monte Carlo
Rally in a 914-6.*

Types 911-2.0/911 S-2.5

The successful activities of the Porsche private owners with the standard and tuned 356 models came to an end after a period of nearly 15 years, but the new 2-litre 911 soon took over. Production and sales of the six-cylinder model began in September 1964 and, little more than three months later, a factory-prepared car took part in the Monte Carlo Rally. Although it was not yet eligible for the GT Group, the new car entrusted to Peter Falk and Herbert Linge, two of the factory's development engineers and testers, acquitted itself beautifully, and after covering 4,600 gruelling rally kilometres, (2,858 miles) it finished fifth overall! Thus the 911's sporting career began just as successfully as the career of the 356, when the only car of its type in the race won its class at Le Mans in 1951. But the 911 was not the best-placed Porsche in that year's Monte Carlo Rally: Eugen Böhringer and Rolf Wütherich drove a Porsche 904 GTS into second place, beaten only by the Makinen-Easter Mini-Cooper!

Thereafter, the 2-litre 911 went from success to success. They were particularly successful in long-distance events, in which the advantages of the air-cooled six-cylinder and the reliability of the Zuffenhausen product were especially valuable. The factory drivers of the 1960s, particularly the Finn Pauli Toivonen, the Briton Vic Elford and the German driver Günther Klass, scored innumerable victories and obtained several national titles.

In 1967, the British pair Vic Elford and his navigator David Stone became European Rally Champions, driving a 170 bhp 2-litre 911 S, while the hitherto little known Polish driver Sobieslav Zasada became European Touring Car Champion in the same year, driving a 912.

Other successes were no less spectacular: for the first time in the history of motor sport, a car fitted with a production automatic transmission (Sportomatic) won an internationl speed event first time out. This is what a 911 did when Hans Herrmann, Vic Elford and Jochen Neerpasch won the 86-hour Marathon de la Route on the Nürburgring.

At the end of 1967, Porsche built a small series of a racing version of the 911, called 911 R, of which the factory kept three for its own use, while the remaining 19 were sold to selected customers. According to the sporting regulations, the 911 R was technically a prototype, but it was actually based on a production body shell into which a Carrera-6 engine developing 210 bhp was dropped and which weighed only 830 kg (1,830 lb) thanks to its extremely spartan equipment and the use of many plastic components. Eventually the factory did not really 'push' the model. In the Targa Florio of 1969, one of them was used as a guinea pig with a four-camshaft six-cylinder engine, but except for a victorious factory entry in the Tour de France, that was the 911 R's last official appearance.

Porsches were particularly successful in rallies. In 1968 Pauli Toivonen, usually driving without factory assistance, won the European Rally Championship with a factory-prepared 911 T and Porsche became the Rally Champion manufacturer, although this was not yet officially recognised. In the Monte Carlo Rally, 911 Ts took first and second places overall with the crews Vic Elford/David Stone and Pauli Toivonen/Martti Tiukkanen. In recognition of the exceptional performances of Porsche 911 models in long-distance races, the FIA honoured the Stuttgart factory with the International Constructor's Trophy for GT cars.

The 1969 season started no less successfully with first and second place again in the Monte Carlo Rally. This time victory went to the Swedish team of Björn Waldegaard/Hans Helmer, followed by the French crew of Gérard Larrousse/Jean Perramond. The Swedish team confirmed their performance four weeks later, winning the Swedish Rally, while the French answered with victory in the Neige et Glace Rally. The entry list for the 1969 Touring Car race on the Nürburgring was typical of the complicated classification of various Porsche 911 models in different homologation groups. The race was won by the Dutchmen Gijs van Lennep and Toine Hezemans, driving a Group 5 car, while fifth place was taken by Kremer-Gall, driving a privately owned 911 which won the Touring car classification!

Successes continued to pour in. Sobieslav Zasada won the 2,110-kilometre (1,320-mile) Polish Rally with a 911 T, and the French pair composed of Chasseuil and Ballot-Léna, a genuine private entry, won the Spa 24 Hours race from prominent factory teams. The 5,000-kilometre (over 3,000 miles) Tour de France Automobile was won by works driver Gérard Larrousse and his new co-driver Maurice Gelin, sharing a 911 R. The same team was again victorious, this time as private entrants of a factory-owned 911 R, in the Tour of Corsica in which they beat the factory entered and assisted teams of Alpine, Ford and Lancia. The 1970 Monte Carlo Rally was a repetition of the previous year's: again, the Porsche team took the first two places, headed by Björn Waldegaard, who also won the Swedish Rally and the Austrian Alpine Rally in quick succession. With Larrousse finishing sixth in the RAC Rally, in spite of various problems, the Rally Championship was again Porsche's. The tool of the achievement had been a specially prepared 2.2-litre 911 S.

From 1971 on, the stage for Porsche's sporting successes slowly shifted from international rallies to racing tracks. In its racing version, in which its capacity had been increased to 2.3 litres, the 911 S engine developed a good 240 bhp and its reliability earned it many successes in long-distance racing. No wonder then, that the winner of the Porsche Cup, which in 1971 was organised for the second time, came from the circuit exponents. Porsche dealer and tuning specialist Erwin Kremer, who won the cup, won the GT class in the races counting towards the World Championship of Makes at Monza, Spa and the Nürburgring. In addition, he won the Nürburgring 500 km (310 miles) race, the 1,000 km (620 miles) races in Paris and Barcelona as well as the 6 Hours of Jarama. Progressively, Porsche moved out of production car racing in order to better concentrate on sports car and prototype racing, while continuing to offer competitive versions of production models to private owners. The last event officially supported by the factory with 911 models was the Tour de France of 1970. The car entered was a 260 bhp 2.4-litre model weighing only 780 kg (1,720 lb). Some factory support was also provided in later years for a 2.2-litre 911 S and later for a Carrera RS in the Safari Rally and also in the Monte Carlo Rally.

For private owners taking part in competitions, small series of special models were produced. The last competition version of the 911 with the old body was offered in 1972. It was a lightened 911 S with a 2.5-litre engine developing 270 bhp and it cost DM 49,000. But even in its first season, it became clear that this 2.5-litre model would not be able to resist the pressure of its competitors. Specially in the touring car class, ever faster cars were being developed and the Porsche 911 almost became an 'also ran'. To remedy this embarassing situation, the Carrera 2.7 RS was developed for the 1973 season. It was followed, one year later, by the formidable Carrera 3.0 RS.

General description: Type 911-2.0 'Monte Carlo'

Coachwork and chassis
The body of the first Monte Carlo cars was generally very similar to that of the production models. Those bright red cars were equipped with an artificial leather and cloth covered passenger seat with a headrest. The driver sat in a bucket seat similar to that used in the Type 356 C competition model. The interior trim was moderately simplified, while rubber fasteners kept the front cover firmly closed. Seat belts were provided for driver and co-driver. A second reservoir doubled the capacity of the windscreen washer, while an anti-mist plastic panel was stuck on the rear window. A towing eye was welded to the rear of the body, while the rear bumper was fitted with a step bar and two grab handles were also welded to the body. A tool box was provided between the seats and there was a left foot rest for the driver. The regulator was deleted from the heating system. A second speedometer cable was fitted, ready to be connected, and the windscreen wipers parked on the co-driver's instead of the driver's side.

There were also a rear window wiper, a Tripmaster, a lighter wooden steering wheel and a 100-litre (22-gallon) fuel tank. The Teroson underbody sealing, the anti-drumming material and the sound-insulating mats were deleted.

The running gear was modified as follows: the MacPherson struts, including dampers, were of Boge manufacture; there was a rear anti-roll bar and the brake discs were unshielded. There were also larger rear brake calipers, racing brake fluid was used, the front brakes were fitted with cooling air pickups, and there was a throttle pedal to stop to relieve the load on the linkage, which itself had specially secured connections.

Engine
The standard 2-litre, six-cylinder engine was tuned to increase its power from 130 to nearly 160 bhp. The modifications included polished intake ports, increased compression ratio, different camshafts, different carburettors on polished intake manifolds, platinum-pointed spark plugs, a different exhaust silencer, free venting of the oil tank, a lightened flywheel, a specially prepared generator and special spark plug caps.

Transmission
The five-speed gearbox was standard, but with lower gearing. Different clutch linings took care of the slightly increased power and the gearbox primary shaft was from the 904 racing car. A ZF limited slip differential was fitted.

Only three months after
production started, the
911-2.0 took part in its
first international rally.

Linge and Falk drove a
Porsche 911/2.0 in its
first sporting event: the
1965 Monte Carlo Rally.

Racing successes were
scored at Nürburgring
(right) and Spa.

General description: Type 911 S-2.0 'Rally'

Coachwork and chassis

As originally used for rally work in 1967, the 911 S-2.0 was not much different from standard. The dark red factory cars were fitted with a heated rear window and a rear wiper, with Catacolor glass all round and a reclining passenger seat with a cylindrical headrest. The driver sat in a normal bucket seat. The front bumper reinforcements (read 'ballast weights'!), the fog lights, the 'emergency' seat squabs, the anti-drumming material, the sound-damping mats and the velvet carpets were deleted.

Some components were added, such as a 100-litre (22-gallon) fuel tank replacing the standard part, and an outside thermometer. The instruments were slightly modified and experimental front brake calipers with non-standard pistons were used. The rear brakes remained standard, but racing brake fluid was specified. Front suspension struts incorporating Koni dampers were fitted and special throttle linkage connections were again used.

Engine

The power of the engine Type 2000 S was raised from 160 to 170 bhp thanks to air intake pipes of 34 mm (1.34 inches) diameter, larger air corrector jets, harder sparking plugs and a nearly free exhaust system.

Transmission

Another gear set providing lower gearing was provided in the standard five-speed gearbox. The limited slip differential and the half-shafts were from the Type 904.

General description: Type 911 R-2.0

Coachwork and chassis

A small special series of 911 R ('R' for racing) was built by the Stuttgart coachwork factory of Karl Baur in co-operation with Porsche. The sheet metal gauge remained unchanged, but the door and front and rear cover hinges were manufactured in aluminium. The covers themselves were glass fibre reinforced plastic as were the front mudguards and both front and rear bumpers. The oil connections leading from the engine to the oil cooler located in one of the front mudguards and back were led through the rocker panels. The external shape of the front mudguards remained unchanged as the plastic material did not require rolled wheel opening edges, but the rear wheel openings were pushed out slightly to accommodate the wider rims.

The windscreen was only 4 mm thick and the Plexiglas side windows only 2 mm. The door windows were fixed, but incorporated a pivoted panel, as in the Porsche 906, while the fixed rear quarter window had ventilating louvres as well as a water gutter. The rear window was 2 mm thick Plexidur.

Differences from the standard 911 included an aluminium oil tank mounted ahead of the rear axle, with its vent and filler cap in the right-hand rear body panel. Special Scheel bucket seats were fitted and the rear squabs were deleted. The independent petrol-electric heater was offered only as an option. There was no sun visor on the passenger side and the 100-litre (22-gallon) fuel tank (steel or plastic to choice) had an external filler. The electricals were little modified from the 911 S, but the instrument panel was simplified. Ashtray and cigar lighter were deleted and only three circular dials (speedometer, tachometer and a combined instrument) and a centrally located fuel level warning light remained. There was a 'Monza' steering wheel (without a horn button, which was moved to the dashboard) and both the steering column stalks and the ignition switch remained, the latter however without the steering lock.

If the standard white colour was not desired, the customer was requested to specify his colour choice at least three weeks before the completion of the car.

The running gear and, among others the dampers, anti-roll bars and suspension torsion bars remained as standard. Larger brake calipers were fitted to take care of the increased performance and the sporting destination of the 'R'. Girling racing brake fluid was specified and the standard rim widths were 152 mm (six inches) at the front and 178 mm (seven inches) at the rear.

Engine
The Type 901/22 engine was used. Basically, it was similar to the standard 911 S-2.0. The air-cooled flat-six unit had an eight-bearing forged crankshaft and developed 210 bhp at 8,000 rpm. The cylinder heads were light alloy and the bores of the light alloy cylinders were chromium-plated. The two overhead camshafts (one for each bank of cylinders) were chain driven. Two electric pumps fed the fuel to the two Type 46 Weber three-choke carburettors. The lubrication was by the dry sump system. The 12-volt alternator had a capacity of 840 watts and its shaft was extended to carry the engine cooling blower. The twin ignition system was partly transistorised. In most of its details, the engine was similar to the 906 (Carrera-6) engine.

Transmission
The Nürburgring gear set was standard in the five-speed gearbox, but two other sets were available. A 6:32 crown wheel and pinion assembly was available as an alternative to the 7:31 combination. The gearbox shafts were from the 906 (Carrera-6) and the limited slip differential drove Nadella half-shafts with special universals, also accommodating length variations, mounted on the differential side. The single plate clutch was specially modified.

Pauli Toivonen in the 1968 Castrol Rally: 911-2.0 with fuel injection and long wheelbase.

Porsche 911 T-2.0: overall winner of the 1968 Monte Carlo Rally, driven by V. Elford/ D. Stone.

305

Porsche 911 S-2.0. French-owned car in the 1969 Lyon-Charbonnières Rally.

306

1969 Spa 24 Hours race: Chasseuil/Ballot Léna won with a private 911-2.0.

Porsche 911 R-2.0. First model of the 'R' (Racing) series. Weight: 830 kg (1,830 lb).

308   *Side views of the Porsche 911 R. Above: Production model. Below: Prototype.*

Doors, covers, front mudguards and both bumpers were glass fibre.

This 911 R driven by Gérard Larrousse won the Tour de France Automobile in 1969.

310

Tour de Corse 1969. A works-entered 911 R with four-camshaft engine.

Porsche four-camshaft, six-cylinder, 2-litre engine: 230 bhp.

911 R with Sportomatic, winner of the 84-hour Marathon de la Route in 1969.

General description: Types 911 S-2.2/2.3

Coachwork and chassis

For the 1970 racing and rally season, the 2.2-litre 911 S became the base for most competition versions. While the engine was kept almost standard for rally work (as in the case of the Safari rally), the racing version had its capacity increased by 52 cc while its power went up from 180 to 240 bhp. The racing 911 S (internally known as 'ST') differed from the standard model in several ways: thin gauge sheet metal was used for the roof panel, for both rear side panels and for the seat pan back and side panels. The following body parts were deleted: the seat slide supports on the central backbone, all standard seat belt anchorage points, the heater ducts, the ashtray, the glove box lid and the tubes for the front and rear cover opening cables. Door and bumper decorative mouldings were also deleted, as were the front and rear cover locks, the foglight recess covers, the front torsion bar protections, the covers giving access to the rear torsion bars and the sun visor on the passenger side. Sheet metal joints were not filled, the body was not undersealed and both the rubber and sound damping felt mats were deleted. Even the paint was kept as thin as possible to reduce weight.

Parts were available for further lightening and modifications, such as: plastic front cover, plastic front and rear bumpers, front mudguard extensions, aluminium doors of which the frame was 0.75 mm thick steel, and Plexiglas for all windows, except the windscreen.

The front end of the car was stiffened by a transverse bar between the strut consoles in the luggage compartment. A special rally or circuit fuel tank of 80 or 110 litres capacity (17.6 or 24.2 gallons), which could be filled through an aperture in the front cover, was available to replace the standard 62-litre (13.6-gallon) tank with filler in the left front mudguard. For rallies, forged light alloy wheels with a 152 mm (6-inch) wide rim at the front and 178 mm (7-inch) at the rear were used, while 178 mm and 228 mm (9-inch) wide rims were fitted for circuit work. Further optional competition equipment included a supplementary petrol-electric heater (rallies only), a ventilating fan, two Recaro sports seats, tape to cover the moulding fitting holes, simplified internal trim, thinner windscreen glass, lighter knee protection padding, rubber fasteners for front and rear covers, a supplementary battery (rallies only), an aluminium roll-over bar, a space-saver spare tyre, and steel mudguard side extensions to cover the wider rear wheels.

For long distance rallies, such as the Safari, the special preparation of the 911 S was as follows. The lightened standard body was further reduced in weight by the use of glass-fibre reinforced plastic components, such as the front cover and the front and rear bumpers. All glass areas were Plexiglas, except for the windscreen. The co-driver sat in a sports seat and the driver in a Recaro bucket. Further equipment included: a reading lamp, a Speed Pilot, a socket for a portable lamp, air horns, Plexiglas covers for the additional lights, 100-watt headlight bulbs, a large map pocket, a tool bag secured to the rear bulkhead, three jacks, complete rally tools, a special tool for quick-changing the front suspension struts, two fire extinguishers, a fire extinguishing jet in the bell housing, a straight-through silencer, a wire mesh protection for the oil tank, and splash flaps at the rear.

The normal production running gear was little changed. The front suspension used the standard torsion bars as well as the standard 15 mm (0.6 inch) diameter anti-roll bar. Toe-in was zero, camber −30'. Koni front struts were used and in many cases the standard brakes were replaced by those of the 908.02 racing model. The rear suspension torsion bars (23 mm/0.9 inch diameter) and anti-roll bar (16 mm/0.6 inch diameter) were also standard parts. Basic settings for the rear axle were also standard with 0° toe-in and −1°30′ negative camber. The dampers were Koni, aluminium brake calipers replaced the cast iron originals, and the hub studs were longer than standard.

Some special equipment was used for the Safari rally, such as reinforced Koni 'tropical' shock absorbers, while the wishbones, the steering and its linkage were reinforced; 20 or 21 mm diameter (approximately 0.8 inch) front torsion bars were used. There were reinforced rear semi-trailing links and attachment brackets. In contrast with the racing version, there was no special protection for the brake pipes, but the front strut consoles were reinforced and both the front and rear running gear were protected by an aluminium underpan. Spare clutch and throttle cables were fitted and the cog-belt driving the injection pump was enclosed in a protective cover.

Engine

For rallies, the 2,195 cc engine remained as standard, developing 180 bhp at 7,200 rpm. The racing version had its cylinder bores increased by 1 mm to raise the capacity to 2,247 cc. With a compression ratio of 10.3:1 it produced 240 bhp at 7,800 rpm. The crankcase was pressure cast in magnesium alloy. The cylinders had chromium-plated bores and the cylinder heads were of aluminium alloy. The forged crankshaft ran in eight bearings. The connecting rods were steel and thin shell bearings were used both for the main bearings and big ends. The engine had dry sump lubrication and was fed through two electric fuel pumps. Injection was by a Bosch twin-row, six-plunger pump, while the twin ignition system was also of Bosch manufacture.

Transmission

The five-speed gearbox and differential unit were mounted in a single casing. Various gear sets were available. The final drive was by spiral bevel and crown wheel through a limited slip differential of Powr-Lok pattern. The wheels were driven through half axles incorporating two constant velocity universals, also taking up the length variations. The single plate dry clutch was reinforced.

313

Porsche ST-2.2, a lightweight version of the 911 S-2.2.

The basic 911 S model was offered with optional glass-fibre and Plexiglas parts.

314

In the British RAC Rally of 1970, Gérard Larrousse took fifth place with this ST model.

Driving a 2.2-litre ST, Waldegaard and Helmer won the Alpine Rally.

1970: Waldegaard winning the Swedish Rally (left) and (below) Larrousse, second in Monte Carlo Rally behind Waldegaard's similar car.

General description: Type 911 S-2.4 (Tour de France)

Coachwork and chassis

Floor pan, body structure and rear mudguards were standard, but bare of any protecting or soundproofing material. Side and rear windows were Plexiglas. The front mudguards, doors, covers and bumpers were all glass fibre. The interior was strictly functional, regardless of appearance. All non-structural parts were lightened, some of them by drilling. Exceptionally light bucket seats were fitted, and where in the standard car the 'emergency' seats were located, there was only bare metal.

No important modifications were made to the chassis and running gear, except at the front where there was an additional tube linking the front strut consoles. The light alloy wheels were 7 × 15 inches front and 9 × 15 inches rear, made by Minilite. The brakes, featuring four ventilated discs, were standard. Weighing only 789 kg (1,739 lb) this was the lightest 911 ever built, still keeping the standard floor pan and running gear.

Engine

The engine was more highly developed than for other 911 S competition models. In addition to the 1 mm bore increase, the stroke was increased from 66 to 70.4 mm (2.6 to 2.77 inches) giving a total capacity of 2,395 cc. The connecting rod material was titanium. The injection system was replaced by two three-choke Webers. The compression ratio was 10.3:1 and the ignition was transistorised. The valve timing was as for other 911 racing engines and the exhaust silencer was more symbolic than effective. At 8,000 rpm, the power was 245 bhp, giving a top speed of 243 km/h (151 mph).

Transmission

The first four gears in the five-speed gearbox were low geared and very closely spaced, with a rather large step to fifth gear. The final drive ratio was 7:31. A limited slip differential with 40 per cent locking factor was fitted and the single plate clutch was reinforced.

General description: Type 911 S-2.2 (Safari)

Coachwork and chassis

The body and running gear were very close to standard. For the East African Safari, the following additions were made: a reading lamp for the co-driver, a Twinmaster, an additional floor-mounted button for the external air horns, and accommodation for route maps and notes. The car was also fitted with a master switch inside the passenger compartment (an external switch was also provided), spare ignition system units, additional wide beam and long-range lights, two jacks, a special wheel brace, a hand winch, emergency spares, a fire extinguisher, special tools, a partly padded roll-over bar and safety harnesses for driver and co-driver.

The standard running gear with special Bilstein dampers was raised and an additional engine oil cooler provided under the left-hand front mudguard. An aluminium underpan protected the front and rear axles as well as the engine and the transmission. The oil tank was specially protected and spare oil lines were fitted for quick connection in case of necessity. The front cover hid a 100-litre (22-gallon) fuel tank as well as a separate 20-litre (4.4-gallon) spare tank. There were three fuel pumps of which two were normally in use with the third kept for emergencies. Low gearing reduced the maximum speed to about 180 km/h (112 mph).

Engine
The engine was a standard 911 S giving 180 bhp at 7,200 rpm.

Transmission
Standard five-speed gearbox with Monte Carlo ratios (top speed 112 mph). The differential had a 40 per cent locking factor.

General description: Type 911 S-2.5

Coachwork and chassis
The body was largely identical to the standard 911. The black interior trim was simplified, however, and the two seats were buckets. The mudguards were widened front and rear to accommodate racing wheels and tyres. The front glass fibre bumper was in one piece with an air dam. The roof and interior panels were covered with black felt. The steering wheel of only 380 mm (15 inches) diameter was padded and leather covered. A 10,000 rpm tachometer was fitted and the 110-litre (24.2-gallon) fuel tank had a large filler protruding through the front cover.

The front suspension was by MacPherson damper struts and lower wishbones, while semi-trailing arms were fitted at the rear. The front torsion bars were longitudinal, the rear ones transverse. The dampers were hydraulic, double acting, incorporated in the struts at the front. There were quickly removable anti-roll bars front and rear. The four radially ventilated disc brakes were operated by twin (one front, one rear) circuits and racing brake pads and brake fluid were specified. The running gear was lowered and the rim widths were seven inches front and nine inches rear, with tyres of the dimensions 4.75/10.00-15 and 4.30/11.60-15, respectively.

Engine
The standard 2.4 911 S engine was modified within the frame of the International Sporting Regulations. The crankcase, crankshaft and connecting rods remained standard. The modifications were the following: bored-out light alloy cylinders giving a capacity of 2,492 cc, with appropriate racing pistons; cylinder heads with polished intake and exhaust ports and larger valves; Bosch racing injection system or twin Weber Type 46 IDA carburettors to choice; racing camshafts; racing exhaust system; specially reinforced clutch and transistor twin ignition system. A power of 270 bhp at 8,000 rpm was claimed by the makers, with a maximum torque of 26.5 mkg (193 lb/ft) at 6,300 rpm.

Transmission
The transmission remained standard, but all gear pairs were interchangeable. A limited slip differential was bolted to the 7:31 final drive gears. A separate oil pump lubricated the gearbox by jets. Each half-shaft incorporated twin constant velocity universals, also accommodating length variations.

Lightest-ever 911: the 780 kg (1,720 lb) ST used in the 1970 Tour de France. It had a 2.4-litre engine and produced 245 bhp.

318

Larrousse drove the ultra-light prototype into second place.

Porsche 911 S Safari, 2.2 litres: 100-litre (22-gallon) tank and separate reserve tank.

Body and running gear were very similar to the standard 911 S.

319

The Porsche 911 S-2.2 in the 1971 Safari Rally, driven by Swede Aake Andersson.

The body of the Porsche 911 S-2.5 was based on the standard 911 S with a 2.4-litre engine.

The front and rear wheel arches were flared and the combined front spoiler and bumper was made of glass fibre.

911 S racing version: the 2.5-litre engine produced 270 bhp.

This 911 S had its engine oil cooler mounted ahead of the small front spoiler.

In the Monte Carlo Rally of 1972, two Porsche 911 S-2.5s were entered with the help of an outside sponsor.

322

The 'Monte' cars were prepared in the factory's tradition, but remained unsuccessful.   323

324

911

Year	Body	Model Type	Chassis no	Engine type	Gearbox type	Cyl	Bore × stroke	Cap-acity	HP (DIN) at rpm	Torque (mkg) at rpm	Comp ratio	W.base (mm)	Track fr/ rear (mm)	Length (mm)	Weight (kg)
1965	Coupé	911-2.0 'Monte'	303075-076 303085	901/02	902/2	6	80 × 66	1991	160/6600	18,2/5200	9.8:1	2211	1367/1339	4163	1030
1967	Coupé	911S-2.0 'Rallye'	30665S-657S	901/30	901/30	6	80 x 66	1991	170/7300	18,5/5200	10:1	2211	1367/1339	4163	1030
1967	Coupé	911R-2.0	307670-671/ 305876 11899001R- 118990019R	901/22	901/54 901/50 901/53	6	80 x 66	1991	210/8000	21/6000	10,5:1	2211	1370/1370	4100	800
1970	Coupé	911S-2.2 2.2 'Rallye'	9110300001- 0003 9110300949- 0950	911/02	901	6	84 x 66	2195	180/6500	20,3/5200	9,8:1	2268	1374/1355	4163	960
1970	Coupé	911S- 2.3	9110300001- 0003	911/20	901	6	85 x 66	2247	240/7800	23/6300	10,3:1	2268	1374/1355	4163	840
1970	Coupé	911S- 2.4 'Proto'	911030949	911/21	901	6	85 x 70,4	2395	260/8000	25/6500	10,3:1	2268	1402/1421	4100	790
1971	Coupé	911S- 2.2 'Safari'	9111300637 9111300683 9111300612 9111300589 9111300561	911/02	901	6	84 x 66	2195	180/6500	20,3/5200	9,8:1	2268	1374/1355	4163	980
1972	Coupé	911S- 2.5	9112300041/ 047	911/73	915	6	89 x66	2466	270/8000	26,5/6300	10,3:1	2271	1402/1421	4147	960
				911/70		6	86,7x70,4	2492	270/8000	26,5/6300	10,3:1				

Types Carrera 2.7/934 Turbo

At the end of 1972, the famous name of 'Carrera RS' was revived for a new model destined to become immensely successful, although it was little more than a 911 S fitted with a slightly larger engine and weighing just over 900 kg (1,984 lb). By the end of 1973, private owners and works drivers of this model were able to claim victory in three international and seven national championships in all parts of the world.

In the GT category the Carrera RSR found no opposition, and races counting towards the European GT Championship of 1973 turned into a Porsche festival. The races were nevertheless very exciting and were contested by a large number of cars. Most of the time they turned into epic battles between Group 4 Carrera private owners, but there were exceptions: the races in Imola and Hockenheim were both won by factory-entered De Tomaso Panteras driven by Mike Parkes and Clay Regazzoni respectively. Eventually the German driver Clemens Schickentanz and the Frenchman Claude Ballot-Léna dead-heated in the championship, while the 58-year old Sepp Greger won the GT class of the European Hill Climb Championship, driving his own Carrera RSR.

As a test for the Carrera RS 2.7 in dusty off-road rallies, Porsche entered two factory cars for the formidable Safari Rally in East Africa. Both cars, driven respectively by the Swedish team of Björn Waldegaard/Hans Thorszelius and the Polish team of Zasada/Bien failed to finish, but only minor defects caused their retirement. Only a few weeks later the Finn Leo Kinnunen drove one of the Safari cars into third place in his homeland's 1,000 Lakes Rally. It was finally left to a private team, composed of hotel owner Gert Behret and his co-driver Willy-Peter Pitz, to win the 1973 German Rally Championship and prove the suitability of the Carrera 2.7 RS for that type of event. To win the championship, Behret and Pitz took seven class victories and three overall victories.

In all, Carrera RS drivers clinched national championships in seven different countries. Specially creditable was the victory of the American driver Peter Gregg in the Trans-Am series, run to rules rather similar to the European Touring Car Championship in which the Carrera had to fight off the large capacity Camaros and Corvettes. In addition, Gregg clinched the American IMSA Championship for GT cars.

In 1974 the domination of the two Cologne-based private teams of Erwin Kremer and Georg Loos grew on most of the world's racing tracks. Special credit must go to Loos for bringing drivers of such high international reputation as Tim

Schenken, Jody Scheckter and Arturo Merzario into GT racing. Porsches also won the GT class in most of the sports car races counting towards the World Championship of Makes, which earned the company the FIA World Cup for GT cars. But Porsche still had not digested the failure of the two Carreras in the Safari Rally, so one of the previous year's cars was again entered for Björn Waldegaard and Hans Thorszelius who, this time, dominated the event until very near to the finish. They were very unfortunate in that the only serious defect of the running gear (a broken half-shaft) happened at night, in a tremendous downpour, and the repair took so long that they had to be content with second place.

While the Safari car was still the previous year's model, the new Carrera RS 3.0 and RSR 3.0 were again dominating the standard GT and special GT classes in European racing. Driving alternatively for the Kremer and Loos teams, John Fitzpatrick won the European GT Championship following a very successful season. In the European Hill Climb Championship too, a Carrera RSR was again victorious, this time with hill-climb specialist Tony Fischaber, while Peter Gregg made sure of winning two American National titles again.

But 1975 was even more fascinating for Carrera RSR supporters, especially in America where BMW had decided to put an end to the Porsche supremacy in the IMSA series which had gone to Porsche drivers for five consecutive years. To achieve their aim they entered factory cars driven by Formula 1 drivers in all important races. Even General Motors began to find the Porsche domination somewhat embarrassing and provided private entrants with the means to make their Chevrolet Corvettes, Camaros and Monzas ever faster and more reliable, but none could stop the Porsche drivers: Peter Gregg, who had won the series three times, and his co-driver Hurley Haywood won eight of the 14 races, while the BMW factory entries won five times and one race was won by a Chevrolet Corvette. Second and third place in the IMSA Championship also went to Porsche drivers who all headed BMW works driver Hans Stuck.

But the 1975 season ended with many more titles for the Carrera RSR, the 3-litre engine of which developed some 345 bhp at the end of the season. Among those titles were the European GT Championship, won by the German driver Hartwig Bertrams; the European Hill Climb Championship for GT cars which went to the Swiss Jean-Claude Bering; the FIA World Cup for GT cars; and the German Rally Championship, which was won by Rainer Altenheimer and Hanno Menne who drove a standard production Carrera RS.

That, however, was the end of the Carrera era in international racing, an era which had lasted for only three years. For 1976, Porsche offered its customers a new 'bomb': a racing version of Germany's fastest production sports car: the Porsche Turbo. To stay ahead of the opposition this 485 bhp thoroughbred which Zuffenhausen offered for no less than DM 108,000 was to become the absolute weapon. As for so many other Porsche racing models, the Daytona 24 Hours race run at the beginning of the year, was the 934 Turbo's maiden race. A single car faced the formidable competition from American Touring and 'Stock' cars, as well as from the 480 bhp BMW factory coupés and innumerable Carrera RSRs. For a long time the Germans Sepp Greger, Egon Evertz and Helmut Lässig held fourth or fifth places, until all the oil escaped from the oil cooler which had been damaged in a previous race incident, and ruined the engine. But the show the team put up was convincing enough: the Turbo was a worthy successor to the Carreras of 1973 to 1975.

General description: Type Carrera 2.8 RSR

Coachwork and chassis

Over 1,000 of the basic Carrera 2.7 RS were sold, but only 49 of them were rebuilt to proper racing specifications. Those were quite enough to earn the model world-wide fame.

The structure of the RS and RSR models was basically similar to the 190 bhp 911 S-2.4. But in order to achieve a competitive power-to-weight ratio, the Carrera was much lightened. Unstressed body panels were of thinner gauge steel, but in contrast to earlier years a large-scale use of plastic components was avoided. Plastic was retained only for the bumpers and for the 85-litre (18.7-gallon) fuel tank (circuit version 110-litre/24.2-gallon with a central filler protruding through the front cover). The wing (fender) extensions (at the rear nearly three inches wider than in the 911 S) were of steel.

Sound proofing mats were deleted, tin filler was used most sparingly during the assembling procedure of the body, the bucket seats for driver and co-driver were as light as they could reasonably be made, the 'emergency' seats and squabs were deleted, and the door lock mechanism was simplified. Of the two batteries housed in the front mudguards of the standard car, only one was retained. The standard window glass was replaced with more expensive, but thinner safety glass (Glaverbel). The interior was trimmed with black felt glued to the metal and perfectly plain door trim panels were used, while the arm rests were replaced by simple leather door pulls.

The front air dam was shaped to accommodate the oil cooler of the racing version. A tail spoiler was also fitted: it increased the maximum speed and improved the straight line stability and general handling. The running gear of the racing version remained as in the production model, but with the following exceptions: the rubber bushes of the rear suspension arms were replaced by Delrin and Unibals. The standard 26 mm (one inch) diameter rear torsion bars of the Carrera RS were retained, but auxiliary coil springs were added round the shock absorbers. The front suspension was also basically 911, but with an auxiliary spring round the struts. The front and rear anti-roll bars were quickly adjustable and removable, while harder settings were used for the shock absorbers.

The braking system of the racing version was basically similar to that used on the 917 racing car for short distance racing. The discs were not only radially ventilated, but also extensively drilled. The calipers were of light alloy with racing linings. Provision was made for varying the front/rear braking distribution.

For racing, light alloy wheels with 228 mm (nine inch) wide rims front and 279 mm (11 inch) wide rims rear were used, shod with racing tyres of the dimensions 230/600-15 and 260/600-15 respectively.

Engine

For the production version, the bore of the 911 engine was increased from 84 to 90 mm (3.3 to 3.54 inches), increasing the total capacity to 2,687 cc. For racing 2 mm larger bores were used, increasing the capacity to 2,806 cc. The crankcase, crankshaft and connecting rods were the same as in the 911 S. Racing camshafts were used, providing different valve timing and running in four instead of three bearings, but the valves remained standard. The injection pump also remained unchanged, except for settings. Twin ignition was used and the cooling fan was slightly reduced in diameter. The engine oil temperature was kept down by an oil cooler mounted in the front air dam. No effort was spared to make this the most powerful engine ever to propel a 911 and over 300 bhp was obtained at 8,000 rpm with a compression ratio of 10.3:1. The maximum torque went up to 26 mkg (190 lb/ft) at 5,100 rpm.

Transmission

The clutch lining material and the clutch disc diameter remained as in the standard car, but for cushioning the drive, steel springs were used instead of rubber. The diaphragm spring pressure was also increased. As in the 911-2.7, the transmission housing was magnesium. The gears were cooled by oil jets, the temperature of which was maintained at a reasonable level by a separate cooler. The gearbox shafts and the gear change mechanism were standard. The limited slip differential had a locking factor of 80 per cent and there was a wide choice of ratios for each of the five gear sets.

Below: Porsche Carrera RSR 2.8. A small series of these 300 bhp cars were built. Bottom: Experimental Carrera 2.8 with long-tail body, running as a prototype. Only one was built.

328

Porsche Carrera RSR 2.8 with lowered front air dam. Driver is Peter Gregg.

Beautifully prepared Carrera 2.8 from the American Roger Penske organisation. Driver: George Follmer.

The cockpit too was extensively lightened: only black felt hid the bare metal.

Six-cylinder, 2.8-litre engine (throttle valve version) with twin ignition.

General description: Type Carrera 2.7 Safari

Coachwork and chassis

The body structure and its equipment were standard Carrera RS. Special equipment for the 1973 Safari works entry was as follows: special rally equipment including a reading lamp, Twinmaster, shelves for helmets and route cards, special tools, a hand winch, a roll-over bar and a safety harness for driver and co-driver. The external appearance was altered by the additional bumper bars front and rear, large auxiliary lamps mounted on the matt black front cover, externally mounted two-tone air horns, exterior filler cap on the side of the front cover, accessible through a protective rubber cover, while a robust aluminium undershield protected the front and rear axles, as well as the engine and transmission.

The running gear was basically standard, but the ride height was slightly increased and Bilstein dampers were fitted. In addition to special settings, they also had supplementary suspension travel stops. The front torsion bars were standard 19 mm (0.75 inch), but the 24 mm (0.94 inch) rear bars were 1 mm thicker than standard and were pre-stressed.

The four 6 × 15 forged light alloy wheels were shod with 185/70 HR 15 M&S tyres. The four radially ventilated disc brakes remained standard, but the fuel tank had a capacity of 100 litres (22 gallons): on African tracks, the 997 kg (2,200 lb) car did little more than 4 km/l (11 miles to the gallon) at rally speeds.

Engine

The engine was entirely standard, but was well protected against dust. The power of the 2.7-litre six-cylinder with Bosch plunger pump injection was 210 bhp at 6,300 rpm with a compression ratio of 8.5:1. The Bosch ignition system was by high frequency capacity discharge and a complete spare installation was fitted.

Transmission

The Porsche five-speed gearbox was driven through a single plate Fichtel & Sachs clutch with a steel spring hub, sintered metal linings and a stronger diaphragm spring. The low gear ratios limited the maximum speed to 210 km/h (131 mph) and the transmission oil was circulated by a pump through an additional cooler, in view of the high stresses caused by the sand and mud and the high temperatures to be anticipated. The 2.7 Safari car was able to accelerate from 0 to 100 km/h (60 mph) in less than six seconds and only 24 seconds were required to reach 200 km/h (125 mph). The differential had a locking factor of 40 per cent.

Porsche Carrera RS 2.7. The 1973 Safari car was basically standard.

Non-standard features included supplementary bumpers and lights, air horns and increased ride height.

332

Under the front cover: 100-litre (22-gallon) fuel tank and separate 20-litre (4.4-gallon) reserve tank, plus 6-litre (1.32-gallon) screenwasher reservoir.

In 1974 the Safari Porsche 2.7 carried sand ladders on the roof.

General description: Types Carrera RS 3.0/ RSR 3.0

Coachwork and chassis

As with the 2.7-litre Carrera RS, its 3-litre successor was lightened by the use of thin gauge steel, simplified equipment and some plastic components to get the weight down to approximately 900 kg (1,984 lb). Thin gauge steel was used for the external roof and door panels, for the seatpans and for the instrument panel. Several parts were made of GFK plastic, such as: the front bumper with integral air dam and air cooler cut-out, rear bumper, luggage locker cover for which the standard locking system was retained, engine compartment cover with integral spoiler and soft rubber spoiler surround. In this case too, the standard lock was retained. In the racing version, the tail spoiler was even larger and the GFK bumpers were modified to follow the contours of the larger wheel opening extensions. In the RS road version, the front mudguards were also widened to accommodate 228 mm (9-inch) wide wheels at the front and 279 mm (11-inch) wide wheels at the rear.

The windscreen remained standard, but the other glass areas were of special thin glass. The rear quarter windows were not pivoted. The interior trim was very similar to the 2.7-litre version with black felt-covered metal surfaces, plain door trim panels with no armrest and leather straps for closing the door and operating the lock. An adjustable Recaro bucket seat with an adjustable backrest was provided for the driver, while the co-driver sat in a Recaro racing seat. Black felt was also glued on to the roof panel and the instrument panel was similar to the standard Carreras, except for the lack of a clock. Four-point safety belts were fitted and mountings provided for the installation of a roll-over bar. The racing RSR version differed from the basic model in that it had a special Recaro racing seat with a high squab and headrest. Holes were provided in the driver's seat for the passage of the 76 mm (3-inch) wide six-point seatbelt. A 10,000 rpm tachometer was fitted and a Heinzmann fire extinguishing installation. There was a roll-over bar, a 110-litre (24.2-gallon) flexible safety tank and twin fuel pumps.

The window frames and the external mirror were matt black eloxided, while the headlight surrounds matched the car's finish. There were no sound-proofing mats and the underpan was only partly treated with rust-proofing material. The air strut counter-balancing the front cover was deleted and the road version fitted with the standard 80-litre (17.6-gallon) tank with a recess for the 152 mm (6-inch) wide spare wheel and space-saver tyre.

The roadgoing RS version came with Pirelli CN 36 tyres, of the dimensions 215/60 VR 15 on 203 mm (8-inch) wide rims at the front, and 235/60 VR 15 on 228 mm (9-inch) rims at the rear. For racing, 9-inch front rims and 356 mm (14-inch) rear rims are used with appropriate tyres. At the end of the 1975 racing season, most of the faster cars used front and rear rims 51 mm (two inches) wider than in the original version.

A total of 109 Carrera RS 3.0s were sold worldwide at a price of DM 64,980 each. Of these, 50 were rebuilt for racing or rallying at a cost of at least DM 30,000.

The running gear of the RS 3.0 was very similar to that of the 1973 Carrera RSR The front cross member was aluminium, the steering arms were reinforced and so were the Bilstein damper struts. The steering box was slightly lowered and the toe-in reduced to zero. Front torsion bars of 19 mm diameter (0.75-inch) were fitted in conjunction with a 18 mm thick non-adjustable anti-roll bar. At the rear, the short steel semi-trailing arms were reinforced and pivoted on solid spherical joints. The Bilstein dampers had the same setting as in the Carrera RS 2.7. Rear torsion bars of 26 mm (one inch) diameter were used with an 18 mm diameter non-adjustable anti-roll bar and standard trailing arm pivots. Auxiliary coil springs were available for racing, there being a choice of steel or titanium springs, the latter costing just DM 1,000 each. When titanium springs were fitted, they went with light alloy dampers.

The braking system was similar to that of the Porsche 917. The four-piston Porsche brake calipers were finned transversally and the brake discs were ventilated both axially and radially. A balancing arm with adjustable fulcrum point permitted any choice of front/rear braking distribution. The hand lever operated a small drum brake on the rear wheels.

The running gear of the 3-litre RSR differed only in a few points from that of the road version. More precise geometry was provided by the use of Delrin instead of rubber bushes for the front and rear suspension arm pivots. Centre-lock hubs were provided, taking magnesium alloy wheels of 917-pattern. The front was slightly lowered by mounting the stub axle slightly higher on the strut. Wider front brake calipers were used to take thicker pads for long-distance racing.

Engine

With a bore of 95 mm (3.75 inches) and a stroke of 70.4 mm (2.8 inches), a capacity of 2,992.55 cc was obtained. With a compression ratio of 9.8:1, the standard model produced 230 bhp at 6,200 rpm. Whereas the 2.7-litre models had a magnesium alloy crankcase, an aluminium alloy crankcase was used for increased strength in the Type 911/77 engine. The crankshaft was forged and ran in eight plain bearings, as did the steel connecting rods. Pistons, cylinders and cylinder heads were aluminium alloy. In each bank of cyclinders, one overhead camshaft operated two valves per cylinder by means of rockers. The camshafts were driven by a twin roller chain each. The tank of the dry sump lubrication system had a capacity of 16 litres (3.5 gallons), a front oil cooler being included in the system. The intake system comprised a triple throttle valve housing with a matching intake riser block, an air filter and a cog-belt driven, twin row, plunger injection pump. The electrical installation and exhaust system were as in the standard 911.

The RSR engine (Type 911/75) was specially tuned to develop 330 bhp at 8,000 rpm. The maximum torque was increased from 28 mkg (204 lb/ft) at 5,000 rpm to 32 mkg (233 lb/ft) at 6,500 rpm. The compression ratio went up to 10.3:1. The crankcase and crankshaft were unchanged from the RS version. Pistons, cylinder and cylinder heads were aluminium. They were generally similar to the RS model, except for the provision of a second plug hole in the combustion chambers, the RSR version having a twin ignition system. The valves, their diameter and their springs were the same as in the road version, but the ports were polished. The valve gear was basically similar to the standard version, but the four-bearing camshaft had the same cam profile and gave the same timing as in the old Carrera-6. There was also an additional oil filter.

A cog-belt driven, Bosch mechanical injection pump was used, but the air intake system was considerably modified, the throttle valves being replaced, on either side, by a throttle slide with appropriate intake trumpets. There was no air

336   *Side and rear views of Carrera RS 3.0 from which the RSR version was derived.*

filter. The exhaust pipes of either group of adjacent cylinders converged into a single tail-pipe, there being two tail-pipes in all. The Bosch twin ignition system was of the magnetically triggered electronic type and an electronic tachometer with a tell-tale needle was fitted.

Transmission
An oil pump was already standard on the RS 3.0 five-speed gearbox. A serpentine cooler was mounted in the left-hand front wing. The capacity of the system was 3.75 litres (6.6 pints). The limited slip differential had an 80 per cent locking factor. Gearbox and final drive ratios were standard, but a large choice of other ratios was available. The Fichtel & Sachs clutch was largely similar to the standard production type, except for the reinforced diaphragm spring, similar to that of the 2.7-litre RSR version. In the racing version, this was replaced by a Fichtel & Sachs single-disc racing clutch providing increased pressure. The clutch disc had a steel spring hub and Cerasintered metal linings were fitted. The gearbox remained as in the RS version.

Externally the RSR version does not differ very much from RS, but the widened fenders are obvious. Thin gauge steel panels and spartan equipment reduced the weight to 900 kg (1,984 lb). Note large rear spoiler and air outlets in front and rear mudguards.

337

Carrera RSR 3.0 centre-lock front hub and long-distance brake.

The engine oil cooler is recessed in the large air dam. Also note larger racing rear spoiler.

With slides replacing the throttle valves, the power of the 3-litre Carrera RSR engine was finally raised to 340 bhp.

Carrera RSR driver's working place with 10,000 rpm tachometer and 300 km/h speedometer.

General description: Type 911 SC 'Safari'

'We are going to Africa because Porsche wants to fulfil a long nurtured ambition' said sports manager Manfred Jantke when Porsche sprang a surprise and announced that they were entering factory cars for the 26th Safari Rally in Kenya. 'We have won almost everything from the World Championship of Makes to the Le Mans 24 Hours Race and from the Monte-Carlo Rally to the Can-Am Championship. However, one trophy is still missing from our collection: the one presented to the winner of the Safari Rally.'

Three times Porsche had entered cars in the most celebrated of all African rallies, considered to be one of the toughest in the world. The result was a second, a fourth and again a second place—nothing to be ashamed of, but only enough to whet the appetite of an ambitious team. So, after three years of retirement, the Porsche management decided to make another attempt. Two cars, both 3-litre 911 SC's finished in the colours of Martini, the company's sponsor, especially prepared and with a huge ground clearance, were to fight it out in the Kenyan dust during the Easter holidays of 1978. Twenty eight cm (nearly 12 inches) ground clearance, an enormous suspension travel and a massive underpan were to enable the 1,200 kg cars to procede at speeds of up to 200 km/h (125 mph) across the African deserts and tracks, to crawl through the notorious red mud and to cross rocky fords. However, good though a car may be, little can be expected from it if it is not entrusted to a crew fully familiar with African conditions. Porsche was lucky to be able to employ the dream crew of Waldegaard and Thorszelius who, in 1974, had driven a Porsche into second place and who had also won the event outright in 1977—unfortunately not in a Porsche. Getting them was a stroke of sheer luck because the team was under contract to Ford that year but the company agreed to release them for the event because Ford had not entered a works team themselves. The second Martini Porsche was entrusted to Preston Jr/Lyall, one of the top crews in African rallies. On paper, with 250 bhp on tap, the lovingly prepared 911 SC seemed unbeatable. They were not only lighter, faster and safer than any of their opponents but also tougher. Drivers like Waldegaard and Preston were certainly as good as any, if not superior. The organisation in Kenya was handled by Preston Senior, himself a former Safari winner. Weissach had sent specialists on rally preparation such as Jürgen Barth, Ing Roland Kussmaul and the top development engineers Bott and Falk, together with a swarm of mechanics from Weissach. Nine and a half tons of material, including the two rally cars themselves had been flown in. The two 911s were in permanent radio contact with the headquarters and two airplanes relentlessly followed the cars throughout the event.

However, once again, it was not to be. The biggest reason for Porsche's defeat was one of the rear suspension arms. Previous Safaris had made the Porsche development engineers aware of the stresses they have to bear and they had taken great care to make them as strong as possible. They had even gone so far as to protect these cast aluminium parts from possible stone damage by enveloping them in fibreglass reinforced plastic. But with Waldegaard well in the lead, picking his way from one rut to the other, one of the arms broke: the ruts were very hard and a lateral blow was more than the arm could take.

The repair took more than one hour and, to cap it all, weak shock absorbers had to be replaced and a seized throttle linkage had to be repaired, dropping Waldegaard to fourth place. Preston Junior was not quite as unlucky. His only troubles were broken drive shafts and weak dampers. But this was enough to lose him first place to the surprise winner Jean-Pierre Nicolas in his Peugeot 504.

With its complete rally equipment, the 911 SC Safari weighed 1,180 kg. This rather high weight was a result of numerous items of extra equipment such as a full protective underpan, additional lights, reinforced running gear, special Dunlop Safari tyres on seven inch wide forged light alloy wheels, twin Recaro bucket seats, a roll-over cage, two 2.5 kg fire extinguishers, two warning triangles, a first aid box, a cross-shaped wheel brace, a hydraulic jack, a second spare wheel inside the passenger compartment, a reading lamp for the co-driver, a Twin-Master, additional fresh air hoses for driver and co-driver, twin thermos bottles, a complete Repa safety harness and a two-way radio installation. The special equipment included a 110-litre fuel tank, a 20-litre (4.4 gallon) oil tank and a 16-litre (3.5 gallon) water tank for the headlight washers, both in the front luggage compartment.

911 SC 'Safari' had nearly 12 inches ground clearance.

342

The cars were well protected against stones and animals— weight with equipment: 1,180 kg.

911 SC 'Safari' cockpit had very complete equipment.

20-litre oil tank and 16-litre water tank in 'luggage compartment'.

3-litre engine had plunger pump fuel injection and developed about 250 bhp.

General description: Type 934 Turbo RSR

Coachwork and chassis

It was plainly obvious that the new Turbo RSR was a very close relative to the production model. Externally it differed mainly by the lateral plastic wheel arch extensions which, in conformity with the rules, were 50 mm wide and 100 mm high (approximately 2 × 4 inches) all around the standard wheel opening. Another identification mark was the front air dam which included openings for the two intake air coolers, for the central oil cooler and for the brake ventilation ducts. A few body reinforcements allowed by the rules were hardly visible, while the front cover had to be opened to see the aluminium tube cross bracing the car's front end, which notably increased the torsional strength of the body.

A better weight distribution was obtained by moving the oil tank into the luggage compartment, next to the 120-litre (26.4-gallon) safety fuel tank to FIA specifications, to the battery and to the fire extinguishing system which together filled the luggage compartment. The fuel tank was fitted with a quick refuelling nozzle, as required for long-distance racing. The interior equipment was rather plain. Gauges for the boost pressure, fuel pressure and fuel injection pressure were added to the instrument panel, while the tachometer and the oil pressure and temperature gauges were standard. A racing seat developed by Porsche and the now mandatory safety equipment consisting of a roll-over bar and a six-point safety belt were also provided.

A first series of 30 cars to this specification was made and sold for DM 108,000 each. As the new rules allowed only few changes to be made, compared with the standard model, the modifications were limited to adapting the suspension to the requirements of racing by more precise location of the moving parts, even harder springing, different damping characteristics, the use of some reinforced parts and of racing brakes. As, partly in view of the stricter rules, the production Turbo already featured slightly modified front and rear suspension geometries, compared with the other models of the 911 range, no change was required in this field.

Precise rear wheel movements were ensured by the stiff cast aluminium semi-trailing arms of the production Turbo, but even more stiffness was provided by the replacement of the sound and vibration absorbing rubber bushes of the production car by solid spherical joints. At the front, too, the suspension struts and wishbones were mounted on solid joints and plastic bushes respectively. There was no need to replace the hub bearings, so strong were they in the production car.

The springing and damping was adapted to the considerable weight of the car, which was the minimum of 1,120 kg (2,470 lb) without fuel required by the new rules. The production torsion bars remained in place, but were supplemented on each side by an auxiliary coil spring coaxial with the suspension strut. The spring abutment was notched to provide ride height adjustment. Adjustable anti-roll bars were used front and rear, the rear one being tubular.

As in previous racing models, the steering gear remained standard as did the track rods and joints. In contrast, special racing brakes were used. They were borrowed from the 917 model and had large size radially ventilated discs and deeply finned aluminium calipers. The front and rear brake circuits were linked by way of a balance bar, so that front and rear braking distribution could be adjusted.

Further cooling of the discs was provided by two flexible pipes directly leading the air from the openings in the front air dam to around the discs. The standard hubs were replaced by special reinforced centre lock hubs: not only were they stronger, but they also allowed quicker wheel changes.

Three-piece alloy wheels were used in which the inside and outside parts of the rim were bolted to the wheel centre. In contrast to previous racing models of 911 origin, these wheels were 406 instead of 381 mm (16 instead of 15 inches) in diameter. The increase was a concession to the tyre width limitations imposed by the current rules, while the minimum weight, also imposed by the rules, went up considerably. Not only did the larger tyre diameter provide a greater safety margin, in the long run they might also allow the use of larger brakes.

Engine

Thanks to the experience gained with the 2.14-litre 'Turbo-Carrera' racing model of 1974 and with the development of the production Turbo engine, no major problems were encountered in developing the 3-litre turbocharged engine of the 934. Such important items as the crankcase, the crankshaft, the connecting rods and the cylinder heads were basically standard Turbo parts, some modified within the frame of the rules, enlarged cylinder head ports being a point in case. The camshafts were specially developed for racing, but the valves had the same head and stem diameter as the standard ones. In view of the extension of the oil circulation to the turbocharger, the scavenge side of the oil pump was increased in size.

Completely new ground was explored by using the Bosch K-Jetronic injection system for a racing engine. The biggest problem was how to accommodate the air flow meter, which has to pass twice the output of the standard unit within the limited dimensions of the engine compartment. The shape of the air passages before and beyond the meter were arrived at after long test-bed developments, while the problem of the metering itself within the available space was solved by replacing the metering disc with a metering cone, preceded by a tranquillising chamber. The deciding factor in the location of the turbocharger and its accessories also being space, the installation was generally similar to that of the production Turbo. The turbocharger and the waste gate were mounted between the engine and the rear rocker panel, while the throttle valve was located in the blower output line—in the racing car between the blower and the intercooler.

Another major problem was how to accommodate the intercooler to cool the blower output before it reached the cylinders. As no solution could be found for the accommodation of an air-cooled intercooler, as had been used in the 2.14-litre Turbo-Carrera, someone came up with the suggestion of cooling the blower output with water. This was received somewhat sceptically, but calculations indicated that this should be feasible by using twin radiators located in the front airdam and adding a water pump to circulate the coolant through several yards of piping. The weight penalty would be around 20 kg (44 lb), but this was acceptable in view of the high minimum weight required by the rules. An experimental car featuring a maze of tubes and hoses (nicknamed 'the Water Power Station' by the factory staff) showed great promise, the temperature of the air reaching the engine being reduced from 150° to 50°C. In the final version, the water pump was belt-driven from one of the camshafts and the water circulated through the two front radiators cooled the blower output in two intercoolers mounted above the three intake pipes of each cylinder bank.

In order to improve the air flow and its distribution over the engine, the cooling air blower was mounted horizontally as in the experimental car of 1974. This blower and the limitation of the intake pressure to 1.3 bar (18.5 lb per square inch) provided an adequate thermal safety margin.

The turbocharger was of the same type as used previously in the 917 Turbo, in which, however, twin turbos were used, one to feed either bank of six cylinders. Both the ignition system and the waste gate (the latter, however, with a different setting) were standard components. With a capacity of 2,993 cc and a compression ratio of 6.5:1, the official output was 485 bhp at 7,000 rpm. It was known, however, that at the end of 1976, this was in fact raised to some 580 bhp in the cars raced by the more prominent racing organisations, mainly by modifying the waste gate settings to obtain a higher boost pressure.

Transmission

There were few alterations to the four-speed gearbox of the production Turbo, of which the shafts, gears and final drive had been designed for a torque output of 65 mkg (475 lb/ft). The synchronising system was also standard, but a gearbox-driven oil pump circulated the transmission oil through a cooler located in the rear spoiler. The pressure differential between the upper and the lower faces of the latter provided a sufficient air flow through the cooler.

To make the best of the cool oil, this was jetted on to the most highly stressed gears. As the latest rules only allowed three different ratios, including the standard one, for any set of gears, Porsche offered three different ratios for any of the four gear pairs, plus a choice of three final drive ratios. The differential locking factor was 80 per cent.

Compared with the standard model, the gear lever travel was considerably reduced and more precision provided by mounting the engine and transmission unit solidly into the body shell. Design and dimensions of the clutch were the same as in the production car; only the diaphragm pressure was increased while, as in all Porsche racing clutches, sintered metal linings replaced those made of an organic compound.

Annual modifications

1980-1981

At first sight, Porsche's type 934 racing Turbo remains externally very little different from the production Turbo, type 930. A look under the sheet metal however, reveals important modifications and detail improvements.

In the passenger compartment, the rear emergency seat is left out and the simplified instrument panel informs the driver of only the most essential functions, such as boost pressure, engine revolutions and oil pressure. The driver sits in a racing bucket seat and the aluminium tube roll-over cage not only protects the driver but also increases the car's rigidity.

All windows are glass because in Group 4 the use of plexiglass is not allowed if not fitted as standard. The engine compartment is full to the brim. For increased efficiency, a horizontal fan wheel replaces the vertical cooling fan. The two water-cooled intercoolers are arranged directly over the intake stacks. They are connected to two radiators integrated in the front air dam and serve to cool the air fed to the engine, increasing its density and reducing the thermal stresses of the engine.

The most important modification to the engine is the increase in cooling capacity. The crankshaft and the bore and stroke dimensions of 95 × 70.4 mm are unaltered from the standard model. But the intake and exhaust valves resting on bronze alloy seats are larger and the compression ratio is raised from 6.5 to 7:1.

The biggest contribution to the power increase however is the modified turbocharging installation. The larger turbo enables the boost pressure to be raised to 1.7 bar (24 psi), more than twice the pressure used in the production 930. A 22-litre (4.8 gallon) oil tank and a large oil cooler keep the oil temperature at a reasonable level.

The running gear required only comparatively minor modifications for racing. Stiffer Bilstein gas filled dampers, additional coil springs and adjustable anti-roll bars front and rear are partly responsible for racing car-like cornering speeds to which the 10.5 inch wide front and 12.5 inch wide rear rims make an important contribution, though handling in fast curves is not always without problems.

The flat-6 engine produces about 600 bhp at 7,200 rpm. It drives the rear wheels through a 4-speed box which is basically standard but has different ratio and includes an 80% limited slip differential. The Porsche 934 Turbo weighs at least 1,130 kg in racing trim (as required by the Group 4 regulations) and can reach 305 km/h (190 mph) on a suitable gear ratio.

Production model derivation is obvious in this side view of a racing 934.

The 485 bhp turbocharged Porsche 934 was offered for DM 108,000, ready to race.

Porsche 934s were often entered for Group 5 races. They were then fitted with the Type 935 rear wing, with wider wheels and larger mudguard extensions to cover them.

Above and below: Front and rear views of turbocharged Porsche 934: the outside openings in the air dam contained the radiators of the heat exchangers. The mudguard extensions were made of glass fibre and riveted to the standard body.

	911 2.4/2.7	Carrera 2.7 RS	2.8 RSR	Carrera 2.7	2.7 Safari	3.0 RS	3.0 RSR	Turbo RSR	Turbo
Engine									
Crankcase	Magnesium	As 911	As 911	As 911	As 911	Aluminium	Aluminium	Mg (Le Mans alum)	Aluminium
Crankshaft	Stroke 70.4	As 911	As 911	As 911	As 911	As 911	As 911	Stroke 66 as 911	As 911
Con rod	Steel	As 911	As 911	As 911	As 911	As 911	As 911, 2.0, Titanium	As 911	As 911
Camshaft	3 bearings	As 911	Modified timing and lift, 4 bearings	As 911	As 911	As 911	Modified timing and lift, 4 bearings	Modified timing and lift, 4 bearings	4 bearings
Valves	46/40 Ø	As 911	As 911	As 911	As 911	Larger Ø	As 3.0 RS	Ø as 911, 2.0 Litre	As 3.0 RS
Injection	2.4 mech 2.7 K-Jetronic	As 911	As 911	As 911	As 911	Mechanical	Mechanical	Mechanical	K-Jetronic
Ignition	Single with breaker	Mechanical	Twin with breaker	Mechanical	Mechanical	Mechanical	Twin, no breaker	Twin, no breaker	Single, no breaker
Cooling blower	11 blades	As 911 Serpentine	Ø smaller	As 911 Serpentine	As 911 Serpentine	As 911	As 2.8 RSR	As 2.8 RSR/horiz	Modified ratio Serpentine
Oil Cooler	–	Serpentine	Front	Serpentine	Serpentine	Front	Front	Front	Serpentine
Running gear									
Front axle	MacPherson	As 911	As 911	As 911	As 911	As 911	As 911	Modified wishbones, different geometry	As 911, geometry as Turbo RSR
Rear axle	Semi-trailing arms	As 911	Modified geometry	As 911	As 911	As 2.8 RSR	As 2.8 RSR	Fabricated alumin semi-trailing arms	New cast alloy arms, geometry as 2.8 RSR
Pivot	Rubber	As 911	Delrin/Unibal	As 911	As 911	As 911	Delrin/Unibal	Unibal	As 911
Springs, front	Torsion bar 19 Ø	As 911	As 911 + auxil spring	As 911	As 911, with bump stops	As 911	As 911 + auxil spring	Coil spring	As 911
Springs, rear	Torsion bar 23 Ø	As 911	Torsion bar 26 Ø + auxil spring	As 911	As 911 with bump stops	Torsion bar 26 Ø	As 2.8 RSR + auxil spring	Coil spring	As 3.0 RS
Dampers	Hydraulic, double acting	As 911, different setting	As 911, different setting	As 911	As 911, different setting	As 2.7 RS	As 2.8 RSR	Different setting	As 2.7 RS
Brakes, front	Cast-iron calliper 911	Aluminium calliper 911	917 short distance	As 911	As 911	As 2.8 RSR	917 long distance	917 long distance	As 2.7 RS
Brakes, rear	Cast-iron calliper 911	As 911	917 short distance	As 911	As 911	As 2.8 RSR	917 long distance	917 long distance	As 2.7 RS
Ventilated brake discs	Plain	As 911	Perforated	As 911	As 911	Perforated	Perforated	Perforated	Perforated
Rim width	6"/6"	6"/7"	9"/11"	6"/7"	5½" f M+S tyres	8"/9"	10½"/14"	10½"/17"	7"/8"
Clutch									
Diameter (mm)	225	As 911	As 911	As 911	As 911	As 911	As 911	As 911	240
Lining	Organic	As 911	As 911	As 911	Sintered metal	As 911	Sintered metal	Sintered metal	As 911
Damper	Rubber	As 911	Steel spring	As 911	Steel spring	As 911	Steel spring	None	Steel spring
Spring pressure	Standard	Higher	Higher	As 2.7 RS	As 2.8 RSR	As 2.8 RSR	Higher	Higher	As 3.0 RSR
Gearbox									
Housing	Magnesium	As 911	As 911	As 911	As 911	As 911	As 911	As 911	New magnesium housing
Jet lubrication + cooler	–	–	Yes	–	Yes	Yes	Yes	Yes	–
Lim slip diff	Optional	As 911	80%	As 911	40%	80%	80%	80% or solid	As 911
Half shafts	Constant velocity	As 911	As 911	As 911	As 911	As 911	As 911	Universals + rubber doughnuts	As 911
Gear selector	Aluminium	As 911	As 911	As 2.7 RS	As 911	As 911	As 911	Simplified, with gate	As 911
Body									
Wheel arches, width	Standard	Rear widened	Front and rear widened	As 2.7 RS	As 911	As 2.8 RSR	Plastic extensions front and rear	Rear wider than 3.0 RSR	As 3.0 RS
Rear spoiler	–	Duck's tail	Duck's tail	Tray spoiler opt	Duck's tail	Tray spoiler	Tray spoiler	Aerofoil	Tray spoiler
Interior trim	Standard	Simplified	Spartan	De luxe	Simplified	Simplified	Spartan	Racing	De luxe
Weight (without fuel)	1025 kg	900 kg	917 kg	1037 kg	1000 kg	900 kg	917 kg	820 kg	1085 kg

Carrera 2.7 RS / 2.8 RSR / 3.0 RS / 3.0 RSR / 934 Turbo

Year	Body	Type	Chassis no	Engine type	Gearbox type	Cyl	Bore × stroke	Capacity	HP (DIN) at rpm	Torque (mkg) at rpm	Comp ratio	W'base (mm)	Track fr/rear (mm)	Length (mm)	Weight (kg)	No produced
1973	Coupé	Carrera 2.7 Safari	9113600288/285	911/83	915	6	90x70,4	2687	210/6300	26/5100	8,5:1	2271	1372/1394	4147	980	2
1973	Coupé	Carrera 2.8 RSR	9113600386-1549	911/72	915	6	92x70,4	2806	300/8000	30/6500	10,3:1	2271	1402/1421	4147	900	49
1974	Coupé	Carrera 3.0 RS	9114609001-9109	911/77	915	6	95x70,4	2993	230/6200	28/5000	9,8:1	2271	1437/1462	4235	900	109
1974	Coupé	Carrera 3.0 RSR	9114609001-9109	911/74 911/75	915	6 6	95x70,4 95x70,4	2993 2993	315/8000 330/8000	32/6500 32/6500	10,3:1 10,3:1	2271	1472/1528	4235	920	109
1976	Coupé	934 Turbo	9306700151-0180 0540	930/75	930/25	6	95x70,4	2993	485/7000	60/5400	6,5:1	2269	1481/1496	4291	1120	31
1977	Coupé	935 Turbo	9307700901-9307700913	930/72	930/51	6	92,8x70,4	2857	590/7900	60/5400	6,5:1	2271	1502/1558	4680	970	13
	Coupé-US	934 Turbo	9307700951-9307700960	930/73	930/25	6	95x70,4	2993	540/7000	60/5400	6,5:1	2271	1481/1496	4680	1120	10
1978	Coupé	911 SC 3.0 Safari	9113300789 9118301416 9118301476 9118301474	911/77	915/R	6	95x70,4	2994	250/6800	30,5/5500	9,1:1	2272	1369/1379	4291	1300	4

Type 924 'Rally' (from 1978)

At the end of September 1978, Porsche's Official Sport Adviser Jürgen Barth (32), was enjoying a glass of beer with Porsche technicians Roland Kussmaul (37) and Helmut Ristl (34). The discussion centred on the possibility of entering a new generation Porsche, the 924, in the Monte Carlo and other rallies of 1979. A little later, Alex Janda (36) the Sales Manager of the Porsche dealership of Spindler in Würzburg joined with them and even found a sponsor and an enthusiastic workshop owner prepared to look after the team.

The budget for entering two reasonably well prepared Porsche 924 Turbos in the Monte Carlo rally was estimated at around DM 120,000, including the two 924s to be obtained at a special discount price.

From the end of November 1978 on, Barth, Kussmaul and Ristl spent all their evenings preparing the two Turbos. Kussmaul alone worked for more than 600 unpaid hours. But suddenly came horrible news: due to a 6-week strike in the steel industry, Porsche had been forced to reduce its production. The 400 units required for the homologation of the 924 Turbo could not be produced before the end of the year, for homologation from January 1 1979 on. In spite of Jürgen Barth's good contacts (he is responsible for the homologation formalities at Porsche), the FISA (the ruling body in international motor sport) and President of the Federation Jean-Marie Balestre, remained unmoved. The 924 Turbo was not homologated until February 1, one week after the finish of the Monte Carlo. The only possibility was to replace the 924 Turbo engine with an aspirated 924 unit. However, such items as the Turbo's running gear and modified brakes as well as the lightened dashboard, which all had been homologated for the normal 924, were able to be retained. By that time, most of the technical modifications had been made: reinforced front wishbones and rear suspension arms, five-speed gearbox, four ventilated disc brakes, an installed spare ignition system and a second fuel pump were all part of it. Fender extensions to cover the 15 inch racing tyres were only required at the front end.

'For a 1,000 kg car, the power is clearly rather low,' said Jürgen Barth, 'but our entry in the Monte is only a development exercise. Things won't get serious until the Safari rally where we can use our turbocharged engine.' Unfortunately, in this first event in which it ran with the 170 bhp engine, driven by Barth and Kussmaul, the Porsche suffered running gear troubles.

The first class victory for a Porsche 924 came in the Australian REPCO rally in July 1979. This 12,349 miles mammoth event led from Melbourne to Melbourne through deserts, forests, fords and mountains, and included 8,235

352

miles of special stages on dirt roads. Barth and Kussmaul in this case drove a normally aspirated 924 prepared by Australian Porsche dealer Alan Hamilton. In spite of minor technical problems and an accident during which the car rolled over completely, they managed to drive their car into eighth place in the general classification and first in the 2-litre class.

Later, after an absence of more than ten years, Barth again took part in a German rally. Driving a Porsche 924 Turbo, the car he had used in practise for the Safari, and with co-driver Christa Herrmann, he entered the Rheinhessen Rally, counting towards the German rally championship of 1979. On asphalt especially, the Barth/924 combination was spectacular indeed, partly owing to the tyres which Barth had decided to use for the entire rally—road going radial tyres! In spite of being delayed by the oil feed to the turbocharger which came loose, the Porsche was placed 14th among 70 finishers. But in spite of all the efforts of Barth and Kussmaul to persuade Porsche to make an official come-back to international rallying in 1981 for which they would have benefited from the experience gained with the turbocharged and atmospheric 924, the company management decided against it. The only step taken in that direction was to offer customers a special version of the 924 Carrera GT (based on the 1980 Le Mans car), suitable for rally and racing.

January 1979: The 924 Rally, still with atmospheric engine, in its first outing, the Monte Carlo Rally. Crewed by Jürgen Barth and Roland Kussmaul.

Porsche 924 Rally driven by the author with atmospheric engine in 1979 'Monte'.

Lightweight instrument panel carries only the indispensable gauges.

354

Rally computer and light switches in front of co-driver.

Porsche 924 Rally ready for 1979 Monte Carlo Rally.

Water and oil coolers of nearly standard 125 bhp engine in 924 Rally car.

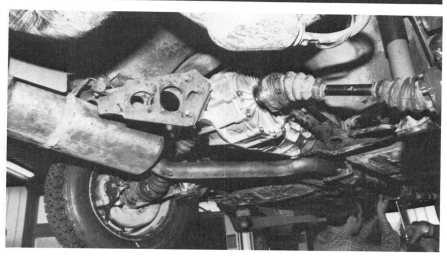

Rear suspension arm, five-speed gearbox and rally running gear.

A 170 bhp turbo-charged engine was first used in 1979 Safari Rally.

In spite of spartan appointments, the car weight exceeds 1,000 kg.

356

Turbo engine required only minor changes to the controls.

924 Rally-Turbo attracts little attention.

Car equipped for various events in which it was crewed by Barth-Kussmaul in 1981.

357

The privately prepared car resembles the 924 GTR which was produced at a later date.

Jürgen Barth's 924 Rally, regularly updated, ready for its third season of competitions.

Type 924 SCCA (from 1979)

In the summer of 1979, Weissach produced a racing version of the 924 suitable for the American SCCA series. This was the first new generation Porsche designed to run in this popular series in which the 356 and the 911 had started their sporting career in the USA. The racing 924 was built to class D-Production regulations of the Sport Car Club of America (SCCA) open to slightly modified production cars. The competitors must qualify for the Great Final on the road Atlanta circuit in Georgia by running in several qualifying races.

The car, developed in Weissach under Ing Rainer Wüst, was intended to be a model for selected USA dealer teams and tuning shops. The first cars were handed over in September 1979 to the competition department of Porsche-Audi in New Jersey. This made it possible for a number of modified 924s to be ready for SCCA events of 1980 in which the main opposition came from the Triumph TR7 and Datsun 2000.

As these cars are mainly intended for popular motor sport, they are largely based on production parts in order to keep the cost as low as possible. The body is stripped of all inessential items, including the entire upholstery, leaving only sheet metal around the driver, but outside, a plastic air dam and fender extensions are added. The weight in racing trim is 970 kg (2,138 lb).

The welded-in roll cage also aids body rigidity. Inside the 924 SCCA nothing flammable is left, only the plain sheet metal, while the successful Porsche racing bucket seat made of Nomex material was taken from the Type 934/935. Modified 924 instruments, a lightened gear selector mechanism and an electric master switch are the main items of equipment. The car itself is in fact much lighter than the 970 kg stipulated by the American homologation rules and it carries over 90 kg (198.4 lb) of lead located in the cockpit so as to improve the weight distribution.

The running gear incorporating larger wheel bearings and rear coil springs was specifically designed for racing, while the twin circuit brakes are taken from the 924 Turbo. 7J × 14 racing wheels are used front and rear, shod with the Good Year racing tyres also required by the rules.

The Audi-made four-cylinder in line engine of 2,039 cc capacity is up-rated to 180 bhp at 7,000 rpm by the use of homologated special parts. In this connection, Wüst says that at least another 30 bhp would have been necessary to stress the engine to the limits of its possibilities. Compared to the normal production model, the most important mechanical change is the use of a Bosch—Kugelfischer fuel injection system and a larger section intake manifold permitting the revolution limit of the engine to be raised substantially. A slightly increased bore and a 11.5:1 compression ratio contribute to the power increase. No fan accelerates the air circulating through the water radiator and the additional oil cooler. A wide selection of ratios is available to adapt the Porsche five-speed gearbox, incorporating an 80% limited slip differential, to all racing circuits. The dry single plate clutch is a Fichtel & Sachs unit with sintered metal linings while the safety fuel tank contains 50-litres (11 Imperial gallons).

Within the D-production SCCA series, the 924 quickly achieved success: after having qualified in several local races to take part in the Grand Final, a US prepared 924 won the final at the end of 1980 and another finished fourth.

In 1981, the 924 got support from the 924 Turbo which however must run in the C-production class. A further modified version will be eligible for the GTO category of the IMSA series (2.5-3.0-litre class).

The 2,039 cc engine was developed to produce 180 bhp at 7,000 rpm.

Porsche 924 SCCA—development work began in summer 1979. In 1980 it won the D-Production category of the SCCA-Series in the USA.

The body was lightened considerably to get the car's weight down to 970 kg. The racing running gear is made up of reinforced standard parts.

360

The roll cage is integrated into the body to increase its rigidity.

Modified 924 instruments, lightened gear lever, centralised electrical system.

Type 924/Group 4 (1979)

In the course of the 1979 racing season, a well prepared Porsche 924 running in Group 4 appeared on Germany's racing circuits. Its preparation was the work of 36-year-old Friedrich Winkelmann from Essen, an amateur racing driver who had prepared his car in his own small Porsche service shop, with the help of the Pierburg company (Solex), the carburation specialists, who had taken care of the engine.

This racing 924 offers an excellent driving position, with all the controls at easy reach. The Fichtel & Sachs single plate racing clutch with sintered metal linings is quite light by racing car standards and starting presents no problem. The steering is almost as light as in the normal road car and even the brakes which operate without a servo are not excessively heavy. Ventilated disc brakes, borrowed from the 924 Turbo and the 928, are used front and rear to avoid any fade problems in spite of the car's 950 kg (2,094 lb) weight—a figure exceeding the allowed minimum weight by over 140 kg (308.6 lb).

The handling characteristics were finalised with the help of the Bilstein company, using their gas filled dampers. The general tendency is towards slight oversteer, the resulting drift being easily controllable.

The Audi 4-cylinder engine is tuned along conventional lines: higher compression (12:1), thanks to the help of different pistons, a Schrick camshaft, larger valves, a Pierburg racing injection system and a fabricated 'bunch of bananas' exhaust manifold result in an output of 195 bhp at 7,100 rpm and a maximum permissible engine speed of 8,000 rpm. The torque characteristics are nevertheless very good and 100 km/h is reached from rest in about 5.5 seconds.

In Group 4, the 924 is, however, handicapped not only by its comparatively modest power but also by the ratios of its production five-speed gearbox, which make it unsuitable for racing and by its too tall final drive ratio.

The Winkelmann 924 runs front and rear on composite wheels of 241 mm (9.5 inches) and 267 mm (10.5 inches) width respectively, shod with Good Year racing tyres. The 80% limited slip differential is of ZF manufacture.

This Group 4 924 has now little future in Europe. It remains the work of an enthusiastic idealist but is outclassed in both circuit racing and rallies by Porsche's own 924 Carrera GT whose performance cannot be matched by any normal 924.

Type 924 Carrera GT-Le Mans (from 1980)

In the first week of October of 1979, the countdown began for the project 924 Le Mans under the leadership of Dipl Ing Norbert Singer (41). That was already very late but another six weeks went by before Singer's task was exactly defined: he was to develop a racing version of the 924 Turbo, to be run in the 1980 Le Mans 24 Hours race and which could afterwards be further developed to be eligible, with only minor modifications, for Group 4 racing, for the new Group B to be implemented in 1982, for the GTO category of the American IMSA series and for the C-Production category of American SCCA races.

In February 1980, the first prototype was loaded on a transporter heading for the Paul Ricard circuit, in the South of France. There the car was to be submitted to various test runs, mainly regarding the running gear and the engine. Very few problems cropped up in the course of those tests and after its return to Weissach, the next points on the programme were tackled. The first step was to send the car to the Volkswagen wind tunnel in Wolfsburg. The results indicated that the body could be left virtually as it was. The drag coefficient turned out to be a very satisfactory 0.35. The next step was four engine endurance runs over 30 to 35 hours on the test beds. For these tests, the Le Mans programme was used. That means that a four-minute Le Mans lap is simulated, implying 1 min 15 s at full load and full speed (6,300 rpm) every lap to simulate the Le Mans straight.

Almost simultaneously, an endurance run started on the climatic roller test bed in Weissach. Here various weather conditions can be simulated, including side and head winds. Drivers drive in two-hour shifts in which the racing car is accelerated and braked as if it were on the Le Mans course, reaching its maximum speed and being braked hard in quick succession.

To be safe in case of torrential showers in the race itself, the crew took the opportunity provided by the bad weather at the beginning of 1980: first a 924 Turbo racing car was sent out to the Weissach circuit where various development engineers drove it as close as possible behind a Porsche 928 S driven fast and raising huge sprays of water. Then the car was left overnight in the rain with the bonnet removed! Starting the car next morning was no problem.

After the 1,000 km test on the destruction tracks of the Weissach proving ground were completed without problem in only one and a half days, people began to get suspicious: things were going too well!

In April 1980 the crew again went to the Paul Ricard circuit for an endurance test which, in view of the encouraging results achieved, was to be extended from 24 to 30 hours. It was finally interrupted after 'only' 28 hours when the experimental aluminium transaxle tube linking the engine to the rear mounted gearbox broke. The average lap time achieved during the endurance test which took place on the full Paul Ricard circuit was under 2.10 minutes, with some fast laps around 2.05 minutes. This compares with average times of round 2.10 minutes for the 2.8-litre Carrera (at the end of 1972) and 2.05 minutes for the Porsche 934 Turbo in spring 1976.

In the four months between the two Paul Ricard tests, the three-dozen strong crew under Norbert Singer had done a lot of work developing a real racing car from the roadgoing 924 Carrera GT.

The first step in the development was to measure a raw body for torsional stiffness and make it more rigid by fitting a roll cage especially designed to reinforce the weaker parts of the structure. This immediately made the 924 almost twice as rigid as the 935! Externally, the body remained almost unchanged, but inside, the instrument panel was completely redesigned with most of the switchgear on the central console. The entire electrics of the car were centralised on an aluminium board installed on the passenger's side. All connections were of the pull-out type, allowing the entire board to be replaced in a matter of seconds.

The position of the Audi 2-litre four-cylinder engine remained unchanged, but the turbocharger was moved to the left, with the exhaust running under the engine to the right. For reasons of rigidity, the front transverse member was welded to the body structure, so that in case of necessity, the engine had to be lifted out from above. The entire engine and transmission unit was mounted rigidly in the body.

The modified running gear incorporated Bilstein gas filled spring-damper units, similar in their principle to those used in the type 935. The springs themselves were made of titanium and so were the tubular drive shafts borrowed from the 935. Steel was retained for the redesigned rear suspension arms. The final drive was solid: as in other Porsche racing models, there was no differential, but an oil-cooler, located in the transaxle tube tunnel was added to the five-speed gearbox.

The centre-lock hubs came from the 935 and the brakes were similar to those originally developed for the 917/10, but featured the reinforced calipers of the 936. Weight in Le Mans trim was less than 930 kg (2,050 lb) without fuel.

Weissach reckoned that if all went well, a place among the first 10 finishers would be a great success. It must not be forgotten that with only 310 bhp, maximum speed was only 280 km/h (175 mph) and with every lap the 924 would lose 15 seconds to a good 935 on the Le Mans straight only.

Porsche originally planned to entrust the three cars to three teams from different nations: Great Britain, USA and Germany. The drivers were to be chosen with regard to their loyalty to the Porsche marque and their successes at the wheel of Porsche cars. From Britain, Ton Dron, Andy Rouse and Derek Bell were invited. The car bearing the stars and stripes was to be driven by Peter Gregg and Al Holbert, while the German car went to Jürgen Barth and Manfred Schurti, a citizen from Lichtenstein, germanicised for the occasion. Unfortunately, following a road accident, Peter Gregg was unable to drive so that Derek Bell had to be paired with Al Holbert.

Practice of the Le Mans Carreras was uneventful. Small spoilers were added to the windscreen wiper arms to keep them down at speed, a fuel tank gasket had to be replaced and a slightly lower geared fifth gear was fitted, raising the maximum speed to 286 km/h (178 mph).

The best lap times during Wednesday practice were around 4.07 minutes, just two seconds slower than the time calculated by the computer in Weissach. It was raining when the race started, always an advantage for comparatively slow but good handling cars, and even after the rain stopped, 2½ hours later, the track did not dry up for several hours and the Carreras picked up place after place, until, after eight hours of racing, the three cars were lying 10th (Barth-Schurti), 14th (Holbert-Bell) and 15th (Dron-Rouse). The situation was to improve further and there was a time when the cars lay in sixth, seventh and eight positions. Even the low tyre pressure warning installation, used for the first time, worked perfectly. This is an electronic device, comprising a sensor in the wheel rim, signalling any eventual drop of air pressure to a high frequency receiver carried by the brake caliper and operating a warning light on the dash board. But fate was to strike already before half distance: a hare ran across the track in front of Barth's car and demolished the water radiator, which took nearly half an hour to replace. After this nothing of importance happened before 9.35 on Sunday morning, when the US car came in with a suspect sounding engine. A rapid investigation showed that cylinder number one had no compression. The mechanics lay it still but after this, with only three cylinders at work, the lap times increased by about half a minute. Sometime later, similar symptoms paralysed the car of the British team. Orders were immediately given to all Carreras to slow down and the perfectly healthy Barth-Schurti car was given the lap time schedule of 4.15 minutes while the Dron-Rouse car lapped in 4.30 and the Holbert-bell car in 4.45 minutes. At this pace, all three cars managed to finish the race from which 30 of the 55 had retired. In spite of their problems the 924 Carrera GTs were placed 6th, 12th and 13th.

Looking back, the result of this first large scale involvement of the 924 in racing was quite satisfactory. The aerodynamic design proved to be particularly effective, no large additional spoilers or wings being required. The fuel consumption too was very satisfactory: with one tank-full, the cars were able to cover 21 laps, which compares to 11-14 laps achieved by the admittedly faster Porsche 935 on the same 120-litre (26.4 gallon) tank capacity. And quite obviously, the 924s could have done even better. The new Kugelfischer electronically controlled injection pump which cuts off the fuel supply completely when the accelerator is released, was not ready in time for the Le Mans race and a normal mechanical pump had to be used.

The 1980 Le Mans race also proved to be a useful step in the development of the future Porsche 944, a prototype of which was to be entered at Le Mans the following year.

924 Rally/924 SCCA/924 Le Mans/924 Carrera GT-Le Mans/924 Carrera GTR

Year	Body	Model Type	Chassis no	Engine type	Gearbox type	Cyl	Bore × stroke	Capacity	HP (DIN) at rpm	Torque (mkg) at rpm	Comp ratio	W'base (mm)	Track fr/ rear (mm)	Length (mm)	Weight (kg)	No produced
1978	Coupé	924 Rally	9247100016 9248100013 9248100015 9248100019	M 31/01	G 31/01	4 4 4	86,5/84,4 86,5/84,4 86,5/84,4	1984 1984 1984	170/5500 140/5800 150/5800	25/3500 16,8/3500	7,5:1 11,5:1 11,0:1	2400 2400	1418/1392 1418/1392	4212 4212	1184	4
1979	Coupé	924 Rally	93A0190001	M 31/50	931/30	4	86,5/84,4	1984	210/6000	28,5/3500	8,5:1	2400	1477/1476	4212	1050	1
1979 SCCA	Coupé	924	92A0490001-16	M 31/50	931/30	4	87,7/84,4	2039	180/7000	20/5750	11,5:1	2400	1513/1466	4320	970	16
1980	Coupé	924 Le Mans GTP	924 001 924 002 924 003 924 004	924 GTP	937/50	4	86,5/84,4	1984	320/7000	39/4500	6,8:1	2400	1534/1504	4200	930	4
1981	Coupé	924 Carrera GTR	93BS72001- 0025	924 GTR	937/50	4	86,5/84,4	1984	375/6400	41,3/5600	7,0:1	2400	1534/1504	4244	945	25

The Porsche 924 Carrera GT-Le Mans was first seen in the famous 24 hours race of 1980.

The countdown for the 924 Le Mans project started in October 1979.

366

The body was optimised in the Volkswagen wind tunnel—$c_d = 0.35$.

Externally, the standard shape is widely retained, but much weight is saved.

Turbocharged and modified Audi four-cylinder 2-litre engine developing 320 bhp at 7,000 rpm—it gave no trouble in preliminary endurance tests, but was not quite so reliable at Le Mans.

The position of the engine is the same as in the standard car, but the turbocharger is moved to the left and the exhaust pipe feeding the turbine passes under the engine, which is rigidly mounted.

The rear suspension arm is made of steel; the tubular drive shafts are titanium, 'borrowed' from the Type 935.

Three Carrera GTs started in the Le Mans race of 1980—all finished.

368

Jürgen Barth and Manfred Schurti drove 'their' 924 into sixth position.

Types 924 Carrera GTS/GTR (1980-1981)

Type 924 Carrera GTS

After having completed the 400 units of the 924 Carrera GT required for its homologation in Group 4, Porsche produced a small series, further developed within the frame of the Group 4 regulations for competition purposes. This was called the 924 Carrera GTS.

Its turbocharged 2-litre engine developed 245 bhp DIN at 6,250 rpm, using a 1 bar (14 psi) boost. Its maximum torque of 34 mkg (247 lb/ft) was obtained as low as 3,000 rpm. The car accelerated from 0 to 100 km/h (62 mph) in only 6.2 seconds and had a maximum speed of 250 km/h (155 mph).

Tuned for a sporting performance, the front running gear consisted of a McPherson front suspension while the rear suspension incorporated aluminium semi-trailing links with coil springs. Bilstein gas filled dampers and anti-roll bars were used front and rear. The internally ventilated and additionally perforated discs of the twin circuit braking system and the hubs were identical with those of the 911 Turbo.

As can be gathered from the foregoing, comfort was entirely sacrificed to satisfy handling requirements, that is, unless the racing seats borrowed from the Porsche 935 could be thought of as comfortable! Interior trim was black felt throughout and even the meagre sound-proofing material of the 924 Carrera GT was deleted to bring the weight down to 1,121 kg with a full 120-litre tank. The car could be bought for DM 110,000 and could be licensed for road use on an individual basis.

Type 924 Carrera GTR

For serious competition work, the 924 Carrera GTS could also be obtained in rally and racing trim, when the suffix GTS became GTR. The rally kit comprised an engine developing 280 bhp and increased ground clearance. A protective underpan and a roll-over bar were included in the price of approximately DM 145,000. World rally champion Walter Röhrl drove a works prepared 924 GTR in several rallies of 1981 on a private basis.

The racing version was a direct development of the 924 factory cars which were successfully entered for the 1980 Le Mans 24 Hours race. The car was said to be down to the 945 kg (2,083 lb) minimum weight limit without fuel, but all the privately owned, but factory prepared cars which ran at Le Mans in 1981 weighed-in at just over 1,000 kg (2,204 lb). Power was raised to an impressive 375 bhp at 6,400 rpm while the maximum torque was raised to 41 mkg (298 lb/ft) at 5,600 rpm. A maximum speed of 290 km/h (180 mph) was claimed and the car was said to accelerate from rest to 100 km/h (62 mph) in only 4.7 seconds. Such performance called for powerful brakes: those of the legendary 917 and 935 models. Costing DM 180,000, this was the most expensive 924 to be marketed.

The racing version featured such special equipment as a larger rear spoiler, 11.75 × 16 inch centre lock BBS wheels front and rear, adjustable front and rear anti-roll bars, sintered metal clutch linings and solid drive (ie, no differential), in contrast to the 40% limited slip differential of the rally version. A different camshaft, higher boost pressure and a plunger pump fuel injection system were mainly responsible for the increased power of the engine which, in addition, had dry sump lubrication. A 120-litre (26.4 gallon) flexible safety tank was standard in both versions.

Below: Walter Röhrl and Christian Geistdorfer, world rally champions in 1980, occasionally drove this works-prepared Porsche 924 GTR in European rallies as private entrants. Bottom: Porsche 924 GTR to IMSA specifications entered by the factory in the Le Mans 24 Hour Race of 1982 in which it finished eleventh overall, driven by Rouse and Schurti.

Type 924 GTP Le Mans (1981)

In addition to the two Porsche 936s, one of which won the race, Porsche again entered two production based 924s for the 1981 Le Mans 24 Hours race. But while one of those cars was almost identical with the model raced successfully the previous year, one of them had a completely new, Porsche designed engine. In fact the car was not a 924 at all, but a prototype of the soon to be announced Porsche 944, modified for racing.

Except for the wider rear wheel arches required to accommodate the 14 × 16 inch wheels instead of the 11.75 × 16 inch of the 924 GTR entered by private teams, the external appearance and the structure of the 944 forerunner were almost identical with the 924 GTR. The centre lock front wheels were also the same, but in view of the 924 GTP's higher performance, the brake discs were of larger diameter.

The car's most interesting feature was, of course, its completely new four-cylinder engine installed at an angle of 45 degrees to the right, of which the iron-coated pistons ran directly in the unlinered cylinder bores. The block had the bore centres at the same distance as the type 928 V-8, and with an even larger bore of 100 mm and a stroke of 78.9 mm, the engine's capacity was 2,479 cc. A completely new cylinder head featured twin cog-belt driven overhead camshafts and four valves per cylinder. In order to balance the normally unbalanced forces of the second order specific of a straight four, which would lead to heavy vibration in such a large engine, twin balance shafts rotating at twice the crank-shaft's speed in opposite directions, driven by another cog-belt, were housed on either side of the cylinder block. These shafts which are part of the production 944 specification, were not very popular with the racing engineers because of the very minimal friction losses they cause, but removing them produced such violent vibration that they were finally retained, even in the racing engine.

This was fed through a single KKK turbocharger of which the output was led through an air-to-air intercooler before reaching the intake manifold, the boost pressure used in the race being 1.1 bar. Probably for the first time in history, a racing engine featured a combined, fully electronic ignition and timed fuel injection system in which the ignition advance and the quantity of fuel injected were controlled according to engine speed and load by a computer integrating signals given by sensors recording the boost pressure, the intake air temperature and the engine speed. The throttle valve was on the intake side of the compressor and in order to ensure the fullest possible air flow, no air flow meter was used, the quantity of fuel injected being controlled by the integration of intake manifold pressure and air temperature. No less than 2,000 combinations of ignition advance and injector timing were programmed in this installation, developed in cooperation with Bosch.

The car which weighed approximately 950 kg (998 kg in full Le Mans trim) made its first tests in spring 1981 on the Paul Ricard circuit when the boost pressure of 1.3 bar (18.2 psi) providing no less than 450 bhp, proved to be more than the engine could take for 24 hours. For the race itself, it was dropped to 1.1 bar (15.5 psi), which still provided some 420 bhp at 6,800 rpm, the car being geared not to exceed 6,200 rpm on the straight. In this form it proved completely reliable and, driven by Jürgen Barth and rally world champion Walter Röhrl, it finished 7th overall and had the honour of being the car which spent least time in the pits: 56 minutes—hardly more than strictly necessary for the 21 refuelling operations which, with the fuel flow of 50 litres/minute in the refuelling installation, took over 2½ minutes each, taking into account the time spent driving slowly in the pit lane.

RACING CARS

Formula 2/Formula 1

In practice for the Formula 2 race which took place on the Nürburgring in 1957, the fastest time was set by a Porsche which was really not a Formula 2 car. With an only slightly modified Spyder RS, on which the alterations did not go far beyond removing the lights, Edgar Barth took pole position in 10 minutes 2.2 seconds. In the race itself he was narrowly headed for some time by Roy Salvadori driving a Cooper-Climax single-seater, but when the Briton was forced to retire, Barth led the race to the finish. One year later, on the occasion of the Formula 2 race preceding the French Grand Prix on the fast Rheims circuit, Jean Behra drove another Spyder in which the steering had been moved to a central position. Apart from this and the absence of lights, this car did not differ from the Porsche Spyders used for sports car racing either, but again it won, heading the cream of the Formula 2 brigade.

These two successes encouraged Porsche to build a real Formula 2 car. The first example was completed in the winter 1958/59 and during test runs in which Wolfgang von Trips drove the car at the Nürburgring, it got down to the quite remarkable time of 9 minutes 29 seconds. Unfortunately the car's first official outing in the Monte Carlo Grand Prix lasted for only two laps, when Trips hit a wall. A new car was built for the Formula 2 race at Rheims, but meanwhile the French driver Jean Behra, who had been part of the Porsche team in sports car races of 1958 and who was sadly killed on the Avus track in Berlin the following year, had had a Formula 2 car to his own design built in Italy with Porsche's backing. Valerio Colotti, an engineer from Modena, was responsible for the actual design of the single-seater called Behra-Porsche. This was a central-engined car and all its important components, such as engine (from the RSK Spyder), gearbox and front and rear suspensions were of Porsche origin. As other commitments prevented Behra from driving his car at Rheims, he entrusted it to Hans Herrmann who finished second behind Moss driving a Cooper-Climax. In third place came Joakim Bonnier, driving the official Porsche entry.

Only a short time later Moss tested the further improved Porsche single-seater on the British Goodwood circuit and expressed his admiration for its roadholding and its brakes—drum brakes to be precise! Moss' enthusiasm prompted Rob Walker, his entrant, to buy a Formula 2 Porsche which was, of course, finished in

Walker's dark blue scheme, with a white stripe across the nose.

It took five races for the long-expected victory to materialise on the British circuit of Aintree. Three times already the great day seemed to have arrived: in Syracuse Moss had been leading easily when a valve broke. In Brussels he won the first heat, but spun in the second and had to be content with second place overall. At Goodwood, Moss' Porsche came second, 6.5 seconds behind a Lotus; at Pau, Gendebien drove the car into third place behind Jack Brabham and Maurice Trintignant, both driving Coopers, but in this event he never looked like having a chance. For the race at Aintree the factory had entered two additional cars, all of which finished, Porsches taking first, second and third places! They were driven by Moss, Bonnier and Graham Hill.

In the Solitude Grand Prix, close to the factory's premises, and watched by 250,000 spectators, no fewer than five Formula 2 Porsches faced the starter. Of them only one—John Surtees deputising for Moss, still recovering from an accident in the Walker Porsche—did not finish. The others took second, third fourth and fifth places behind von Trips' Ferrari. On this occasion, Dan Gurney drove a works car with a new body. The chassis and engine remained unchanged, but the nose was slightly lower and the back had a stepped shape. It is of interest that Trips' disc-braked Ferrari had the same braking points as the drum-brake Porsches.

Five Porsches were again entered for the Formula 2 German Grand Prix on the Nürburgring. In this case, the 'Manufacturers' Cup' (an unofficial F2 championship) was at stake. Jo Bonnier's victory in a works Porsche clinched the championship for Zuffenhausen.

Almost automatically, the Formula 2 Porsche became a Formula 1 as the 1961 season began and the engine capacity limit for Formula 1 was reduced from 2.5 to 1.5 litres. But it was clear that to be competitive in this premier racing formula, a new engine would be necessary. This had become very evident when the lone F2 Ferrari dominated the Porsches in the Solitude race the previous year. Porsche's old four-cylinder had reached the limit of its development potential and a new flat-eight was laid down, which first ran on the testbed in December 1960. It was a completely new unit, although it remained faithful to the two major characteristics of Porsche power units: air cooling and opposed cylinders. The 180 bhp at 9,200 rpm announced by Porsche was something of an understatement.

An entirely new chassis was designed. Its longer wheelbase, wishbone front suspension and coil springs were major departures from previous Porsche practice. When it first appeared on a track, however, it stood alone by still having drum brakes.

Porsche's first Formula 1 race took place in Brussels, on April 9 1961. It was a great disappointment, as neither of the two cars entered—still with the old four-cylinder engine—finished. But the race had shown that the old four-cylinder engine was still competitive against the British makes. Ferrari was another problem, as the Syracuse Grand Prix showed when the then almost unknown young Italian Giancarlo Baghetti headed the four-cylinder Porsche to the finish.

The debut of the eight-cylinder engine had been scheduled for the Monaco Grand Prix, but its development had taken more time than expected and Porsche ran cars with a new chassis, slightly modified body and a four-cylinder engine with fuel injection instead of carburettors. Bonnier's and Gurney's cars had a wheelbase of 2.30 m (7 feet 6½ inches), while Herrmann's car was only 2.26 m

(7 feet 5 inches). Herrmann had difficulties with the gear change linkage, Bonnier had to retire with a defective injection system due to the formation of air bubbles, while Gurney finished fifth, two laps behind the winner.

What the slow and winding course in the Principality had suggested became obvious on the faster course winding its way through the dunes of Zandvoort. Neither the Porsche's engine nor the chassis were able to match the opposition. After Monte Carlo the entire fuel feed system had been modified and baffles had been added to the tanks, but the cars were still uncompetitive. Gurney finished tenth and the Dutch driver Godin de Beaufort, driving an older carburettor car, was just able to keep Herrmann's fuel-injection factory car at bay. Perhaps this was the reason why the works Porsches were back to carburettors in the Belgian Grand Prix in which they put up a better show, Gurney and Bonnier finishing sixth and seventh respectively.

At Rheims—a lucky circuit for Porsches—the old four-cylinder very nearly gave Porsche its first victory in Formula 1. In an exciting slipstreaming finish, Dan Gurney was beaten by only one tenth of a second by Giancarlo Baghetti's Ferrari, after the three other cars from Maranello had retired. At Solitude Porsche was again second, this time just beaten by Innes Ireland's Lotus. In that race Edgar Barth drove an experimental car in which the four-cylinder engine had a horizontal cooling blower as developed for the new eight-cylinder. Thanks to a modified body it also had a slightly smaller frontal area. This prototype was also fitted with Porsche's own disc brakes. Their calipers were light alloy on the front wheels and cast iron on the rear ones.

Even on Porsche's home circuit, the Nürburgring, success remained elusive. Bonnier had a puncture, then his engine blew up. Herrmann fell back with a slipping clutch, and Gurney, Porsche's last hope, collided with Graham Hill's BRM and could not do better than seventh place.

In March 1962 a completely new Formula 1 car, at last powered by the eight-cylinder engine, had its first trial runs. The new car had torsion bar and wishbone independent suspension front and rear, and disc brakes of Porsche's own design. On the same day another car was also tried with a four-cylinder engine featuring direct fuel injection. This Michael May-developed unit produced some 20 bhp more than previous engines—in all, over 180, it is said. The eight-cylinder first appeared in the Dutch Grand Prix at the Zandvoort circuit. After two years of development, Porsche had produced a low-built and elegant car which immediately made an excellent impression. Its frontal area was much reduced compared with previous models; unfortunately, however, luck was not on Porsche's side: Dan Gurney, the team's fastest driver, went off the road and fell a long way behind.

Another four weeks were spent testing and developing before two cars were sent to the French Grand Prix on the Rouen circuit. On this difficult course Dan Gurney was sixth fastest in practice and, after 20 race laps, was running third, thereafter taking the lead when the two leadings cars both retired. One can imagine the jubilation in the Porsche camp when the American took the chequered flag to present Porsche with its first Grand Prix victory. Next day the team's mechanics were almost unrecognisable, having shaved their beards which they had sworn they would keep until the car had achieved its first victory.

This resounding success drew a quarter of a million spectators, hoping for a repeat performance, to the Nürburgring for the German Grand Prix. Neither rain nor fog dampened their enthusiasm. Unfortunately the Swabes did not quite fulfil their hopes. Only 4.4 seconds behind Graham Hill's BRM and a car's length behind John Surtees' Lola, Gurney could do no better than present them with third place.

Neither did the following races fulfil their hopes: one had to admit that Porsche could not quite make the same impact in Formula 1 as previously in Formula 2. At the end of the 1962 season, the Stuttgarters quietly made it known that, from then on, they would only occasionally take part in F1 races. But in fact the American Grand Prix of 1962 was to be the last race for which a Formula 1 Porsche was entered.

There were three main reasons for this withdrawal: one was that the special components required for the very specialised Formula 1 machines were extremely difficult to obtain from the German suppliers, especially at the short notice required by the F1 involvement. This was the reason why Porsche cooperated with the British branches of Dunlop and BP, when it would have been much more convenient to deal with their German branches. The second reason was that it proved impossible to compete continuously in three different categories of racing: single seaters, sports prototypes and GT cars. The third reason was economic: the takeover of Reutter Bodies, which had nearly as many employees as the Porsche company itself, required a capital investment incompatible with the continuation of Formula 1 activities.

It was generally felt and regretted that Porsche had given up the struggle prematurely. But who knows if, some day, they will not try their luck again in this most prestigious of all forms of racing?

General description: Formula 2

Coachwork and chassis

There is no need for a complete description of the Formula 2 Porsche's immediate forerunner: the 'central drive' Spyder. Except for the driving position, it was almost identical with the Type 1500 RSK.

The aluminium sheet body of the true Formula 2 car was hand-beaten on a wooden rig, and covered the extruded steel tube space frame. The complete car weighed around 470 kg (1,036 lb). The driver was faced with a three-spoke steering wheel through which he could see the central tachometer, flanked by the oil pressure and temperature gauges. The fuel tank had a capacity of 100 litres (22 gallons) and the car's maximum speed was approximately 250 km/h (155 mph).

A slightly narrower front track than in the two-seater was obtained by the use of more sharply angled trailing arms, while the rear suspension was by angled double wishbones. The front springs were transverse bundles of leaf springs working in torsion (four in all), while coil spring and damper units were used at the rear. The dampers, all double-acting, were of Koni manufacture, and there was a front anti-roll bar.

The ZF worm and peg steering had twin symmetrical track rods, and its ratio around the central position was 16:1. The front tyres were 5.50 × 15 R and fatter 6.00 × 15 R tyres were used at the rear. The drum brakes had an internal diameter of 280 mm (11 inches) and an effective braking area of 558 cm² (six square feet) at the front and 372 cm² (four square feet) at the rear. Operation was by twin circuits and the handbrake lever operated the rear brakes by cables.

In 1959, the rear suspension was modified by adding a radius rod to the angled lower wishbones.

Engine

The engine, Type 547/3, of 1,498 cc capacity, was almost identical with the Types 550 and 718 Spyder engines. In its original Formula 2 version with a 9.8:1 compression ratio, it produced over 150 bhp at 7,800 rpm. The four-stroke, flat-four engine had individual light alloy cylinders of which the bores were chromium-plated, spigoted to an aluminium alloy crankcase. The built-up crankshaft ran in three roller bearings and one ball bearing. The big ends also ran on rollers while a floating gudgeon pin was inserted in the little end. The pistons were alloy forgings and carried one oil scraper and three compression rings.

The two one-piece light alloy cylinder heads carried two camshafts each and there was one intake and one exhaust valve per cylinder, in V-formation and fitted with twin concentric coil springs each. They were operated by slave-type tappets interposed between the valve stem and the camshaft. The latter were driven off the crankshaft by a horizontal shaft and two pairs of bevel gears on each side.

A twin radial blower, V-belt driven from the camshaft, provided efficient air cooling. Lubrication was by the dry-sump system with a separate oil tank and a full-flow filter. The energy for the twin ignition system was provided by a battery. The two circuits were entirely separate, with twin distributors driven off the crankshaft. The firing order was 1-4-3-2. Fuel was fed to the two twin-choke, Type 46 IDM 1 Weber carburettors by an electric pump. Later, at the factory's request, the Swiss fuel injection expert Michael May modified the engine to operate with direct fuel injection. At the beginning of the 1962 season the four-camshaft engine, Type 547/6, produced 187 bhp from 1.5 litres. One engine built up from brand-new parts even reached 189 bhp.

Transmission

The Type 718 gearbox had six forward ratios, all synchronised, and one reverse. First was not merely a starting gear, but could effectively be used in the course of a race. Both the gearbox shafts and the differential were included in a barrel-type aluminium housing. The final drive was by spiral bevel and crown wheel and a limited slip ZF differential.

General description: Formula 1

Coachwork and chassis

The main structure of the car consisted of an extruded steel tube frame covered by an aluminium sheet external skin. The aluminium tanks were located on either side of the cockpit and in the nose. To facilitate access to the cockpit, the steering wheel was removable. The small instrument panel carried a tachometer and gauges indicating the oil temperature and pressure. The weight of the complete car, without fuel, was 452 kg (996.5 lb), just 2 kg (4.4 lb) above the minimum weight required by the rules. The top speed was around 270 km/h (170 mph).

The running gear featured unequal length wishbone independent suspension front and rear. The rear arm of the front suspension lower wishbones was carried far back to improve rigidity under braking. After the Dutch Grand Prix at Zandvoort, a similar stay was added to the top wishbone. The suspension was controlled by longitudinal torsion bars and rocker-operated dampers inside the body structure, front and rear, where anti-roll bars were also to be found. The rack-and-pinion steering was of ZF manufacture and the tyres were 5.50 × 15 R front and 6.50 × 15 R rear. The disc brakes were of Porsche's own design in which the disc was, in fact, a large diameter ring with the caliper bridging the inside, so that a larger disc could be accommodated in any given wheel.

Before the eight-cylinder Formula 1 car was introduced, Porsche had run in 1961 a Formula 1 model in which the torsion bars had been replaced by co-axial coil-and-damper units, but a reversion to torsion bars was made for the 1962 season.

Engine
The eight-cylinder engine, Type 753, had a bore of 66 mm (2.6 inches) and a stroke of 54.6 mm (2.2 inches), giving a capacity of 1494.4 cc. With a compression ratio of 10:1, it produced 180 bhp at 9,200 rpm. The crankcase was made of aluminium alloy, as were the separate cylinders of which the bores were chromium-plated. The forged crankshaft had nine bearings of which one was a roller. The big ends carried tri-metal thin shells and the little ends ran on bronze bushes. The pistons were light alloy forgings with one oil scraper and two compression rings. The four overhead camshafts (two for each bank of cylinders) were operated by horizontal shafts and bevel gears. There were two valves per cylinder, each assisted by twin concentric coil springs.

Cooling was by a horizontal turbine, made of plastic. Lubrication was by the dry sump system with a separate oil tank. The Bosch twin-ignition system had two completely independent circuits, incorporating two coils and one distributor each. The distributors were driven by an intermediate shaft. Mixture was provided by four twin-choke Weber carburettors of 38 mm (1.5 inches) diameter.

Transmission
The monoposto used Porsche's own, Type 718, six-speed gearbox, an improved version of the transmission used in 1961. The gear clusters and differential were incorporated in a common, barrel-shaped aluminium housing. The final drive was by spiral bevel and crown wheel, a ZF limited slip differential and twin universal driveshafts to the rear wheels.

Racing a central-drive Spyder, Edgar Barth won an F2 event at the Nürburgring in 1957.

378

Front view of the central-drive Porsche Spyder RSK, the forerunner of Formula 2 Porsches.

Spyder was standard, except for the central driving position.

Edgar Barth racing the central-drive Spyder as an F2 car in the German Grand Prix of 1958.

Porsche Formula 2 prototype, built in 1959. Chassis No 718-2-01.

The first F2 car still looked a bit clumsy—not only from the rear.

380

The modified version of the F2 car for 1960. Note the twin trailing link front suspension.

Under this well-vented tail, the four-cylinder engine produced nearly 190 bhp.

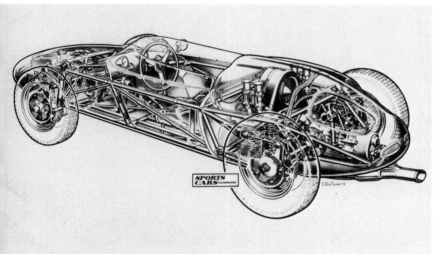

Cutaway view of the F2 championship-winning 1960 monoposto.

381

Dan Gurney driving the experimental 'flat nose' works F2 car at Solitude in 1960.

This experimental 1961 F1 chassis with wishbone front end did not quite live up to expectations.

Formula 1 Porsche four-cylinder (718-2-05) which ran in the 1961 Monaco Grand Prix.

382

New Formula 1 chassis for 1962 with four Porsche-designed disc brakes.

Testing of the eight-cylinder Formula 1 car began in March 1962.

The eight-cylinder engine had a horizontal cooling fan.

383

First race for Porsche's eight-cylinder 1,500 cc Grand Prix car was the 1962 Dutch GP at Zandvoort.

The eight-cylinder Porsche of 1962 was much slimmer than the 1961 eight-cylinder Formula 1 car (right).

The 1962 car (right) had a much smaller cross-section than the 1961 Formula 1 model.

Experimental four-cylinder F1 engine for 1962 with fuel injection and horizontal cooling blower.

1961 four-cylinder, 1.5-litre Formula 1 engine with vertical cooling blower.

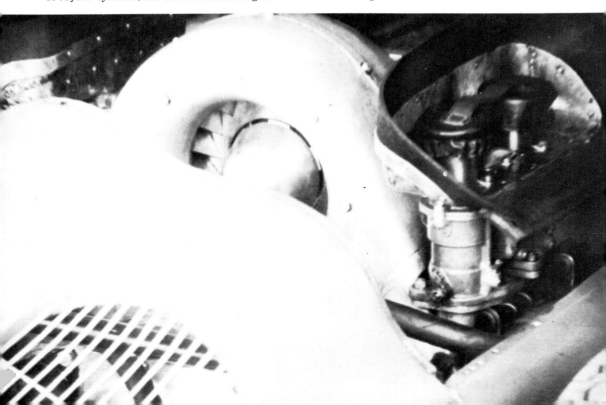

Michael May-modified engine (180 bhp) in revised F1 car, early 1962.

For comparison: the 1961 Porsche monoposto with Dan Gurney driving.

Eight-cylinder engine, Type 753 with four twin-choke carburettors: 180 bhp from 1,500 cc.

Formula 2/Formula 1

Year	Body	Model Type	Chassis no	Engine type	Gearbox type	Cyl	Bore × stroke	Cap-acity	HP (DIN) at rpm	Torque (mkg) at rpm	Comp ratio	W.base (mm)	Track fr/ rear (mm)	Length (mm)	Weight (kg)
1958	Spyder	F2-718	718201-718204	547/3	718	4	85 × 66	1498	150/7800	14,9/6300	9,8:1	2200	1300/1260	3350	470
						4	85 × 66	1498	165/7800	15,1/6300	10,3:1				
1960	Spyder	F2-718/ 787	718205	547/3	718	4	85 × 66	1498	150/7800	14,9/6300	9,8:1	2200	1300/1260	3350	470
1960	Mono-posto	F2-787	78701	547/6	718	4	85x66	1498	190/8000	15,0/6500	10,3:1	2300	1300/1290	3420	456
			78702	547/6	718										
1961	Mono-posto	F1-804	80401-80404	547/6	718	4	85 x 66	1498	190/8000	15,0/6500	10,3:1	2300	1300/1330	3600	450
1962	Mono-posto	F1-804	80401-80404	753	718	8	66 x 54,6	1494	180/9200	15,6/7200	10:1	2300	1300/1330	3600	455

From Glöckler Porsche to RS 61

Even before the Porsche factory produced a sports car specially built for racing, a private owner had broken the ground. He was Walter Glöckler, a VW dealer in Frankfurt who, during the winter of 1949, had teamed up with his works manager, Ing Ramelow, to build a racing open two-seater based on Porsche mechanical units and for which the body workshop Weidenhausen, sited just across the road, built a well-proportioned body. Thanks to its very light tubular frame the car weighed under 450 kg (992 lb). As the 1,086 cc VW-Porsche engine running on methanol produced 58 bhp, this provided quite a respectable power-to-weight ratio.

With this car, soon generally known as the 'Glöckler Porsche', Walter Glöckler became a German champion in 1950. It even powered other drivers to champion titles in the two following years! Meanwhile Walter Glöckler had built himself another car, based on a 1,500 cc Porsche engine, with which he won the German championship in this very competitive class. Methanol helped to produce 98 bhp, enough to endow this Glöckler Porsche with a maximum speed of 210 km/h (133 mph). This second car was later sold to America, where it earned many more victor's laurels. Meanwhile, however, competition from abroad had become more formidable and Glöckler's private venture could not be expected to deal successfully with such competition. This could only be met by a proper, factory-made car, on which work was started in Zuffenhausen in the winter of 1952. This mid-engined car was largely inspired by the Glöckler Porsche, but at the same time work was also started on the design of a completely new four-camshaft engine which was to make history and was the work of Dr Ernst Fuhrmann, who was to become Porsche's managing director 20 years later.

The new car was driven in the Eifel Race of 1953 by Helm Glöckler—Walter's cousin—but still powered by the standard 1500 S engine of which the power was slightly increased thanks to the use of methanol-based fuel. In the Le Mans 24 Hours race, however, for which two of the new cars had been entered, commercial fuel was mandatory and in order to increase the speed which could be achieved with little more than 75 bhp, a streamlined top was adapted to the two tubular-framed 'Spyders'. These dead-heated for first place in the 1,500 cc class and were timed on the straight at a speed just under 200 km/h (125 mph). As the Glöckler Porsches, the Le Mans coupés had their aluminium body made by Weidenhausen in Frankfurt and the complete cars weighed 560 kg (1,234 lb). These Le Mans Cars and the Glöckler Porsches were thus the direct ancestors of the Type 550 'Spyder' which was to acquire celebrity in the second half of the 1950s.

The two Le Mans cars were then entered—without their coupé top—for the sports car race preceding the German Grand Prix at Nürburgring. Thanks to the use of methanol fuel, their 1500 S engine developed 98 bhp and Hans Herrmann did the fastest lap in 11 minutes 2 seconds. An even more interesting car, however, had been seen during practice for this race: a similar Spyder powered for the first time by the new four-camshaft engine. It was driven one week later by Hans Stuck Sr in the Freiburg-Schauinsland hill climb.

The true Type 550 Spyder with the 1,498 cc four-camshaft engine, Type 547, did not make its first official appearance before 1954. Although it was generally known as the 'Spyder', the cars were officially called 1500 RS, following Dr Porsche's special request. The body was built by Weinsberg and in order to identify the externally identical works cars they had the area in front of their tail lights finished in different colours. In the case of Hans Herrmann, the colour was mostly red and his cars were known as 'red tails'.

The first racing appearance of the 550 Spyder was on the 1954 Mille Miglia in which Hans Herrmann and Herbert Linge finished sixth overall, in spite of being slightly delayed by some minor troubles. For Le Mans, a Type 550 was entered with a 1,300 cc engine, Type 547/1. Except for its smaller capacity, it was identical to the 1,500 cc version and developed 93 bhp at 5,500 rpm, with an 8.0:1 compression ratio. Maximum torque was 9.3 mkg (68 lb/ft) at 4,000 rpm.

At the end of 1954, a first batch of 550 Spyders was sold to private owners. Their bodies were built by Wender in Reutlingen, but mechanically they were almost identical to the works cars. Their 1.5-litre four-camshaft engines produced 110 bhp at 6,200 rpm. The price was DM 24,600. Altogether slightly more than 100 of this model were sold, a large proportion going to the USA. The first Type 550 sold in Germany went to Kurt Ahrens Sr. The 550 Spyder was successfully used by the factory, up to the end of the 1957 season, but the model continued to be successful in the hands of private owners up to the beginning of the 1960s. In the Avus race of 1954, the 1.5-litre Spyders went nearly as fast as the pukka Formula 2 cars. The top drivers took the famous banking at approximately 190 km/h (120 mph) and the works driver Richard von Frankenberg lapped the course at an average of 198.8 km/h (123.5 mph).

In the Eifel race of 1955 at the Nürburgring, however, the factory Porsches had to accept an unexpected defeat. They were beaten on their home course by Edgar Barth, driving an East German EMW. Fortunately the Le Mans 24 Hours race presented them with an opportunity to make good, when the four 1.5-litre Spyders entered—and fitted with new, larger brakes—all finished. The two coupés featuring an 1,100 cc four-camshaft engine also met with success, taking the first two places in their class.

For the Avus race of 1955 the 550 to be driven by Richard von Frankenburg incorporated a few improvements, aimed at increasing its speed and power to take on the East German EMW team. The power of the engine was raised from 110 to 125 bhp. A five-speed gearbox was fitted and the coachwork was modified in details. The maximum speed was increased to around 255 km/h (160 mph). In the race deciding the German championship, Edgar Barth and Richard von Frankenberg fought wheel to wheel, raising the enthusiasm of the 30,000 spectators. Only when the the throttle linkage of Barth's EMW broke was the issue settled in favour of Frankenberg, who clinched the German 1,500 cc Sports Car Championship for 1955.

For the Mille Miglia of 1956, the 550 was so drastically improved that it was renamed 550A. For this long-distance race, the A-types were to have a space

390

frame, a modified rear suspension and a four camshaft engine of which the power was increased to an honest 130 bhp. A five-speed gearbox with the latest baulking mechanism was also developed. Only one car with the reinforced frame could be readied in time, however. It was allocated to Hans Herrmann and weighed only 515 kg (1,135 lb). The other 500A cars received the other improvements, but still used the old ladder-type tubular frame weighing alone 16 kg (35.3 lb) more than the space frame. A twin circuit brake system was also used . . . and proved unexpectedly troublesome.

The first race of the new Spyder was the 1000 km Race at the Nürburgring, where it finished fourth overall. But much more sensational was its performance in the Targa Florio in which the Italian driver Umberto Maglioli drove the 1,500 cc car to a resounding overall victory. This success was all the more remarkable due to the fact that the decision to race in Sicily had been taken only 11 days before the race, as a result of the good performance put up by the new Spyder at the 'Ring. Porsche's effort for the race consisted in sending down their racing manager Huschke von Hanstein, a single car, two mechanics and the driver. The 1500 RS ran in practice and in the race without any problem, pitted only for refuelling—even the Continental racing tyres lasted through the 720-kilometre (448-mile) long race—and won with almost 15 minutes in hand. In Porsche's racing history, this was then by far the biggest and most satisfying success. When the triumphant team returned home all production came to a halt. Almost all the company's employees gathered on the factory's forecourt and paid an enthusiastic tribute to the winners. Stuttgart's Mayor celebrated the occasion with a speech and an obviously very moved Dr Ferry Porsche thanked all his colleagues.

At the end of the 1956 season a new prototype Spyder appeared in the Solitude race staged in Stuttgart's immediate outskirts. It differed from the normal 550A mainly in its shortened wheelbase (only two metres, 6 feet 6.75 inches) a narrower track and body and a modified rear suspension. The wheels were located by two asymmetrical triangular wishbones each, the springing medium remaining transverse torsion bars and telescopic dampers. The frame was reinforced by a transverse member over the rear suspension. 'Micky Mouse' was not very successful, however, and after it burned out following a spectacular accident on Berlin's Avus track, no replica was built.

The racing season of 1957 began with a sensation: the EMW cars from East Germany which for many years had been Porsche's toughest opponents, were withdrawn from the racing scene following the decision of the German Democratic Government to withdraw their contribution of an estimated 60 million East-Marks per year to the development of the racing cars and the maintenance of the team. The two EMW works drivers, Edgar Barth and Alfred Rosenhammer, were immediately signed up by Porsche.

Some time after the season had begun, at the Nürburgring 1000 km race, a jealously kept secret was revealed only a few minutes before the start of practice: a revised version of the 550A Spyder. It had the same wheelbase as its predecessor, but it was lower built, and had two small tail fins. It became known as the 1500 RS-K Spyder (or Type 718) after the K-shaped reinforcement of the front cross tube assembly carrying the torsion bars and trailing arms. Even though, in later years, the diagonal reinforcement tubes were deleted again, the name remained.

As all previous Spyder models, the RS-K could be bought from the factory, either new or from the factory team. In the commercially available 1958 model, the 1,498 cc engine developed 142 bhp at 7,500 rpm, the power being increased to 148 bhp at 8,000 rpm for the following year. Approximately 30 were sold.

Beginning with the 1958 season, Porsche concentrated on running the RS-K which did remarkably well in the first race of the year, the 1000 km of Buenos Aires: driven by Stirling Moss and Jean Behra it finished third overall, headed only by two 3-litre Ferraris. The same result was achieved at Sebring by Harry Schell and Wolfgang Seidel, and the car did even better in the Targa Florio where Behra and Scarlatti drove it into second place. These and other excellent results in long distance races brought Porsche second place in the World Championship of Makes. Particularly creditable were the results obtained at Le Mans where of the five Spyders entered, four managed to finish in third, fourth, fifth and ninth places. Only a Ferrari and an Aston-Martin—both of 3-litre capacity—headed the Porsche armada. Of the four cars which reached the finish, the third placed (and another which was eliminated by a crash) had the engine capacity increased to 1,588 cc. In order to avoid the piston troubles which had plagued Porsche the previous year, the compression ratio of all the engines was reduced from 9.8 to 9.4:1 for this particular race.

The debut of the 1500 RS-K with central steering in the Formula 2 race preceding the French Grand Prix at Rheims ended in triumph. Driving this otherwise completely standard Spyder, Jean Behra won the race, beating the cream of the pedigree single seaters of the period. For the occasion, the cockpit opening had been faired-in and spats were fitted to cover the rear wheels in order to improve the streamlining. The 1,500 cc engine of this car developed 164 bhp.

A year later, in 1959, Porsche went back to Rheims, but this time with real Formula 2 cars having exposed wheels. Two Spyders with central steering were also entered for Wolfgang von Trips and Colin Davis. But this time Porsche's fastest driver, Edgar Barth, had to be content with third place behind Moss' Cooper-Borgward and Herrmann's Behra-Porsche. Porsche's worst year at Le Mans was in 1959 when none of the factory or privately entered Spyders finished. Their retirement was, in every case, caused by a broken crankshaft.

They did not fare much better in 1960 when all four factory Spyders retired with various troubles. The only Porsche to finish was the Linge/Walter Abarth-Carrera which saved the day for Zuffenhausen by taking 11th place overall and a class victory. In order to compensate for the very high, full-width windscreen made compulsory by the rules, which reduced the Spyder's speed to an unacceptable extent, the Porsche engineers had done a lot of experimenting to improve the streamlining until the loss in speed was only 100 rpm (approximately 2.5 mph). The result was a car looking very much like a coupé without the roof panel. In case the inside of the windscreen was obscured by rain or mist, an additional wiper was fitted on the *inside* of the glass!

Two of the streamlined RS 60s were bored out by an additional 0.5 mm in order to raise the engine's capacity to 1,605 cc, putting them in the 2-litre class, while another RS 60 had a 1,500 cc engine fitted. These cars weighed just over 600 kg (1,322 lb) and reached a maximum speed of 225 km/h (140 mph).

For the Targa Florio of 1961 Porsche produced an engine bigger than the 1.7-litre unit which had been developed meanwhile. Its capacity was just under two litres and externally it did not differ from the smaller power unit. This engine, which was barely more powerful than the 1.7-litre but had a much fatter torque curve, was used for two cars. One of them, driven by Joakim Bonnier and Dan Gurney, finished second overall.

In the Nürburgring 1000 km race, Porsche's big problem which had been ever more clearly recognised by the insiders reached a climax. The four-cylinder engine, which had been designed in the years 1952-53, had obviously reached the limit of its development potential. It had been hoped to make do with this engine until the new eight-cylinder was ready, but the Formula 1 development programme running parallel with the engine developments had taken up too much of the engineers' time. In spite of the wet and cool weather, two of the three works cars suffered engine trouble and had to retire, while the third just limped home!

No wonder that, only a few weeks later, the Porsche team heading for Le Mans was not in a particularly cheerful state of mind. Five cars had been entered for the 24 Hours race: there were two new coupés powered by a 1.7- and by a 1.6-litre engine, an open Spyder with the 2-litre unit and two Abarth-Carreras. To finish at any cost was the order of the day, and to achieve this all cars except the open Spyder had been fitted with very 'civilized' plain bearing engines, as normally used for ordinary Carreras. The Spyder nevertheless acquitted itself very well, reaching the finish in fifth position overall, driven by Masten Gregory and Al Holbert, heading the Porsche contingent. Barth and Herrmann's much-loved RS coupé finished seventh and the Abarth-Carrera of Pon/Linge came home 10th.

The great day of the eight-cylinder's first outing at last came with the Targa Florio. The 2-litre version used produced an honest 210 bhp and proved to be quite reliable. In fact it was not the engine but the new disc brakes which doomed the Porsche's effort when success was almost in sight: from the fourth lap on (the race was run over 11 laps of the 72 kilometre/44.8 mile circuit) the brakes gradually became less efficient, slowing the car considerably. Two eight-cylinders had been entered: a Spyder and a coupé in the 1961 Le Mans form. This wore an unfamiliar red livery, having been lent to the Italian Scuderia Serenissima, but it outlasted the Spyder which Dan Gurney crashed into a wall on the second lap, and finished third despite its failing brakes.

At the Nürburgring, one of the two eight-cylinders again finished third in the 1000 km race, while the second car had to retire two laps from the end when its six-speed gearbox became unusable. For Le Mans no eight-cylinder was entered, the factory concentrating on its 1.6-litre Carreras. Its efforts were rewarded with seventh and 12th places overall, which earned Porsche the World Championship for GT cars in the 2-litre class.

The first big international victory for the eight-cylinder engine came in the 45th Targa Florio in 1963. The winning car was driven by the Swedish-Italian team of Joakim Bonnier and Carlo Mario Abate. But while this second victory in the Targa Florio was being celebrated, a completely new sports racing car was being prepared in Zuffenhausen to replace the now famous Spyder, the career of which had lasted a whole decade: the Porsche 904 GTS, first raced in the Sebring 12 Hours race of 1964. Not only did the new model win its class in its first race, but its first appearance in Europe was an even more resounding success when Colin Davis and Baron Antonio Pucci won the Targa Florio outright, ahead of another identical car, after the two eight-cylinder Spyders had retired with rear suspension troubles and a broken half-shaft respectively.

With this race, the career of the Spyder on the world's racing circuits had come to an end, but some of them continued to earn successes in the European Hill Climb Championship which, at that time, was supported by several manufacturers. The most successful of them was the 2-litre eight-cylinder car at the wheel of which Edgar Barth became European Hill Climb Champion both in 1963 and 1964—and which eventually became known as 'Grandma'!

393

The Glöckler Spyder
was the ancestor of
all Porsche racing
Spyders.

Spyder with
1.5-litre engine.
W. Glöckler won
the German
Championship
with it in 1952.

Cockpit of the
Glöckler-Porsche.
This very well-
made car weighed
under 450 kg
(992 lb).

General description: Types 550/550A

Coachwork and chassis

The first 550 models were built by Porsche in 1953 both in open and closed versions. The coupé was aerodynamically superior to the Spyder, even when fitted with only one small aero screen. In the open model, the long fairing behind the driver's head was intended to serve both as a headrest and to smooth the turbulence created by the windscreen, but it could not fill the depression behind the car, which would have been necessary to reduce the air drag.

Wind tunnel tests carried out on models to finalise the shape of the Spyder produced some unexpected results. To improve the air flow through the engine bay, an air intake was installed behind the seats, first with the opening facing forward, then with the same opening facing rearward. Rather surprisingly, the latter arrangement gave the better results. A wool staple held in the air stream ahead of the model was fed into the inverted funnel without any outside help, while with the opening facing forward, it obstinately refused to enter the opening.

The one-piece external skin of the Type 550 Spyder was made of aluminium sheet smoothly extending from the nose over the mudguards to the car's tail, thus contributing to the overall stiffness of the structure, based on a ladder frame made up of steel tubes assembled by welding. The doors, which were hinged at their forward edge and had their lock at the opposite end, were also made of aluminium. Both external door handles could be locked from outside by means of a key, the car still being, in principle, suitable for road use.

The front and rear covers both had invisible hinges and a stay to hold them automatically in the open position. They could be opened only from inside the car by means of a cable. An air intake grille was provided in the engine bay cover and the laminated glass windscreen was slightly curved. The upper part of the windscreen frame was provided with two fittings to which the all-weather top with transparent rear panel (or hard top) could be attached. The entire windscreen could be removed in a matter of minutes.

The dash panel was welded to the structure of which it was a stressed element and carried the switches controlling the windscreen wiper, the instrument lights and the headlights, the generator, oil pressure and main beam warning lights, the ignition switch, a plug socket and starter button. Warm air was fed through the main chassis members from the engine to the cockpit interior, from where a flap could be operated to open or close the system. Two additional slides inside the cockpit could be operated to regulate the air flow. No provision was made for defrosting.

The two bucket seats could be adjusted longitudinally. Behind them a step in the floor could be used as an emergency seat, but no rear squab was provided. Rubber mats covered the bare metal in the front foot well, over the central backbone, in the rear compartment and on the door sills.

The Spyder's top could either be folded or completely removed. It was made of light convertible top material. The interior door trim panels were made of hard paper and imitation leather, and other visible metallic surfaces were covered with 'bouclé' carpet material. The upper part of the dashboard, the instrument cowl and the protection around the cockpit opening were also covered with imitation leather. The central windscreen tensioner carried the rear view mirror.

The independent front suspension was by twin trailing arms and transverse torsion bars made up of bundles of spring leaves. An anti-roll bar was also provided. At the rear, the swinging half-axles were controlled by trailing arms operating transverse cylindrical torsion bars. Double-acting telescopic dampers were fitted all round. The worm and peg steering gear had a ratio of 14.1:1 (2.4 turns from lock to lock).

The brake pedal operated four drum brakes of 280 mm (11 inches) diameter hydraulically. The front brakes were of the two-leading shoe type. All wheels were of the dimensions 3.50D—16 carrying 5.00-16 Rs tyres at the front and 5.25-16 RS tyres at the rear. Early cars weighed around 550 kg (1,212 lb), later increasing to 590 kg (1,300 lb). The 550 Spyder had a top speed of approximately 220 km/h (138 mph), and 100 km/h (60 mph) was reached from rest in just under ten seconds. In racing, the 68-litre (15-gallon), front-mounted tank with quick-action filler provided a range of approximately 350 kilometres (220 miles).

The 550 A model, which first appeared in 1956, differed from its predecessor in the following main particulars: the ladder-type frame was replaced by a steel tube space-frame which was both stiffer and lighter. It weighed 43 kg (95 lb), a saving of 16 kg (35.3 lb) over the tubular ladder frame. The weight of the complete body was reduced by no less than 27 kg (60 lb) to 63 kg (139 lb), thanks to the fact that the space-frame allowed a large part of the body frame to be deleted. Torsional stiffness of the frame was trebled and the beam stiffness was five times that of the ladder frame.

At the same time, the rear suspension was changed from a normal swing axle to a low pivot swing axle, while a front anti-roll bar was added. These modifications considerably improved the car's handling. The springing medium remained transverse laminated torsion bars at the front and cylindrical torsion bars at the rear.

The brakes were constantly being improved by increases in drum diameter and lining width. The original Porsche Spyder had leading and trailing shoe front and rear brakes, but a change was soon made to two leading shoe front brakes. The front drum diameter was increased from 230 to 280 mm (nine to 11 inches) and the rear brake drums were similarly increased, although the front drums were wider: 60 mm (2.36 inches), compared with 40 mm (1.57 inches) for the rear drums. The 550 A had twin braking circuits and weighed 530 kg (1,168 lb) excluding fuel, but including the compulsory spare wheel, and its engine originally developed 135 bhp. The car would cover a kilometre from a standing start in 26.6 seconds and reach a terminal speed of 205 km/h (127.5 mph). Maximum speed was approximately 240 km/h (150 mph). The fuel tank now had a capacity of 80 litres (17.6 gallons), the auxiliary tank fitted for long distance races increasing this to 130 litres (28.6 gallons).

Engine

In late summer 1952, the first drawings were laid down for a completely new engine which had become necessary to fight off the ever-increasing competition put up by Borgward and Osca in the 1,500 and 1,100 cc classes respectively. Mainly responsible for the design of the new engine was Porsche's current managing director, Professor Ernst Fuhrmann. The new engine, known as the Type 547, had four shaft-driven overhead camshafts. The flat-four engine had an aluminium crankcase and produced 110 bhp at 7,800 rpm in its original 1,498 cc version. The separate cylinders and the heads were also of aluminium alloy. Two Solex 40 PJJ twin-choke down-draught carburettors produced the mixture. The valves were in V-formation and the crankshaft was of the Hirth built-up type, running in four roller bearings. From the beginning, the engine had twin ignition with two plugs per cylinder, two distributors and two coils. The distributors were driven directly and in line with the upper two camshafts. Later, a different drive was used with the two distributors arranged in V-formation and driven by bevel gears from the rear of the crankshaft. Air cooling was provided by a vertical, V-belt driven blower with twin intakes. Lubrication was by forced feed and dry sump with a separate 8-litre (14-pint) tank. The electric system was fed by a 6-volt battery and the dynamo had an output of 160 watts. The engine was ahead of and the gearbox behind the rear wheel axis.

For the 550 A used as from 1956, the power of the basically unmodified engine was raised to 135 bhp at 7,200 rpm. The compression ratio went up from 9.5 to 9.8:1 and the Solex carburettors were changed for Weber 40 DCM twin-choke down-draught carburettors. A change was also made to a 12-volt electrical system.

Transmission
The first Spyders made in 1954 had a normal Porsche synchromesh four-speed gearbox, but in the British Tourist Trophy race of 1955, Richard von Frankenberg had an experimental five-speed box which was adopted as the Spyder's standard gear from 1956 on. First gear, however, was only a starting gear, contained in a small separate housing. It was not synchronised and could be selected only after operating a catch, just as for reverse gear. Although the synchronisation of the other gears was exemplary, all the works drivers normally used double declutching methods—as they still do today—for which the single dry plate clutch was thankful. The final drive was by spiral bevel gears and wheelspin was reduced by a ZF limited slip differential.

Side view of the Type 550 Spyder with coupé top shows good streamlining.

Prototype of Porsche 550
with coupé top. It
weighed 550 kg (1,212 lb).

Rear view of Type 550
coupé for 1953 Le Mans
(first version).

398

With the 1500-S pushrod
engine slightly modified
to produce 82 bhp, the Le
Mans coupé could achieve
a speed of 200 km/h
(124 mph).

Rear view of 1953 Le Mans coupé. The body was all aluminium and the complete car weighed only 560 kg (1225 lb).

Inside view of the 1953 Le Mans coupé reveals the efforts to save weight.

Below left: The two coupés shared the victory in 1,500 cc class after 24 hours' racing.

Below: Space could be found for only the fuel tank and the spare wheel in the nose of the Le Mans coupés.

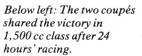

Experimental 1953 Spyder with high tail.

This 550 Spyder ran in slightly modified form in several overseas races.

400

Porsche Type 550 Spyder: its first official appearance with the new four-camshaft engine came in 1954.

The Type 550 was powered by the original 1.5-litre, four-camshaft engine with an output of 110 bhp.

At the end of 1954, the 550 Spyder was offered in this form to private owners at DM 24,600.

The frameless aluminium body of the Type 550 was supported by this tubular ladder frame.

Later 550 Spyders had a lower tail and an aerodynamically more efficient front end.

For 1956, the Type 550 A Spyder was developed from the 550.

A tubular spaceframe replaced the 550's ladder frame in the 550 A.

A low-pivot swing axle replaced the 550's normal swing axle.

405

Spyder 550 A-1500 RS with streamlined headrest.

1.5-litre Spyder at the 1956 Targa Florio. It was driven to an unexpected overall victory by Umberto Maglioli.

Count Berghe von Trips/Maglioli in the 1,000 km race at the Nürburgring in 1956: it was the 550 A's first appearance.

Targa Florio winner Umberto Maglioli at the Nürburgring in the curtain raiser to the 1957 German GP.

Specially made for the 1956 Le Mans 24 Hours race: the 550 A-1500 RS with coupé top.

408   *Technically, the Le Mans coupés differed little from the works Spyders.*

The famous Type 547, 1.5-litre, four-camshaft engine. Power progressed from 110 to 150 bhp.

General description: Type 718 (RS-K)

Coachwork and chassis

The successor to the 550 A Spyder had a lighter space frame assembled from extruded steel tubes by welding. The body was generally lower and had a lower aerodynamic drag than the RS Spyders. Originally, the RS-K featured a metre wide and 20 cm high windscreen (39.37×7.87 inches), as required for sports cars by the racing rules. To reduce the drag, the screen was extended on either side of the cockpit. Ahead of the front wheels, the body progressively became narrower and contained the two headlights, protected by Plexiglas covers. The engine oil surface radiator was under the nose. Otherwise the front of the vehicle was perfectly smooth and devoid of any large air intakes. It contained the compulsory spare wheel and behind this was an 80-litre (17.6-gallon) fuel tank, the quick filler of which protruded through the front cover. The oil filler was on the right-hand side, just ahead of the rear wheel. A prominent feature of the rounded tail were the two air intake grilles. A panel with four louvres, on either side of the body, ahead of the rear wheels led air to the large drum brakes.

The external shape of the body was modified several times. Vertical tail fins were fitted on fast circuits and there was also a so-called 'aerodynamic hump' which was either a fairing behind the driver's head or extended over the full width of the cockpit. In some cases—as in Le Mans 1958—the passenger's seat was covered with an aluminium cowl. The car's weight was just under 530 kg (1,168 lb).

Compared with the previous model, the front suspension was improved. The trailing arms were less offset to match longer torsion bars and the hub carriers were pivoted in spherical joints instead of multiple bushes. The steering column had two universal joints because of the central location of the steering gear, from which the wheels were controlled by two symmetrical track rods. The steering wheel was still on the left, but the arrangement made it easy to move into the centre line in case the car should start in Formula 2. The rear suspension was now by variable rate coil springs with concentric telescopic dampers. The suspension travel was increased and the rear swinging half-axle suspension was modified to lower the pivot, while the half-axles were each located by a longitudinal Watt's linkage avoiding any toe-in variations. The peripheral brake drum fins were abandoned in favour of angled transverse fins making an angle of 30 degrees to the car's transverse axle. They were the so-called 'Turbofins'. The footbrake operated the four drum brakes of 280 mm (11 inches) diameter over a twin hydraulic circuit, while the handbrake operated the rear brakes mechanically. The total braking area was 930 cm^2 (10 square feet).

Engine

The Type 718 power unit was a development of the Type 550's engine, with the power increased to 142 bhp at 7,500 rpm. One year later another 6 bhp had been found and 148 bhp was obtained at 8,000 rpm. In actual racing, the drivers were not allowed to use more than 7,600 rpm for any length of time, but in emergencies up to 8,000 rpm were permissible for very short periods. The two Weber twin down-draught carburettors, Type 40 DCM, were later changed for Types 46 IDM.

Transmission

A single-plate dry clutch was used in conjunction with a five-speed gearbox contained in a barrel-type housing. It was controlled by a central lever and the four upper gears were synchronised. Final drive was by spiral bevel and crown wheel and there was a vast choice of gearbox and final drive ratios.

General description: Types RS 60/RS 61

Coachwork and chassis

The RS 60 and RS 61 models did not differ drastically from the 718. The aluminium two-seater Spyder body was built around the space frame made up of welded extruded steel tubes. The two doors were hinged at their front end and the windscreen was laminated glass. There were two bucket seats and the front and rear covers were fully removable. The two fuel tanks, located under the front cover through which their filler protruded, had a capacity of over 80 litres (17.6 gallons). The new Spyders had a new, rounded and lower front end. There was a fairing behind the driver's head. Two large grilles were incorporated in the tail and enough space was provided behind the engine to hold the compulsory 'suitcase'. The car's nose was completely smooth, except for the small openings to cool the front brakes and the oil radiator. The headlights were protected by Plexiglas covers.

For Le Mans a new body was developed, looking like a flat and elongated coupé of which the roof panel was missing. For the 1961 race, the superstructure which previously ran to meet the rear air intake grille was more or less halved in length. For the same race, the later well-known Le Mans coupé was also developed. The lower part of the coupé was identical with the Spyder RS 61, but a hard top was added that ended approximately at rear wheel hub level. The RS 61 Spyder was successfully raced, mainly in the European Hill Climb Championship until 1964. It was with one such Spyder, nicknamed 'Grandma' and powered by an eight-cylinder engine, that Edgar Barth won the European Hill Climb Championships of 1963 and 1964.

The front suspension was by twin trailing arms working transverse laminated torsion bars clamped in their centre. At the rear, the wheels were located by twin oblique wishbones. In this case, coil springs concentric with the telescopic dampers were used. The dampers themselves were twin-acting Konis front and rear and there was a front anti-roll bar.

The ZF-Ross worm and peg steering gear operated two track rods of equal length. Its ratio was 16:1 around the central position.

The tyre dimensions were 5.50-15 R at the front and 5.90 or 6.00-15 R at the rear, mounted on 4.00 J × 15 alloy rims. The foot brake had twin hydraulic circuits and operated on 280 mm (11 inch) drums. The handbrake was mechanical on the rear wheels.

The RS 61 had a completely new rear suspension with two triangular wishbones on either side, the lower one being additionally located by a longitudinal radius rod. The front axle trailing links were more offset than before and the chassis frame also became slightly wider to meet an FIA requirement. The 25 cm (ten inch) high windscreen had a similar origin. Another important detail was the lengthened wheelbase, increased from 210 to 220 cm (82.67 to 86.6 inches).

Engine

The Type 547 four-camshaft engine which had powered the Types 550 and 718 was also used in the Types 718 RS 60 and RS 61. For the latter, the engine capacity was raised from 1.5 to 1.6 litres (exactly 1,587.5 cc). The smaller version of the four-cylinder engine produced an honest 150 bhp at 7,800 rpm with a compression ratio of 9.8:1 while its 89 cc larger successor developed at least 10 bhp more at the same speed.

The two engines had many common features, such as the aluminium alloy crankcase and separate cylinders, the latter with chromium-plated bores, the built-up crankshaft running in three roller and one ball bearing. Compared with the previous models, the crankshaft was of a stronger design. The big ends were also on rollers, while the little ends were fitted with a floating bronze bush. The pistons were stamped light alloy with one scraper and three compression rings.

The valves were operated by twin overhead camshafts for each bank, via pivoted tappets. The camshafts were shaft-driven and the two valves per cylinder arranged in V-formation were each reclaimed by twin coil springs. The mixture was provided by two Weber Type 46 IDM 1 down-draught twin-choke carburettors to which the fuel was fed by an electric pump. A filter was incorporated in the fuel tank and the pressure limiting valve was provided with a water separator.

Cooling was by a twin-flow radial blower, V-belt driven from the crankshaft. Engine lubrication was by a dry sump system. The battery provided the energy for the twin ignition system of which the two circuits were entirely independent and the two distributors were driven from the rear of the crankshaft.

The eight-cylinder engine, Type 771 was also used. It is fully described in the chapter devoted to the Porsche Types 904 to 908.

Transmission
A barrel-type magnesium housing contained the Type 718 gearbox and differential. Of the forward gears, only first was not synchronised. The selectors were operated through an appropriate linkage by a ball-mounted lever in the centreline of the car. Final drive was by spiral bevel and crown wheel, a ZF limited slip differential and half shafts featuring twin universals each.

412

Left, the RSK Spyder, Type 718. Right, the Type 550 A-1500 RS, its predecessor.

*Umberto Maglioli
at the wheel of a
1500 RSK at the
Freiburg-
Schauinsland hill-
climb of 1957.*

*Small tail fins were
added to the RSK
Spyder for the
Sebring 12-Hour
race.*

414   *Front and rear views of the 'Sebring Spyder' with tail fins and supplementary lamps.*

On the Avus track, where maximum speed is all-important, spats were used to cover the rear wheels.

Le Mans 24 Hours race, 1958. Edgar Barth (at the wheel) and Paul Frère drove this 1500 RSK Spyder into fourth place overall. Note faired-in passenger seat.

Bird's-eye view of 1959 RSK Spyder with wrap-round side windows.

416

The spaceframe of the RSK was lighter than the Type 550 A's. It was made of extruded steel tubes.

Four-camshaft engine fitted with air filters over the intakes.

417

Externally, the Porsche RS 60 differed little from its predecessor, the 1500 RSK, but had wishbone rear suspension.

Rear view of RS 60: the compulsory luggage compartment is ahead of the two large air intake grilles.

The 1,500 cc engine was mounted just aft of the cockpit.

The new Spyders had more flowing lines and a modified, better-streamlined rear cover.

Nürburgring, 1,000 Km race, 1960: Phil Hill in the RS 60 Spyder.

Only the air intakes for brake and oil radiator cooling spoil the clean front.

Spyder RS 60 for the 1960 Le Mans race with 'open air' coupé top.

Edgar Barth drove this Le Mans coupé in 1960. Note inside windscreen wiper.

For the 1961 Le Mans race, the rear end of the 1960 model's top was cut off.

This coupé ran in the prototype group at Le Mans in 1961. Except for the top, it was a normal RS 61.

424   *This RS 61 coupé was also powered by the 1,500 cc, four-camshaft, four-cylinder engine. Power was 150 bhp.*

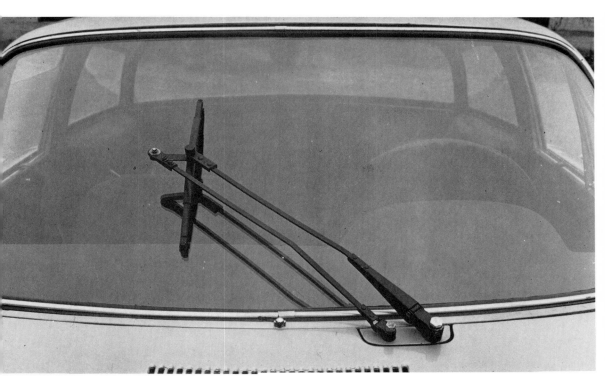

High-speed, parallel-action screen wiper, first seen on Porsche RS 61 coupé.

2-litre, eight-cylinder engine, Type 771, in Spyder RS 61. It developed 210 bhp at 8,400 rpm.

426 *Eight-cylinder RS 61 coupé for the 1962 Targa Florio.*

Eight-cylinder RS 61 Spyder. It won the 1963 Targa Florio.

Because of its long career, the eight-cylinder RS 61 Spyder became known as 'Grandma'.

2-litre, eight-cylinder, Type 771 engine, first seen in the Targa Florio of 1962.

Glöckler-Spyder/550/718 (RS 60-61)

Year	Body	Model Type	Chassis no	Engine type	Gearbox type	Cyl	Bore × stroke	Capacity	HP (DIN) at rpm	Torque (mkg) at rpm	Comp ratio	W.base (mm)	Track fr/rear (mm)	Length (mm)	Weight (kg)
1950	Spyder	Glöckler	–		VW	4	73,5 × 64	1086	58			2000			445
1954	Spyder	550-1500RS	5500001-5500015	547	718	4	85 × 66	1498	110/7800	12,1/5000	9,5:1	2100	1290/1250	3600	550
1955	Spyder	550-1500RS	5500016-5500090	547/1	718	4	85 × 66	1498	110/6200	13,2/5300	9,5:1	2100	1290/1250	3600	590
1956	Spyder	550A-1500RS	550A0101-0104 0111-0113 0131	547/1	718	4	85 × 66	1498	135/7200	14,8/5900	9,8:1	2100	1290/1250	3600	550
1957	Spyder	550A-1500RS	550A0114-0144	547/1	718	4	85 × 66	1498	135/7200	14,8/5900	9,8:1	2100	1290/1250	3600	550
1958	Spyder	718-1500 RSK	718001-718034	547/3	718	4	85 × 66	1498	148/8000 142/7500	14,9/6300	9,8:1	2100	1290/1250	3600	530
1959	Spyder	718-RS 60	718051-718064	547/3 547/4 547/5	718	4 4 4	85 × 66 87,5 × 66 87,5 × 66	1498 1587 1587	150/7800 160/7800 180/7800	14,3/6600 15,0/7000 15,5/7500	9,8:1 9,8:1 9,8:1	2200	1290/1250	3700	550
1960	Spyder	718-RS 61	718065-718078	547/3 547/4 547/5	718	4 4 4 4	85 × 66 87,5 × 66 87,5 × 66 88 × 66	1498 1587 1587 1605	150/7800 160/7800 180/7800	14,3/6600 15,0/7000 15,5/7500	9,8:1 9,8:1 9,8:1	2200	1290/1250	3700	550
1961	Coupé 'Le Mans'	718-RS 61	718044-718045	547/3 547/4 547/5 587/3	718	4 4 4 4	85 × 66 87,5 × 66 87,5 × 66 92 × 74	1498 1587 1587 1966	150/7800 160/7800 180/7800 185/7200	14,3/6600 15,0/7000 15,5/7500 21,5/5000	9,8:1 9,8:1 9,8:1 9,8:1	2200	1290/1250	3700	590
	Coupé 'Le Mans'	718GTR	718046-718047	771/0 771/01	718		76 × 54,6 80 × 54,6		210/8400 270/8600	19,6/6600 23,5/7000		2335	1300/1280	4020	670
1962	Spyder	718	718046-718047	771/0 771/01	718		76 × 54,6 80 × 54,6		210/8400 270/8600	19,6/6600 23,5/7000		2335	1300/1280	4020	640

Types 904/908.03

The 904 is a milestone in the development story of Porsche competition cars. Also known as Carrera GTS, this central-engined car was completely new and belonged to an entirely new design philosophy, except for its power plant. In order to comply with the homologation regulations of the time for Grand Touring cars, a batch of 100 cars was laid down. To make sure that they would be sold, the cars were offered at the exceptionally low price of DM 29,700, but in fact it aroused so much interest among private owners that a second series of 20 cars had to be built, of which 16 were sold. The remaining four were not completed and were later used for spares.

During the development phase, three prototype 904s were built with a 160 bhp, Type 547 Carrera engine for the initial tests which took place at the end of August 1963 on Porsche's own Weissach track which had just been completed. These were followed by many test runs on the Nürburg and Hockenheim Rings. How quickly development progressed is indicated by the fact that at a certain stage, a development 904 lapped the Nürburgring in 9 minutes 55.9 seconds—a very creditable performance for a 2-litre sports car at the time—but only four weeks later, this time was cut down by no less than ten seconds.

There could be no question, however, of Porsche resting on their laurels as the Sebring 12 Hours, in February 1964, was to be the 904's first race. This made it imperative to freeze the project by the end of November 1963 and to start with the production of the new model for which the glass fibre body was made by the Heinkel aviation works in Speyer.

The first 12 Porsche 904 GTSs to be completed went straight to the USA. At the beginning of 1964, 102 cars of this model had already been ordered; 31 went to the United States, five to Holland, four to Great Britain, nine to Switzerland, 15 to France, seven to Italy, four to Belgium and one each to Argentina and Spain. The remaining 25 cars stayed in Germany, ten of them being kept by the factory for its own use.

Private owners bought the car with the Type 547 engine tuned to produce up to 185 bhp, but six- and eight-cylinder engines (Types 901 and 771 respectively) were fitted to many of the factory cars, this being part of the engine development programme designed to replace the ageing four-cylinder.

The new car was immediately successful. Even before it was homologated in the GT Group, the Americans Briggs Cunningham and Lake Underwood won the 2-litre class outright in the Sebring 12 Hours race. Only a few weeks later, a duly homologated sister car, driven by Colin Davis and Antonio Pucci, won the Targa Florio outright, followed by the Linge-Balzarini sister car.

The 904's reliability was one of the car's more appealing features. Up to a dozen of these models could be seen at the start of long-distance sports car races, and most of them used to be in the results. In the first year, successes were scored at Spa, Le Mans, Rheims, Nürburgring and in the Tour de France. In January 1965, Eugen Böhringer and navigator Rolf Wütherich demonstrated the 904 GTS's amazing versatility by finishing second in the Monte Carlo Rally, only just missing victory!

By the end of 1964 development work on the 904 had become more intensive while the defence of the Porsche colours in the GT class was progressively left to private owners. Works entries for the 1965 Targa Florio offered interesting variations on the 904 theme. Klass/Pucci won the GT Group with a normal production 904 while a similar car fitted with the six-cylinder engine developed from the 911 took third place with Maglioli and Linge. Less satisfactory results were obtained by the two eight-cylinder prototypes. A 904-based Spyder, powered by the eight-cylinder, Type 771 engine, and a similarly powered 904 coupé both had to retire. The conclusion drawn from this race was that the Type 901 six-cylinder engine was the more promising power unit for long-distance racing.

Meanwhile, however, a new tubular-framed hillclimb car pointed to the line of thought followed by the Porsche development team when it came to replacing the 904 GTS.

Starting from the now well-proven 904 coupé, Porsche developed an eight-cylinder Spyder for the European Hill Climb Championship of 1965. It was generally known as the 'Kangaroo' because of its rather strange shape, but it weighed only 570 kg (1,256 lb)—120 kg (265 lb) less than the coupé. After a few development runs in April 1965, the car was first entered for the Targa Florio in which it finished second, driven by Gerhardt Mitter and Colin Davis, headed only by a 3.3-litre Ferrari. This was a very successful debut, but it could not hide the fact that the chassis was insufficiently stiff. Following this experience with the first Kangaroo, which later served as a factory development car, two new cars were built in which improvements were incorporated. They were sent to the Trento-Bondone Hill Climb, counting towards the European Championship, where the two drivers Mitter and Fischaber had to settle for third and fourth places, behind Scarfiotti's Ferrari and Hans Herrmann's Abarth. This was a severe blow, but the cars' lack of stability was confirmed in the following events in which, in spite of further development work, Mitter's Porsche could not touch Ludovico Scarfiotti's Ferrari.

The consequence was that, three races before the end of the European Hill Climb championship, the decision was taken to undertake the design and construction of a completely new car. Work was started only two weeks before the Ollon-Villars hill climb. The only component the new car inherited from its predecessor was the gearbox. Even the eight-cylinder engine was modified by a new exhaust system, although for the event Mitter eventually opted for the older arrangement which proved to provide more torque. The platform frame of the 904 Spyder gave way to a completely new, lighter, tubular space frame. The suspension was completely new and as 330 mm (13 inch) diameter rims were to be used—but were not available from former models—time was saved by buying a set of complete wheels from Lotus boss Colin Chapman. Pressure of time also dictated the use of the springs and dampers of the old 904 Spyder, settings remaining unaltered, there being no time for any development testing.

Day and night, engineers and mechanics worked to get the so-called Lotus-

Porsche ready for the Ollon-Villars hill climb. Surely, the Spyder would have been more competitive if the unions hadn't flatly refused to let the mechanics work over the weekend, which they were entirely willing to do! A solution was thought to have been found by sending the crew on a 'business trip' to Böblingen, near Stuttgart, where Gerhardt Mitter had his garage. Unfortunately, the trick didn't work and the idea had to be abandoned.

Consequently, there was not the slightest chance of trying the car before official practice began and when the times for the two runs were added, Mitter had lost to Scarfiotti's Ferrari by 2.5 seconds, which finally put the European Championship out of his reach. More development had been put into the car by the time the Gaisberg Hill Climb came round, for which the weight was brought down to 488 kg (1,076 lb) without oil—a remarkably low weight for a 250 bhp car—although much better was yet to come! Unfortunately, fog made a direct comparison between Scarfiotti's Ferrari Dino V6 and the 'Lotus-Porsche' impossible. But it was this car, designed and built in two weeks, which became the basis for the 906 and 910 models, especially where the chassis and running gear were concerned.

As 50 identical cars had to be completed to qualify for the newly created 'Sports Car' group, Porsche's target was to build the required number of the new Type 906 before the 1966 season began. As there was a surplus of 904 suspension parts it was decided that, in order to save costs, they should be used for the 906, which explains why the suspensions of the 904 GTS and of the 906 were virtually identical. For the new model, however, a coupé of no more than one metre (less than 40 inches) overall height, a tubular space frame was used to carry the glass fibre body. The centrally mounted six-cylinder engine initially produced just over 200 bhp and endowed the 906 with a maximum speed of 280 km/h (175 mph). The list price of the 906, also called 'Carrera-6' was DM 45,000. For a full-blooded racing car this was a very tempting proposition and orders came in unexpectedly quickly, so that the batch of 50 cars originally planned had to be extended. A second series of 15 cars was built and altogether 52 Carrera-6 to normal specification, nine powered by a six-cylinder fuel-injection engine and four with a 2-litre eight-cylinder engine were built, the two 'non-standard' types being eligible only for the prototype group. In this case, too, success was immediate: even before the model was homologated in the 'Sports Car' group, an early example driven by Herbert Linge and Hans Herrmann was entered as a prototype in the American Daytona 24 Hours race and won the 2-litre class. The 50th Targa Florio was the new car's first European race. The factory prepared five of them, of which one was privately entered. Two of them running in the Sports Car group, were 'standard' Carrera-6s while the other three ran in the prototype group. Two of them were fitted with a fuel-injection version of the six-cylinder engine which produced about 15 bhp more than the carburettor version, while a 2.2-litre-cylinder, Type 771, was installed in the fifth car. The overall winner was the privately entered 'standard' 906 driven by Willy Mairesse from Belgium and Herbert Müller from Switzerland.

Five cars were again prepared for the Le Mans 24 Hours race, two of which were the standard 906 models. The others, which ran as prototypes, all had the fuel-injection six-cylinder engine installed, producing 220 bhp at 8,200 rpm, which in addition to their higher power output also had a better torque in the lower engine speed ranges. The 906 prototypes also had a new, longer tail which made the cars slightly heavier (they weighed approximately 710 kg—1,565 lb), but improved the aerodynamics to the extent of increasing the maximum speed by some 15 km/h

(10 mph). Four of the five Carrera-6s entered reached the finish, closely grouped and taking not only fourth to seventh places overall, but also winning both the Sports Car group and taking first place in the Index classification for the best overall performance in relation to the engine capacity.

The last race of the season, run at the Hockenheim Ring, provided an opportunity for interesting experiments. The shape of the long-tail car was further improved and as experiments with aluminium brake calipers and beryllium brake discs had been successful, three cars were entered with this equipment and easily won the race.

Development of the hill climb cars also continued. A new model was built, based on the Ollon-Villars Spyder and fitted with a higher windscreen to meet the modified rules. A hard-top was also tried. While the Ollon-Villars car had had a slightly longer wheelbase than other Porsche racing models—a modification dictated by the makeshift running gear—the new car, now called 910, was back to Porsche's traditional 230 cm (90.55-inch) wheelbase, while the now entirely Porsche-designed and made running gear implied slightly different track measurements. The 330 mm (13-inch) rim diameter of the Ollon-Villars car was, however, retained in place of the 381 mm (15-inch) wheels of the Carrera-6.

The maiden outing of the 910 was the Italian Trento-Bondone hillclimb, counting towards the European Hill Climb Championship. With the eight-cylinder, Type 771, 2-litre engine installed, the 910 had a weight of exactly 575 kg (1,268 lb), as prescribed by the rules. For long-distance racing, however, the well-proven Type 901 six-cylinder engine was used in most cases. Such six-cylinder models were very successful in the Daytona 24 Hours and the Sebring 12 Hours races in the USA. In the former event, factory drivers Hans Herrmann and Josef Siffert finished fourth overall, and at Sebring Gerhardt Mitter and his American co-driver Scooter Patrick took third place overall, headed by only two 7-litre Fords.

Porsche did not intend to sell the 910 to private owners or have it homologated in the Sports Car group, where it would have been a hard nut to crack for Carrera-6 owners, who would not have been too pleased after having spent so much money on a new car only one year earlier. For this reason, the 910 was run only by the factory in 1967 and, being eligible for the prototype group only, never was in direct competition with privately owned Carrera-6s. As, however, Porsche had made a rule of running only brand new cars in all important races, as far as possible, many cars which had done only one race were sold to customers who entered them privately, in direct competition with the factory. As, by the end of 1967, 28 cars had been made and the FIA decided to reduce the production required for homologation in the Sports Car group from 50 to 25, the 910 automatically qualified as a 'Sports Car' from the beginning of 1968.

At the Targa Florio of 1967, a new engine variant appeared in one of the six 910s sent to Sicily by the factory. While three of the cars used the now well-known, Type 901 fuel-injection six-cylinder, the three others were eight-cylinders in which the capacity of the Type 771 engine had been increased to 2.2 litres, while the carburettors had been replaced by a fuel-injection system. The effort was, no doubt, worthwhile, Porsche cars taking the first three places. The winners were Rolf Stommelen and Paul Hawkins, two drivers who had never been to the Targa before and had been entrusted with one of the 2.2-litre cars. Cella/Biscaldi and Neerpasch/Elford were second and third respectively with six-cylinders.

But even before the season ended, on the occasion of the Le Mans 24 Hours race and, later, in the Brands Hatch 6-Hours race, an even newer model was added to the Porsche entries: the Type 907. This, however, did not stop the development of the 910 which continued to be used for international hillclimbs, where the very liberal rules provided an ideal opportunity for trying out new ideas. One of them was the aluminium tube space-frame, first used in a 910 Spyder entered for the Ollon-Villars hillclimb. Further weight had been saved by the liberal use of titanium, and the engine incorporated several magnesium castings, while some comparatively lightly stressed shafts were even made of aluminium. The oil tank had a capacity of ten litres (17.6 pints) and the fuel tank contained only 15 litres (3.3 gallons). With a full oil tank, the car weighed only 420 kg (926 lb).

More development took place for the 1968 hillclimb season, concentrating mainly on the use of exotic metals which finally brought down Gerhardt Mitter's car to the astounding weight of 382 kg (842 lb) as it appeared at the Montseny hillclimb in Spain.

It is doubtful, however, if the final steps taken to lighten the car actually improved it. With so much power (270 bhp) and so little weight on the front wheels, front end adhesion under strong acceleration was very much at a premium, and a new car was hastily built while the 1968 season was still in progress. This was the 909 which Rolf Stommelen drove in the Gaisberg event, the penultimate race in the European Hill Climb Championship. There was no time to make the new car quite as light (430 kg—948 lb) as its predecessor, from which it mainly differed by having its five-speed gearbox between the engine and the differential, instead of overhung at the rear. Thus not only the gearbox, but also the engine and driver were moved forward—the driver in fact so far that the pedals protruded ahead of the front wheel axis. An interesting weight-saving trick was the replacement of the fuel tank and pump by a pressurised fuel accumulator. This consisted of a football-sized titanium sphere containing a pressurised rubber ball fitted with fuel. Quite unexpectedly this device proved troublesome and both at Gaisberg and Mont Ventoux, Stommelen had to give best to Mitter who drove the older 910. The 909 ran only in those two events, but it was nevertheless a significant model, being the ancestor of the extremely successful 908/03 which appeared in 1970.

The Porsche 907 was first seen in the middle of 1967. It was not very different from the 910, except for its shape. Zuffenhausen had not been too happy with the aerodynamics of the 904 and 906, while the 910 'just happened' without any help from the wind tunnel. In fact the main reason why the 907 came into being at all was to achieve a lower drag, and it is significant that it was first used at Le Mans, where very high speeds are reached. It had a long-tail body which gave a lower drag coefficient than the long-tail 910 and the same as the long-tail 906.

Another difference was that the 907 had right-hand drive in view of the slightly better weight distribution and driving position this provides on circuits used in the clockwise direction—which are the vast majority. The front suspension was also different, providing a variable spring rate by the angled position of the spring instead of variable pitch coils and thus saving weight, while ventilated front brake discs were used. These had been successfully tried on an eight-cylinder 910 at the Nürburgring 1000 km race of 1967.

Two long-tail 907 cars were sent to the Le Mans 24 Hours race. Using the fuel-injection six-cylinder engine, they were officially timed by the organisers on the long Hunaudières straight at speeds of 298 km/h and 302 km/h (185 and 187.6 mph) and the Herrmann/Siffert car finished fifth overall at an average speed of 201 km/h (125 mph) for the 24 hours! This sensational performance earned the car first place on Index and second place in the classification based on an efficiency formula (fuel consumption/distance/weight). After this, the only other occasion when a 907 ran in six-cylinder form was in the Brands Hatch 6-Hours race of 1967, where the short-tail version driven by Neerpasch/ Herrmann finished fourth.

For the 1968 season, the 2.2-litre eight-cylinder engine had, at last, achieved the reliability required for long-distance racing, as was confirmed in the first two races at Daytona and Sebring, where, after 24 and 12 hours' racing the Porsches took the first three and the first two places respectively. Daytona was also the occasion for another important development: one of the cars had an aluminium tube frame and many titanium parts, both used for the first time in a long-distance race; but for the failure of the generator, it would have won. Also for the first time, all cars were fitted with a device which has, since, found its way into many production cars: a brake pad wear warning light.

In the summer of 1967, it transpired that the FIA intended to limit the capacity of prototypes to three litres, while allowing a 5-litre capacity for so-called 'Sports Cars' (minimum production 25 units), and this prompted Porsche into designing an entirely new 3-litre, eight-cylinder racing engine.

Less than a year later the new engine, Type 908, for which Dipl-Ing Hans Mezger was responsible, made its first public appearance at the Le Mans pre-practice in April 1968. Two of them had been dropped into accordingly modified long-tail 907 models, outwardly almost identical with true 907s, bearing the chassis numbers 908.000 and 908.002. The 908 was born.

The new cars were far from being trouble-free, not only at the Le Mans trials, but also in private practice sessions at the Nürburgring and Monza. The two cars sent to Monza for the first World Championship race of the European season fared no better: Siffert/Herrmann and Mitter/Scarfiotti finished 19th and 11th respectively after endless troubles. All the greater was everybody's surprise when, only three weeks later, a 908 (now fitted with 381 mm/15-inch diameter wheels instead of the previous 330 mm/13 inches) won the Nürburgring 1000 km race, driven by Siffert and Elford, a success for which the troublesome practice sessions had given little hope.

This boosted the morale of the overworked racing department, where all efforts were now concentrated on preparation for the Le Mans race. The task seemed really overwhelming, but luck was on Porsche's side: because of the students' rebellion in May 1968, the race was postponed three months to September, leaving the development crew with a little more time to solve their biggest problems.

The main steps in the 908's development can be summed up as follows: aluminium tube frame and mobile tail spoilers at Watkins Glen; various modifications to the front and rear suspensions and their geometry; experiments with a lighter gearbox featuring a magnesium housing. But in spite of endless testing with short and long-tail cars, there were still some doubts about the 908's reliability in a 24 hour race. Though four of these were entered by the factory, the entry list also included three privately entered long-tail 907s. Although not officially 'works' cars, they had been prepared by the factory, just in case . . . that this was not a vain precaution is shown by the results: in second place, behind Luciano Bianchi's and Pedro Rodriguez' winning Ford GT40, came the 'private' 2.2-litre 907 of Spoerry and Steinemann, while the Stommelen/Neerpasch 908 was only third.

In 1969 it was the 908's turn to play the role of the rearguard car to its successor, the Porsche 917, but as the rules no longer required a spare wheel and a 'luggage locker' for prototypes, while the minimum weight limit had been dropped, the coupé body was abandoned in favour of an open Spyder, Type 908.02.

Because of insufficient testing facilities during the winter months, both American long-distance races at Daytona and Sebring ended in disaster for Porsche. At Daytona none of the five 908s entered reached the finish, in most cases because of exhaust system and timing chain breakages. At Sebring the chassis broke on four different cars. Two were retired, but when it came to the fourth, mechanics had become so proficient in repairing the frame that the car still finished third, driven by Stommelen and Buzetta.

After the conclusions had been drawn from these incidents, reliability was found: at Brands Hatch three 908 Spyders filled the first three places driven by Siffert/Redman, Mitter/Schütz and Elford/Attwood. But in spite of this and other successes, the development engineers were still not really satisfied with the 908, and in time for the Nürburgring 1000 km race, a reshaped 908.02 Spyder, nicknamed 'the sole' was produced. Of the three cars prepared, however, two crashed in practice. The only remaining car was allotted by ballot and fell to Herrmann/Stommelen.

Subsequent investigation indicated that the reason for the crashes was that the new body shape created insufficient downthrust. The remedy was to fit spoilers to either side of the car's nose. How necessary these were was indicated by the unfortunate accident in which the Finnish private driver Hans Laine was killed when his car just took off on the fast Döttinger Höhe section of the Nürburgring because one of the front spoilers had broken away.

A return to coupé bodies was made for Le Mans. They were long-tail cars of which, however, the mobile rear spoilers had been disconnected and firmly fixed, following the CSI's ban on mobile aerodynamic devices, inspired by accidents in the Formula 1 Spanish Grand Prix. In addition to the coupés, there was also an open 'sole', modified by the addition of a long tail carrying two vertical fins. The body modifications alone made the car 20 km/h (12.5 mph) faster than the original 908.02 Spyder and some 10 km/h (6 mph) faster than the short-tail 'sole'. Unfortunately this car, driven by Siffert and Redman, did not last long: the tubes provided for gearbox ventilation on the coupés had been left off and the red-hot gearbox seized up.

Meanwhile every effort was made to make the immensely powerful 917 competitive to take over from the 908 in World Championship events, but as it was feared that the big car might be too unwieldly for very winding courses, Porsche also got busy on a new 908 development, the Type 908.03, and by the end of 1969 all the 908.02 cars were sold to private drivers or teams.

A full-scale model of the new car had already been completed in the summer of 1969. It had practically nothing in common with its forerunners, except for the 3-litre eight-cylinder engine producing 350-360 bhp. Only the very best units were passed off with 370 bhp—and there were very few of them. But in a car weighing only 545 kg (1,201 lb), even that relatively modest power provided an excellent power-to-weight ratio, and although the model was entered for only four races in 1970 and 1971, it won three of them—the 1970 Targa Florio and the 1970 and 1971 Nürburgring 1000 km races—and only rotten luck prevented it from scoring a 100 per cent success by winning the 1971 'Targa'. The 1971 car was virtually identical to the original version, from which it differed mainly in the two added tail fins and the replacement of the 330 mm (13-inch) rear wheels (which the 908.03 had inherited from its direct ancestor, the Type 909 hillclimb Spyder) by

381 mm (15-inch) wheels, the 13-inch front wheels being retained.

By that time a new 3-litre racing engine had been fully developed, but was never raced. Porsche, having decided to withdraw from the World Championship of Makes, starting in 1972, had no need of the new engine which had air-cooled cylinders, as before, but water-cooled, four-valves-per-cylinder heads.

At the end of 1971 most of the 908.03 cars still in existence—altogether only 11 were built—were sold at prices ranging from DM 150,000 to 180,000. Some of them were used for hill-climbing, but they suffered from the fact that, due to a minimum weight of 650 kg (1,433 lb) having been imposed, they had to carry substantial ballast to make them over 100 kg (220 lb) heavier than in their original form, and much of their competitiveness was lost. Only the German privateer Reinhold Jöst was consistently successful with 908.03s, right up to 1976! His main asset was the old car's reliability in long-distance races, in which he did extremely well. Unfortunately some of this reliability was lost when, at the beginning of 1975, Jöst exchanged the car's original eight-cylinder engine for a 2.1-litre six-cylinder, Type 911 turbocharged engine producing approximately 500 bhp and entered it for World Championship and Interserie races: neither Jöst, nor two other teams which also entered old 908.03 models with the turbocharged engine, had the necessary experience of turbocharging to achieve success.

General description: Type 904 GTS

Coachwork and chassis

In order to reduce costs, it was decided that the 904 GTS—a mid-engined two-seater coupé—would have neither a tubular space frame, nor an aluminium body. Instead it got a pressed steel frame made up from rectangular-section longitudinal and cross members assembled by spot welding—rather cheaper than welding tubes together—to which the glass fibre body was bonded. All the chassis component parts had a simple shape, to facilitate repairs.

The glass fibre-reinforced plastic body was hand-made in appropriate moulds—a simple method which does not require such highly specialised labour as aluminium beating. In addition to being inseparably bonded together, the frame and the body were additionally tied by bolts at the front and rear ends. They formed a structure which proved to be surprisingly stiff in view of the lightness of the assembly: the frame weighed about 45 kg (100 lb), the glass fibre body about 100 kg (220 lb).

The interior was pretty spartan and there was no window winding mechanism: the door windows were simple sliding Plexiglas panels. The seats were only thinly upholstered and as they were part of the body, greatly contributing to its torsional stiffness, they were not adjustable: the pedals and the steering column were adjustable for reach instead. In spite of the low seating position the forward view was excellent, benefitting from the low front end containing the 110-litre (24.2-gallon) fuel tank and the spare wheel, lying almost flat.

Large shelves were provided in the doors which reached down to only a few inches from the ground, which made it impossible to open them with the car parked alongside a high kerb. The single and large parallel motion windscreen wiper remained fully efficient up to speeds of around 250 km/h (160 mph). Side-wind sensitivity was very low and straight line stability was excellent at all speeds.

At either end, the suspension was by unequal length wishbones of which the pivot axis was not parallel with the car's longitudinal axis, and coil springs concentric with a telescopic damper. At the rear the location was completed by twin forward-facing radius rods on either side. The wishbones were pivoted in rubber bushes and there was an anti-roll bar at either end. A tandem brake master cylinder operated the twin braking circuits, the disc brakes themselves being those of the standard 911, but with larger diameter discs. They were of Ate-Dunlop manufacture.

The wheels were of 381 mm (15-inch) diameter with a choice of 127, 140, 152 and 178 mm (5-, 5.5-, 6- and 7-inch) wide rims on which 185-15 radial tyres or racing tyres (front 5.00-15, rear 5.50-15) could be mounted.

Engine

Originally the 904 had been designed to take the new flat-six engine, as used in the 911, but it was finally decided to retain the old 2-litre, Type 587 'Carrera' four-cylinder. The main reasons for this late decision were that spare parts for the four-cylinder engine were available around the world and that most racing mechanics were familiar with the old unit, over 200 of the 2-litre version alone having already been built at the time the 904 GTS was first announced.

In its latest form, the four-camshaft engine produced 180 bhp in racing trim (road trim 155 bhp) which gave the 650 kg (1,433 lb) car a power-to-weight ratio of 3.6 kg/bhp (277 bhp per ton). According to the magazine *Auto Motor & Sport* which road-tested the car, the 904 GTS could reach 100 km/h from rest in 5.5 seconds, 160 km/h in 12.4 seconds and 200 km/h in 21.2 seconds (0-60 mph in 5.3 seconds, 0-100 mph in 12.5 seconds and 0-125 mph in approximately 21.7 seconds). It covered the kilometre from a standing start in 24.8 seconds and reached a maximum speed of 252 km/h (156.6 mph).

Even in racing trim—with an (highly illegal!) open exhaust—the car remained quite tractable in normal traffic. The clutch was quite progressive and the engine could be accelerated from as low as 1,000 rpm, although pulling power did not become really evident before 4,500 rpm were reached.

Here is just a reminder of the main technical data of the Type 587 'Carrera' engine which, in the 904, was turned 180 degrees, being installed ahead of the rear wheel axis, with the gearbox overhung at the rear: air-cooled flat-four engine with aluminium alloy cylinders, but ferrous bores; twin shaft-driven overhead camshafts in each aluminium alloy head, operating two valves per cylinder in V-formation; forged crankshaft running in three main bearings in a light alloy crankcase. Dry sump lubrication with oil cooler located in the car's nose. Twin Weber (also Solex) down-draught twin-choke carburettors, 12-volt battery, 450-watt direct current generator. Twin ignition with twin distributors and coils.

Transmission

The 904 GTS had a newly developed five-speed gearbox, Type 904, featuring a heavily ribbed light alloy barrel housing. The five forward and the reverse gears were selected on three planes, first and reverse (in the same plane) being protected by an appropriate catch, while the upper four gears were arranged in the usual H-pattern. The gearchange was rather heavy and vague and clean changes required some attention from the driver.

The engine's power was transmitted through a single-plate diaphragm clutch and the ZF limited slip differential was of the 'Powrlok' multiple-disc type. The half-shafts had twin universals of which one was of a special Nadella design accommodating length variations.

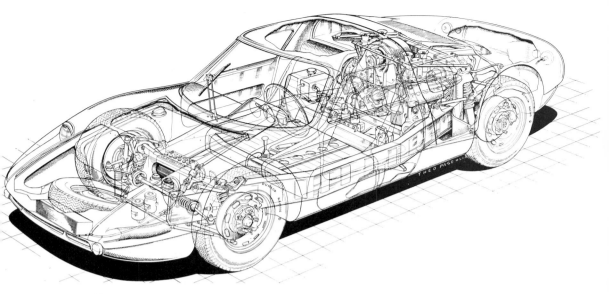

Porsche 904 GTS: cutaway view of the four-cylinder sports racing car.

Front view of the 904 GTS prototype.

Top: Bird's-eye view showing car with raised tail panel.

Above: Left, Porsche 904 GTS with glass fibre body; right, its chassis.

Tail view of early 904 GTS with 160 bhp Carrera engine.

MON- A 270

For economic reasons, the 904's frame was made up of fabricated, rectangular section steel members.

Nearly 120 Porsche 904 GTSs were built and bought for DM 29,700.

Private owners usually ran the 904 with the Type 587, 185 bhp four-cylinder engine.

442   *In the 1964 Le Mans race, Porsche ran a 904 with the eight-cylinder, Type 771 engine.*

For 1965, the air intakes of the engine compartment and for brake cooling were increased in size.

443

The Type 901, six-cylinder, 210 bhp engine was used only in factory cars.

General description: Type Elva-Porsche

Design and development work on the 904 had prevented Porsche from keeping the racing Spyder really up to date, even when fitted with the eight-cylinder engine. As a stop-gap to compete in the European Hill Climb Championship, Porsche turned to the British Elva company which had bought 15 Porsche four-cylinder racing engines for its own cars, and acquired a chassis from them. Into this one of the eight-cylinder engines was dropped to make a hillclimb car weighing only 520 kg (1,146 lb), some 170 kg (375 lb) less than the eight-cylinder version of the 904!

With this car, generally known as 'Elva-Porsche', Edgar Barth won the Rossfeld Hill Climb in 1964, but for the following races he went back to his old love, the veteran Spyder, 'Grandma' as it was known. The Elva-Porsche was taken over by Swiss driver Herbert Müller, but in none of the hillclimbs in which he took part could he get the better of Barth and 'Grandma'.

Hill-climbing rivals: Edgar Barth in the Type 718 Bergspyder (left) and Herbert Müller in the Elva-Porsche.

General description: Type 906

Coachwork and chassis

The two-seater body covering the tubular space frame had gull-wing doors. The nose was very low and protruded far ahead of the front wheels. The entire rear part was hinged at its rear end and, when raised, uncovered the complete engine transmission. The cockpit was very simple, weight having been saved everywhere. Both the driver's seat and the steering column were adjustable for reach. There was only one instrument, the tachometer, facing the driver and deeply shrouded to prevent glare.

The external shape was dictated by the efforts to reduce air drag, as exemplified by the deeply rounded windscreen, the cut-off tail (Kamm principle) and the Plexiglas covers over the head and directional indicator lights. The roof progressively merged with the tail, the part over the engine being transparent and louvred to allow air to be aspirated into the engine compartment. The spare wheel was accommodated at the extreme front end, in front of the oil radiator. Dunlop Racing tyres (5.50 L-15) were used at the front, while at the rear the new Dunlop dimension of 5.50 M-15 was fitted to 228 mm (9-inch) wide rims. The 'luggage room' compulsory for sports cars, according to the CSI rules, was located at the extreme rear, behind the gearbox.

The front suspension was by unequal length wishbones having their pivot axis angled to the centre-line of the car. The coil springs were concentric to the double-acting telescopic dampers and an anti-roll bar was fitted. The uprights had adjustable spherical bearings at both ends.

At the rear the wishbones also had an angled pivot axis, and a coil spring and damper arrangement similar to their front counterpart. Precise location was ensured by twin forward-facing radius arms on either side and roll stiffness was controlled by an anti-roll bar.

The use of 381 mm (15-inch) diameter wheels had economic reasons: a second series of 904 GTS had been planned, but was never built. For this, complete sets of brakes and suspension parts had already been obtained, and Dr Porsche insisted that they should be used for the 906 for which, however, wider rims were specified: 7K × 15 front and 9K × 15 rear.

While in spring 1966 the first cars were being delivered to their owners, scoring immediate successes, the development staff concentrated on three particular spheres in which improvements were sought: weight reduction, improved handling and engine developments. Titanium progressively replaced steel for many running gear parts (such as hubs) while beryllium brake discs were tried.

For Le Mans, the so-called 'long-tail' version was developed, which mainly differed from the normal car in its longer and slimmer nose and its considerably extended tail.

Engine

The Carrera-6 engine in fact differed more from the basic 911 power unit than a casual glance indicated. One important difference was that the crankcase of the 901/20 racing engine was cast in magnesium instead of aluminium, as in contemporary 911s. The pistons, connecting rods, cylinders and valve gear were also different, although the basic layout remained the same as in the standard product. The flat-six engine was air-cooled by an axial blower and had one overhead camshaft per bank. The mixture was provided by twin three-choke Type 46 IDA Weber down-draught carburettors fitted with 42 mm (1.65 inch)

445

chokes. A single Marelli distributor controlled the twin ignition system.

The oil tank of the dry-sump lubrication system had a capacity of 14 litres (three gallons). Only special oil with a high film strength and an anti-frothing additive could be used. The crankshaft was a standard production part, but the flywheel was lightened from six to 3.5 kg (13.2 to 7.7 lb). Instead of the standard forged steel connecting rods, titanium rods were used in the 901/20 engine, bringing the weight down from 550 to 400 grammes (19.4 to 14.1 oz). The Mahle pistons were aluminium alloy forgings and the light alloy cylinders had porous chromium-plated bores, the pores being provided to better retain the oil on the cylinder walls. The cylinder heads were aluminium castings basically similar to the production 911 S parts, but the ports were reshaped and polished by hand, while a second plug hole was provided in the combustion chambers.

Both intake and exhaust valves were sodium-filled for better cooling (only the exhaust valves in the standard 911) and were of a larger diameter. The camshafts were soft-nitrided castings, as in the production engine, but provided much larger overlaps.

Care given to details and the use of lighter materials reduced the weight of the 901/20 engine by no less than 54 kg (119 lb) compared with the standard 911.

Transmission

The fully synchronised Type 906 five-speed gearbox was controlled by three selector rods. It shared its magnesium alloy barrel housing with the ZF limited slip differential. Six different sets of gears, each pair individually interchangeable, were mentioned on the homologation form, which also mentioned three different final drive ratios. This provided an enormous number of combinations to choose from. The gearbox ratios could be changed without removing the transmission from the car: only the rear cover and intermediate flange had to be undone.

The clutch was similar to that of the 911, except that the disc had damping springs only to absorb torsional vibrations, but was axially rigid and had bonded linings. Operation was by a Bowden cable.

Bergspyder developed from the 904, with eight-cylinder engine. It finished second in the 1965 Targa Florio and became known as 'Kangaroo'.

The 906.010 tubular space-frame Bergspyder with Lotus F1 running gear replaced the 904 Spyder.

447

Porsche 906
Carrera 6: a
tubular space-
frame-based coupé
with a six-cylinder
engine.

The 50 units
required for
homologation as a
'sports car' were
sold almost
immediately.

448

Private owners
could drive the car
away after paying
DM 45,000.

Distinctive features of the 906 were its gull-wing doors, the flat, sloping front and the high mudguards.

Low drag was the key word when the 906's body was shaped.

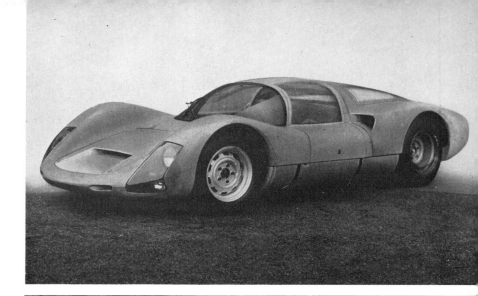

The tail sloped smoothly towards the rear where it was cut-off sharply (Kamm principle) The upper part of the tail unit was louvered Plexiglas.

The rear wheels were located longitudinally by two radius arms on each side.

450

The cockpit was kept as simple as possible. The driver's seat and the wood-rimmed steering wheel were adjustable.

Private owners drove six-cylinder models, but eight-cylinder engines were used in some of the works cars.

Side view of a 'private' 906: the model's career spanned several years.

Long-tail version of the Carrera 6: three experimental cars were built in 1966.

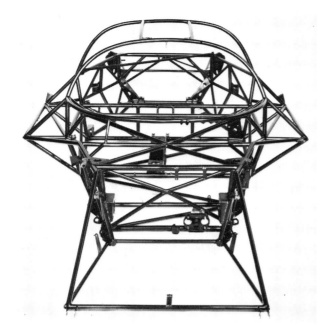

Front and side views of the 1966 Porsche Carrera 6 spaceframe.

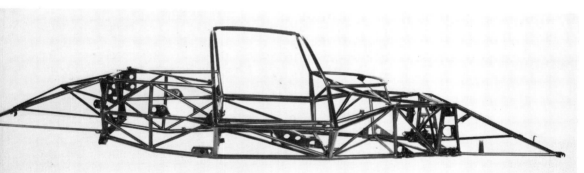

Engine, Type 901, as fitted to the 906, with Weber carburettors and twin ignition. Power was 210 bhp.

General description: Type 910

Coachwork and chassis

The glass fibre body was bonded to the tubular space frame. It was a two-seater coupé which could easily become an open car by removing the roof panel. The two doors were hinged at their front edge and the tail was pivoted at the back. It could be lifted to give access to the engine and transmission, these being ahead and astern of the rear wheel axis respectively. The spare wheel was accommodated under the front cover.

Wheels of 330 mm (13-inch) diameter were the first used for the 910, their rims being 203 mm (eight inches) wide at the front and 241 mm (9.5 inches) wide at the rear. They were magnesium die-castings and considerably lighter than the pressed steel wheels of the 906. The centre-lock hubs—the first time the system was used by Porsche—had a light alloy locking nut, an arrangement which was to be retained for all racing Porsches to the present day. The racing tyres were 5.25-13 at the front and 7.00-13 at the rear. The 1,430 mm (56.3-inch) front track was notably wider than the Carrera-6's 1,337 mm (52.6 inches), but the rear track remained virtually unchanged. Racing damper-spring units were used front and rear, incorporating variable rate coil springs. The front and rear anti-roll bars were infinitely adjustable, while the rack-and-pinion steering had a ratio of 13:1, giving two turns of the steering wheel from lock to lock.

A balance bar operated the two master cylinders of the twin braking circuits, providing an adjustment for front-and-rear braking force distribution. Ventilated front brake discs were first used on the eight-cylinder cars entered for the Targa Florio of 1967. In the last race for which Porsche entered a 910, the Brands Hatch 6-Hours race of 1967, the cars were fitted with quick-change calipers in which a pivoted bridge piece had only to be moved against spring action to free the pads.

Engine

As the 910 was first used in international hillclimbs, the model started life as a 2-litre, eight-cylinder-engined Spyder. The Type 771 engine had an exact capacity of 1,981 cc and an output of 270 bhp at 9,000 rpm with a compression ratio of 10.4:1. For long-distance racing, however, the Type 901, 2-litre, six-cylinder was more usually fitted. For the 1967 Targa Florio, a more developed version of the eight-cylinder Type 771 engine was used. This had a capacity of 2.2 litres (exactly 2,195 cc with bore and stroke dimensions of 80 × 54.6 mm) and featured fuel injection. It also produced 270 bhp, but at a lower engine speed (8,600 rpm) than the 2-litre hill climb engine.

This new eight-cylinder engine weighed 145 kg (320 lb) and had a specific output of 123 bhp/litre. Its crankcase was a magnesium casting, the cylinders were Chromal (aluminium with chromium-plated bores) and its cylinder heads were of aluminium alloy. There were two valves per cylinder and two overhead camshafts per bank. The camshafts ran in ball bearings and were shaft-driven. The forged crankshaft ran in nine plain bearings, and forged titanium connecting rods were used. The horizontal cooling blower was also shaft-driven. The engine had dry sump lubrication and fuel feed to the Bosch injection system was by twin electric pumps. The platinium-pointed plugs were fired by a transistorised twin ignition system.

The six-cylinder engine, Type 901, had 80 × 66 bore and stroke dimensions, giving a capacity of 1,991 cc. It produced 220 bhp at 8,000 rpm with a compression ratio of 10.3:1. Its weight was 135 kg (298 lb) and its specific output 111 bhp/litre. There was only one camshaft per bank of cylinders and it was chain-driven. The crankshaft ran in eight plain bearings and the cooling blower was belt-driven.

Transmission
The Type 906 five-speed gearbox shared its magnesium barrel housing with the disc-type limited slip differential. All five gears had Porsche split-ring synchronisation and were rod-operated from the central lever. For long-distance racing, the Giubo 'doughnuts' incorporated in the half-shafts were replaced by metallic Nadella universals with splines taking up the length and variations. These shafts proved to be rather troublesome and were reinforced several times.

General description: Type 910 Bergspyder (Mountain Spyder)

The 910 'Bergspyder' used for international hill climbing (European Hill Climb Championship) in 1967 and 1968 differed in some aspects from the long-distance 910 and became more and more different as time went by. The use of a thin gauge, doorless body, of a low windscreen, of a small (15-litre/3.3-gallon) fuel tank, the widespread use of titanium parts and other weightsaving modifications brought the weight of the eight-cylinder Bergspyder down to just over 500 kg (1,102 lb). One Bergspyder was built with an aluminium tube frame.

From race to race, further weight was saved. Beryllium brake discs were fitted and this alone saved 14 kg (31 lb). Lighter wheels were tried, the body was lightened even more, more steel was replaced by titanium and even the eight-cylinder engine was lightened by the ever more extensive use of aluminium and magnesium, until at the end of 1967 the complete aluminium-frame car weighed only 419 kg (924 lb), with no fuel but with a full oil tank.

But more was to come in the following year. One move was to delete the dynamo, while the small lead battery was replaced with a lighter silver version. Even the front coil springs were deleted and replaced by a single, much lighter, cross-mounted Z-shaped torsion bar! Mobile rear spoilers, controlled by the rear suspension, were fitted to improve the rear wheel adhesion. The car entered for Mitter in the Montseny hill climb must have set a record for lightness, weighing-in at 382 kg (842 lb), although in the timed runs a stronger fuel tank and a heavier battery were used for safety.

In the last races of the season, the weight of the Bergspyder with a full oil tank was around 400 kg (882 lb)—light enough to enable the 270 bhp engine to power Mitter to his third title of European Hill Climb Champion.

Ollon-Villars hill-climb car with Lotus wheels and hubs. It was the forerunner of the 910.

Front view of spaceframe Lotus-Porsche. Only the running gear was from the Formula 1 Lotus.

For long-distance racing, the 910 used the Type 901/21 six-cylinder fuel injection engine.

In 1967, the 910 was only eligible for the 'Prototype' group. This is an eight-cylinder version.

The Porsche 910 had a short but successful career. This is the Targa Florio winner for 1967.

Front view of a normal 910: it could be used in open or closed form.

This 910, owned by Swiss driver Dieter Spoerry, was a closed version.

458

The 910 was the first Porsche fitted with 33 cm (13-inch) diameter wheels and centre-lock hubs with light alloy nuts.

Porsche 910 Bergspyder in 1967 form. It weighed less than 500 kg (1,102 lb) with the eight-cylinder engine.

459

Gerhard Mitter at the 1967 Freiburg-Schauinsland hill-climb: he could rely on 270 bhp.

Porsche 910 Bergspyder as used in 1967.

1968 version of the 910 Bergspyder with mobile rear flaps. It finally weighed only 382 kg (842 lb)! This view shows how the rear flaps tended to equalise the load carried by the rear wheels in a corner.

2-litre, six-cylinder, 220 bhp engine with Bosch fuel injection, as fitted to the 910 for long distance racing.

General description: Type 907

Coachwork and chassis

There were no fundamental differences between the 910 and the 907, which was little more than a 910 with an aerodynamically improved body. As it had also been recognised that right-hand steering provided an advantage in races run in the clockwise direction, the steering column was moved accordingly. The chassis remained as in the 910, but the front coil springs and coaxial dampers were rearranged to provide variable rate springing without having recourse to variable pitch coil springs. Several coils—and thus weight—could be saved by this modification. Ventilated front brake discs were used from the beginning. Originally, the 907 had the same wheels—front rims 203 mm (eight inches), rear rims 241 mm (9.5 inches) wide—as the 910, but for 1968, 305 mm (12 inch) wide rear rims were used, except at Le Mans where aerodynamic reasons dictated a return to the narrower size.

Engine

The same 2-litre, six-cylinder Type 901, and 2.2-litre, eight-cylinder Type 771 engines were used as for the 910.

Transmission

The Type 906 five-speed transmission was the same as in the Type 910.

461

1968 version of short-tail 907. It had right-hand drive and a lower drag than the 910.

These views of a Type 907 emphasise its similarity with the 910.

462

In 1968, the 907 had wider rear wheels than in 1967 and a different nose. Short-tail version at Nürburgring.

In the 1968 Monza 1,000 km race, Mitter and Scarfiotti drove a long-tail 907 (seen here at Hockenheim).

A long-tail 907 was fitted with a 2.2-litre, eight-cylinder engine for the 1968 Le Mans race.

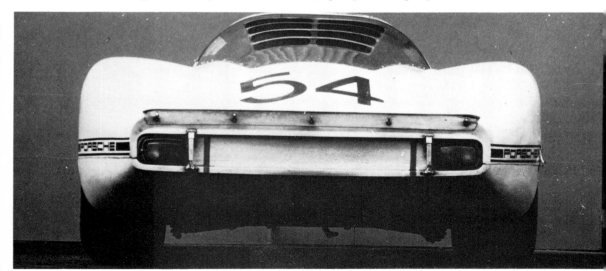

Front view of Porsche 907 long-tail, 1968 version.

Type 771, eight-cylinder engine with fuel injection (2 litres, 270 bhp), as fitted to hill-climb Spyders, Types 910 and 909.

465

General description: Type 909 Bergspyder (*Mountain Spyder*)

Coachwork and chassis

The open glass fibre body was bolted to the aluminium tube space frame. Two front-hinged doors gave access to the seats. The front and rear structures were detachable. Two mobile flaps (spoilers) connected with the rear suspension were fitted to the rear of the car in an effort to maintain a constant rear wheel grip. The 909 was to be the successor of the 910 Bergspyder, the drastic weight saving on which had made it more and more a handful for the drivers. To achieve a better weight distribution without forsaking the lightness achieved by the 910, the gearbox was moved to a position ahead of the rear wheel axis, which moved the engine forward correspondingly, so that the driver now sat with his feet ahead of the front wheel axis which itself had been moved back about 38 mm (1½ inches). The weight of the 909 was 430 kg (948 lb).

The suspension was by transverse wishbones and radius arms front and rear, and progressive rate coil spring-and-damper (double-acting) units. The front springs were made in titanium and both front and rear anti-roll bars were infinitely adjustable. The rack-and-pinion steering had a ratio of 12.2:1. Beryllium brake discs were fitted to all wheels and to compensate for the reduced rear weight bias, 305 mm (12-inch) wide rear rims were used to provide adequate grip, 203 mm (8-inch) rims being used at the front. The tyres were 4.75/10.00-13 and 6.00/12.00-13 front and rear respectively.

Despite the fact that, apart from testing, the 909 was only entered for two hill climbs and never won because it could not be fully developed in time, it was nevertheless significant as the ancestor of the very successful 3-litre 908.03 which appeared two years later.

Engine

In its two events, the 909 was powered by the Type 771 2-litre, eight-cylinder

Porsche 909 Bergspyder with the gearbox ahead of the final drive. It weighed 430 kg (948 lb).

engine which, in its latest form, produced 275 bhp at 9,000 rpm, ie, 5 bhp more than before. The extra power was obtained by a slightly raised compression ratio and the higher rev limit permissible for the short duration of a hill climb. Unfortunately the novel fuel feed system used (pressurised accumulator—see under Porsche 910) proved unsatisfactory and did not allow the engine fully to demonstrate its power.

Transmission

The five-speed gearbox was modified to adapt it to its new position ahead of the differential unit, but otherwise this Type 909 transmission was similar to the Type 906. All gears had Porsche split-ring synchromesh. Final drive was by spiral bevel and crown wheel through a disc-type limited slip differential, and universally jointed and splined half-shafts. The single-disc dry clutch had a diaphragm spring.

General description: Type 908

Coachwork and chassis

When, in October 1967, the FIA set the engine capacity limit for prototypes at three litres (and Sports Cars at five litres), Porsche was fairly well prepared. Previous rumours had hinted at this move and no time had been lost: as early as July 1967 design was started on a completely new 3-litre, eight-cylinder engine (Type 908) which was to be dropped into a chassis derived from the Type 907, to become the 908 coupé. The first tests with the new 3-litre engine took place at the Le Mans trials in April 1968, when two such engines were installed in 907 long-tail cars, numbered 908.000 and 908.002, with none too convincing results. The first short-tail 908 to be built (908.001) was also virtually identical with a 907, including its 330 mm (13-inch) diameter wheels.

The first appearance of the new model (in 908 K short-tail form) with 381 mm

The 909 was first raced at Gaisberg in 1968. It was never fully developed, but was the forerunner of the 908.03.

(15-inch) wheels and more appropriate, larger cast iron brake discs (with aluminium calipers) was at the Nürburgring 1000 km race. Later, at Watkins Glen, one of the cars had an aluminium tube frame, and weighed 20 kg (44 lb) less than its steel tube brothers. The lighter frame was adopted for all cars built as from chassis number 908.012.

Before the 1969 Le Mans race, both the short- and long-tail coupés were again examined in the wind tunnel. The long-tail cars (which had the same frontal area as the short-tail version) were fitted with a rear girder consisting of two tail fins connected by a wing incorporating a mobile flap on either side. These were connected to the rear suspension, in the same way as in the hillclimb cars. Exhaustive test runs also led to the use of reinforced front uprights, stronger half-shafts and a stronger gearbox primary shaft, larger half-shaft flange bolts and a new, more heavily ribbed gearbox housing for better heat dispersion. As run at Le Mans, the long-tail cars weighed just over 700 kg (1,543 lb) and reached 320 km/h (200 mph) down the straight. Because, however, the new international rules included neither a spare wheel nor a minimum weight where protoypes were concerned, no short-tail coupés were entered, Spyders being run instead.

The first 908.02 Spyder had been tested in the wind tunnel at the end of 1968. It had the advantage of being about 100 kg (220 lb) lighter than the long-tail coupé, but it had a higher drag. Its aluminium tube space frame was very similar to that of the coupé, but in the first version two diagonal tubes were deleted from the rear part of the structure. As a result of exhaustive tests, all Spyders were equipped with titanium front stub axles and titanium hubs all round. Another novelty was an air valve fitted to one of the aluminium frame tubes. This made it possible to pressurise the frame and check it for cracks or failures by measuring the pressure drop after a given time—a practice which is continued to the present day.

For the Nürburgring 1000 km race of 1969 Porsche produced a new Spyder, nicknamed the 'sole' because of its flat and straight shape. It had a higher front and a higher waistline than its predecessors. A long-tail version of this Spyder ran at Le Mans driven by Siffert/Redman and was nearly as fast in a straight line as the three long-tail cars! In order to reduce its sensitivity to side wind, the long-tail Spyder sported twin tail fins.

Meanwhile, the 917 had matured enough for Porsche to risk racing it, and by the end of 1969 it became clear that the career of the 908 had come to an end, and all cars still in existence were sold to private owners. As, however, the bigger and much more powerful 917 might not be the ideal answer to such winding courses as the Targa Florio and the Nürburgring, a new Spyder was developed with just those two courses in mind: the 908.03.

It was, in fact, a completely new car, rather reminiscent of the Type 909 'Bergspyder', for which only the 3-litre engine was carried over from the previous 908 series. The first wind tunnel tests on models date back to 1968, but the project was subsequently shelved in favour of the 917 and 908.02 developments. As the 908.03 was to run only on slow circuits, it could be very specialised and every effort was made to keep it as small and as light as possible. Its polyurethane body, for example, weighed only 12 kg (26.5 lb)! Widespread use of titanium and other lightweight materials kept its total weight down to 545 kg (1,201 lb) with the full complement of oil.

The 908.03 had 330 mm (13-inch) diameter wheels with 9.5 and 14.5 wide rims front and rear respectively. For 1971, 381 mm (15-inch) rear wheels were used, which required different uprights, and the rim width was increased to 279 mm and 432 mm (11 and 17 inches). After running the 908.03 in two races (which they won) in 1970, the cars were shelved for almost a year. Then they were readied for action again, virtually unaltered, except for the bigger wheels and the addition of tail fins. This and some additional safety equipment raised their weight to 565 kg (1,246 lb). At the end of the season some 908.03s were offered to selected customers. As late as 1975, three of them appeared in events counting towards the World Championship of Makes, now with a turbocharged engine, similar to the unit which had powered the factory's Carrera prototype in 1974—a 2.1-litre flat-six developing at least 450 bhp. The engines had been adapted to the old cars by the service department of the Stuttgart factory. The cars were almost unrecognisable, having been extensively rebodied with front and rear sections from the unsupercharged 917 Can-Am Spyder providing urgently needed downthrust. A large air intake box provided the intercooler with the necessary cooling air and was later modified several times on all three cars built. The aluminium tube frame had to be locally reinforced in view of the increased performance, and slightly extended rearwards to carry the tail section and its large wing.

Engine

In July 1967 the engine experts started designing the Type 908 3-litre, eight-cylinder engine and only four months later the first engine was assembled. First time on the test-bed it produced 320 bhp, and after four months of development it had become sufficiently reliable to try its luck in long-distance racing. In Monza—the engine's first race—the power was up to 335 bhp and in the final version, the best examples developed nearly 370 bhp, still with two valves per cylinder and four chain-driven camshafts. Other solutions were tried experimentally, but never raced.

The valves were all sodium-filled for improved cooling and the compression ratio was 10.4:1. A peculiarity of the dry sump lubrication system was that the lubricant was fed axially to the front end of the drilled crankshaft to lubricate the big ends, while the main bearings were fed from the main oil gallery. The connecting rods and their bolts were of titanium. Pressure of time dictated the use of the same bore and stroke dimensions as in the six-cylinder engine, ie, 84 $\times$ 66 mm, but before the Le Mans race, the bore was increased by one millimetre to bring the capacity close to the 3-litre limit.

The cylinders and heads were made of aluminium, the crankcase and all covers of magnesium alloy. The complete power unit weighed 178 kg (392 lb). The firing order originally chosen having produced severe vibrations, it was altered after the first race in Monza. Experimentally, a crankshaft was machined to have hollow crankpins and appropriate balance weights were added. In the course of further development, the following modifications were made: a new, more heat resistant magnesium alloy was used for the crankcase, the injection pump was modified to include a space cam, twin belts were used for the cooling blower drive, the alternator mounting was modified to reduce vibration and different starting motor and generator were used.

A new (flat) crankshaft was finally used to balance out the second order forces which still caused severe vibration. In this it was successful, although it considerably complicated the exhaust system. The engines with the flat crankshaft could easily be recognised by the injection pipes which were crossed over the pump instead of being symmetrical.

For the 908.03, the engine remained practically unchanged. The only modification was the addition of a fluid coupling incorporated in the hub driving the cooling blower, aimed at preventing V-belt breakages caused by sudden engine speed variations. A further development never left the experimental shop: it was a four-valve-per-cylinder engine which had water-cooled heads in order to cool the valves adequately (with four valves, the passages for cooling water were inadequate). The engine was fully developed on the test-bed, but unfortunately performance figures are not available.

Some old 908.03s were fitted, in 1975, with a turbocharged 2,142 cc, Type 911 six-cylinder engine, as used by the factory in the 1974 Carrera prototype, to run in World Championship races. Some of these cars even ran in the Interserie with 2.7- and 3-litre engines (for specifications, see '930 Turbo Prototype').

Transmission
The transmissions used in the 907 and earlier models were not strong enough to transmit the torque of the 3-litre engine. As a stopgap, a six-speed box designed for use in the 'Bergspyder' (but never used) was fitted in conjunction with a small diameter triple-plate clutch at the far end of the box, driven by a plain shaft. The low inertia of the clutch allowed very quick gear changes. From the clutch, the drive to the gearbox was taken through a pair of quickly interchangeable gears, facilitating the alteration of the overall ratios. The twin universal half-shafts were divided by a cushioning Giubo doughnut. Unfortunately this transmission weighed 25 kg (55 lb), which was considered excessive. Consequently a new five-speed box, Type 916, was developed, in which the gears, rather than permanently running in oil, were jet lubricated by means of a small gear pump and appropriate pipes.

On the 908.03 turbocharged cars, the problem of the inadequate gearbox rating was solved more or less satisfactorily by adding an oil cooler with an appropriate circulating pump to the lubrication system. The original half-shafts were replaced by those from the unsupercharged 917-10.

*Porsche 908 short-
tail coupé with
mobile rear flaps
and added front
spoilers (1968).*

*Porsche 908 long-
tail coupé with tail
fins, aerofoil and
mobile rear flaps.*

As late as 1972, a privately entered long-tail 908 (with modified front) finished third at Le Mans.

The long-tail coupés entered for Le Mans in 1969 had a maximum speed of 320 km/h (199 mph).

472

Porsche 908.02 Spyder, derived from the 908.01 coupé model for the 1969 season.

With no minimum weight imposed for 1969, the 908 Spyder was lightened to 630 kg (1,389 lb).

Porsche 908.02 Spyder competing in the Nürburgring 1,000 km race of 1969.

In the middle of the 1969 season, an aerodynamically improved 908.02 was produced. It was nicknamed the 'Sole'.

The 'Sole' had a straighter waistline and higher scuttle than its predecessor.

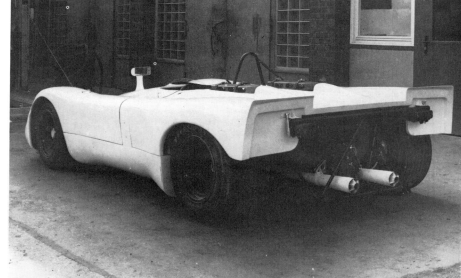

474

Frenchman Claude Ballot-Léna driving a 908.02 Spyder owned by Sonauto, the French Porsche importers.

The long-tail version of the 908.02 was nearly as fast as the long-tail coupés on the Le Mans straight.

The extended tail and the fins of the 1969 Le Mans 908.02 Spyder are clearly visible.

Porsche 908.03 Spyder. In factory hands, it was raced only four times in 1970-71.

The 908.03 originally weighed only 545 kg (1,202 lb) and had 33 cm (13-inch) diameter wheels.

The driving position was very far forward (1970 Targa Florio).

Private owners—and notably Reinhold Jöst— successfully used the 908.03 long after the factory had disposed of them. This picture was taken in 1973.

The 908.03 reappeared almost unaltered in 1971, except for the tail fins and 38 cm (15-inch) rear wheels.

477

The 908.03 as run in the 1971 Targa Florio. Pedro Rodriguez is at the wheel.

Vic Elford driving the winning 908.03 in the 1971 Nürburgring 1,000 km race.

908.03s were entered by John Wyer's Gulf racing team in 1970 and 1971.

Modified 908.03 with Porsche 917-10 rear aerofoil, driven by Reinhold Jöst in the Spa 1,000 km race of 1975.

Co-author Jürgen Barth driving a modified 908.03.

In 1975, some 908.03s appeared with a turbocharged engine. This one is driven by Leo Kinnunen.

Porsche 908.03 with large intercooler air intake (Enna 1975).

Herbert Müller driving a 908.03-Turbo. The engine is a 2.14-litre flat-six of approximately 450 bhp.

At the Hockenheim Interserie race of 1975, Jöst tried a smaller air intake.

480

At Enna, Jöst used a long-tail on his 908.03-Turbo.

*Driving a long-tail
908.03 powered by
its normal 3-litre
eight-cylinder
engine, Jöst
finished fourth at
Le Mans in 1975.*

*The eight-cylinder
racing 3-litre.
From the initial
310 bhp, its power
went up to
370 bhp.*

481

904/Elva/906/910/907/909/908

Year	Body	Model Type	Chassis no	Engine type	Gearbox type	Cyl	Bore × stroke	Capacity	HP (DIN) at rpm	Torque (mkg) at rpm	Comp ratio	W.base (mm)	Track fr/rear (mm)	Length (mm)	Weight (kg)
1964	Coupé	904GTS	904007-904106	587/3 587/3-S	904/0 904/1 904/2 904/3	4 4	92 × 74 92 × 74	1966 1966	180/7800 155/6900 185/7200	20,5/5000 19,0/4800	9,8:1 9,8:1	2300	1316/1312	4090	650
1964	Coupé	904-8 904-6	904001-904006	771/1 901/20	904/0 904/1 904/2 904/3 904/0	8 6	80 × 54,6 80 × 66	2195 1991	270/8600 210/8000	23,5/7000 20,0/6000	10,2:1 10,3:1	2300	1314/1312	4090	640
	Spyder	Elva	–	771/1 771/0	904/0	8 8	80 × 54,6 76 × 54,6	2195 1981	270/8600 260/8800	23,5/7000 21,0/7500	10,2:1 10,5:1	2286	1270/1350	3500	520
1965	Spyder	906-8	906007/08/09 906004	771/0 771/1	909	8 8 8	76 × 54,6 80 × 54,6 76 × 54,6	1981 2195 1981	260/8800 270/8600 260/8800	21,0/7500 23,5/7000 21,0/7500	10,5:1 10,2:1 10,5:1	2300	1338/1402	4113	650
	Spyder 'Lotus'	906-8	906010	771/0	909	8	76 × 54,6	1981	260/8800	21,0/7500	10,5:1	2300	1340/1410	3580	500
1966	Coupé Coupé-LH	906-6	906101-906158 906001-003 (906151-153)	901/20	906	6	80 × 66 80 × 66	1991 1991	210/8000 220/8000	200/6000 21,0/6400	10,3:1	2300	1338/1402	4113 4600	675 710
	Coupé Spyder Coupé-LH	910-6 910-8 910-8 910-6	910001-910012 910013-910028 910030-910034 910020-910021	901/21 771/0 771/0 901/21	906 909 909 906	6 8 8 6	80 × 66 80 × 54,6 76 × 54,6 80 × 66	1991 2195 1981 1991	220/8000 270/8600 272/9000 220/8000	21,0/6400 23,5/7000 21,5/7100 21,0/6400	10,3:1 10,2:1 10,4:1 10,3:1	2300	1430/1380 1430/1401 1430/1401 1430/1401	4113 3860 4600	600 450 620
1967	Coupé	907-8	907001-004 907011 907022-907032	771/1 771/0	907	8 8	80 × 54,6 76 × 54,6	2195 1981	270/8600 260/8800	23,5/7000 21,0/7500	10,2:1 10,4:1	2300	1462/1403	4033	600 575
	Coupé-LH	907-6	907005-008	901/21	907	6	80 × 66	1991	220/8000	21,0/6400	10,3:1	2300	1462/1403	4650	600

904/Elva/906/910/907/909/908

Year	Body	Model Type	Chassis no	Engine type	Gearbox type	Cyl	Bore × stroke	Capacity	HP (DIN) at rpm	Torque (mkg) at rpm	Comp ratio	W.base (mm)	Track fr/ rear (mm)	Length (mm)	Weight (kg)
1968	Spyder	909-8	909001-002	771/0	909	8	76 × 54,6	1981	275/9000	21,5/7100	10,4:1	2264	1470/1464	3448	430
1968	Coupé	908.01	908000-012 908017	908	907-6 916	8 8	85 × 66 85 × 66	2997 2997	310/8000 350/8400	30,0/6600 30,0/6600	10,4:1 10,4:1	2300 2300	1484/1456 1462/1454	4020 4020	650 660
	Coupé-LH	908.01	908000 908002-004 908013-016 908022-026 908029-031	908	916	8	85 × 66	2997	350/8400	32,5/6600	10,4:1	2300	1484/1456 1486/1454	4650 4839	650 680
1969	Spyder	908.02	90802002/009 90802006-008 90802010-019 90802024/028	908	916	8	85 × 66	2997	350/8400	32,5/6600	10,4:1	2300	1486/1454	4000	600
	Spyder-LH	908.02	90802005/014 90802024-028	908	916	8	85 × 66	2997	350/8400	32,5/6600	10,4:1	2300	1486/1454	4400	620
1970	Spyder	908.03	90803001-013	908	910	8	85 × 66	2997	350/8400	32,5/6600	10,4:1	2300	1504/1510 1542/1506 1542/1564	3540	545
														3540	565
1975	Spyder	908.03 Turbo	90803008/011	911/78	910	6	83 × 66	2142	450/8000	46,0/5500	6,5:1	2300	1542/1506	3540	670

483

Types 917/917-30

When the FIA decided to limit the engine capacity of prototypes running in the World Championship of Makes to three litres, sports cars (minimum production 25 units) were allowed a limit of five litres. Whereas Porsche had expected the 3-litre limit, in view of which the 908 engine was designed, the 5-litre limit for sports cars was a surprise, it being generally thought that the 5-litre cars would be at a tremendous advantage. Porsche still thought, however, that very light 3-litre cars might have a chance, until it was learned that Ferrari was preparing to build a batch of 25 sports cars. This sparked Porsche's decision to build a car eligible in that class too, the Type 917.

Design started in July 1968 and it was planned initially to use a 12-cylinder engine of 4.5-litre capacity. This capacity handicap was accepted because it made it possible to use the same cylinder dimensions and material, the same pistons, the same connecting rod length, the same valves and the same timing as for the 908 engine. For similar reasons, the chassis was a very close relative to the 908.02 and the time saved by using so many existing components made it possible to have the first car ready in time for the Geneva motor show which opened on March 13 1969, where it was offered at a price of DM 140,000. At the end of April, the 25 cars required for the homologation in the sports car group by the CSI were lined up in the factory court!

In May 1969, Mitter drove the new car—a short-tail version—in its maiden race in the Spa 1000 km race on the Belgian Francorchamps circuit, but a broken valve stopped it after the first lap. Two weeks later, Frank Gardner and David Piper were invited to drive the same car in the Nürburgring 1000 km race with orders to finish at all costs—which they did, in eighth place. At Le Mans, only three months after the 917's first outing, a long-tail version created excitement when it led the race for more than 20 hours before retiring.

After the first half of the 1969 season, however, an important conclusion was drawn: the efforts put into racing the 908 and 917 models was more than the factory's technical staff could cope with, especially as, at Porsche, the development of both racing and production cars is carried out by the same department. A partner had to be found to run the still underdeveloped 917 in the World Championship of Makes in the following two years. The choice fell on John Wyer Automotive Engineering, the company based in Slough and supported by the Gulf Oil Company. The collaboration was initiated, starting from 1970, when the factory also could rely on another private organisation, that of Porsche-Salzburg, headed by Dr Porsche's sister, Kommerzialrat Louise Piëch. In the following year, the Austrian team changed hands to become the Martini Racing Team. There was an important difference, however, between Wyer's link with the factory and the other teams': Wyer was served directly by the experimental department while the other teams (including Porsche-Salzburg) were dealt with by the sports service department.

The 917 scored its first victory in the Austrian 1000 km race of 1969 in Zeltweg, when Josef Siffert and Kurt Ahrens beat all comers in a short-tail car entered by Baron von Wendt. In the following year's first race, the John Wyer team triumphantly inaugurated its collaboration with Porsche by taking the first two places in the Daytona 24 Hours, the drivers being P. Rodriguez/Kinnunen and Siffert/Redman. Up to the end of 1971, when the 917 was banned from European racing by a change of rules excluding all cars over 3-litre capacity, no fewer than 36 short-tail, two Spyders and five long-tail cars were made! Of 24 World Championship races for which the 917 was entered from 1969 to 1971, it won 15 while the 908 won four, so that Porsche were beaten on only five occasions. The Wyer-Gulf team won 11 races with its blue and orange cars, Porsche-Salzburg won one race in 1970—albeit an important one, Le Mans—and the Martini team which succeeded it won two.

Porsche's programme with the 917 cost an estimated DM 15 million, ie DM 350,000 per car when related to the 43 cars of the 917 family produced over the period. It is not surprising therefore that from the initial DM 140,000, the price of a 917 short-tail car, ready to race, had risen to DM 280,000 in 1971, while a 917-10 Spyder cost DM 325,000 and the turbocharged version DM 450,000.

After nearly 20 years' uninterrupted participation at Le Mans, the 917 eventually presented Porsche with the most prized victory of all when Hans Herrmann and Richard Attwood drove their Porsche-Salzburg entered short-tail car over the finishing line in 1970, a performance which was rewarded by a triumphal drive through Stuttgart's town centre to the town hall.

After three consecutive victories in the World Championship of Makes, in the years 1969 to 1971, Porsche decided to retire from the series. From 1972 the engine capacity for World Championship racing was again limited to three litres, which would not have deterred the men in Zuffenhausen had not a minimum weight limit of 650 kg (1,433 lb) been imposed. Without this limit, the power handicap inherent to an air-cooled engine could have been accepted and compensated for by light weight—an art in which the factory excelled. But 650 kg were a good 100 kg (220 lb) more than could be achieved in Zuffenhausen—the 908.03 had proved it—and they opted out.

Meanwhile, starting in summer 1969 and under the cover of 'private entries', the company had been gaining experience in a new sphere of racing: the Can-Am Championship. Works driver Josef Siffert had thought that a well-prepared 917 would have been competitive in this series, then dominated by two-seater cars powered by huge American, production-based engines of anything between seven and eight litres capacity. A Spyder version of the 917 was built very quickly on a virtually unmodified coupé chassis, and although Siffert could take part in only seven of the series' 11 races, he finished fourth in the final championship placings. Only one 917 PA (PA stood for the American entrant Porsche-Audi) was built and it did not run in 1970 because Porsche were too busy winning the World Championship of Makes to devote time to the Spyder, but when it became known that the FIA would limit the engine capacity to three litres in 1972 and that the Can-Am was to be included in the FIA calender, they became more interested. Obviously, however, a more powerful car was needed than the 917 PA to meet the opposition which mainly came from McLaren whose 8-litre Chevrolet-engined cars (over 750 bhp for 700 kg—1,543 lb) reigned supreme at the time.

The new car—an entirely new Spyder from which the later 917-10 was a direct development—started its career in the middle of 1971. Its 5-litre engine was good enough to earn it third place in its first race, at Watkins Glen, headed by two McLarens. After six races Siffert was sixth in the Championship and had successfully finished in every race, never lower than fifth. But after the brilliant Swiss driver was killed at the wheel of a Formula 1 BRM at Brands Hatch, the Spyder was withdrawn.

Following the successful experience with John Wyer, Porsche forged a similar arrangement for its American campaign of 1972, the partner in this case being the Roger Penske organisation, for which the factory provided the brand new 917-10. Its driver was to be Indianapolis winner Mark Donohue.

At the beginning of the season the chances of the 'Panzer Porsches', first seen in Mosport, Canada, were not rated very high. Certainly the turbocharged, 5-litre flat-12 was said to produce a resounding 1,000 bhp, but up to then no turbocharged car had ever been successful on normal racing circuits, Indianapolis being a very special case where cars are driven at an almost constant speed.

Porsche had this very much in mind when the turbocharged engine was developed, turning their efforts less towards the achievement of very high power than to good throttle response—excessive response times being the stumbling block of all turbocharger installations. Today, they have acquired such experience that they even produce a very successful turbocharged road car (930 Turbo).

As the complicated correlations between engine and turbocharger performance on the race track could not be successfully reproduced on the test-bed, they had to be understood and solved by long and innumerable track tests in the course of which the response time was progressively reduced, down to previously unsuspected levels.

The first turbocharging experiments were carried out on the 4.5-litre engine which, from the start, was equipped with two turbochargers—one per bank of cylinders. When the development was concluded, 850 bhp was obtained and the engines were mainly used in the Interserie races, the European equivalent of the Can-Am. For Can-Am itself the 5-litre engine was used, the extra capacity being considered essential to face the McLaren opposition. The bigger engine differed from the 4.5-litre mainly in its bore and stroke dimensions, the former being increased from 85 to 86.8 mm (3.35 to 3.4 inches) and the latter from 66 to 70.4 mm (2.6 to 2.77 inches). The additional 500 cc brought a surplus of no less than 150 bhp!

Unfortunately Mark Donohue, who had played a great part in the development tests, had a serious accident with the 917-10 Turbo and became unavailable for the entire 1972 season. He was replaced at short notice by George Follmer who apparently immediately felt at home in this, for him, entirely new car, and won the Can-Am Championship outright by a large margin. The following year Donohue was fit again and Porsche built him the 917-30, the most powerful car ever to appear on a racing circuit. In 1972 Follmer had beaten the McLarens in most of the races, but the Porsche's margin over their opponents was not such that they could rest on their laurels. For this car, of which only two were built, the engine capacity was increased to 5.4 litres, raising the power to over 1,100 bhp. Finished in Penske sponsor Sunoco's colours, the 917-30 had a longer wheelbase, a wider front track and a slightly narrower rear track (the latter following a change in the rules, limiting the car's overall width to 210 cm (82.67 inches) than its predecessor. The body became slightly longer too and the tank capacity was increased to 400 litres (88 gallons)! The weight went up by 20 kg (44 lb) to 800 kg (1,764 lb). From the cockpit, Donohue could control the boost pressure to increase the power output momentarily even further, if necessary, and he could also alter the rear anti-roll bar stiffness.

Another 917 Spyder variant had appeared in Europe during the 1971 season. To make them more suitable for the Interserie, 917 coupés were fitted with an open body and a 5-litre unsupercharged engine. For cost and time reasons, all chassis parts and mechanical units were carried over from the coupé, but the Ate brakes were replaced by Girlings. Radical weight saving brought the weight down to 730 kg (1,609 lb) (there was no minimum weight rule in Group 7). These cars were replaced by the 917-10 for the 1972 Interserie.

While the Turbo-Porsche which won the Can-Am series twice in succession was ever more criticised in America for 'spoiling the sport', Europe seemed to take a different view. But when the Can-Am rules for 1974 were changed in such a way that turbocharged cars were robbed of all chance of success, similar—if not quite as drastic—measures were taken in the European Interserie. Porsche was left with no choice but to pull out, but 917-10 Turbos, with their engines limited to 4.5 litres, were still seen in private hands in Europe until they were finally excluded at the end of 1975.

In the end, instead of providing the Can-Am with a new lease of life the anti-turbo rules proved to be its death knell and it was abandoned after 1974 for lack of spectators. As large-engined turbocharged cars were also excluded from the Interserie from 1976 on, the fabulous Porsche 917 and its turbocharged variants can, today, only be seen in museums.

But before the 917-30s were pushed behind museum's doors, Mark Donohue took one of the two cars to the Talladega race course and beat the absolute lap record set up by a racing car on a race track, at a speed of 355.846 km/h (221.1 mph).

General description: Types 917 K (short-tail)/ 917 LH (long-tail)

Coachwork and chassis

The Porsche 917's body was made of glass fibre reinforced plastic. The main structure was bonded to the aluminium tubular space frame, while the front and rear structures were detachable. The outer skin was only 1.2 mm thick, but critical parts such as the doors and the engine cover, were reinforced with aluminium tubes or polyurethane foam.

The windscreen was made of 4.2 mm (0.165 inch) thick laminated glass while the door windows were Plexiglas. The body panel extending over the engine was made of transparent Plexidur to provide rearward visibility and was louvred to permit the entry of air into the engine compartment. The complete body, including all covers, seats, transparent areas, aerodynamic devices, electric cables and (in the case of the long-tail car) the tail extension weighing alone 12 kg (26.5 lb) weighed only 95 kg (209 lb).

The rack-and-pinion housing was in magnesium, the rack itself in Aluknet, an aluminium alloy. The ratio was approximately 11.4:1.

Researches into the effect of aerodynamic forces on a racing car's road behaviour led to the adoption of mobile flaps which, after some experiments, were used only at the rear. They were controlled by the rear suspension in such a way that they increased the downforce when rear wheel adhesion was reduced and decreased it when the suspension was compressed. Unfortunately, the CSI banned such mobile devices as from June 1969 (although the 917s were allowed to use them at Le Mans by special permission) and they had to be abandoned.

The driver's seat consisted of two parts: the shell and a removable seat pan individually shaped for each driver and which was changed when one driver took over from the other in long-distance races. The seat was adjustable for reach and the steering column both for reach and height.

Flexible tubes carried fresh air into the cockpit. In addition to the tachometer and the oil pressure and temperature gauges, the instrument panel carried warning lights for fuel level, generator charge, oil pressure and brake pad wear.

The fuel tanks, with a total capacity of 140 litres (30.8 gallons), were made of aluminium sheet and carried as panniers on either side of the cockpit, where they contributed to lowering the car's centre of gravity. They were connected by a thick tube, so that the car could be filled up from either side or simultaneously from both sides.

The homologation in the Sports Car group (implying that at least 25 had been built) included the long-tail version, consisting of a short-tail car with a quickly removable tail extension. Neither shape, however, was very satisfactory, but the factory cars remained unchanged throughout the 1969 season. Only David Piper's privately owned 917 short-tail appeared at the end of the season—at Kyalami—with modified rear spoilers.

For 1970 the factory cars were drastically modified. The front end was little changed, but from the central part of the cockpit backwards the waistline was raised in a nearly continuous line over and behind the rear wheels. The Plexidur cowl was deleted, leaving the cooling blower and the air intake pipes in the open air. The first car that appeared with this configuration was again David Piper's, in the Buenos Aires 1000 km race. Two weeks later the works cars first appeared in Daytona in John Wyer's colours and for the Le Mans 24 Hours race, the Wyer-Gulf cars sported a small spoiler across the car's tail. As this car proved to be more stable and not very much slower in a straight line than the long-tail version, Wyer used this type of car for most of the races in 1970.

In the following year, fins were added to the tail which was somewhat lowered, reducing the drag by some 15 per cent, but the finned tail was only occasionally used by Wyer. High glass fibre air boxes were also tried over the air intakes, but they brought no improvement and were never used in races.

An interesting cross between the short- and long-tail versions was the Porsche 917-20, of which only one example was built. The design of this car attempted to achieve the low drag factor of the long-tail version without exceeding the length of the short-tail car. Its shape was a joint effort by Porsche and the French SERA company. Noteworthy were the large lateral overhang and the rounded edges of the wheel housings. The car appeared in the Le Mans trials in April 1971, brand new and completely untried, and won the 3-hour race concluding practice driven by Willi Kauhsen. In the actual 24 Hours race it proved to be faster than the wind tunnel tests had suggested, but unfortunately it crashed during the later stages of the race, when very well placed.

Before that, Porsche had already collaborated with SERA on the development of the two long-tail cars which were entered for Le Mans in 1970 by Porsche-Salzburg and the Martini Racing team. The latter car had been lent to that organisation (which did not yet represent Porsche officially) because John Wyer did not trust the 'long-tails'. This particular car finished second with Larrousse and Kauhsen.

But Porsche felt that the car needed still further development and for the 1971 Le Mans race new bodies, made of very light polyurethene foam-reinforced plastic material were made. Compared with the 1970 cars, the front was modified by the addition of an air dam, the brake cooling ducts and oil cooler air intake were modified and so were the front wheel openings and housings. The cockpit ventilation was improved, the 'Coke bottle' hump over the rear wheels was lowered and the rear fins modified. The handling was so much improved that even Wyer was persuaded to enter two of these cars. With one of them, Jack Oliver lapped the course in practice at 250.457 km/h (155.66 mph) and was timed on the straight at 386 km/h (240 mph)!

In 1970 a new rule made it necessary to reduce the tank capacity to 120 litres (26.4 gallons). These could be contained in a single safety tank, on the right-hand side of the car.

The type of suspension and its geometry are directly dependent on the characteristics of the tyres and their dimensions. As in all Porsche racing cars, beginning with the 906, all suspension parts of the 917 were pivoted in Teflon linered, solid spherical (Unital) bushes and adjustable ball joints. The suspension itself was by transverse wishbones front and rear, combining light weight with great flexibility in the choice of geometries. Anti-roll bars were used front and rear to control body lean and consequent undesirable wheel camber changes. The 381 mm (15 inch) diameter wheels were magnesium castings, carried by titanium hubs. The coil springs, mounted coaxially with the gas-filled dampers, were also of titanium.

A four-piston brake caliper was developed specially for the Porsche 917. The piston carriers bridging the two calipers were aluminium, but the calipers were titanium. The pads had an area of 60 cm^2 (9.3 square inches) each and were 18 mm (0.71 inch) thick, while the radially ventilated disc itself had a thickness of 28 mm (1.1 inch). Front and rear brakes were separately operated by twin circuits, each with its own master cylinder. The more highly stressed front brakes were additionally cooled by air ducted from the front of the body.

No important running gear changes were made for 1970, except for detail modifications dictated by the development of even wider tyres and by the efforts to improve the straight line stability. Rim width varied with the circuits, normal combinations being 267 mm (10.5 inches) front and 381 mm (15 inches) rear or 305 mm (12 inches) front and 432 mm (17 inches) rear.

Porsche devoted great care to the brakes of the 380 km/h (236 mph) 917. Wyer fitted Girling brakes with four-piston calipers to his cars in 1970 and Martini followed suit in 1971. Larger pistons were fitted to the Porsche-Salzburg cars which retained Ate brakes. The new Ate brakes also had twin titanium calipers (later aluminium) to which the piston carriers were bolted. Further development led to the use of discs made of copper-chrome alloy. They were lighter than the cast iron discs but were rather heat sensitive, so that they could be used for the less highly stressed rear brakes only. They were actually used successfully in Daytona, in 1970, but a more reliable and cheaper means of increasing the braking efficiency and reducing the weight was to drill the ventilated cast iron discs, in a certain pattern, right through the cooling ducts and, vanes. Such drilled discs were used throughout the 1971 season, except at Le Mans.

With the car bearing the chassis number 917.030, built in January 1971, tests were undertaken with anti-lock brakes and the car equipped with the Teldix-developed electronic device was entered for the last long-distance race of the season, the Austrian 1000 km race at Zeltweg. The Martini Porsche Racing-entered car was driven by Gérard Larrousse and Helmut Marko. In practice the device worked satisfactorily, the main problem being the drivers who found it difficult to adapt their technique to the anti-lock brakes and take advantage of the possibility they offer to brake notably later and enter curves with the brakes still firmly applied. Unfortunately a tyre failure caused the car's retirement in the race itself. The car was then used for another year for anti-lock brake tests and was later bought by Count Gregorio Rossi—part-owner of the Martini & Rossi concern—who had it adapted for road use and drives the car between Paris and his various estates!

Engine

The Porsche 4.5-litre, flat-12 Type 912, was an air-cooled four-stroke engine with twin overhead camshafts per bank of cylinders and fuel injection. The cylinders had the same dimensions as in the Type 908 3-litre engine (85×66 mm). In view of the unit's considerable length, the power take-off was in the middle of the crankshaft, where a 32-teeth gear meshed with a 31-teeth gear driving the power take-off shaft. The long crankshaft, which would be the source of considerable torsional vibrations with the power take-off at one end (as is normal practice), was thus turned into two shorter crankshafts with a much higher fundamental vibration period, putting resonance periods outside the speeds reached by the engine. In addition, the centre of the crankshaft coincided with the node of the fundamental torsional vibration, where the amplitude was virtually nil. As all auxiliary drives, including that of the gear-driven camshafts, were also taken from this place, no vibrations were transmitted to other engine components. The crankshaft had six crankpins (each carrying two big ends side by side) and eight main bearings, a configuration which is not only simple, but also leaves room for thick webs providing an excellent rigidity.

The crankshaft existed in two forms. One was forged in one piece, in which the central gear was cut. The second consisted of two half-crankshafts of soft nitrided tempered steel welded to the hardened gear in an electron ray welding machine. The crankcase, made of a special magnesium alloy, was split vertically along its centre-line. The 130 mm (5-inch) long (from big to little end axis) connecting rods were made of forged titanium, a material also used for the big end bolts. The cylinders were forged aluminium with machined fins and chromium-plated bores. The chrome layer was porous, so as to retain the oil and improve lubrication of the forged alloy pistons.

There were two plugs per cylinder, twin platinum electrodes being specified. The single cylinder heads were aluminium sand castings. The four camshafts were spur gear driven from the central crankshaft gear, the five intermediate gears on either side running in needle bearings. The one-piece camshafts all ran in nine plain, 2 mm thick, steel-backed bearings.

An axial blower, made of glass fibre-reinforced plastic, provided the engine cooling air. Its outside diameter was 330 mm (13 inches) and it had six 58 mm (2.3-inch) high blades.

At the Italian World Championship race run at Monza in April 1970, the 917 appeared for the first time with a bigger engine. Its bore had been increased by

1 mm to 86 mm (3.386 inches), while the stroke had gone up from 66 to 70.4 mm (2.6 to 2.77 inches), giving a total capacity of 4,907 cc (instead of 4,494 cc). There were no other modifications, but the power went up from 580 to 600 bhp.

For 1970 a new exhaust system was also developed, in which all exhaust pipes from one bank of cylinders merged into a single megaphone tail pipe and in which all individual pipes had exactly the same length, measured from the exhaust valve to the merging point, a requirement which involved quite a lot of clever plumbing.

Meanwhile, titanium intake valves had been developed to the stage of raceworthiness and were widely used. Quick wear (or even breakages) of the blower driving gears was checked by the use of an elastic blower wheel hub. The pistons were cooled by 1 mm diameter jets located near the main bearings and fed from the main oil gallery. Tapping five to ten per cent off the total quantity of oil circulated by the pressure pump lowered the piston crown temperature by 30-35°C.

The cooling blower was driven through bevel gears from the layshaft running parallel to the crankshaft. At 8,400 rpm engine speed, corresponding to peak power, it delivered 2,400 litres (146,461 cubic inches) of air per second, absorbing 17 hp. The engine's maximum power being 580 bhp, this represented only three per cent of the total power. Of the blower output 65 per cent served to cool the cylinder heads and 35 per cent the cylinders.

For the 12-cylinder, a new 12-plunger injection pump was developed by Bosch, incorporating a space cam. The injection pipes were all nylon, of 6×2 mm, the length being equal for all of them. In order to prevent the throttle slides from sticking, they were ball-mounted. The intake pipes and the engine cover plate were of glass fibre materials.

The engine had twin ignition, the two distributors being located at the front end of the left-hand, and at the rear end of the right-hand, crankcase half. The four separate ignition circuits were all fully transistorised. The firing order was 1-5-12-3-8-6-10-2-7-4-11, resulting in equal firing intervals in any group of three cylinders and greatly simplifying the exhaust system.

The dry-sump lubrication system comprised no fewer than seven pumps: one pressure and six scavenge. They served to keep the engine as 'dry' as possible. A thermostat incorporated in the pressure line fed the oil to a cooler whenever the temperature exceeded 90°C. The oil for big-end lubrication was fed axially to the crankshaft, as in the 908. The tension in the electrical circuits was 12-volt, the 45 Ah battery being kept charged by an 860 watt alternator. For night racing a second, similar generator was fitted.

At the end of the 1970 season Ferrari came out with his Type 512 M, intended to give the Porsche 917 a run for its money and with which Jacky Ickx actually beat Jo Siffert's works 917 in a race not counting for the World Championship of Makes. This Porsche countered with a larger-capacity engine. The bore was increased from 86 to 86.8 mm (3.386 to 3.417 inches) to raise the capacity to 4,998 cc, just 2 cc off the allowed limit. The new engine first appeared in April 1971 at the Brands Hatch 1000 km race. In addition to the increased bore, there was another important change: the Chromal cylinders were replaced with Nikasil (aluminium alloy cylinders with their bore coated with nickel/silicium carbide). Thanks to the reduced friction provided by the new material, the engine produced an extra 30 bhp.

There was no capacity limit in the Can-Am series at the time Porsche turned its attention to it, in 1972. This made it possible to push the engine up to 5,374 cc by increasing the bores to 90 mm (3.54 inches), and from 630 bhp the power went up once more, to 660 bhp at 8,300 rpm.

Transmission

In some races five, in others four gears were used. If the box contained five gear sets, there was a catch in the selector mechanism to prevent the driver inadvertently selecting the wrong gear. All forward gears were Porsche-synchronised. The triple-plate dry clutch was bolted to the engine power take-off shaft and the starter crown gear was mounted on the clutch housing.

A multiple-disc limited slip differential was used. Its locking factor could be altered, but usually 75 per cent was used. The engine and transmission unit was carried in the frame by three rubber supports and welded-on gearbox supports. The half-shafts featured two universal joints, one damping 'doughnut' and approximately 400 mm long (15.75 inch) ball splines.

Initially the five-speed gearbox was used in conjunction with a Fichtel & Sachs triple-plate clutch, but in the course of the season the clutch was changed for a Borg & Beck of similar type which was more reliable. The initial weakness of the gearbox housing, which tended to crack, was looked after by increasing the number of stiffening webs.

When the turbocharger was added, a transmission oil cooler was fitted.

Porsche 917 long-tail: the car was never raced under the pictured Gulf-Wyer colours.

Short-tail version of the 917. 800 kg (1,764 lb), 520 bhp, 320 km/h (199 mph).

*Below: Second race of the 917 ended with eighth place in the 1969 Nürburgring 1,000 km.
Bottom: Jo Siffert driving a Porsche 917 in the 1969 Austrian 1,000 km race on the
Zeltweg circuit.*

Le Mans 1969: first race for the long-tail 917. Driver is Jo Siffert.

In the Porsche factory's forecourt: the 25 Porsche 917s required for homologation in the 'sports car' group.

Porsche 917 short-tail winning the 1970 Le Mans 24 Hours race.

Side view of 1970 917 short-tail. It no longer has the Plexidur engine cover and the body is wedge-shaped.

Further modified Porsche 917 with additional small tail spoilers.

At Daytona, Pedro Rodriguez drove a 917 short-tail with an additional rear aerofoil and 43 cm (17-inch) wide rear rims.

Jo Siffert driving a Wyer-team 917 in the 1970 Spa 1,000 km race.

For the 1971 Le Mans 24 Hours race, the 917 short-tail cars sported tail fins on a lowered rear body.

The tail fins were used in most of the 1971 races.

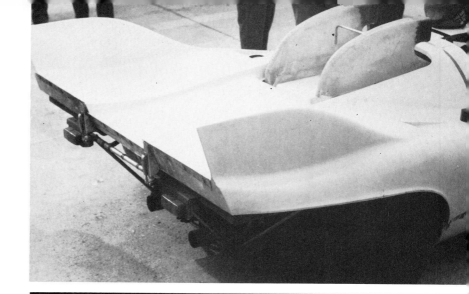

Ram air intakes were tried in the course of development tests, but were never used for actual racing.

498

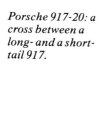

Porsche 917-20: a cross between a long- and a short-tail 917.

The body shape was a joint development of Porsche and the French Sera company.

The 917-20 had never raced before it came to the Le Mans trials in 1971, but won the 3-hour event rounding off the day.

Rear view of the 917-20 which only ran at Le Mans in 1971.

1970 Le Mans experimental car. The body is almost entirely closed.

500

This view of the experimental 917 long-tail car shows the total enclosure of the engine.

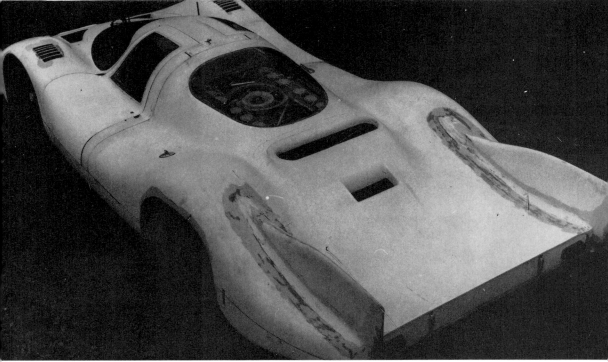

This improved
version of the
long-tail 917 was
run at Le Mans in
1970.

1971 Le Mans
long-tail car with
new nose section
and rear wheel
spats.

Rear view of the
1971 long-tail 917
which was raced
only at Le Mans.

Side views of the 1971 long-tail coupé. Maximum timed speed was 388 km/h (241 mph).

12-cylinder, Type 912 engine (left). The 16-cylinder shown on the right was fully developed, but never raced.

View of the cockpit of a 917 which earned Porsche the World Championship of Makes in 1970 and 1971.

503

12-cylinder engine in 917 coupé. This engine was built in capacities of 4.5, 4.9, 5.0 and 5.4 litres.

General description: Type 917 PA Spyder

Coachwork and chassis

The open two-seater body was made of epoxy material, bonded to the aluminium tube space-frame. The two doors were hinged at their front edge and the tail section pivoted at its front end. The steering was on the right-hand side. The car was built in great haste in August 1969 to enable factory driver Jo Siffert to take part in the remaining Can-Am races of the season. The idea was that the 917 PA (PA stood for the American entrant Porsche-Audi Vertriebsgesellschaft) should compete in those races in order to assess the chances a full factory entry might have in the series. Thus the fact that the car was not an immediate winner had little importance, especially as its creators knew perfectly well that it could not compete in weight and power with the specialised Can-Am cars, notably McLaren's. The PA differed from the 917 coupé only by its lighter, open body. Instead of 140 litres (30.8 gallons) its tanks contained 180 litres (39.6 gallons) of fuel and the car weighed 780 kg (1,719 lb) ready to race, but without fuel.

The general body outline was a wedge, but there had been no time to try it in the wind tunnel: it was just based on the experience gained with the 908.03. Except for wider rims and lighter brakes, the 917 PA had exactly the same technical specification as the coupé which won the Austrian 1000 km race at Zeltweg in 1969.

As more experience of the American races was gained the Spyder was progressively developed, and for the 1971 season a new Spyder was built and equipped with the 4.9-litre atmospheric engine. It was largely based on the original 917 PA, but had a completely different nosepiece, while the tail carried two large vertical fins, similar to those used in 1971 on the 908.03 and on the 917 K.

The main chassis data were very similar to those of the 917 coupé. Front and rear suspensions were by double transverse wishbones, triangulated by radius arms facing forward. The telescopic spring/damper units used progressive rate titanium coil springs, the variation being obtained by the use of progressively variable section wire. The dampers were, of course, double-acting. Front and rear anti-roll bars were tubular and infinitely adjustable. The rack-and-pinion steering gear had a ratio of 11.4:1. Front and rear hydraulic brake circuits were independently operated by twin master cylinders, a balance bar operating the cylinders making the pressure distribution adjustable. The wheels were cast magnesium with a central locking system. Their diameter was 381 mm (15 inches) and the rim width was 267 mm (10.5 inches) front and 381 mm (15 inches) rear, carrying tyres of the dimensions 4.25/10.20-15 and 12.5/26.0-15 respectively.

This second Spyder driven by Siffert in America was the base for the Porsche 917-10 used for Can-Am racing in 1972, both with the 5.4-litre unsupercharged engine (for private owners) and with the turbocharged unit. In contrast, the three 917 cars which participated in the 1971 Interserie were near relatives of the original 917 PA of 1969. Only the car raced by Jürgen Neuhaus—the 1970 Interserie champion—in 1971 was modified and fitted with two tail fins. 917 Spyders were used with turbo and atmospheric 4.5- and 4.9-litre engines in the Interserie up to 1975, only a change of rules putting a stop to their activities.

Engine

The engines used in the 917 PA were 4.5- and 4.9-litre flat-12s, absolutely identical with those of the 917 coupés. They were fully described under the heading '917'.

Transmission

A four- or five-speed gearbox shared its barrel housing with the limited slip differential of the multi-disc type. All forward gears were Porche-synchronised. Right-hand gear lever was ball-mounted and operated the selectors by means of rods. Twin universal half-shafts incorporating ball-mounted splines and a cushioning 'doughnut' were employed and the final drive was spiral bevel.

General description: Types 917-10/917-30

Coachwork and chassis

The chassis of the 917-10, also known as Can-Am Porsche, was a development of the 917 coupé frame. It was built up from aluminium tubes welded under the protection of argon. The body shape was dictated entirely by the need for optimum stability and handling; in a racing car, aerodynamic factors are just as important as the running gear. Both the nose piece and the large rear wing were aimed at obtaining the largest possible down-force to improve adhesion. At high speeds this force reaches several hundred pounds. Unfortunately, the down-force is obtained at the cost of a higher drag, as illustrated by the fact that with nearly twice as much power and lighter weight, the Can-Am Porsche was slower than the 917 coupé—especially the long-tail version. At the Californian Riverside speedway, the straight-line speed of the turbocharged Can-Am car was 'only' 343 km/h (213 mph), compared with the 386 km/h (240 mph) achieved by the 630 bhp long-tail coupé on the Le Mans straight.

505

All 917-10s sold to private customers had an epoxy material body bonded to the aluminium tube space-frame. The various reinforcements required to accept the turbo-engine's extra power increased the weight of the bare frame to just over 60 kg (132 lb). But for the Roger Penske team, officially representing the factory in American races, a car (917-10/011) was built around a magnesium tube frame weighing only 45 kg (100 lb) inclusive of all lugs!

The increased power also put additional demands on the chassis. Braking was particularly critical and for the 917-10 Porsche finally decided to make their own brakes. The aluminium four-piston calipers grew large reinforcing and cooling fins and the 28 mm (1.1-inch) thick discs, made of special cast iron material and radially cooled by internal vanes, were also laterally drilled in order to improve cooling, improve wet weather response and reduce weight.

Whilst, in accordance with the CSI ruling of the time the 917 coupé had a 120-litre (26.4-gallon) fuel tank, the 917-10 Turbo had two tanks of a total capacity of 300 litres (66 gallons), later increased to 330 litres (72.6 gallons).

As in 1972, the first Can-Am race of 1973 took place on the Canadian circuit of Mosport, and here the 917-30 was used for the first time. There were no drastic changes, but the wheelbase was increased from 2,316 mm (917-10) to 2,500 mm (917-30) (91.2 to 98.4 inches). This naturally implied some body modifications and the front end was changed to the shape used on late 1972 unsupercharged 917-10 cars. The tail was not only lengthened to match the longer wheelbase, but it was also extended behind the rear wheels to take an even larger wing. The drag coefficient consequently dropped from $C_x = 0.65$ to $C_x = 0.60$ and the maximum speed consequently rose from 343 to 370 km/h (213 to 230 mph) with the 5.4-litre turbo engine fitted. The fuel tankage was increased from 330 to 400 litres (88 gallons) and the weight also rose slightly to a good 800 kg (1,764 lb), some 20 kg (45 lb) more than the weight of the 917-10.

Engine

The basic engine from which the turbocharger unit was developed was the flat-12 which powered the 917 in races counting towards the World Championship of Makes from 1969 on. The decision to make a turbocharged version was sparked by the FIA's decision to limit the engine capacity in World Championship racing to three litres, starting from 1972. Following the 917 Spyder's tryout in the Can-Am series of 1969 in which it was driven by Jo Siffert, Porsche decided to make an attack on the series in 1972. While the 917-10 made its entry in the European Interserie with unsupercharged 5.0- and 5.4-litre engines, the turbocharged version was used in the Can-Am from the beginning of the season.

The basic engine remained almost unchanged in the turbocharged version. The first trials were made with the 4.5-litre version, from which 850 bhp was obtained. This was the engine used for the Interserie in 1972 to take over from the larger-capacity unsupercharged versions, but for the Can-Am the 5-litre turbocharged version, yielding 1,000 bhp, was used from the start. For 1973 a 5.4-litre version of the turbo engine was developed and run throughout the Can-Am season. It developed over 1,100 bhp at 7,800 rpm and produced a maximum torque of 112 mkg (820 lb/ft)! The weight of the complete unit, including the twin turbos, was 285 kg (628 lb).

As the flat-12 engine of the Porsche 917 was fully described under the heading Porsche 917, we shall limit ourselves here to a description of the main differences between the atmospheric and the turbocharged engines. In the atmospheric engine, the power take-off shaft diameter was 22 mm (0.866 inch) if the shaft was made of steel and 24 mm (0.944 inch) in the case of a titanium shaft. In the turbo unit, the shaft was always steel and 24 mm in diameter. The cooling blower driving gears were interchanged to provide a 29 per cent higher blower speed, increasing the blower air output from 2,400 litres/second in the case of the unsupercharged engine to 3,100 litres/second in the turbo engine. This increased the power absorbed by the blower from 17 to 31 hp. Further modifications were directly linked to the turbocharging installation: the intake trumpets were replaced by pipes, each incorporating a throttle valve to replace the throttle slides, and the shape of the piston crown was flatter in order to reduce the compression ratio drastically from 10.4 to 6.5:1.

The turbocharged engine had different intake camshafts, while the exhaust camshafts remained unchanged. As in the unsupercharged engine, each bank of six cylinders had regular firing intervals which made it possible to treat them as two separate six-cylinder engines, fed by entirely separate turbocharging installations. The exhaust gases from one cylinder bank were thus fed to the turbine of one of the turbochargers which, in turn, drove its blower feeding the compressed air to a plenum chamber surmounting six intake pipes, each with its own throttle valve. The forward ends of the plenum chambers were linked in order to compensate for possible differences in the boost pressure provided by the two superchargers.

The two turbochargers were adjusted to produce a high boost at comparatively low engine speeds. This meant that, under full load, the pressure had to be limited at high engine speeds. The pressure reduction was obtained through the use of a bypass valve (waste gate) mounted upstream of the turbine and controlled by the boost pressure. When the maximum permissible boost was reached, the valve opened and allowed the exhaust gases to escape into the atmosphere, bypassing the turbine. The bypass valve was operated by a membrane acting on a spring of which the preload could be adjusted by a screw. Increasing the preload raised the maximum boost, as the valve would only operate at a higher pressure. A pressure rise of only 0.1 atm (1.4 psi) increased the engine power by some 50 hp! Hence the name 'screwdriver tuning' the racing drivers gave it. In Donohue's works car, the waste gate setting could be altered from the cockpit, enabling the driver to modify the boost pressure and the power at his disposal during a race!

Normally the 5.0- and 5.4-litre engines (1,000 and 1,100 bhp respectively) were run at 1.4 to 1.5 atm boost (20 to 22 psi). The air fed to the engine had a temperature of approximately 150°C, while the exhaust gas temperature at the turbine entry was approximately 1,000°C. The turbochargers were standard proprietary parts, normally used in commercial vehicle Diesel engines. The only difference was that in, the case of the 917-10, the turbocharger shaft was mounted on ball, rather than plain bearings. At full load its speed was 90,000 rpm.

In addition to these modifications, a fuel injection pump with larger diameter plungers had to be used to increase the quantity of fuel injected proportionally to the increased air throughput, and a boost pressure sensitive delivery control had to be incorporated; thanks to the low compression ratio and the negligible boost pressure at low engine speeds, a fixed ignition timing could be used. In the development stage, sticking exhaust valves, due to overheating, caused problems. They were solved by shortening the valve guide, chromium-plating the valve stem, increasing the clearance between the valve in its guide and drilling a small lubrication hole in the guide. Obviously, the exhaust system had to be modified to feed the turbocharger turbines. If related to more normal power outputs, the fuel consumption of the Can-Am cars, which varied between 3.7 and 2.88 miles per gallon (3.0 and 2.37 miles per US gallon) according to the race course, was not all that extravagant!

The 4.5-, 5.0- and 5.4-litre turbocharged engines used in the Spyders were virtually identical except for bore, stroke and power output. Their main data were as follows:
4,494 cc—85 × 66 mm—850 bhp at 8,000 rpm—620 lb/ft at 6,600 rpm
4,998 cc—86.8 × 70.4 mm—1,000 bhp at 7,800 rpm—730 lb/ft at 6,400 rpm
5,374 cc—90 × 70.4 mm—1,100 bhp at 7,800 rpm—820 lb/ft at 6,400 rpm
Unsupercharged engines used in the Spyders were identical with those of the 917 coupés.

Transmission
In order to transmit the increased torque of the turbocharged engine a completely new, reinforced gearbox, Type 920, was conceived. It was laid down purely as a four-speed box, but was otherwise very similar to the 917 box. It was fully synchronised and incorporated a pump circulating the oil through a cooler which fed it under pressure, both through the hollow gearbox shafts and to jets spraying the final drive bevel gears. The splines were deleted from the titanium half-shafts to save weight, the 'doughnuts' being left to compensate for length variations. The three-plate clutch was inherited from the 917 almost without modification, only the diaphragm spring being reinforced. The cars were run with either a multi-disc type limited slip differential or solid drive (no differential at all).

The Can-Am Spyder was driven by Jo Siffert. Note side exhaust of this early version.

Porsche 917 PA Spyder (PA = Porsche-Audi of America): first version of the Can-Am car.

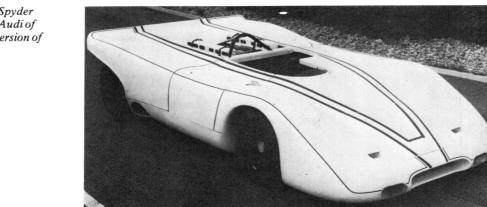

Views of the 12-cylinder engine, Type 912, in 4.5-litre form, as fitted to the 917 PA Spyder.

The Can-Am Spyder with modified front and small tail spoilers.

Below: Porsche 917 Spyder as run in the 1971 Can-Am series: new nose, tail fins, 4.9-litre engine. Bottom: 917 Spyder with 908.03-type tail fins. This is, in fact, a modified coupé.

The so-called 'Interserie 917' was also raced without the fins.

Below: The 917 Spyders used 4.5- and later 4.9-litre engines. Bottom: The European Spyders—this one driven by Ernst Kraus—dominated the Interserie races.

Cutaway view of Porsche 917-10 Spyder with 5-litre turbocharged engine, developing 1,000 bhp.

The ancestor of all Porsche 917-10s. This car was originally fitted with a 5.4-litre engine.

Front view of first Porsche 917-10. This type was raced in both Can-Am and Interserie races.

The still all-white 917-10 undergoes development tests by American driver Mark Donohue.

513

In the States the factory was officially represented by the Roger Penske organisation. In Europe the cars were all privately entered.

Porsche 917-10 with turbocharged 12-cylinder engine (right) and with normally aspirated engine (below right).

Porsche 917-10 with different fronts: right for the Turbo, below right for the normally aspirated engine.

Porsche 917-20: a cross between 917-10 and 917-30. Its wheelbase could be varied and it was built for experimental purposes. Driver is H. Müller.

Cockpit of a 917-10. The tachometer and boost pressure gauge are the most important instruments.

Porsche 12-cylinder engine with turbocharger. This is the 5.4-litre Type 912-52.

Top, side and front views of a Porsche 917-30. Only two were built. They ran in the Can-Am races and had a wheelbase 19 cm (7.5 inches) longer than the 917-10.

Cockpit of a 917-30. The gauges on the left indicate the fuel and supercharger output pressures.

Rear view of Porsche 917-30 with the tail removed.

By lapping the Talladega track at 355.846 km/h (221.112 mph), Mark Donohue set up a new world record in the 917-30.

History of Type 917 racing cars (use and duration)

Car	Duration/Distance	Use
917.001	250 km	Tests/Exhibitions/Museum
917.002	400 km	Le Mans pre-practice 1969
	2,080 km	Rough track tests/Scrapped
917.003	350 km	Le Mans pre-practice 1969
	100 km	Practice Spa 1969
	1,380 km	Tests at Nürburgring 1969
		Scrapped after accident
917.004	1,230 km	Practice/Race Nürburgring 1,000 km
	170 km	Tests
	7 h 25 m	Practice/Race Brands Hatch 1970
		Sold
917.005	280 km	Practice/Race Spa 1969
		Sold
917.006	1,550 km	Tests 1969
	380 km	Practice Le Mans 1969
	25 h	Roller endurance test/Scrapped
917.007	2,550 km	Practice/Race Le Mans 1969
		Sold
917.008	4,840 km	Practice/Race Le Mans 1969
	900 km	Tests 1969
	450 km	Tests 1970
	2,030 km	Rough track endurance test 1970
	20 h	Roller endurance test
917.009	1,320 km	Practice/Race Zeltweg 1969 (1st)
	12 h 15 m	Practice/Race Sebring 1970
	6 h 25 m	Practice/Race Monza 1970
	5 h 35 m	Practice Silverstone and Zeltweg 1970
	15 h 30 m	Practice/Race Sebring 1971
917.010	1,350 km	Practice/Race Zeltweg 1969
		Sold to David Piper
917.011	30 h 30 m	Pre-practice Daytona 1969
	2,300 km	Practice/Race Daytona 1970
	200 km	Pre-practice Targa Florio 1970
		Scrapped after accident
917.012	5 h 15 m	Pre-practice Daytona 1969
		Sold
917.013	3 h 15 m	Practice Daytona 1970
(917.034)	13 h 25 m	Practice/Race Sebring 1970
		Filming at Le Mans 1970
		Accident
917.014	22 h 40 m	Practice/Race Daytona 1970
(917.023)	5 h 40 m	Practice/Race Spa 1970 (1st)
	9 h 20 m	Practice/Race Watkins Glen 1970
	2 h 15 m	Tests at Goodwood
		Sold
917.015	26 h 45 m	Practice/Race Daytona 1970 (1st)
(917.035)	9 h 10 m	Pre-practice/Practice Sebring 1970
	1 h 05 m	Practice Brands Hatch 1970
	1,090 km	Pre-practice Monza 1970
	1 h 30 m	Practice Spa 1970
	280 km	Tests Nürburgring
	2 h 50 m	Practice/Race Watkins Glen 1970 (1st)
	1 h 10 m	Tests at Goodwood
		Sold
917.016	8 h 45 m	Practice/Race Brands Hatch 1970 (1st)
	6 h 00 m	Practice/Race Monza 1970 (1st)
	0 h 35 m	Tests at Goodwood 1970
	3 h 40 m	Practice/Race Le Mans 1970
	8 h 05 m	Practice/Race Watkins Glen 1970 (1st)
	2 h 30 m	Practice/Race Imola 1970
	4 h 50 m	Practice Daytona 1971
	1 h 10 m	Practice Sebring 1971
	4 h 45 m	Pre-practice Le Mans 1971
	0 h 50 m	Practice Monza 1971
	3 h 00 m	Practice Spa 1971
	1 h 55 m	Practice Zeltweg 1971
917.17	5 h 05 m	Practice/Race Spa 1971
	12 h 25 m	Practice/Race Le Mans 1971
	8 h 10 m	Practice/Race Daytona 1971
	5 h 55 m	Practice/Race Monza 1971
	4 h 50 m	Practice/Race Zeltweg 1971
917.018		Sold
917.019		Sold (1st Sebring 1971)
917.020		Sold
917.021		Sold
917.022		Sold (1st Le Mans 1970)
917.023		Sold
917.024		Sold
917.025		Sold
917.026	1 h 15 m	Tests at Goodwood
(917.030)	5 h 15 m	Practice/Race Le Mans 1970
		Sold
917.027	1,500 km	Tests
Spyder	57 h 30 m	Roller endurance test
917.028		Sold
Spyder		

Chassis		Event
917.029	7 h 50 m	Practice/Race Buenos Aires 1971 (1st)
	8 h 35 m	Practice/Race Brands Hatch 1971
	6 h 35 m	Practice/Race Spa 1971
		Scrapped after fire tests at Hockenheim on February 18 1974
917.030		Tests
	450 km	Practice/Race Zeltweg 1971
	1,580 km	Sold to Count G. Rossi
917.031	4 h 25 m	Practice/Race Imola 1970 (1st)
	8 h 40 m	Practice/Race Zeltweg 1970 (1st)
	14 h 50 m	Practice/Race Sebring 1970
	26 h 10 m	Practice/Race Le Mans 1971
917.032	2,080 km	Endurance test
	1,720 km	Tests
917.034	32 h 00 m	Roller endurance test
	24 h 45 m	Practice/Race Daytona 1971 (1st)
	5 h 50 m	Practice/Race Monza 1971 (1st)
	7 h 35 m	Practice/Race Zeltweg 1971 (1st)
917.035	6 h 20 m	Practice/Race Buenos Aires 1971
	4 h 20 m	Practice/Race Brands Hatch 1971
	6 h 30 m	Practice/Race Spa 1971 (1st)
917.040LH		Scrapped after accident
917.041LH	230 km	Pre-practice Le Mans 1970
		Scrapped after accident
917.042LH	3,490 km	Practice/Race Le Mans 1970
	2,390 km	Tests
917.043LH	1,870 km	Practice/Race Le Mans 1971
	5,090 km	Practice/Race Le Mans 1970
	1,785 km	Tests
917.045LH	890 km	Pre-practice Le Mans 1971
	15 h 10 m	Practice/Race Le Mans 1971
917.051	17 h 00 m	Rough track 1971
	740 km	Rough track 1971
		Scrapped
917.052	200 km	Pre-practice Le Mans 1971
	1,020 km	Rough track 1971
		Scrapped
917.053	5,830 km	Practice/Race Le Mans 1971 (1st)
		Museum
917/20.001 'Swine'	930 km	Pre-practice Le Mans 1971
	440 km	Tests 1971
	2,970 km	Practice/Race Le Mans 1971
		Museum

NB: All cars had aluminium tube frames, except 917.051/52/53 which had magnesium tube frames.

Types 917/10 and 917/30

(Alu = Aluminium tube frame; Mg = Magnesium tube frame.)

917/10.001	Alu	Development car
917/10.002	Alu	Sold to W. Kauhsen in 1972
	Alu	Sold to Jo Siffert
917/10.003	Alu	Accident at Nürburgring (W. Kauhsen)
		Sold to R. Penske in 1972
		Resold to B. Rinzler in 1973
917/10.004	Alu	Sold to Wihuri Racing (L. Kinnunen) 1972
917/10.005	Alu	Sold to R. Penske in 1972
		Resold to B. Rinzler in 1973
917/10.006	Alu	Sold to Vasek Polak in 1972
		Resold to H. Wiedmer in 1973 (accident)
917/10.008	Alu	Sold to P. Gregg in 1972
		Resold to H. Haywood 1973
917/10.010	Mg	Development car. Endurance test. Scrapped
917/10.011	Mg	Sold to R. Penske 1972
		Accident at Road Atlanta (Donohue)
917/10.015	Alu	Sold to W. Kauhsen in 1973
917/10.016	Alu	Sold to E. Kraus in 1973
917/10.017	Alu	Sold to G. Loos in 1973
917/10.018	Alu	Sold to Vasek Polak in 1973
917/30.001	Mg	Development car with variable wheelbase. Reconverted to 917/10 specifications, except for front part of body and wider front track
917/30.002	Mg	Sold to R. Penske in 1973
917/30.003	Mg	Sold to R. Penske in 1973

917/917 PA/917 Spyder/917-10/917-30

Year	Body	Model Type	Chassis no	Engine type	Gearbox type	Cyl	Bore × stroke	Cap-acity	HP (DIN) at rpm	Torque (mkg) at rpm	Comp ratio	W.base (mm)	Track fr/ rear (mm)	Length (mm)	Weight (kg)
1969	Coupé	917-4.5	917001-917025	912/00	917	12	85 x66	4494	560/8300	50/6800	10,5:1	2300	1526/1533	4290	800
	Coupé-LH												1488/1457	4780	830
	Spyder	917PA	917028	912/00	917	12	85 x66	4494	560/8300	50/6800	10,5:1	2300	1488/1457 / 1584	3905	775
1970	Coupé	917K4.5	917001-917053	912/00	917	12	85 x66	4494	580/8400	52/6800	10,5:1	2300	1564/1584	4140	800
		-4.9		912/10		12	86 x70,4	4907	600/8400	56/6500	10,5:1		1564/1584		
		-5.0		912/11		12	86,8x70,4	4999	630/8300	60/6500	10,5:1		1526/1533		
		-5.4		912/12		12	90 x70,4	5374	660/8300	65/6400	10,5:1		1564/1584		
	Spyder	917-4.5	917027	912/00	917	12	85 x66	4494	580/8400	52/6800	10,5:1	2300	1564/1584	4100	780
		-4.9		912/10		12	86 x70,4	4907	600/8400	56/6500	10,5:1				
		-5.0		912/11		12	86,8x70,4	4999	630/8300	60/6500	10,5:1				
		-5.4		912/12		12	90 x70,4	5374	660/8300	65/6400	10,5:1				
1970	Coupé-LH	917LH-4.9	917042-043	912/10	917	12	86 x70,4	4907	600/8400	56/6500	10,5:1	2300	1564/1584 / 1526/1533	4780	800
1971	Coupé-LH	917LH-4.9	917026/045 917042-043	912/10	917	12	86 x70,4	4907	600/8400	56/6500	10,5:1	2300	1564/1584	4780	800
	Coupé	917-20-4.9	91720001	912/10	917	12	86 x70,4	4907	600/8400	56/6500	10,5:1	2300			
1972	Spyder	917-10 TC 4.5	91710001-018	912/50	920/10	12	85 x66	4494	850/8000	87/7600	16,5:1	2316	1620/1638	4385	750
		TC 4.9		912/51	920/50	12	86,8x70,4	4999	1000/7800	100/6400	6,5:1	2500		4562	
		TC 5.4		912/52	920/50	12	90 x70,4	5374	1100/7800	112/6400	6,5:1				
		6.5	917027	917	917	16	86 x70,4	6543	755/8200	73,4/6800	10,5:1				
1973	Spyder	917-30 TC	91730002-003	912	920/50	12	90 x70,4	5374	1100/7800	112/6400	6,5:1	2500	1670/1564	4562	800

Types Carrera RSR prototype/ 936 Turbo-Spyder

The factory-prepared Carrera's racing debut began with a sensation: two RSR versions of the new model were sent to the Daytona 24 Hours race of 1973, even before the model had been homologated as a GT car, to be driven by Mark Donohue/George Follmer and Peter Gregg/Hurley Haywood.

After 16 hours of racing, the sensation had crystallised: in spite of the opposition from the much faster and more powerful Matra and Mirage prototypes, the two Carreras occupied the first two places. Engine problems prevented the Donohue/Follmer car from reaching the finish, but Gregg/ Haywood won outright.

For the following World Championship races, the factory itself took over and entered cars for eight races in the colours of its sponsor, Martini. In order to try out new developments, many of which were incorporated in the 1974 Carreras, at least one car was always entered as a prototype. Against the superior power of the Matra, Ferrari, Mirage, Alfa-Romeo and Lola prototypes, the Martini Porsche team could offer only a fascinating reliability.

Only once in the whole season, at the Monza 1000 km race of 1973, did the Swiss Herbert Müller and the Dutchman Gijs van Lennep fail to finish a race. In all others, they were to be found high up in the classification, without ever having experienced any trouble or having been involved in an accident. In two races they were particularly successful: they won the Targa Florio outright and two other Carreras finished fourth and sixth. No less impressive was Müller and van Lennep's fourth place at Le Mans. The final World Championship placings had Porsche in third place behind Matra and Ferrari. In most of the World Championship long-distance races privately owned Carreras won the GT group, which earned Porsche the FIA Cup for Grand Touring cars. Porsche also won the World Cup for Speed and Endurance for the successes achieved in long-distance racing for the seventh time!

For the 1974 season the Porsche engineers were faced with a bitter dilemma. They had no 500 bhp engine to beat the French and Italian cars, not to mention the fact that the Carrera, despite some drastic lightening, was still much heavier than its prototype rivals. The only solution would have been to build a new prototype, but at the end of 1973 there were signs that, as from the beginning of 1975, a change of rules would intervene and only production-derived cars would be eligible for World Championship events. The idea of developing an expensive new prototype was therefore abandoned. It was decided instead to capitalise on the experience gained with the 917 Turbo which had been excluded from the

Can-Am series and to drop a turbocharged, Type 911 six-cylinder engine into a Carrera RSR. For this, a basically standard Carrera body was used, an enormous rear wing creating the required down-force.

From this point on, Porsche's aim in the World Championship races was less to win the events (which the Turbo-Carrera would be unable to do, unless the opposition from the faster prototypes broke down), than to gain experience for the 'production derived racing car' required by future Group 5 regulations. Once again, the works entries were Martini-sponsored and one car driven by van Lennep and Müller was entered for most races, with a second car in support in some of them driven by Helmuth Koinigg and Manfred Schurti.

Although the Porsche coupé developing close on 500 bhp was severely handicapped by its frontal area and its weight, it was fast and reliable enough to score very respectable results. Nine starts produced two second places, one in the Le Mans 24 Hours race and one in the Watkins Glen 6-Hours race. In both cases the Porsche was headed only by one of the very fast Matra prototypes. In the entire season, van Lennep and Müller retired only twice. In the World Championship of Makes, Porsche ran second up to one race before last. But as sufficient experience had been gained, the cost of sending the team to South Africa was not thought to be worthwhile and Porsche dropped a place for the benefit of Mirage-Ford. Unfortunately, the start of the World Championship of Makes, based on production cars, was postponed to the beginning of 1976 and the factory decided to stay out of racing for one year.

The time was not lost, however, as the Group 5 rules eventually turned out to be rather different from what had been generally expected, and this was important when laying down the specifications of the Type 930 Turbo road car, on which the Type 935 racing car was to be based.

In 1976, the first year of the new formula, only Porsche came up with a car that had been specially developed for it. The strongest competition came from ex-Group 2 BMW coupés, modified to suit the new Group 5. The cars were prepared at their Munich-based factory and three or even more cars were entered for most races, in the hope that the faster but solitary Porsche coupé might suffer from teething troubles and allow the BMWs to prevail. Porsche, on the other hand, found little support from private teams, only the Kremer brothers having prepared their own version of a turbocharged Group 5 Porsche to help the factory meet the opposition.

In fact BMW's strategy nearly succeeded as differences in the interpretation of the new rules forced Porsche hastily to introduce some modifications required by the CSI, which impaired the car's reliability, so that BMW won several races and the championship was only decided in Porsche's favour in the penultimate race of the series, at Watkins Glen. Following this success, it was decided to build a small series of 15 replicas of the championship-winning Group 5 car for private customers.

In spite of the problems which arose around technical regulations, Porsche had successfully achieved its aim of winning the World Championship of Makes for the fourth time, in this case with a car based on a production model. But in 1977, things turned out to be not as easy as had been expected. Out of eight races counting towards the World Championship of Makes, the works-entered Martini Porsches won only four. This partly resulted from the fact that because strong competition was not expected, the factory decided to enter only one car per race, which made the factory entries vulnerable to the slightest mishap. Fortunately, although this took some glory away from the Porsche team, it did not take away the precious World Championship points. Private Porsche 935 teams took up the challenge and had a successful season earning the points for Porsche. Fate even divided the laurels between the most meritorious and most appropriate teams! The Daytona 24 Hours race was won by the American team of John Graves/Hurley Haywood/Dave Helmick driving an old Carrera RSR(!), the Nürburgring race was won by Rolf Stommelen/Toine Hezemans/Tim Schenken on a Porsche belonging to the Loos team and in the second German World Championship race at Hockenheim, the victor was a Kremer Porsche 935 driven by Bob Wollek/John Fitzpatrick/Claude Haldi. Only the race held at Mosport (Canada) was not won by a car made in Zuffenhausen: the winner was a BMW.

Before the 1976 season began, it was difficult to assess if the new Group 5 would provide good racing and for some time it was feared that the World Championship based on this Group might be called off owing to a lack of participants. Just in case, the decision was taken in Autumn 1975 to build a Spyder to the new Group 6 regulations to run in the races of the World Championship of Sports Cars in which the main force was the Alpine Renault. The new car, called 936, was a winner from the outset and dominated most of the races in which it ran.

The first climax came in the 1976 Le Mans 24 Hours race, for which two Martini sponsored 936 Spyders were entered. Though one of them had to be retired after 14 hours' racing, the other car driven by Jacky Ickx and Gijs van Lennep won the race by a large margin.

The following year of 1977 brought more drama as after an 18 hour long furious drive, the Martini Porsche 936 number 4 charged through the field from its 41st position into the lead, again beating the Alpine Renaults. The drivers were Jacky Ickx, Jürgen Barth and Hurley Haywood. Their victory aroused the kind of enthusiasm that had been seldom seen before. For Ickx, who had driven one of the most difficult and best races in his career, this was the fourth Le Mans victory, but Porsche too had been successful four times in the most celebrated long distance race in the world.

By the end of 1977, it was clear that the World Championship of Makes based on Group 5 cars would never be a great success. For Porsche, this was a good reason to withdraw its 935 works cars and leave the racing to private 935 owners. In 1977, private Porsche teams had won the German Racing Championship (Rolf Stommelen, Loos Porsche), the German Rally Championship (Kuhn/Hopfe, Carrera RS), the Trans Am Championship in the United States (Peter Gregg, Porsche 934), the European Hill Climb Championship (Anton Fischhaber, Carrera RS), as well as a number of important international overall and class wins.

1978 was again a Porsche year. In addition to their six victories in the World Championship of Makes, Porsche cars took five international and 21 national championships, underlining Porsche's position of most successful sports car in the world.

The tremendous achievements of 1978 coincided with the climax of the restlessly pursued development of the 911, started in 1973 with the intention of making the car an absolute weapon in Groups 4 and 5. In contrast to the original decision, a Martini sponsored 935 factory car, was entered in a few selected races. Powered by its new 6-cylinder engine, featuring four camshafts and four valves per cylinder, the 935/78 was easily the fastest Group 5 car of the year. In the World Championship series, it won its first race, driven by Jochen Mass and

523

Jacky Ickx in Silverstone. In the final race of the series in Vallelungs, Italy, Ickx and Schurti had to retire with only a few laps to go and victory in sight when the toothed belt driving the injection pump broke.

The World Championship of Makes for 1978 was won for Porsche by the private teams of Georg Loos and the Kremer brothers. After the dramatic Watkins Glen 6 Hours race held in pouring rain, had been won by the Porsche of Hezemans, Fitzpartrick and Gregg, followed by the similar 935 of Stommelen, Schurti and Barbour which both beat the BMW of Stuck and Quester, the World Championship of Makes was firmly in Porsche's hands.

Further titles which went to Porsche included two European Hill-Climb Championships, won by the brothers Jean-Marie and Jacques Almeras (934 and 935), the FIA Gran Turismo Cup, won by Angelo Palavicini (934) and the American IMSA Championship which was won by Peter Gregg (935)—not to mention the many national championships won on Porsche cars.

On the rally scene too, Porsche obtained two remarkable successes. Jean-Pierre Nicolas scored a surprise win in the Monte-Carlo Rally driving a privately entered 911 Carrera 3.0 and beating all the factory supported teams, while Preston/Lyall and Waldegaard/Thorszelius took second and fourth places in the Safari Rally. Of the 70 starters in this gruelling event, only 9 reached the finish in Nairobi, among them the two works entered 911 SCs.

An astonishing feat was achieved by the German driver Reinhold Jöst: he succeeded in winning the European Sports Car Championship driving a modernised Porsche 908/03, a car made in 1970 into which a Porsche Turbo engine had been dropped. This, and meticulous preparation, was enough to make the old but agile 908 (a car which had won the Targa Florio) still the car to beat, after eight years of hard racing.

524

In 1978, Porsche's most up-to-date racing car, the 936, was entered in the Le Mans 24 Hours race only. In the two previous years, Porsche had been able to beat Renault in their fight for supremacy, but this time the French team made the grade. In the two 936s powered by the new 4-valve engine, fifth gear surrendered to the increased torque and power of the new engine. In each case, the repair cost more than half an hour and the 936 driven by Wollek/Barth/Ickx and Haywood/Gregg respectively finished second and third to the Renault driven by Pironi and Jaussaud. However, the fastest car down the famous Le Mans straight was neither a Renault nor a 936: it was Porsche's 935/78 which, in practice, was timed at a speed of 365 km/h (227.5 mph).

1979 was again a success year for Porsche. More than 20 national, international and world championships were won by Porsche cars entered and run by private teams or drivers. The Championship of Makes went Porsche's way for the seventh time. Out of ten Championship races, Porsche won nine and averaged four cars among the first six past the finishing line. The most successful team in the World Championship series was formed by Fitzpatrick, Schurti and Wollek who won at Mugello, Nüburgring and Silverstone (where Heyer replaced Schurti), while the Whittington brothers together with Klaus Ludwig won at Watkins Glen and Le Mans. The works team was unlucky in the only two races for which cars were entered: an accident put paid to the chances of the only 936/79 running under Essex sponsorship in Silverstone and in Le Mans minor defects caused the retirement of the two similar cars entered. These failures, were however, more than made up by the remarkable performance of privately entered Porsches in the Le Mans race, won by a 935 prepared by the Kremer brothers. Four Porsches finished in the first four places.

Probably the most attractive Group 5 championship of 1979 was the German Racing Championship. Perfect preparation, inspired driving and the indispensable little bit of luck made Klaus Ludwig and the Porsche-Kremer team an unbeatable combination.

In America, the IMSA series for modified production cars (largely similar to the European Group 5 cars), is considered to be the major drivers championship. Out of the 15 races of the 1979 series 14 were won by Porsche drivers, eight of them by Peter Gregg in his Brumos sponsored Porsche 935. This was his sixth title in the nine-year history of the series.

The same drivers and cars which compete in the IMSA championship are eligible for the Trans Am championship. This SCCA series comprises seven races on the North American continent from Mexico to Canada and was also dominated by Porsches. It was won by a large margin by John Paul who drove a 935.

As in the previous year, Jean-Marie and Jacques Almeras were declared European Hill-Climb champions in Groups 4 and 5 respectively, driving a 934 and a 935 powered by a Carrera atmospheric engine.

General description: Type Carrera RSR prototype

Coachwork and chassis
It had been the factory's policy for several years to leave the defence of its colours in the GT Group to private teams. The Carrera RS 2.7 had been developed to give them a better chance, but in this case the factory stepped in too. In most of the races for which Carreras were entered by the factory however, they ran in the Prototype Group where they were not in direct competition with customers' cars. Initially the cars were virtually to normal RSR specifications, but as time wore on more and more modifications were introduced.

The body structure of the Martini Racing Porsche remained largely standard, but the running gear was progressively developed. Among the newly developed parts were the lighter and stiffer aluminium rear semi-trailing arms which were adopted for all production Porsches, starting with the 1974 models. For the racing version, the rubber bushes in which the arms pivot were replaced by Unibal spherical joints. At the front, the upper suspension strut location was made adjustable, so that caster and camber could be optimised, while the stub axles were mounted slightly higher on the strut, thus reducing the ride height. The Porsche-designed and constructed four-piston brake calipers, the ventilated and perforated brake discs and the titanium hubs were borrowed from the 917-10 Turbo. So were the centre-lock magnesium wheels, except for their narrower rims: front 228 mm (nine inches), rear 279 mm (11 inches), the limit being dictated by the CSI regulations on mudguard width.

The standard torsion bars remained unchanged, but the suspension was considerably stiffened by variable rate titanium springs mounted concentrically with the Bilstein dampers. The inner pivot of the rear semi-trailing arm was moved rearwards to increase camber variations and prevent the outside rear wheel leaning excessively with the body in curves.

Even faster steering and adjustable front and rear anti-roll bars were also fitted, in addition to the normal racing equipment, such as a 120-litre (26.4-gallon) fuel tank with quick-action filler cap, an integral fire extinguishing system with multiple jets, a roll-over bar and various other items.

One of the first steps of the development was to increase the mudguard width over the limit allowed in the GT group, so that 279 mm (11 inch) wide rims could be fitted at the front and 356 mm (14 inch) rims at the rear. The small rear spoiler (the so-called 'Duck's tail') of the standard Carrera was extended on either side and for the Zeltweg 1000 km race even vertical fins were added. Glass fibre doors and front cover, Plexiglas side windows and leaving off the spare wheel reduced the weight to 890 kg (1,962 lb)—50 kg (110 lb) less than the GT version.

Engine

The rear-mounted engine, developed from the standard 2.7-litre Carrera RS, was used in three different stages of tune. Initially, it was a normal Carrera RSR of 2,806 cc and 300 bhp. Then the bore was increased by 3 mm to 95 mm (3.74 inches), the stroke remaining 70.4 mm (2.77 inches), which increased the power to 315 bhp, and when the throttle valves were replaced by slides, the power went up to 330 bhp.

The cylinder heads were basically similar to the standard parts, but had a second plug hole for the twin ignition. The ports and valves were larger than in the standard Carrera and racing camshafts were used. The compression ratio was 10.3:1 and the six-plunger Bosch injection pump incorporated a space cam to govern the quantity of fuel delivered. For reasons of cost, the connecting rods were not made of titanium: they were standard steel parts, polished to improve their fatigue strength.

The racing version used a large oil cooler mounted under the front bumper, rather than the smaller serpentine cooler housed in the right-hand front wing.

Transmission

The Porsche five-speed box, Type 915, was used. It was a standard part, except for the gear ratios and the fact that a special front cover was used, incorporating an oil pump circulating the lubricant through a separate cooler. A single plate racing clutch and a limited slip differential were also part of the racing equipment.

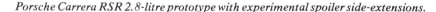

Porsche Carrera RSR 2.8-litre prototype with experimental spoiler side-extensions.

Carrera with additional vertical rear fins (1973).

Development started with this factory-owned Carrera RSR in 1973.

The cars usually ran in the Prototype group, allowing new developments to be tried out.

Rear view showing the first developments which eventually led to the finalisation of the Carrera 3-litre.

General description: Type Carrera RSR-Turbo

Coachwork and chassis

The basic similarity between the Turbo-Carrera's body and that of the standard model was obvious. But a closer examination revealed more differences than the addition of the spectacular rear wing. The rear mudguard extensions widened the 161 cm (63.38 inches) wide 911 body (in its original version) to an imposing two metres (78.74 inches). Another striking modification was the deletion of the rear quarter windows. The panel replacing them incorporated a NACA air inlet feeding air into the engine compartment, which it reached via large diameter tubes. (Early in the 1973 season these covers did not exist.) Another modification was to raise the rear part of the roof, which was made flatter, improving the aerodynamic flow. In the new roof the rear window was no longer recessed, but flush with the roof panel and bonded.

There were more modifications under the plastic and steel skin. The fuel tank, for instance, was moved from the front into the cockpit where it took the place of the rear seats and even slightly protruded into the front passenger area. The opportunity was taken to use a 120-litre (26.4-gallon) safety tank, completely protected by aluminium sheet. The oil tank was moved from the rear to the front of the car. These modifications reduced variations in the car's weight distribution during the course of a race and hence provided a more constant road behaviour.

The roll-over cage was also much more elaborate than in the Group 4 Carrera. Not only was it a full cage (chosen because of the location of the fuel tank within the passenger area), but it was made of aluminium tubes to reduce weight. The driver had two additional instruments to check: a boost pressure gauge and a governing pressure gauge.

To reduce the weight to under 800 kg (1,764 lb), the Turbo-Carrera had to be drastically lightened. In addition to the weight-saving already mentioned, a short cut was taken by using paper-thin plastic material for all non-stressed parts of the body such as mudguards, covers and doors. The efforts made to lighten the car went down to the smallest details; for instance, the seat adjustment mechanism was made of titanium, which was both expensive and difficult to manufacture.

In all, four Turbo-Carreras were built. Their speed on the Le Mans straight was 300 km/h (186.4 mph) and they accelerated from rest to 100 km/h (62 mph) in 3.2 seconds and to 200 km/h (124 mph) in 8.8 seconds.

The suspension system was still basically similar to that of the 911 series, although the torsion bar springs were eliminated front and rear to save weight. At the front the deletion of the torsion bars made it possible to use light tubular lower wishbones, and the Bilstein steel suspension struts had an adjustable abutment to take the load of the concentric coil spring. At the rear, the semi-trailing link principle remained, but both the longitudinal arm and the diagonal semi-trailing arm were replaced by a single fabricated and argon-welded aluminium sheet triangle, carrying the wheel hub. In this case too, Bilstein spring-damper units with an adjustable spring abutment were used, but as, in this case, the unit was submitted to axial loads only, it was made of aluminium. No modifications were made to the steering and brakes, which remained as in the Carrera RSR (ventilated and perforated discs, four-piston, ribbed aluminium calipers). One-piece cast magnesium centre lock 381 mm (15-inch) diameter wheels were used with 267 mm (10.5-inch) wide rims at the front and 381 mm or 432 mm (17-inch) rims at the rear, according to race circuit and conditions. Tyre sizes were 245/575-15 and 340/575-15 front and rear respectively.

Engine

The engine capacity limit for the Prototype group was three litres and as a 1.4 coefficient was applied to any sort of supercharged engine, this meant that the capacity limit for the Turbo-Carrera's engine had to be 2,142 cc. This was obtained by using the crankshaft of earlier 2-litre engines giving a piston stroke of 66 mm and combining it with a bore size of 83 mm (2.6 × 3.27 inches).

There was no fundamental difference between the turbo-engine and the well-known RSR engines. For the turbo car the titanium connecting rods, formerly used in the Carrera-6 engine, were unearthed and Nikasil cylinders were used, as had been normal practice for Porsche racing engines for three years. The cylinder heads were machined from standard castings and the camshafts provided slightly less overlap and lift than those of the Carrera RSR.

Development brought no thermal problems. Both the existing cooling blower and the Type 908 front-mounted oil radiator were fully adequate, but the exhaust valve guides 'grew' fins to improve the heat dissipation. In the course of the racing season, however, the virtually standard cooling blower was replaced by a horizontal blower. This made the drive more complicated, two separate V-belts being necessary: one for the blower drive and one for the separately mounted generator. Instead of being driven directly by its V-belt, the plastic blower wheel, mounted on top of the crankcase and providing a more balanced air distribution was now driven from a horizontal shaft through a pair of bevel gears.

The KKK (Kühnle, Kopp & Kausch) turbocharger and its installation were similar to the installation in the Porsche 917-10 Turbo, except for the fact that the single turbocharger fed both banks of three cylinders. This was, however, completed by the addition of an induction air cooler interposed between the supercharger and the single plenum chamber. It was located approximately where the normal Carrera had its 'duck's tail' spoiler and was cooled by the air ducted on to it. It provided worthwhile extra power by cooling the turbocharger output from approximately 160°C to anything between 60 and 90°C according to circumstances.

Both the electrical and fuel injection systems were by Bosch, the mechanical fuel-injection pump being, in principle, similar to the pump used in the standard Carrera, but with an additional control by the boost pressure. The electronic twin ignition installation was similar to the Carrera RSR's.

As it stood at the end of the 1974 season, the 2.14-litre engine had an output of 500 bhp at 7,600 rpm—a specific output of 233 bhp/litre. A maximum torque of 56 mkg (408 lb/ft) was obtained at 5,400 rpm.

Transmission

Rather surprisingly, the Fichtel & Sachs single-plate clutch (with sintered metal linings) used in the Carrera RSR proved well up to the task of transmitting the engine's impressive torque, provided the diaphragm spring was slightly reinforced. The five-speed gearbox, Type 915, remained basically similar to the production unit, but an oil pump was added in the front cover to circulate the oil through a cooler mounted in one of the wide rear mudguards. No differential was fitted, solid drive being used as had already been done in the 917-10 and 917-30 Turbos.

First tests of a turbocharged version of the Carrera RSR in France, at the end of 1973.

'Ghost'-view of six-cylinder Turbo-Carrera RSR prototype.

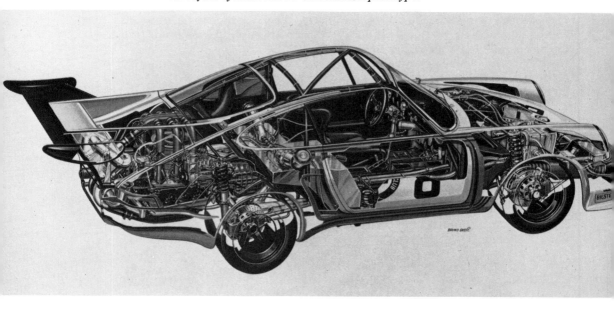

Front and rear views of the first version of the 1974 Carrera RSR-Turbo, with 2.14-litre, six-cylinder engine producing 500 bhp.

Side view of RSR-Turbo. The tail was modified several times.

Helmut Koinigg in the 1974 Nürburgring 1,000 km race.

Open tail cover shows the blower output intercooler.

Purely functional interior of the RSR-Turbo. On the right is the 'horsepower screw'.

533

The fuel tank is immediately behind the driver and protrudes into the passenger's compartment.

The semi-trailing arms were hand-welded aluminium. The half-shafts were borrowed from the 917.

RSR-Turbo front suspension with brake cooling duct for long-distance racing.

534

The nose of the Turbo prototype also contained the oil tank.

First version of the turbocharged six-cylinder with vertical cooling blower.

Later version, with the cooling blower wheel lying flat, provided a better spread of the air flow.

Type 935 (1976-1979)

Since 1976, the World Championship of Makes has been based on the new Group 5 introduced by the CSI, for which modified production cars are eligible. For several years, Porsche had been developing 911-based cars in anticipation of the introduction of this formula. They were raced in 1973 and 1974 and culminated in the current Type 935 racing coupé. The 935 was successful from the word 'go' and, thanks to its performance and stamina, dominated the racing scene in spite of the sporadic efforts of its competitors.

In this connection, it should be mentioned that, in addition to rig tests and thorough testing on the company's own and other racing circuits, every newly developed Porsche racing car must, since 1966, survive a 1,000-kilometre (621-mile) endurance run on a destruction track comprising pot holes, humpbacks and a spring board which brings any weak spot to light. If the car's structure completes this test successfully, it is very unusual for it to break down on the race track. As with all others, the 935 was submitted to this test, as well as to nearly 6,000 kilometres' (3,728 miles') testing on the Paul Ricard track and in Weissach, before it was first raced.

The first races were completely trouble-free. In the third, the clutch was burnt out in an over-zealous start. Following an unexpected decision by the CSI, the location of the intercooler had to be modified. According to the 'Appendix J' rules, the rear spoiler is permitted to differ from that of the production model. This being established, it seemed logical that, in addition to the cooling and induction air openings, the intercooler should also be incorporated in the new spoiler structure, as any designer would normally do. It was not possible to do this in the case of the Type 934, the Group 4 prescriptions calling for the retention of the standard spoiler. But the CSI insisted that, though the spoiler could be modified, the standard (930) spoiler must remain interchangeable with the modified one. The only way of meeting this rule was by fitting less space-consuming water-cooled intercoolers, as in the Group 4 car. This meant designing and testing new intercoolers with their piping and connections; completely retuning the engine on both the test-bed and the track and developing a new space cam for the injection pump, as well as developing and testing an entirely new throttle linkage. To achieve this in the period allocated, ie, between April 9 and May 30 1976, was an impossible task. As an interim solution, Type 934 intercoolers were fitted for the Nürburgring 1000 km race, but the engine was so rough at part throttle that the resulting vibrations caused rapid wear of the distributor drive and rotor, which eventually led to the car's retirement.

In Zeltweg larger radiators and intercoolers achieved the desired results, but a hurriedly manufactured throttle shaft, based on an existing part, broke in all cars so modified, forcing them to retire. Following this, the shaft was made thicker and a modified Group 4 car was still completing an endurance test in Weissach while the race cars were already in the 'plane, *en route* to Watkins Glen, where the good news came through that the outcome was satisfactory. And in fact, the engines ran perfectly in the American race, although the leading car, driven by Ickx/Mass, was delayed by a different mishap. To improve brake cooling, wheel discs incorporating radial vanes to activate the air flow over the brakes had been developed and were fitted to the front wheels only, as the front brakes do the major part of the work. For that reason, only the front brake pads are checked when the car comes into the pit, and this is just what the pit crew did in Watkins Glen. Nobody expected that the better cooling provided by the discs would reduce pad wear to such an extent that after four hours racing, the rear brake pads had worn down to the metal, when there was still plenty of material left on the front pads. This cost an additional, rather prolonged pit stop and first place for Ickx/Mass who lost the race to their team mates Stommelen/Schurti, who were stopped in time for the pad change to be completed without problems and with the shortest possible delay.

In Dijon, the only technical problem was the faulty brake line which cost an additional pit stop. The CSI's decision in April 1976 cost Porsche nearly half a million Marks, not to mention the additional risk to the drivers because of the lack of time to test the hurriedly made modifications.

For Porsche, 1976 was a year of trials. Cars were entered in both the World Championship of Makes and the World Championship of Sports Cars, both of which Porsche won. The experience indicated that there is no room for two such separate championships, the number of front-running entrants being insufficient in either of them. From this, the Stuttgarters drew their own conclusions and decided to concentrate on the World Championship of Makes in 1977, for which a modified version of the 935 was developed.

To back the factory team in 1977, Porsche built a small series of types 935 largely identical with the 1976 works cars, for sale to private teams.

Great promise was displayed by the single works car entered in the first race of 1977, the Daytona 24 Hours, until Jochen Mass had an accident on the famous banking. It was caused by the failure of the right hand rear tyre. After a 30-minute pit stop he was able to resume racing in 22nd position. After an exciting drive through the field, the works 935 had fought its way back into second place when it was finally stopped by a second similar accident in the same place.

Two cars were entered for the second race of the championship series on the Mugello circuit in Italy. One of them was the new 935/77 driven by Mass, Barth and Ickx while Stommelen and Schurti drove the 935/76. In view of previous problems with Italian scrutineers Porsche had had this 935/77 examined in Weissach by delegates of the CSI who issued a certificate of conformity to the regulations. This avoided any pre-race problems.

But 1977 was to be a difficult season for the works team which was plagued by cylinder head gasket failures—of eight races of the World Championship series, the factory cars won four and retired from the others when in the lead twice due to cylinder head gasket failures. The 935/77 was also entered for the Le Mans 24 Hours race where it was to back up the two 936 entries. Unfortunately, after a few hours, a cylinder head gasket blew again and the car had to be retired.

At the end of the 1977 season, Porsche decided to withdraw from active participation in the World Championship of Makes: the management was confident that the private teams using 935s would be able to successfully defend its colours. A factory 935 would only be entered for the Le Mans race.

Nick-named Moby Dick, the 935/78 had been developed specially for the Le Mans race. With its lowered, aerodynamically efficient body and its 3.2-litre, four-valve, six-cylinder engine, it was the fastest 935 ever. In Le Mans, Rolf Stommelen and Manfred Schurti drove it into eighth place after a far from trouble-free drive. Much time had been lost tracing an electrical and fuel feed problem and in the late stages of the event, a crack in the crankcase slowed the car. Before Le Mans, the 935/78 had been tried out in the Silverstone 6 Hours Race which Ickx and Mass had won.

Apart from its lower and aerodynamically more efficient body, the main interest of the 935/78 centres around its modified engine with twin overhead camshafts per bank of cylinders and four-valve cylinder heads. While the cylinders were still air-cooled, the four-valve arrangement did not leave enough room for efficient air cooling, and this is why water cooling was adopted for the cylinder heads. In this new version, the 3.2-litre engine developed 750 hp, enabling the 1,030 kg (2,270 lb) car to reach a maximum speed in excess of 355 km/h (220 mph). As most races are run clockwise, the steering was moved to the right to achieve a better weight distribution.

In 1979, only two Essex sponsored 936 Spyders were entered for the famous French race—for once unsuccessfully. In the following year, the 924 Carrera GT 'Le Mans' made its bow, indicating that the Porsche 911 which in all its forms had been the backbone of Porsche's sporting activities for one and a half decades was getting competition from Porsche's younger generation.

But a Kremer owned and prepared 935 had shown that in 1979, even without the four-valve engine, the 935 was still fast enough to win the most celebrated race in the world, not to mention the innumerable national and international events. The faith Porsche had in the 935 was proved when at the end of 1980, the factory resumed development work on the car in order to provide its customers with even more reliable Group 5 cars for the next two or three years.

General description: Type 935

Coachwork and chassis

Light weight was the main target the development engineers set themselves when developing the Group 5 car. It was built up from the bare body shell of the 930 Turbo which was further lightened as much as possible. All rust proofing and sound deadening material and all internal trim was deleted. The front and rear covers, the doors and the mudguards were all made of GFK plastic material. The front fenders and the front air dam were made in one single, quickly detachable part. At the rear, a long tail could be fitted without modifying the original body shell which, according to the Group 5 rules, must remain unaltered. There were two versions of the car's front: one with the headlights in the standard position and one with aerodynamically more efficient forward-sloping fenders. In this case the headlights were included in the air dam.

The rear wing was made of aluminium and plastic material. It was built up on the standard Turbo spoiler (a requirement of the rules) and had an adjustable rear edge as well as two lateral 'fences'. The intercooler was incorporated in the spoiler part and a support added to take care of the much increased air pressure. The windscreen and the driver's window were safety glass, but all other transparent surfaces were Perspex. A seat was provided for the driver only, there was no roof liner and no spare wheel. Padding was to be found only as sketchy patches on the cockpit side and instrument panels. The roll-over cage and the gear lever, including the knob, were made of aluminium, while the driver's seat supports were of titanium.

Well in sight of the driver was the tachometer and next to it the boost pressure gauge. Within his reach was the famous 'power tap' which can be turned, during the race, to momentarily increase the boost pressure and hence the engine power.

Hunting for any superfluous weight brought the 935 down to under 900 kg (1,984 lb) in racing trim. Only a few months before the new Group 5 rules were enforced did the CSI publish its final minimum weight scale, in which the weight is related to the engine capacity. According to this scale, the Porsche 935, which technically ranks as a 4-litre car (2,856 litres × 1.4 supercharging factor = 3,999 litres) had to weigh at least 970 kg (2,138 lb) without fuel, so that its creators added more than 70 kg (154 lb) ballast which was disposed so as to achieve an almost ideal weight distribution of 47 per cent front and 53 per cent rear. The location of the ballast was decided during the course of the test runs made on the Paul Ricard Circuit in December 1975, when it was accommodated partly at the extreme front end of the car and partly where the passenger's feet would normally be. To additionally load the front end, the 120-litre (26.4-gallon) fuel tank, made of polyester material, the oil tank, the battery and the fire extinguisher were all accommodated under the front cover.

In principle, the rear suspension remained that of the standard Turbo, but there were several detail modifications. The most important was the replacement of the torsion bars by titanium coil springs allowing an appreciable reduction in weight. The anti-roll bar was adjustable from the driver's seat while the car was running. In the front suspension, too, the torsion bars were replaced by titanium coil springs, while the fulcrum points were modified.

The brakes came from the Type 917 racing car and featured four ventilated and perforated discs on which longitudinally ribbed alloy calipers with four pistons each operated. The twin master cylinders were operated from the pedal by means of a balance lever permitting quick adjustment of the front/rear brake pressure. The wheels were one-piece magnesium castings with centre-lock hubs, their dimensions being 279 × 406 mm (11 × 16 inches) at the front and 368 × 406 or 368 × 483 mm (14.5 × 16 or 14.5 × 19 inches) at the rear.

Engine

The six-cylinder turbocharged engine was developed from the standard 930 Turbo unit. From 2,856 cc it produced over 590 bhp at 7,900 rpm and a maximum torque of 60 mkg (438 lb/ft) at 5,400 rpm with an electronic twin ignition system. The maximum boost pressure was 22 psi, but was reduced, in some instances, to 19 psi. Average racing fuel consumption was 5.38 miles per Imperial gallon (4.38 miles per US gallon).

The racing engine used many major standard parts, such as the crankshaft, the crankcase and the valves. The camshafts, the ports, the exhaust system, the cooling blower (horizontal), the lubrication and the connecting rods were all modified. No fewer than five electric fuel pumps supplied the Bosch plunger injection pump feeding the intake manifold-mounted injectors. In contrast to the Group 4 car (Porsche 934), the intercooler was air-cooled, as in this case this bulkier, but much lighter type could be used (until the CSI thought otherwise, when water cooling had to be adopted). The thermostatically governed engine oil cooler was incorporated in the front air dam.

Transmission

The transmission was similar to that of the Group 4 car, except for the absence of any differential, the drive being solid to the two rear wheels. The single-plate clutch with sintered metal linings and coil spring plate hub damper was of Fichtel & Sachs manufacture. For the first time in a model of 911 derivation, the gear ratios of the four-speed gearbox could be changed without taking the engine out of the body shell. The gearbox oil cooler was accommodated in the front part of the right rear fender.

Annual modifications

1977

Porsche entered cars for eight of the nine races counting towards the World Championship of Makes 1977. The first of these races was the Daytona 24 Hours. As this race took place at the beginning of February, the new 935/77 was not ready and Porsche entered a 1976 model. It was identical to the cars used at the end of 1976 but with one exception: the turbocharging installation had been modified to improve throttle response, but still had a single turbocharger.

After the race, the team moved for two weeks' testing on the Paul Ricard circuit in the South of France. Over 2,000 miles were covered by the twin turbo-charged 935/77 without any engine or turbocharger problems, even though the car was driven as fast as possible and always using the maximum permissible boost pressure. The fastest lap was done by Manfred Schurti in 1.53.3 minutes, 3.4 seconds faster than the 935 had done in Spring 1976. The maximum speed too was raised by some 10 km/h (6 mph) and a speed of 305 km/h (189.5 mph) was measured on the straight. Following these tests, a brand new 935/77 was taken to the race on the Mugello circuit in Italy, to be driven by Mass, Ickx and Barth, along with the older 935/76 entrusted to Stommelen and Schurti. Unfortunately, Barth crashed the 77 model after a pit stop, due to failing brakes. Later investigations in the factory revealed traces of seizures in the master cylinder and a defective rubber seal, probably responsible for the incident. In the 1,000 km race on the Nürburgring, the works 935 was again on pole position but after the first routine pit stop, the engine started to loose power. So much time was lost investigating that the car was eventually retired. It finally turned out that the problem was caused by a damaged pressure sensing membrane in the injection pump.

In Watkins Glen (USA) Jochen Mass and Jacky Ickx had an easy win. But four weeks later they were less successful in Mosport (Canada) when 20 minutes after the start, a tyre blew and 30 minutes later the car had to be retired with a blown cylinder head gasket. This problem cropped up several times during the season, a sure indication that the limit of the thermal stresses which the engine could accept had been reached, even though the designed boost pressure of 1.5 bar (21 psi) had never been exceeded. Profound engine modifications were obviously required if more power was to be extracted for the following year.

A heavy rain storm caused the Brands Hatch race to be interrupted after 1.15 hours. It was later restarted and the factory entered 935 had no difficulty keeping ahead of the field. The last race counting towards the World Championship of Makes was run on the Hockenheim circuit. The 6 hour race was split into two 3 hour events, on two successive days. All the teams seemed to treat it as a sprint race and many cars suffered mechanical damage. The works Porsche 935 was no exception—a head gasket blew again. As the organisers offered Porsche the possibility of taking part in the second half of the race, on a 'hors concours' basis, the engine was changed overnight and Schurti won the second half-race in spite of a gear selector failure which forced him to complete the last 50 minutes using 4th gear.

At Le Mans, where the 935/77 had been entered in support of the two 936, the car failed to fulfil its task—again due to the failure of a cylinder head gasket.

1978

For the first time in Porsche history water is used to cool a racing engine, or at least part of it. A 2.8-litre flat-6 prototype engine was developed from previous units with water-cooled cylinder heads featuring four valves each. This ensures adequate cooling, even with higher boost pressures than used to date. The cooling water enters the head on its lower part and exits from the top. Each bank of cylinders has its own water pump driven by one of its two camshafts. Each pump circulates the water to one of two radiators located in the left and right rear fenders. Thanks to the water cooling, which is permitted by the regulations as long as the cylinders remain air cooled*, the temperature of the head, which is welded to the cylinder and does not require a gasket, is lowered by approximately 60°C.

After the prototype 2.8-litre, a 3.2-litre was prepared for the 935/78 while a 2.1-litre engine developed for the 936. A further 1.4-litre turbocharged 6-cylinder (with air cooled, two-valve cylinder heads) was prepared to successfully power the so-called 'Baby Porsche' in two races while more four-valve engines were to be built with a capacity of 2.65 litres to compete in the Indianapolis 500 Miles race of 1980.

The water cooled engines are almost entirely new. From the original 911, only a modified crankcase with larger diameter crankshaft bearings remains. The pistons, the connecting rods, the camshafts—now entirely gear driven—are new. Only the cooling fan, which is again upright, looks familiar but its capacity has been reduced by 2/3 as only the cylinders must be cooled.

The engines run up to 9,000 rpm and are designed to operate at a boost pressure of 1.6 bar (22.5 psi), 1.8 bar (25 psi) being permissible for short periods.

The 935 itself was extensively modified for the 1978 season. Norbert Singer, head of the 935 project, used every opportunity provided by the Group 5 regulations to make the 935 more competitive. The entire lower part of the body was sliced off and the entire car lowered by 6 cm. In the course of this operation, the floor pan disappeared and was replaced by an aluminium frame covered by a very thin layer of fibreglass. The gearbox was turned upside down to reduce the angle at which the drive shafts work. A very rigid roll-over cage virtually forms the chassis. It carries the engine at the rear and a new 120-litre (26.4 gallon) fuel tank at its front end. The engine oil cooler is located in front of the tank and further ahead are the two water radiators of the turbocharger intercoolers.

---

*Group 5 regulations require the 'cylinder block' to be a standard production part (with additional machining allowed), but the cylinder heads can be modified.

1979

After the withdrawal of the two factory entered 936s in the Le Mans 24 hours race in which one of them was disqualified, the private Porsche teams had their big chance. Of the 55 cars which started in the race, more than a third—exactly 21—were Porsches. Right from the start of practice, the Porsche 935 entered by Georg Loos and by the Kremer brothers made it quite clear that they were by no means prepared to wait for the retirement of the Group 6 prototypes to get among the race leaders.

Klaus Ludwig, driving a Kremer 935, had achieved the third fastest practice time, headed only by the two works 936s, and during the race he and his two partners, the Whittington brothers, kept strictly to the pre-established running schedule, completely unimpressed by any of their competitors. They were so fast that, from the beginning of the race, they were hard after the two Ford Mirage M-10s and already at quarter-distance, the Kremer team's number 1 car was leading the race, while another, crewed by Plankenhorn, 'Winter' and Gurdjian was lying fourth.

Kremer finally brought all his three cars home in first, third and 13th position. For a long time, however, the cars of the Loos team were not to be discounted. Between the 8th and the 14th hour, the two Loos cars driven by Schurti/Heyer and Fitzpatrick/Grohs/Lafosse navigated between first and fourth places. But then, at less than one hour's interval, at dawn on Sunday, both Loos Porsches retired with serious engine damages. For the Kremer brothers, the most serious threat had disappeared. But in Le Mans, the race is never won before the 24th hour—almost in sight of the finish, the cog-belt driving the injection pump of the leading car broke. Don Whittington fitted the spare he had in the car but this immediately broke—just as happened to Ickx in the factory 936. Don who is an engineer, refused to be beaten. He removed the belt driving the alternator and adapted it to the injection pump. The belt wasn't the right length but he managed to restart and to drive the car back to the pits. A lot of time was lost but fortunately for the team, the second place Porsche 935 of the American Barbour team were also forced into the pits by a faulty wheel bearing. In the end, Porsches filled the first four places and of the 22 cars which survived the gruelling race, 12 came from Zuffenhausen.

Type 935 Baby (1977)

In spring 1977, Porsche decided to enter an extra-lightweight 935 in the Norisring race in Nuremberg. As the race was for cars up to 2 litres, it was necessary to develop a 1.42-litre turbo engine* and to keep the weight of the complete car as near as possible to the minimum weight requirement of 735 kg (1,620 lb). Development began in great secret in March and with the help of a single turbocharger, 370 hp was extracted from the well-known flat-6 whose capacity had been reduced to 1.42 litres. To save weight, the front and rear parts of the body as well as the floor pan were replaced with an aluminium tube frame integrated into the remaining central part of the body. Before any component was built into the car, it was examined to see if it could not be deleted or at least lightened. After a four-month development period, the complete Baby was pushed on to the scales: the result of 750 kg was very satisfactory.

The car came to the race virtually untested and both the engine and the handling obviously required more attention. As sufficiently low gearing was not available, the 19 inch diameter rear wheels had to be replaced with 16 inch wheels. In practice, Jacky Ickx only achieved 13th fastest time, though, in the race, he moved up to sixth, but was forced to retire as he could not bear the intense heat.

Three weeks later, the Baby took part in its second race on the Hockenheim ring. Intensive development work on the test bed made it possible to broaden the torque curve. Handling was improved by reinforcing the structure composed of the aluminium tube frame and the steel sheet body. The running gear settings were also improved. This resulted in pole position with a 2.8 second lead on the second best time and in a victory for Jacky Ickx who finished 52 seconds ahead of the second car home. The company had proved their point: if Porsche wanted to, they could beat the established runners in the 2-litre class to which the company pays little attention these days. After it had taken part in only two races, the Porsche Baby disappeared into the factory museum.

---

*The rules stipulate that in supercharged engines, the actual capacity is to be multiplied by 1.4.

Side view of the first experimental prototype. The rear aerofoil was modified before the car's first race.

Testing the new car. Note experimental rear end modifications.

544

Porsche 935 in the colours of its sponsors Martini & Rossi.

Interior of the 935: bare metal wherever you look!

Removal of the entire front nosepiece reveals the oil tank and the 120-litre (26½-gallon) fuel tank.

Rear view of the Porsche 935 with large air/air intercooler.

Turbocharged 2.85-litre, six-cylinder engine in the tail of the 935. The 590 bhp engine has a horizontal blower.

546

Rear suspension of 935 with 'long-distance' brake and centre lock hub.

Modified body for the 1977 version of the 935.

Sloping front with recessed left and right rear-view mirrors.

The interior of the 935/77 was almost the same as the previous year's model. Note aerodynamically justified 'running boards' between front and rear mudguards.

Early version of the 935 with headlights in standard position.

Later version with sloping front mudguards.

Third version with modified rear spoiler and squared-off rear fenders (mudguards).

Fourth version (1977): a new tail with flush fitting, more inclined rear window covers the original body. Also note the 'running boards'.

The Porsche 935 Baby
weighed only 750 kg. It
is shown here with the
detachable body parts
removed.

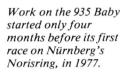

Work on the 935 Baby
started only four
months before its first
race on Nürnberg's
Norisring, in 1977.

550

For Better weight
distribution, oil and
fuel tanks were in the
car's nose.

The turbocharged 1.4-
litre six-cylinder engine
developed 370 bhp. Air
circulation through the
intercoolers was
activated by the
exhaust system.

*First test of a Porsche
935 modified in
accordance with the
Kremer brothers' own
ideas (1977).*

Porsche 935, 1977 Kremer version, driven by Bob Wollek into second place in the German Racing Championship.

In 1978, the lowered
'Moby Dick', powered
by the 3.2-litre 'four-
valve' engine, was built
in Weissach.

The car's aerodynamics
were much improved.

After only four races,
'Moby Dick'
disappeared into
Porsche's private
museum.

Former managing director Professor Ernst Fuhrmann examines the new engine with engine designer Hans Mezger.

3.2-litre flat-six with air-cooled cylinders and water-cooled heads.

554

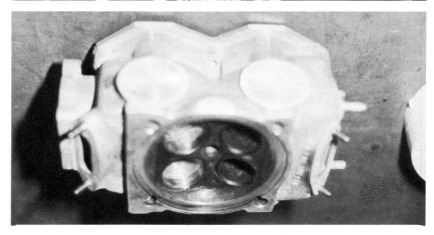

Four-valve cylinder heads provided 750 bhp with reliability—the head was welded to cylinder.

The compact six-cylinder produced 750 bhp at 8,200 rpm from 3.2 litres.

Below: The 'works' Porsche 935/78 in the colours of its sponsors, Martini & Rossi.

In its only Le Mans appearance, the 935/78 was placed eighth after an eventful run.

For better weight distribution on clockwise circuits, the 935/78 has right-hand drive.

556

Rear view of 935/78: weight 1,030 kg, speed over 220 mph.

935/78 in its original form. The doors were later modified to meet the strict regulations which also entailed the use of a different rear aerofoil.

Problems with the new engine dropped the car to eighth place in the 1978 Le Mans race.

1977 Porsche 935 as built for private teams (here a Loos-owned car).

Porsche 935 as modified by the Kremer team in 1979.

Liqui-Moly-sponsored Porsche 935 driven by Rolf Stommelen in 1979.

Porsche 3.1-litre, 720 bhp air-cooled flat-six engine, as developed for private customers.

558

Rear view of Kremer-team Porsche 935 in 1980 version.

Type 936 Turbo (1976-1981)

The decision to participate in the World Championship of Sports Cars was taken in great secrecy, almost overnight, only a few months before the first race was due to be run. It was prompted by doubts about the respective value of the World Championship of Makes and the World Championship of Sports Cars, by rumours that the two series might be amalgamated into a single championship and by comments from France and Italy that Porsche had found an easy way to win the World Championship of Makes (run to Group 5 regulations) where the German cars were unlikely to meet serious opposition, but was not at all keen to meet Alfa-Romeo who had just won the title or the much fancied Renault-Alpines. Porsche's reaction was to hurriedly develop a car to Group 6 specifications, the Porsche 936, to meet the opposition on both fronts. At the time, nobody could suspect that this would be the first chapter of an almost unparalleled success story.

The first meeting of the brand new Porsche with the now well proven Renault-Alpines in the Nürburgring 300 km race was a complete flop. The race was run in pouring rain and less than 3 km after the start, the two Renaults collided and were out of the race, leaving the new Porsche an undisputed leader until the throttle cable jammed and left it to Reinhold Jöst's old Porsche 908/03 to earn the first championship points for the Zuffenhausen factory.

In the following races, the Porsche, Renault and Alfa-Romeo showed very similar performance potentials, however, much to the surprise of everyone, the 936 proved to be the more reliable car. It won the races in Monza, Imola and Pergusa, so that after only four of the seven-race series, the championship was already decided. But, Porsche gallantly defended its laurels in the last three races which the 936 also won.

The victory of the 936 in the Le Mans 24 Hours race only gilded the lily. That year, Le Mans was not part of the World Championship series, but the world-wide reputation of this race makes it at least as important as the World Championship itself and draws entries of unsurpassed quality. Even American 'Stock cars' had come to give battle to the Group 6 Sports Cars of Lola, Mirage, Porsche and Renault and to the Group 5 production cars of BMW, Chevrolet, Datsun, Ford and Porsche, included among the 55 starters. After the victories of Herrmann/Attwood in 1970 and Marko/Van Lennep in 1971, this was Porsche's third Le Mans victory. Although Porsche had chalked up two champion titles, the news came at the end of the season that they would not take part in the Sports Cars Championship of 1977 from which, so rumours went,

Renault also intended to retire in order to better concentrate on the preparation of the all important Le Mans race. The 935 was to be further developed to defend Porsche's title of World Champion of Makes in 1977, but the 936 was to be entered only for Le Mans.

The Group 6 car did not require any major modifications, but it was known that its body was not aerodynamically optimised and following wind tunnel tests, a new body was designed around the slightly modified chassis. The modified cars (no new 936 had been built) were then sent to the Paul Ricard circuit for a 28-hour endurance run, during which timings on the straight showed the modified models to be 24 km/h (15 mph) faster than the previous year's.

The test run was completely uneventful, but Le Mans was a different story. After little more than one hour's racing, the Barth/Haywood car came in with fuel injection pump trouble. A spline had come adrift in the pressure sensing box. The repair took 28 minutes and dropped the car to 41st position. Then, after only 2 hours and 50 minutes racing, a connecting rod broke in the Ickx/Pescarolo 936, putting it out of the race. Ickx then joined Barth and Haywood on the other car which had already begun to pick up places. Well supported by the other two drivers, he drove a fabulous race to put the car back into the lead after 18 hours of racing.

But there was to be more drama. At 15.14 hours with exactly 46 minutes to go, at a time when, fortunately, all the direct challengers were out of the race or far back, Hurley Haywood came in with a seized piston. Ignition and fuel feed to the damaged cylinder were cut off, but nobody knew how serious the damage was. Would the engine restart? Would it be able to do another two laps without which the car couldn't qualify as a finisher? Jürgen Barth, who had known the car from its birth, was selected to drive it over those last two critical laps. He pushed the starter button and the engine immediately responded. It even kept running for two slow laps, enough to give Porsche a fourth Le Mans victory.

When 55 cars faced the starter again in the 1978 Le Mans race, the stage was set for what appeared to be not as much a battle of cars and drivers against each other, as a battle of nations with Germany represented by Porsche and France by Renault in various forms. Having lost the race to Porsche for two years in succession, the state-owned French Renault company, could not afford to be defeated again and had made enormous efforts to come out a winner. The French manufacturer had entered four cars, supported by two Renault V-6 turbo-engined Mirages. Jean-Pierre Jabouille, driving the fastest Renault with a V-6 turbo engine of 2.14 litres was sent out to play the part of the hare. He led the race from the start at a pace far exceeding Porsche's proposed time schedule. The Stuttgart crew had entered three 936, one of which was brand new. Two of them had a new four-valve engine and one the older fully air-cooled two-valve power unit. These cars were to lap in the 3.40 minutes to 3.50 minutes bracket, but Jabouille lapped consistently under 3.40, forcing the Porsches to lap faster than originally planned if they were not to lose contact, and imposing additional stresses on engine and transmission. Things were not made easier for Porsche as after only two laps, Ickx stopped to report a heavy throttle, necessitating the replacement of the injection pump. The mechanics were still at work when Haywood came in with a jammed wastegate. All this put the two cars a long way back.

Hard driving by Ickx and Pescarolo had put their car back into sixth place, when a fifth-gear pinion broke. The repair took more than 40 minutes, which finally put the car out of contention, but Ickx was immediately moved to the other four-valve car, which had up to then been driven by Barth, Wollek and Jöst. Meanwhile, the two-valve 936 had been delayed by the replacement of a turbocharger and when shortly before 11.00 am Jochen Mass crashed the car originally driven by Ickx, Porsche's hopes were virtually dashed.

However, the Renault camp also had problems when, around midday on Sunday, the Type A 443, their fastest car which had a commanding lead, stopped out on the track, with a blown engine. The Bell and Jarier A 442 had broken its final drive and a gearbox repair had dropped. Fréquelin and Ragnotti's similar car down the classification. Both Renault-Mirage cars had lost considerable time with electrical problems, but in the end the Pironi/Jaussaud Renault A 442B crossed the finishing line seven laps ahead of the Wollek/Barth/Ickx Porsche.

Having fulfilled its stately mission, Renault declared a few days later that the company would not in future compete at Le Mans but would concentrate their efforts on the Formula 1 project.

Without Renault Le Mans seemed less attractive to the Porsche management and the entry of two Essex sponsored 936s for the 1979 race was a late decision. It came too late for extensive tests and except for some minor modifications, the cars were identical to the 1978 models. The modifications, mainly concerned the engine which had redesigned intake pipes and throttle valves and also a modified exhaust system, these modifications being aimed at improving the flexibility. In the gearbox a plain set of fifth gear pinions was used in place of the lightened set.

Lapping at between 3.40 and 3.45 minutes, the two Porsche 936s quickly took a commanding lead, but after less than three hours came the first problems: a tyre failure seriously damaged the Ickx/Redmann car and almost at the same time, Wollek came in with a rough engine. It went on into the night on five cylinders but it was retired in the early hours of Sunday. Even before that, the other 936 had been disqualified after Ickx had benefited from outside help when replacing a broken fuel pump cog belt. But Porsche's honour was saved by the two private Porsche teams of the Kremer brothers and American Dick Barbour which finally took first and second place respectively with the drivers Klaus Ludwig and the Whittington brothers on the Kremer car and Rolf Stommelen, Paul Newman and Dick Barbour on the American entered 935. This almost unique success of private teams at Le Mans prompted Porsche's decision not to enter Group 5 or 6 cars for the 1980 edition, but to start a new era based on the development of the Porsche 924 (See Type 924 Carrera GT Le Mans).

General description: Type 936

Coachwork and chassis
The shape of the new Spyder was a cross between a 908.03 and a 917-10 Can-Am Spyder. The three-piece polyester body was carried, in true Porsche tradition, by an aluminium tube space frame. The headlights were incorporated in the front body structure, the central part had two lift-up doors and the pivoted rear section covered the engine while its two raising tail fins carried the aerofoil. It was shaped as a 'cut-off long-tail'. The aerofoil was in two-pieces, the rear one being adjustable, and its rigidity was ensured by an additional central support. The driver's seat was slightly offset to the right of the centre-line and about as far forward as in the 908.03.

Front suspension was by triangulated transverse wishbones, while the rear suspension also incorporated transverse wishbones of which the lower one was triangulated. Both the upper and the lower wishbones were longitudinally located by a long pivoted tubular link. Variable rate coil springs and Bilstein gas-filled dampers were used front and rear. The twin circuit brakes comprised ventilated discs and four-piston light alloy calipers, a balance lever allowing front/rear brake pressure adjustment. The light alloy wheels of 381 mm (15-inch) diameter had a centre-lock hub. Their rim width was 267 mm (10.5 inches) at the front and 15 inches at the rear. The weight was around 700 kg (1,543 lb) and the maximum speed approximately 330 km/h (205 mph). The 160 litres (35 gallons) of fuel were carried in tanks located in the body sides and behind the driver, while the oil tank was placed obliquely behind the driver's seat.

Engine

The engine was the unit successfully used in the factory's 1974 Turbo-Carrera. It was an air-cooled flat-six with the cooling air blower wheel placed horizontally above the engine. A Bosch six-plunger injection pump was used in connection with a KKK turbocharger. Bore and stroke dimensions of 83 × 66 mm gave an effective capacity of 2,142 cc and the engine developed 520 bhp at 8,000 rpm with a 6.5:1 compression ratio and a boost pressure of approximately 1.5 bar (21.5 psi). Maximum torque was 48 mkg (350 lb/ft) at 6,000 rpm. From the turbocharger, located at the extreme rear of the car, two separate pressure pipes, each incorporating an air-cooled intercooler, ran forward to the two banks of cylinders. The crankcase was magnesium alloy and twin ignition was used.

Transmission

An aluminium distance piece approximately 305 mm (12 inches) long connected the engine crankcase to the final drive housing, while the Type 917 five-speed, fully synchronised gearbox was overhung behind the final drive. The three-disc clutch was of Borg & Beck manufacture.

Annual modifications

1977

During the winter 1976-77, serious development work was done on the type 936. A modified body was the result of extensive wind tunnel testing, all the more important as speed can be gained from better aerodynamics without any sacrifice of reliabilty. However, the engines also received attention: both the 935 and 936 engines were equipped with twin turbochargers, each being fed by one bank of cylinders. In the case of the 936, the new installation not only improved the throttle response but also raised the power from 520 to 540 bhp. It is certainly worth mentioning that such power outputs were obtained from an engine directly derived from the production 911 engine, a comparatively simple unit with a single overhead camshaft per bank, two valves per cylinder and a limit of 8,000 rpm. Also worthy of attention is the fact that the two 936s prepared for the 1977 Le Mans race were still chassis numbers 001 and 002, the only two cars built to that date which had been used for all the development tests and the entire racing programme of 1976.

The modifications made to reduce the drag included a reduction of the front track by 50 mm and of the rear track by 30 mm. The wheelbase was increased by negligible 10 mm, but the overall length of the car was increased by 0.5 m and the height reduced by 60 mm for aerodynamic reasons.

1978

The two 'old' cars were again used in 1978 albeit with some important modifications, especially in the engine department. In 1976 and 77, Porsche had easily won the World Championship of Makes with the Type 935 powered by the turbocharged 2.8-litre engine. The same engine was used in the Type 936, but with its capacity reduced to 2.14 litres in order to meet the regulations. This deserves attention because whereas in Group 5 the regulations require the engine to be directly developed from a production unit, the 936 could have used a full-blooded racing unit. The achievements of the 911-based engines are all the more remarkable.

At 640 bhp for the 2.8-litre and 540 bhp for the 2.14-litre version, the limits had not yet been reached as far as mechanical stresses were concerned, but any increase in power would certainly have created thermal problems. Consequently, a development programme was launched to reduce the thermal stresses and significantly increase the power of the engine without going beyond the limits allowed by the Group 5 regulations. This involved far reaching modifications, considerably exceeding those which the 911 engine had seen in, up to then, 14 years of production life.

One of the most important modifications was the use of four valves per cylinder. This considerably reduced the thermal stress of the exhaust valves, but the four valves crowded the cylinder head to such an extent that the space available for cooling air became insufficient. This led to the adoption of water cooling for the cylinder heads. As the separate cylinders are retained, a similar arrangement is adopted for the heads. Instead of having one cylinder head with three combustion chambers for each row of three cylinders, the engine has six separate heads. This unconventional layout has a very important advantage: the cylinder and the head are welded together on an electron beam welding machine, eliminating the troublesome head gasket. What does not exist seldom creates problems!

The flow of coolant runs from the bottom to the top of the heads, ie, from the exhaust to the intake side, ensuring well balanced cooling. Each row of cylinders has its own water pump, driven by the exhaust camshaft. The cooling fan which must now cool only the cylinders, is reduced in size, reducing its output from approximately 1,700 litres per second to 500 litres per second. The critical temperatures of around 280°C which had been measured in the cylinders of the air cooled engine are now reduced to approximately 200°C.

The small included angle of the valves results in a modern, compact combustion chamber with only one central plug. The valves are operated by two camshafts per bank of cylinders through inverted cup tappets instead of rockers. Another modification is the replacement of the timing chains by gears. The high voltage condenser discharge ignition system is also improved, the magnetic trigger being driven by one intake camshaft while the distributor is driven by the other. In its principle, the turbocharging installation remains unchanged. Twin turbochargers are used in both the 2.14-litre and the 3.2-litre versions of the engine, powering the 936 and 935 respectively.

During the winter 1977-1978, the engine test bed number 2 of the Weissach Development Centre worked overtime. But even the first prototype engine convinced the most sceptical that the redesign was a success. There was no difficulty in achieving the power targets the engineers had set themselves, and the development engineers could concentrate on improving the engine's flexibility and reliability.

The test runs before the important Le Mans 24 Hours race were completed with success. In the Silverstone 6 Hours race counting towards the World Championship of Makes, the works entered 935 powered by its 3.2-litre four-valve engine was an easy winner while the 2.14-litre, type 936, successfully survived a 40 hours' endurance run on the Paul Ricard circuit.

In Le Mans, the Porsche crew seemed quite capable of beating the only serious competition provided by four Renault Alpines. But even two new four-valve 936 Spyders, one two-valve 936 and the very fast 935/77 also powered by a four-valve engine, could not avoid a defeat. The 20 minutes making up the difference between defeat and victory was about the time lost in repairing the gearbox, a dealy which had nothing to do with the new engine. In order to meet the characteristics of the new engine, the gearbox ratios had been changed and the lightened fifth gear pinions proved to be fragile. In spite of the time lost changing the gears, Barth, Wollek and Ickx managed to make up some lost ground but at the finish, 7 laps still separated them from the winning Renault Alpine of Pironi and Jaussaud. The two-valve 936 of Haywood-Gregg-Jöst finished a creditable third, but the third Group 6 Porsche was wrecked in an accident from which Jochen Mass escaped unhurt.

1979
The final decision to enter for the 1979 Le Mans race came when the Essex Oil company and its boss David Thieme accepted sponsorship of the venture. Technically the Porsche 936s were much as they had been the previous year. Some development work had been done on the engine, mainly on the intake and exhaust systems, including a modification to the injection pump. The result was increased flexibility of the engine which could now be operated over the wide range between 5,500 and 8,500 rpm. The maximum power remained unchanged at 580 bhp. Thanks to the welded cylinder heads, a boost pressure up to 1.6 bar (22.5 psi) could safely be used. Increased safety was provided by stiffer brake calipers and a brake pad wear warning light. Nevertheless, with the hasty preparation in mind, racing engineer Norbert Singer started the pre race drivers' meeting with the following comments: 'What we do is try to jump very far from a standing start. There is a lot of things we must learn again as we have all been very busy in recent times with production car development.'

In the race, the car driven by Bob Wollek and Hurley Haywood suffered mysterious fuel feed problems and when a cylinder lost its compression on Sunday morning and the car couldn't hold its second place, it was retired. The car driven by Jacky Ickx and Brian Redman lasted an even shorter time. The Briton had hardly taken over from Ickx for his first stint when a tyre burst in the 150 mph curve following the pits. The car spun four times and it was sheer luck that only a radiator was damaged. But it took 1 hour 25 minutes for the car to crawl back to the pits and to be repaired.

Meanwhile, the leading cars were 18 laps away. But Ickx, determined to be first in winning Le Mans five times, did not give up and when, shortly before half distance, it began to rain, he really got the bit between his teeth and picked up place after place. However, suddenly the car stopped on the straight. The cog belt driving the injection pump had broken. Ickx fitted the spare, but after only a few kilometres it broke again at Mulsanne corner. A last desperate move was tried even though it went against the race regulations. A Porsche employee dropped a new belt somewhere near the immobile 936 and Ickx picked it up but the officials had observed the stratagem and the car was disqualified for having benefited from outside assistance.

1980

Twenty four out of the 55 cars lined up for the start of the 1980 Le Mans 24 Hours race are Porsches. Among them the much fancied Group 6 two-seater of Reinhold Jöst and Jacky Ickx. This brand new car is almost identical with the 936 works cars of 1977 and is powered by a two-valve engine developing approximately 520 bhp. Unfortunately, the team lost the race in the early stages by exerting excessive caution for the sake of reliability. Had the car built up a greater lead during the first half of the event, the half hour lost in repairing the gearbox whose fifth gear pinions had broken would not have cost them the victory, which they missed by only four minutes to be beaten by the Le Mans specialist, Rondeau. Nobody had expected such reliability from the Ford-Cosworth Formula 1 engine powering his car and much of the credit is due to the former Siffert mechanic, Heini Mader, who had built up the engine and managed to reduce its typical all destroying vibrations.

1981

1981 was the last year in which the Porsche 936 was eligible for the Le Mans 24 Hours race. Since the previous year, the Le Mans regulations had accepted Group 6 cars without engine capacity limit. Under the leadership of its new managing director Peter W. Schutz, Porsche decided to give the 936 another chance of winning the race. Using components developed for the 1980 Indianapolis 500 Miles race, the factory developed a version of the 'four-valver' similar to the 2,142 cc engine used in 1978, but with a capacity increased to 2,650 cc obtained from a 92.3 mm bore and a 66 mm stroke. With a boost of 1.6 bar (21.5 psi) and larger intercoolers, 620 bhp were obtained at 8,000 rpm.

As the five-speed gearbox had indicated several times that it was hardly capable of dealing with the power of the smaller engine for 24 hours, it could obviously no longer be used and the stronger version originally developed for the turbocharged 917 Can Am cars was fitted instead. Unfortunately, this had only four speeds, resulting in much too wide ratios for a circuit on which speeds range from less than 50 mph in three of the bends to 215 mph on the straight.

In order to accommodate the stronger gearbox, the rear part of the chassis had to be slightly modified, but apart from this, the engine capacity increase and the stronger gearbox, the two 936 Spyders facing Dr. Porsche, who was given the honour of starting the race, were virtually identical with those which had been raced in 1979. Painted in the colours of their new sponsor 'Jules', the two cars were the very original five-year-old 936-001 driven by Mass-Schupan-Haywood and 936-003, first seen in 1978 when Mass crashed it, for Ickx-Bell. An interesting addition to their equipment directly resulting from the disastrous tyre failures of 1979, was a permanent electronic tyre pressure warning device, triggered by a pick-up on the rim and operating a warning light in the case of a pressure drop of 3 psi.

This time, the target Porsche had set themselves was fully achieved, as Ickx and Bell dominated the race from the start and finished 14 laps ahead of their closest rival, a Ford-engined Rondeau. This gave Porsche its sixth and Jacky Ickx his fifth Le Mans victory—an all-time record he was to better in the following year, driving a Porsche 956.

Porsche 936-Turbo. This Spyder was a cross between a 908.03 and a 917-10.

Rear view of the Porsche 936. The body hid a 2.14-litre, six-cylinder engine developing over 500 bhp.

566

Works driver Jochen Mass during development tests of the 936 in 1976.

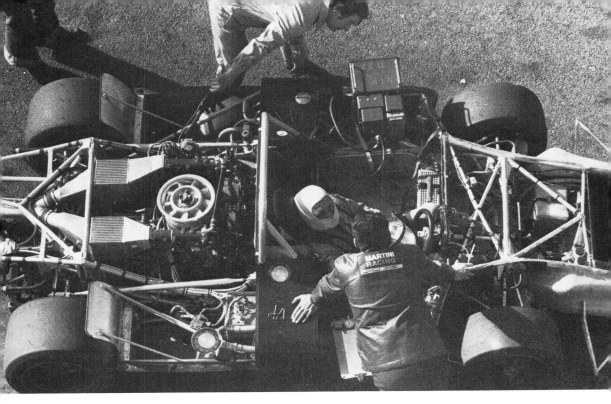

'Naked' 936 shows its main components and their location.

Porsche 936: well-proven aluminium spaceframe and turbo-engine with twin intercoolers (right and left of cooling blower).

This page and top two photographs on facing page: The original Porsche 936 undergoing wind-tunnel tests. Several variants were tested for cockpit cowling, air intake and tail fins.

569

The Porsche 936 as it appeared in its first two races in 1976.

Modified version of Porsche 936, after the CSI allowed a higher rear aerofoil.

570

The 1976 Le Mans-winning 936 had a high dynamic air intake.

Rear part of 936/77 body: two different air intakes are being tried out.

Porsche 936/77: lower, shorter and narrower, plus an additional 20-30 bhp.

Porsche 936/78: first tests of modified body with intakes for lateral radiators.

Ready for Le Mans with the new 'four-valve', 2.14-litre, 580 bhp engine.

Only 20 minutes separated the 936/78 from victory at Le Mans in 1978.

Well-hidden in the tail is the 'four-valve' engine with air-cooled cylinders and water-cooled heads.

1979 version of Porsche 936 was similar to 1978.

The engine develops 580 bhp, and a boost pressure up to 1.6 bar (22.5 psi) could safely be used.

The two factory cars were sponsored by the Essex oil company.

Le Mans 1979: one 936 had fuel feed problems, the other was disqualified.

574   *The Group 6 Porsche entered by Reinhold Jöst for the 1980 Le Mans race was almost identical with the 1977 factory cars. Its 'two-valve' engine developed 520 bhp.*

The INDY Project (1980)

For nearly five years beginning in 1975, Indianapolis was a topical subject at Porsche. Unfortunately, when the project had nearly come to fruition, the USAC (United States Automobile Club) organising the INDY series and the world famous Indianapolis 500 Miles race, ran into internal difficulties which culminated in a split. From this two organising bodies emerged: USAC and a new group called CART. The result was that for technical reasons, Porsche had to cancel its second American campaign, planned for 1980.

The plans were that Porsche was to cooperate with the American Interscope team in running a car not only in the Indianapolis 500 Miles race but in the entire USAC championship series. The partners were no strangers to one another as Interscope had run two Porsche 935s in the IMSA series with the drivers Danny Ongais and Ted Field who won the 1980 Daytona 24 Hours race.

A modified Parnelli chassis served as mobile test bed for the Porsche six-cylinder engine, but work had started on a completely new racing car jointly designed by Porsche and Interscope which was to be built in America. Hawaian born Danny Ongais was to be its driver. Cooperating in the project INDY 1980 were Porsche's old partners Shell, Bosch and KKK. For tyres, Porsche was to rely on INDY specialist Good Year.

Serious work in view of the INDY project started in Weissach in 1978 under the leadership of Helmut Flegl who had been responsible for the successful 917 Turbos which won the Can Am series in 1972 and 1973. Valentin Schäffer was responsible for the development of the INDY engine which was to power the car at an average lap speed of 200 mph. This 2.65-litre engine was developed from the Group 5 and Group 6 four-valve engine which had to be adapted to run on methanol, the compulsory fuel in the INDY series.

The final decision in favour of the American campaign was taken in December 1979, but the project had hardly been announced when new problems cropped up between USAC and CART. After their split which had led to the organisation of two championships in 1979, the two partners resumed negotiations at the beginning of 1980. There were not only personal frictions but also differences of opinion on technical regulations. Among other things, the two bodies disagreed on the maximum boost pressure to be allowed in supercharged engines. For 1980, CART recommended a maximum boost of 60 inches of water for eight-cylinder engines and of 70 inches for four-cylinder engines while USAC wanted 48 inches and 58 inches respectively (10 inches of water = approximately 2.45 psi).

575

Another point of disagreement were skirts: CART wanted them while USAC was against them. Their only point of agreement was the fuel consumption which was not to exceed 1.8 miles per US gallon (approximately 2.15 mpg).

In December 1979, the Americans had informed Porsche that their 6-cylinder would be allowed to run on 60 inches of boost. But following the discussions between CART and USAC, it was announced on April 31 1980 that the maximum pressure allowed for the six-cylinder would be only 48 inches. This made the Porsche engine uncompetitive and the only reasonable decision that could be taken was to withdraw from the 1980 INDY series. Porsche calculated that the 60-inch boost originally allowed would have produced 630 bhp. When USAC published the original Indianapolis regulations, the maximum boost had been reduced to 54 inches for a six-cylinder engine. This would have reduced the power by 60 bhp but the final limit of 48 inches announced in March 1980 was a complete surprise which just made the whole venture hopeless.

The Indy-Porsche went straight into the museum without ever starting in a race.

Carrera RSR prototype & Turbo/935- & 936-Turbo/INDY

Year	Body	Type	Chassis no	Engine type	Gearbox type	Cyl	Bore × stroke	Capacity	HP (DIN) at rpm	Torque (mkg) at rpm	Comp ratio	W.base (mm)	Track fr/ rear (mm)	Length (mm)	Weight (kg)	No produced
1973	Coupé	Carrera RSR 'Proto'	911360019-R1 0020-R2 0307-R3 0328-R4 0576-R5 0588-R6 0686-R7 0974-R8	911/72 911/74 911/75	915	6 6 6	92 x 70,4 95 x 70,4 95 x 70,4	2806 2993 2993	300/8000 315/8000 330/8000	30/6500 32/6500 32/6500	10,3:1	2271	1472/1528	4147	850	
1974	Coupé	Carrera RSR-TC	9113600576-R5 4609016-R9 9101-R12 9102-R13	911/76 911/78	915/50	6 6	83 x 66 83 x 66	2142 2142	500/7600 450/8000	56/5400 46/5500	6,5:1 6,5:1	2271		4235	750 820	
1976	Coupé	935 TC 'proto' Gr.5	9305700002- R15	930/72	930/25	6	92 x 70,4	2806	590/5400	60/5400	6,5:1	2271	1502/1558	4680	970	
1976	Spyder	936 TC 'Gr. 6'	936001/936002	911/78	917	6	83 x 66	2142	520/8000	48/6000	6,5:1	2400	1580/1510	4200	700	
1976	Coupé	935 Turbo	9305700002 (R15) New: 935.001 935.002	930/72	930/25 930/51	6	92 x 70,4	2857	590/7900	60/5400	6,5:1	2271 2265	1502/1558 1500/1560	4680 4655	970 970	Test-car
1977	Coupé	935-77	935.77003/ 04/05	930/78	930/50	6	92 x 70,4	2857	630/8000	60/5400	6,5:1	2271	1502/1558	4680	970	3
	'Baby'	935-77-20	935.02001	911/79	915/2	6	71 x 60	1425	370/8000		6,5:1	2271	1502/1457	4680	750	1
1977	Spyder	936-77	936001/02	911/78	917	6	83 x 66	2142	540/8000	50/6000	6,5:1	2410	1530/1480	4700	700	2

577

Carrera RSR prototype & Turbo/935- & 936-Turbo/INDY

Year	Body	Type	Chassis no	Engine type	Gearbox type	Cyl	Bore × stroke	Cap- acity	HP (DIN) at rpm	Torque (mkg) at rpm	Comp ratio	W.base (mm)	Track fr./ rear (mm)	Length (mm)	Weight (kg)	No prod- uced
1978	Coupé	935-78	9308900011-	930/ 72[1]	930/50	6	92,8×70,4	2857	600/8000	60/5400	6,5:1	2271	1502/1558	4680	970	23
	'Cust- omer'		0033	930/ 78[2]	930/60	6	95×70,4	2994	675/8000	73/5600	6,5:1				1025	
				930/ 79[1]		6	97×70,4	3124	680/8000	72/5600	6,5:1				1025	
				930/ 80[2]		6	95×74,4	3160	720/8000	75/5500	7,0:1				1025	
1978	Spyder	936-78	936003[4]	935/73	917	6	87 × 60,0	2140	580/8500	53/6000	7,0:1	2430	1530/1480	4740	800	1[4]
1979 79[2]	Coupé	935-79	00000009-13[3]	930/	930/60	6	97×70,4	3124	680/8000	72/5600	6,5:1	2271	1502/1558	4680	1025	5
80[2]	'Cust- omer'		00016-17	930/		6	95×74,4	3160	720/8000	75/5500	7,0:1				1025	2
			00022-25 00027-28													6
1978 'Werk'	Coupé	935-78	935006-007	935/3,2[2]	930/60	6	95,7×74,4	3211	750/8200	85/6500	7,0:1	2279	1630/1575	4890	1025	2
1979	Mono- posto	Indy P6B	P6BF 05IP1		Hew- land	6	92,3×66,0	2650	630/9000	57/6400	9:1	2654	1524/1575	4547	680	1
1981	Spyder	936-81	936001 and 936003[5]	935/75	917	6	92.3 × 66.0	2650	620/8000	62/6200	7,0:1	2430	1530/1480	4740	825	2[5]

1) Single turbo. 2) Twin turbos. 3) Delivered as spare bodies. 4) 936001 was rebuilt to 936/78 specifications. 5) 936001 and 936003 rebuilt to 936/81 specifications.

In November 1979, Porsche took the decision to participate in the 1980 Indy-Series with its own car. Its American partners were to be the Interscope team and driver Danny Ongais.

Engine for Indy-Porsche: a turbo-charged 2.65-litre flat-six developing 630 bhp.

The engine was developed from the 'four-valve' unit of the Porsche 935 and 936.

580

First Indy-Porsche was really a mobile test-bed based on a Parnelli chassis.

The Indy engine. Last minute changes of regulations forced Porsche to abandon the project.

The Interscope-Porsche was to compete at Indianapolis and in the USAC Series.

Type 956 (from 1982)

In an effort to restore the World Championship of Makes to its former glory, the FISA drafted completely new regulations for long distance racing, which were implemented from the beginning of 1982. The old Groups 1 to 6 were replaced by the new Groups N, A, B and C, respectively for unmodified production touring cars, modified production touring cars, Grand Touring cars (minimum yearly production 200 units) and two-seater competition cars without any minimum production requirements. For Group C, there was no restriction on either the type of engine used or on its capacity, the main limitation being the fuel consumption allowed. Maximum tank capacity (including fuel lines, etc) was 100 litres and cars were allowed to refuel only five times in the course of a 1,000 km or six-hour race, twelve times in a 12-hour race, and 25 times in a 24-hour race. In addition, the regulations prescribed a minimum weight of 800 kg without fuel, and various internal and external body dimensions as well as some strict safety requirements. In the first year, only Group B and C cars were eligible to compete for the World Championship of Makes, but cars complying with the old Groups 4, 5 and 6, as well as with the IMSA GT and GTX regulations, were allowed to take part in the races in order to fill the field while cars were being designed and prepared to meet the new regulations. Those cars, however, also had to use a 100-litre tank and to comply with the refuelling regulations. Only one type of car was banned from the races: Group 6 cars exceeding 2-litre engine capacity. This meant that the Porsche 936 was finally ruled out.

Porsche welcomed the new regulations, which did away with unrealistic equivalence formulae aiming at equalising the chances of atmospheric and supercharged engines, and put the emphasis on fuel efficiency, a most topical subject and a field in which racing developments could be of direct benefit to production car progress. Work on a new racing car to meet the new regulations had commenced in spring 1981 under Dipl. Ing. Norbert Singer's leadership, even before the regulations were finalised, and the new car underwent its first serious tests on the Paul Ricard circuit in February 1982.

Development was facilitated by the fact that in 1981 the Porsche 936 fitted with the 2.65-litre turbocharged 'four-valve' engine had just about met the fuel consumption requirements of 1982 when it won the Le Mans 24 Hours Race, so that it was decided to use the same basic engine in the Group C car, the Porsche 956. But whereas the 1981 version of the 936 was the last stage of the development of a car designed back in 1975, hurriedly adapted to keep it competitive against equally aged models in the last season in which it would be eligible, the

Porsche 956 was to meet the cream of what the opposition would produce, and in order to make it as competitive as possible nothing could afford to be neglected. Consequently an entirely new five-speed gearbox was designed—evidently using Porsche synchromesh—to reliably transmit the torque of the 620 bhp engine.

The rest of the car, designed from scratch, reflects the requirements of the regulations and the efforts to make use of the ground effect to create down force without the help of the flexible skirts used in Formula One, which are strictly banned by the Group C regulations. In order to achieve the greatest possible down force through ground effect, the car is built to the maximum allowed dimensions of 2 m width and 4.8 m length. This in turn has led to the longest wheelbase ever seen in a Porsche—2.65 m—because the rules require the over-hangs not to exceed a certain percentage of the wheelbase; and it was the require-ment that the top of the windscreen was to be at least 1 m above the ground that, for aerodynamic reasons, led to the 956 being a closed car. However, the biggest departure from traditional Porsche racing car policy is the replacement of the tubular space frame, first seen in the Porsche 906 of 1966 and made of aluminium since 1968, by a riveted and bonded aluminium sheet monocoque construction carrying a traditional three-part body made of plastic materials. It is not without some regret that Porsche abandoned their cherished aluminium space frame construction which was light, efficient and easy to manufacture, but the monocoque lends itself better to shaping a floor structure that generates the required down force, and it would have been difficult to meet the safety regulations, requiring a very impact-resistant structure around the pedals and foot well, using a tubular frame.

The general shape of the car was obtained in the wind tunnel using 1:5 scale models and finalised on a 1:1 model, and while the external shape is in true Porsche tradition, the floor is designed to take the maximum advantage of the air flow under the car to create down force by ground effect. This is why, instead of carrying a full width front air dam, the central part of the 956's nosepiece is shaped to allow a large flow of air underneath the car, of which the bodywork on either side of the central monocoque is shaped to form an inverted wing. As a consequence, the two intercoolers, the two water radiators and the two oil radiators are all located in the upper part of the side pods.

The suspension has been designed to interfere as little as possible with the air flow which, in the case of the rear suspension, has resulted in moving the spring/damper units to a central position, above the gearbox, where they are operated by the rocker-shaped upper wishbones. The lateral radius rods used in previous racing Porsches are dispensed with by using wide base lower wishbones taking the driving and braking forces. As these wishbones are in the path of the air flow, they have been shaped to interfere as little as possible with it, and for the same reason, the well-proven titanium tubular drive shafts, used in racing Porsches since 1969, are replaced by much thinner steel shafts with homokinetic Löbro joints at both ends, as used on Porsche production models. The brakes too have been redesigned: the discs are still both perforated and radially ventilated, but twin calipers are used.

In view of the fact that most races are run clockwise, right-hand steering has been retained, operating through a rack and pinion mechanism.

In the endurance races for which it was designed, during the first year the Porsche 956 faced competition not only from other Group C cars designed to the new regulations by such experienced manufacturers as Ford, who fielded the C.100 and Rondeau (both using a special version of the Ford-Cosworth Formula

One V-8 engine enlarged to 3.9 litres), as well as Lola, Sauber and others, also using the Cosworth engine, Aston-Martin using their own V-8, the Peugeot-sponsored WM team powered by a turbocharged Peugeot V-6, and also Lancia. The Italian manufacturer had taken the opportunity provided by the regulations to build a completely new Group 6 car powered by a 1420 cc turbocharged four-cylinder engine, and thus eligible for the 2-litre class. Since cars in this latter class were allowed a minimum weight of only 600 kg and were not submitted to either windscreen or skirt regulations, those small, open and light Lancias proved to be extremely competitive. They were not eligible for competition in the World Championship of Makes, but their drivers could take points in the World Championship for Endurance Drivers.

Nevertheless, the success story of the Porsche 956 sounds almost like a fairy tale. It started its career in the Silverstone 6 Hours Race, the third World Championship event of the season, after a Rondeau had won the Monza 1,000 km and a Lancia the 1,000 km of Nürburgring. At Silverstone, the sole Porsche 956 driven by Jacky Ickx and Jochen Mass took pole position and shared the front line with Patrese and Alboreto's Lancia. But the pace set by the Porsche, hotly pursued by the Lancia, was such that the distance finally covered in the 6 hours was almost 1,150 km, and to manage the distance with the fuel allowed the Porsche had to slow at the end of the race and leave overall victory to the Lancia. But though finishing second overall, the Porsche was still first in Group C and scored a full 20 championship points. This was the·only occasion when the 956 did not win both the Group C and the general classification, a success story culminating in a 1-2-3 victory in the Le Mans 24 Hours Race in which 28 Group C cars started and where, at their first attempt, all three works cars finished after almost completely troube-free runs. This was the sixth Le Mans victory for both Porsche and Jacky Ickx and the third for his co-driver Derek Bell.

584

Another hard-fought victory of the Porsche over the Lancia, in the 1,000 km of Francorchamps, had clinched the World Championship of Makes for Porsche, but the driver's title was still unsettled between Ickx and Patrese. Consequently Porsche decided to enter a car for Ickx and Mass for the last race of the season the Fuji 1,000 km in Japan, where after a fierce battle Ickx, who in every race had been one of the two drivers of the winning Porsche, finished four seconds ahead of Patrese and obtained his first world champion title.

Paul Frère, 1960 Le Mans winner and respected motor journalist, showed at the wheel of the Porsche 956 that he has not forgotten how to handle super-fast cars.